Bioethics and Society

Bioethics and Society

Constructing
the Ethical Enterprise

edited by

Raymond DeVries

St. Olaf College

Janardan Subedi

University of Miami—Ohio

PRENTICE HALL, Upper Saddle River, New Jersey 07458

Library of Congress Cataloging-in-Publication Data

Bioethics and society : constructing the ethical enterprise / edited
by Raymond DeVries. Janardan Subedi.
    p.   cm.
  Includes bibliographical references.
  ISBN 0-13-531252-3
  1. Medical ethics.   2. Bioethics.   I. DeVries, Raymond G.
  II. Subedi, Janardan.
  R724.B467   1998   97-18359
  174′.2—dc21   CIP

Editorial director: Charlyce Jones Owen
Editor-in-chief: Nancy Roberts
Acquisitions editor: John Chillingworth
Editorial assistant: Pat Naturale
Project manager: Cecile Joyner
Prepress and manufacturing buyer: Mary Ann Gloriande
Marketing manager: Christopher DeJohn
Cover director: Jayne Conte
Cover design: Pat Wosczyk
Copy editor: Betty Duncan

Excerpt on the following page is reprinted by permission of the University of Chicago
Press from Renée C. Fox and Judith P. Swazey, 1984, "Medical Morality Is Not
Bioethics: Medical Ethics in China and the United States," *Perspectives in Biology and
Medicine* 27(3): 336–60. "Counting Sheep" on p. xii from *The Intuitive Journey and Other
Works* (New York: Harper and Row Publishers, Incorporated, 1976). Copyright © 1976
by Russell Edson. Reprinted by permission of Georges Borchardt, Inc., for the author.

This book was set in 10/12 New Baskerville by DM Cradle
Associates and was printed and bound by Courier Companies, Inc.
The cover was printed by Phoenix Color Corp.

 © 1998 by Prentice-Hall, Inc.
Simon & Schuster/A Viacom Company
Upper Saddle River, New Jersey 07458

Printed in the United States of America

10 9 8 7 6 5 4 3 2 1

ISBN 0-13-531252-3

PRENTICE-HALL INTERNATIONAL (UK) LIMITED, *London*
PRENTICE-HALL OF AUSTRALIA PTY. LIMITED, *Sydney*
PRENTICE-HALL CANADA INC., *Toronto*
PRENTICE-HALL HISPANOAMERICANA, S.A., *Mexico*
PRENTICE-HALL OF INDIA PRIVATE LIMITED, *New Delhi*
PRENTICE-HALL OF JAPAN, INC., *Tokyo*
SIMON & SCHUSTER ASIA PTE. LTD., *Singapore*
EDITORA PRENTICE-HALL DO BRASIL, LTDA., *Rio de Janeiro*

. . . [If *bioethics*] *is an indicator of the general state of American ideas, values, and beliefs, of our collective self-knowledge, and of our under-standing of other societies and cultures—then there is every reason to be worried about who we are, what we have become, what we know, and where we are going in a greatly changed and changing society and world.*

Renée C. Fox and Judith P. Swazey
"Medical Morality Is Not Bioethics"

Contents

Chapter Five

PART II: THE SOCIAL ORGANIZATION OF BIOETHICS

Chapter Six

Chapter Seven

Chapter Eight

PART III: DOING BIOETHICS

Chapter Nine

Chapter Ten

Chapter Eleven

PART IV: SOCIOLOGY IN BIOETHICS

AFTERWORD

Preface

Several years ago, the *Los Angeles Times* ran a brief article about a couple who had just moved to Los Angeles from Nevada. Nothing newsworthy here, except that the couple had been proprietors of one of Nevada's notorious "ranch/brothels." Why had they left the brothel behind? Their departure was the result of the birth of their first child, a daughter they named Chastity. As they told the *LA Times*, "A brothel is no place to raise a child."

Morality is socially situated. The decision to become "ethical" is not made in a vacuum: Ideas about right and wrong, proper and improper, are shaped by social context. In the early 1960s there were no bioethicists in the United States. There *were* individuals concerned with moral questions occasioned by medicine and medical research, but they were not known as bioethicists, nor did they have the institutional support of centers for bioethics, professional journals, government commissions, or graduate programs and professorships. Why did American medicine suddenly decide to "get ethical"? Why do we now turn to bioethicists (as opposed to doctors, the clergy, or lawyers) to help us decide the proper way to resolve the dilemmas of health care?

WHY BIOETHICS?

Although bioethics is barely three decades old, it has already become a taken-for-granted part of medical care: "Ethics committees" are now mandatory in U.S. hospitals; a plethora of seminars offer training in bioethics for those who need, or wish, to offer ethical advice; bioethics courses are now a regular part of the curriculum at universities, colleges, and medical schools.

The typical bioethics course is an introduction to the field: Students review "landmark cases," become acquainted with the current theoretical frameworks for ethical decision making, and are given the chance to "play bioethicist," struggling with knotty ethical problems.[1] Students of bioethics are *not* asked to reflect on the meaning of the fact that the body of knowledge they are studying did not exist thirty years ago. The syllabus for "Introduction to Bioethics" does not include one of the most important questions about the bioethical enterprise, a question that directly addresses the nature of morality in our society: How did bioethics come to supplant literature, law, and religion as a source of moral instruction and arbitration in all matters medical?

For centuries we looked to poems, stories, novels, and plays for advice on how to behave ethically. Well over one hundred years ago, writers like Nathaniel Hawthorne and Mary Shelley were doing what we now call bioethics, raising questions about the proper use of science.[2] In 1976, when bioethics was still in its infancy, Russell Edson wrote a strange little poem that reminds us of the moral dangers of biological engineering:

Counting Sheep

A scientist has a test tube full of sheep. He wonders if
*   he should try to shrink a pasture for them.*
They are like grains of rice.
He wonders if the sheep are aware of their tininess, if
*   they have any sense of scale. Perhaps they just think the*
*   test tube is a glass barn . . .*
He wonders what he should do with them; they
*   certainly have less meat and wool than ordinary sheep*
Has he reduced their commercial value?
He wonders if they could be used as a substitute for
*   rice, a sort of wooly rice . . .*
He wonders if he just shouldn't rub them into a red
*   paste between his fingers.*
He wonders if they are breeding, or if any of them
*   have died.*
He puts them under a microscope and falls asleep
*   counting them . . .* [3]

Twenty years after this poem was written, Scottish scientists succeeded in cloning a lamb, Dolly. The moral implications of this event were profound, but in the late twentieth century, we do not turn to poets for guidance or advice. Nor do we ask our priests or pastors to pass judgment on the behavior of science. Instead we seek counsel from the modern-day arbiters of medical morality, bioethicists. Why bioethics?

Some suggest that bioethics is a new way to regulate medicine. The public has always felt a need to patrol the behavior of physicians. The inequality inherent in the relationship between a physician and a sick person, and the frightening possibilities of medical science, create the desire to find some way to regulate the profession. In the nineteenth century, regulations on medical practice were rather benign. We trusted that entry requirements for medical education would admit only those of good character to the profession. We welcomed physicians into our communities and trusted the surveillance that comes with community to check immoral practice. We approved of professional codes of ethics,[4] trusting physicians to police themselves. Early in the twentieth century, as education became more universal and as geographic and social mobility increased the social distance between our physicians and us, we asked the state to regulate medical practice.[5] In the 1970s we added a layer of control known as bioethics. If we view bioethics as the latest form of regulation, the question "Why bioethics?" becomes *two* questions: What social and historical forces created the need for bioethics? How effective is this new form of regulation?

Like the brothel owners who moved to Los Angeles, medicine has, with the advent of bioethics, experienced a sudden shift in its ethical framework. This book explores why—and *how*—medicine has "gotten ethical." As you read these chapters, you will discover that we have no interest here in resolving ethical dilemmas or in helping bioethicists make "better" decisions. We do not concern ourselves with finding the "right thing to do." Rather, we want to know *"Who gets to say* what is the right thing to do?" We are curious about the who, what, where, and when of bioethics: Who are bioethicists? What are they saying? Where are they working? When are they called upon? Simply put, our goal is to examine and measure bioethics as a new way of being moral.

WHY SOCIOLOGY?

We believe that sociology provides the most direct answer to the question "Why bioethics?" The critical, relativizing stance of sociology allows us to see bioethics in the sweep of history and the context of medicine and society. A sociological approach lifts bioethics out of its clinical setting, examining the way it defines and solves ethical problems, the modes of reasoning it employs, and its influence on medical practice. A brief example, drawn from field notes of a study of bioethicists, illustrates the way a sociological perspective broadens our understanding of the bioethical enterprise:

> At a professional meeting of bioethicists, during a session on the withdrawal of care, a panel member suggested that, in the United States, the decision to withdraw care is often made for financial reasons. She asserted that Medicaid patients (whose care is paid for by the government) are often the victims of financially based withdrawal of care. A well-known bioethicist immediately responded, "Can you *document* the withdrawal of care for economic reasons?" The panelist replied by citing a study of Medicaid patients in California that demonstrated limited access to care for people on government assistance. "But where is the *withdrawal* of care?" the bioethicist asked. "Are Medicaid patients

taken out of intensive care units (ICUs) sooner?" "No," the panelist answered, "they never get into the ICU!" "Well then, they haven't had care withdrawn!" declared the bioethicist.

The bioethicist was technically right but sociologically wrong. From the perspective of the clinic, care that is never begun cannot be withdrawn. Hence, there is no need for a "bioethical" decision. However, if we think about the health care system in the United States sociologically, if we compare it to health care systems in other modern nations, we discover that the poor here do suffer from the withdrawal of care in a much more serious way. Not only is adequate care difficult to obtain, but, with recent reductions in federal support for Medicaid, more and more services are in fact being (collectively) withdrawn from the poor.

The sociological perspective is characterized by a desire to "get the whole picture." The habit of challenging explanations given by those being studied, of looking beyond the taken for granted, leads to a stereotype of sociologists as "professional cynics." Given this penchant to scrutinize existing arrangements of power, one would expect sociologists to be anxious to analyze the moral authority of bioethics and to measure its influence on the traditional power and authority of medicine. One would also expect sociologists to be drawn to bioethics because it raises questions about the social bases of morality—a classic sociological concern. Furthermore, in bioethics we find the type of social action that attracts sociologists: the collision of social worlds, power differences, and the social construction of realities. Yet, until recently, sociologists have been conspicuously absent from the world of bioethics. What has kept sociology from turning its gaze on the practice of bioethics?

For one thing, bioethicists are reluctant to have others watch them work, to subject themselves to clinical trials that would validate their claim to expertise.[6] We have experienced this reluctance firsthand. One of us (DeVries) participated in "Bioethics Summercamp," an annual gathering where prominent bioethicists meet to reflect on the state of their profession and to ruminate on bioethical theory. The response to his presence was enlightening. DeVries explains:

> I obtained permission to be in attendance and was properly introduced at the first session. But on the second day of the meeting, I became the subject of concern. Several journalists had asked to attend and had been refused. Why had I ("this sociologist") been granted entrée? The bioethicists called a special session to decide if I could stay. After some debate (to which I was not privy . . . I was asked to wait in the hallway while my fate was decided), the group decided in my favor. I would be allowed to stay if I agreed (1) that the participants at the sessions would not be named in any publications based on my research and (2) to *permit everyone at the meeting (fifty people or so) to review and edit any article I prepared based on the data I gathered there.* One attendee noted the hypocrisy of this request coming from bioethicists who routinely publish conversations taken from clinical settings without the consent (or knowledge) of patients.

But bashful bioethicists are not the only reason for the lack of a well-developed sociology of bioethics. For their part, sociologists have been reluctant to mix themselves up in bioethics. From its beginning, bioethics was seen as a task for philosophers, physicians, and lawyers, not sociologists. Sociologists and bioethicists have, after all, different approaches to the study of medicine: Sociologists attempt to study the medical world as it is, and bioethicists write about medicine as it ought to be. Sociology tends to be a descriptive discipline that eschews explicit moral judgments. Conversely, bioethics is a prescriptive discipline; its basic work is moral evaluation. These innate differences have led to a significant gap between the disciplines that is only now being closed.

Given the general reluctance of sociologists to study bioethics, what drew us to this field? We editors are medical sociologists who have done a good deal of research in other countries. Working in other societies makes one keenly aware that there are alternate ways of doing medicine and of doing bioethics. In the course of our research, we also noticed that only certain ethical problems interested bioethicists. In Nepal, Subedi witnessed the ill effects of the maldistribution of medical resources and the use of unscrupulous means to promote medical technology. Closer to home, DeVries found American physicians using unfair political tactics to prevent midwives from practicing, thus denying many underserved populations access to maternity care. When we looked for the bioethical response to these (and other) ethical problems, we found none. The clinical bent of bioethicists (illustrated in the discussion about the withdrawal of care) leads them to overlook some of the most profound ethical problems of medicine. It became clear to us that bioethics was in desperate need of sociological examination.

THE PLAN OF THE BOOK

In these pages we and our collaborators seek to explain the emergence of bioethics, to describe and analyze the major trends in the field, to look at ethical questions in other societies, to study the way ethical decisions are *actually* reached (as opposed to how they *should* be reached), and to reflect on the way bioethics is organized.

The contributors to this book include sociologists as well as philosophers, political scientists, anthropologists, nurses, historians, and lawyers. Irrespective of their disciplinary background, you will find each chapter has a sociological flavor. The authors place bioethics in its historical and social context, identifying the cultural, political, economic, and organizational forces that give shape to the ethical enterprise.

In Chapter One, Donald Light and Glenn McGee set the book's tone by exposing the "acontextual" bias of moral philosophy and its stepchild, bioethics. Their analysis opens the door to the work of the other contributors, who explain the many ways in which the field of bioethics has been shaped by its context, even as bioethicists claim to "float above culture and class."[7]

Part I looks at the social contexts that engendered bioethics. Bioethicists are put in their social place: Jonathan Imber suggests that bioethicists are the contemporary version of medical publicists, serving as apologists for medicine; Paul Wolpe explains the penchant of American bioethics to defend autonomy (at the expense of justice); Jeanne Guillemin examines the economic forces that shaped bioethics; and Jonathan Moreno and Valerie Hurt sift through documents from early experiments on radiation, showing us the embryonic stages of the ethical idea of "informed consent" two decades before "bioethics" existed.

The articles in Part II focus on the way bioethics is organized, identifying the social forces that act on the practice of bioethics. Charles Bosk and Joel Frader look closely at institutional ethics committees, exploring the way hospital organization shapes ethical decision making. Rob Houtepen presents a detailed history of the issue of euthanasia in the Netherlands. In his account we gain an appreciation of the influence of culture on the content of ethical questions, and we see how an ethical issue gets passed back and forth among players in the health care arena. Dorothy Wertz's description of her international study of the ethical problems that attend genetics gives us a glimpse of the many ways ethics gets done in other societies.

In Part III we see people *doing* the work of bioethics. We see them in clinics, laboratories, and centers of bioethics thinking about and making ethical decisions. Eugene Gallagher and his collaborators use three different pieces of nursing research to make a case for *social bioethics*, a bioethics that considers the social dynamics of the relationships in clinics and labs. Bette-Jane Crigger examines the changing fashions of bioethics, giving us an overview of the work of bioethicists found in professional journals over the past twenty-five years. Karen Gervais looks at the bioethical challenges of a changing America. The increasingly multicultural face of the United States and the shift to managed care demand a response by bioethics, but how can the individualistic, abstract framework of the field accommodate? Gervais offers suggestions based on her experience as the director of an ethics center involved in developing policy in both areas.

By asking questions about how bioethicists gather information, how the field organizes itself, and the ideologies bioethicists bring to their work, the articles in Part IV suggest ways bioethicists can use social science. Raymond DeVries and Peter Conrad show how well-crafted ethnographic analysis and a thorough sociology of the bioethical profession can help bioethics see the disjuncture between their goals and their accomplishments. Bruce Jennings analyzes the intellectual work of bioethics, showing bioethicists how their biases shape their work and the larger field.

In the course of producing this book, DeVries and Renée Fox, one of the first sociologists to examine bioethics in depth, engaged in a conversation (via phone, fax, and express mail) about the history and current condition of the sociology of bioethics. Together they reviewed each chapter, considering its place in the growing field. A summary of these conversations is presented in the Afterword.

We began this preface by noting that, as sociologists, we are not professionally interested in helping bioethicists do their work better. Our intent is to use bioethics and bioethicists for our own social scientific ends: In bioethics we find an ideal arena in which to extend our ideas about the creation and organization of new professions, the social context of morality, and the role of expertise in society. If you read this book closely, however, you will discover a certain paradox in the disinterested approach to bioethics we espouse. When we cast a "cold sociological eye" on the field, we give bioethicists the opportunity to be more effective. At work here is a sociological version of the bioethical idea of "double effect." Our objective is the sociological dissection of bioethics. An unintended and unavoidable outcome of that effort is a better understanding of the bioethical transaction, a sort of "guidebook to effective bioethics." Paradoxically, it is in remaining disinterested that we produce the information bioethicists and their clients need to make medicine a more just and loving enterprise. As cold and objective as we may appear, we are not saddened to think that our work might make this world a better place.

ACKNOWLEDGMENTS

Talk to anyone who has edited an anthology and you will hear stories of woe. You will learn that the editorial task includes the worst features of academic life: broken promises of procrastinating contributors, missing references, improper citations, long hours laboring over someone else's sloppy writing, unwilling permissions editors. But if you get beyond these editorial lamentations, most editors will admit that assembling an anthology also embodies the best of academic life, the very things many of us hoped for when we entered graduate school. What other occasion offers the opportunity to be on the cutting edge of a new field, to weigh arguments, and to engage colleagues in a vigorous dialogue about ideas and issues (rather than departmental policies)?

Going through this process felt, to us, like a *rite de passage*. The task includes the three elements Van Gennep attributed to rites of passage: separation, transition, and incorporation. As scolding editors we felt removed from the community of colleagues; in the midst of the task we had strong feelings of being "between," of being nowhere (*"this project will never succeed; why did we begin?"*); and then, with publication, we reenter the community, our status slightly changed.

Viewing the editorial task as a rite of passage allows us to appreciate the communal nature of academic life. In spite of our academic egos and our blustering, the production of knowledge is a group effort. Acknowledging this we would like to thank the several people who helped us bring this project to light. Our work was made easier by bioethicists who were willing to open their world to sociological inquiry. Particular patience in this regard has been shown by Karen Gervais and Art Caplan. Help with writing was provided by Steven Polansky, Alvin Handelman, Carol Holly, and Charlotte DeVries. Belinda Quick did some sociological snooping on her own, and her notes offered empirical support for some of the observations made here. Eileen Shimota, Jennifer Swift, and Christine Flunker helped with the many clerical details. Robert Wennberg of Westmont College deserves credit for planting the seeds of interest in ethics over two decades ago, seeds that have grown into this book.

A product like this also requires financial support and someone willing to take a chance on publishing something new and completely different. The faculty research grant program of St. Olaf College supported the research that led to this book. The folks at Prentice Hall, notably Nancy Roberts and Pat Naturale, not only took a chance with this book, but remained patient and gracious throughout the process.

Finally, thanks to our contributors and to our families. It was Charlotte, Anna, Rocky, Jesse, Sree, Sonny, and Avik who offered the support and stability we needed to generate this book.

Raymond DeVries
Janardan Subedi

NOTES

1. Visit the web site of the Center for Bioethics at the University of Pennsylvania (http://www.med.upenn.edu/~bioethic/) to see syllabi for "Introduction to Bioethics."

2. See Hawthorne's (1970) short story "The Birthmark," (published in 1843) and Shelley's (1994) *Frankenstein, or the Modern Prometheus* (published in 1818). Bly (1996) has collected a number of literary pieces that impart ethical instruction. Fine examples of writing with bioethical overtones can be found in the work of physician writers Williams (1984) and Selzer (1987). Film versions of ethical narratives are offered by Steven Spielberg's *Jurassic Park* and *The Lost World*. Reaching literally millions of viewers, these movies warn of the dangers of cloning and genetic engineering.

3. See Edson (1976).

4. Because they are intended to regulate the relationship between practitioners (in this case, physicians), professional codes of ethics are better thought of as etiquette.

5. See Abbott (1983) for a thorough discussion of professional ethics and professional regulation.

6. "Ethicists, it seems, have ethical objections to being evaluated," reports Shalit (1997) in a journalistic exposé of bioethics.

7. See Callahan (1997).

REFERENCES

Abbot, Andrew. 1983. Professional ethics. *American Journal of Sociology* 88(5): 855–85.

Bly, Carol. 1996. *Changing the bully that rules the world.* Minneapolis: Milkweed.

Callahan, Daniel. 1997. Bioethics and the culture wars. *Nation* 264(14): 23–4.

Edson, Russell. 1976. *The intuitive journey and other works.* New York: Harper & Row.

Hawthorne, Nathaniel. 1970 [1843]. *Hawthorne: Selected tales and sketches.* San Francisco: Rinehart Press.

Selzer, Richard. 1987. *Confessions of a knife.* New York: Quill.

Shalit, Ruth. 1997. When we were philosopher kings. *New Republic* 216(17): 24–8.

Shelley, Mary W. 1994 [1818]. *Frankenstein, or the modern Prometheus.* New York: Oxford University Press.

Williams, William C. 1984. *The doctor's stories.* Compiled with an introduction by Robert Coles. New York: New Directions.

Contributors

Charles L. Bosk is Professor of Sociology, Senior Fellow of the Leonard Davis Institute of Health Economics, and Senior Faculty Associate in the Center for Bioethics at the University of Pennsylvania.

Julie B. Brown is Assistant Professor in the Medical Assisting Technology Program in the Department of Medical Services Technology at Eastern Kentucky University.

Anna Cholewinska is a doctoral candidate in sociology at the University of Kentucky. Her dissertation focuses on graduate medical training.

Peter Conrad is Harry Coplan Professor of Social Sciences and Chair of the Department of Sociology at Brandeis University.

Bette-Jane Crigger is editor-in-chief of the *Hastings Center Report* and co-director of the Hastings Center project "Value Perceptions and Realities in Managed Health Care," which examines ethical concerns in managed care from the perspectives of managers, health care providers, and patient-members. She is also managing editor of *IRB: A Review of Human Subjects Research*, a bimonthly newsletter devoted to examining ethical issues in biomedical and behavioral research.

Raymond DeVries is Associate Professor of Sociology at St. Olaf College, Northfield, Minnesota.

Renée C. Fox is Annenberg Professor of Social Sciences at the University of Pennsylvania.

Joel Frader, M.D., is Associate Professor of Pediatrics at Children's Memorial Hospital and Northwestern University Medical School, Chicago. He is also a core faculty member in the NWUMS Medical Ethics and Humanities Program.

Eugene B. Gallagher is Professor of Medical Sociology in the Department of Behavioral Science and Sociology, University of Kentucky.

Karen G. Gervais is Director of the Minnesota Center for Health Care Ethics and Professor of Philosophy at the College of St. Catherine, Minneapolis.

Jeanne Guillemin is Professor of Sociology at Boston College. She also directs the HealthQuest Project at Boston College, a federally funded effort to promote new communication technology for health care education.

Rob Houtepen is Associate Professor in the Department of Health Care Ethics and Philosophy, University of Maastricht, the Netherlands.

Valerie Hurt was a Research Associate with the President's Advisory Committee on Human Radiation Experiments. She is currently studying law at the University of Virginia.

Jonathan B. Imber is Professor of Sociology at Wellesley College, Wellesley, Massachusetts.

Bruce Jennings is Executive Vice President of the Hastings Center, a prominent bioethics research institute.

Donald W. Light is Professor of Sociology and Comparative Health Care Systems at the University of Medicine and Dentistry of New Jersey and Rutgers University. Currently he is a Senior Visiting Fellow at the University of Pennsylvania Center for Bioethics.

Glenn McGee is Assistant Professor and Director of Graduate Studies at the University of Pennsylvania Center for Bioethics and Senior Fellow in Health Economics at the Wharton School Leonard Davis Institute.

Jessica Mesman is Director of the International Master's Programme, "European Studies on Society, Science, and Technology," at the University of Maastricht, the Netherlands.

Jonathan D. Moreno is Professor of Pediatrics and of Medicine and Director of the Division of Humanities at the SUNY Health Science Center at Brooklyn. He is also a Faculty Associate of the Center for Bioethics at the University of Pennsylvania and director of its project on Human Research Ethics. During 1994–1995 he was Senior Policy and Research Analyst for the President's Advisory Committee on Human Radiation Experiments.

Pamela Schlomann is Associate Professor of Nursing at Eastern Kentucky University.

Rebecca S. Sloan is Assistant Professor in the Family Health Nursing Department at Indiana University School of Nursing and serves as a nursing research consultant for the Kidney Disease Program at the University of Louisville.

Janardan Subedi is Associate Professor of Medical Sociology in the Department of Sociology and Anthropology, Miami University, Oxford, Ohio.

Dorothy C. Wertz is associated with the program on social science, ethics, and law at the Shriver Center for Mental Retardation. She is principal investigator on a New England Regional Genetics Group project, "Quality Assurance in Genetics: A Collaboration of Consumers and Providers."

Paul Root Wolpe is Senior Faculty Associate and Director of the Project on Informed Consent at the Center for Bioethics at the University of Pennsylvania, where he also serves on the faculty of the Department of Sociology.

Bioethics and Society

CHAPTER ONE

On the Social Embeddedness of Bioethics

Donald W. Light and Glenn McGee

The field of bioethics exists because those who are not bioethicists need help in resolving difficult ethical dilemmas. These dilemmas are spawned in medical institutions, where history, culture, and family interact with professional and institutional power structures and with economic demands. Are bioethicists prepared to weigh all these factors in their deliberations?

Most American bioethicists have been trained in philosophy departments where Anglo-American analytic philosophy holds sway. Analytic philosophy, with its insistence on linguistic strictures and universal moral duties, tends to reduce the complexities of the clinic to the most benign details (patient X requests the discontinuation of treatment Y). As a result of their training, bioethicists are inclined to take an anecdotal approach to the basic "principles" of bioethics. Or, even worse, analytic philosophers turned bioethicists will insert here and there, as suits their argument, a few facts or assertions about the real world. The full range of variables present in a clinical context will be ignored, as will the implications of these variables for defining the issues and finding solutions.

In their important essay on the social and cultural myopia of bioethics, Renée Fox and Judith Swazey (1984, 339, 356) forcefully argue that analytic "moral philosophy has had the greatest molding influence on the field. . . . Within its rigorously stripped-down analytic and methodological framework, bioethics is prone to reify its own logic and to formulate absolutist, self-confirming principles and insights." This sort of bioethics runs the danger of what Chinese scholars have called "playing with emptiness." The result, observed a Canadian bioethicist who directed workshops in the field, is a growing intellectual and practical irrelevance (Hoffmaster 1992).

Our goals in this essay are to identify some of the "bad habits" wreaked by the twenty-year-old dominance of analytic philosophical approaches to ethics and medicine, and to point out several ways empirical social study can change the shape of bioethical research and the discipline of bioethics itself. We are convinced that sociology and the other social sciences have much to contribute to bioethics. Empirical work will show bioethicists the socially constructed nature of the moral issues they are pursuing. The provision of empirical underpinnings for normative work increases the perceptiveness of normative analysis by underscoring its social character. "Social bioethics" improves on "analytic bioethics" by locating philosophical deliberation squarely in the social and institutional contexts that shape moral issues. We demonstrate that a strictly analytic bioethics—one that relies on principles uninformed by a sociological analysis of how moral life is constructed—will never develop workable solutions to moral problems.

The failure of analytic bioethics is particularly evident in bioethicists' attempts to formulate policy and participate in governance. Consider the diligent efforts of a number of moral philosophers who sought to develop and enact policies dealing with do-not-resuscitate (DNR) orders and advanced directives. The "patient self-determination act," the most significant end-of-life decision-making legislation in several decades, was framed by the analytic, deontological model of patients as rational, autonomous individuals. By now it is very clear (see SUPPORT 1995) that these efforts have failed to increase decision-making power at the end of life. Why? Harold Garfinkel (1967), a founder of ethnomethodology, would have said there are "good sociological reasons" for these "bad bioethical outcomes." For example, Robert Zussman (1992) points out that intensive care units (ICUs) vary widely in how often they write DNR orders and in how often the patient is consulted. Renée Anspach's (1993) ethnography of neonatal intensive care units (NICUs) shows that physicians and nurses frequently do not seek informed consent but rather "manufacture assent" with the patient and family and "diffuse dissent."

Much more is missing in the narrow debates about how to construct and enact surrogacy through advance directives: the hierarchical organization of clinical units, the dominance of the culture of physicians (with its predilection for technological intervention and cure) over the culture of nursing, the dynamics of the family, and the necessity for complex and ongoing revision of any treatment plan at the end of life (Hastings 1996; Marshall 1996).

Advance directives do not function as explicit instructions to be carried out by autonomous rational beings. They are better thought of as important guideposts for those entrusted with the care of a suffering person in a rapidly changing, complex situation replete with ambiguous clinical signs, power struggles, value differences, and varied perceptions. Those who wrote the patient self-determination act, its accompanying DHHS instructions, and the many guides to hospital policy covering advanced directives seem to have assumed a different culture from the one encountered by the SUPPORT study and by those who work on ethics in clinical settings. The framers seem to have supposed a "DNR culture" in which patients present as total individuals with fully articulated preferences about sustaining treatments, preferences that would work under any clinical circumstances. These patients would also always present as unambiguously terminal and incompetent, and with relatives who do not fight about outcomes or come from cultures with differing values. Meanwhile in *real* hospitals, the clinical team and family must share the elusive search for meaning and good outcomes within an ambiguous climate of forced trust, with or without advance directives (Zaner 1987).

Several historians and social scientists have argued that the field of bioethics in the United States is rooted in a secular fundamentalism that emphasizes individualism as glue of a highly pluralistic society (David Rothman, Ludwig Edelstein, Leroy Walters, Richard Zaner, and, in these pages, Paul Wolpe). The field's institutional dynamics and funding influenced its shift from a religious to a secular principlism. Bioethics department faculty came to rely on a patchwork quilt of principles to be applied to any case, regardless of its complexity: autonomy, beneficence, and justice. These principles are now overused and diluted. As Fox and Swazey (1984) point out, the most pernicious problem with the preoccupation of analytic bioethics with particular principles is the insistence on the isolated individual and his or her rights:

> In the prevailing ethos of bioethics, the value of individualism is defined in such a way, and emphasized to such a degree, that it is virtually severed from social and religious values concerning relationships between individuals; their responsibilities, commitments, and emotional bonds to one another; the significance of the groups and of the societal community to which they belong; and the deep inward as well as outward influence that these have on the individual and his or her sense of the moral (358).

The development of this concept of the individual, a notion that doomed the advance directive project and that is everywhere apparent in analytic bioethics, stems from the bad habits of moral philosophy as understood and taught in the majority of Anglo-American philosophy departments. Before we can move to a social bioethics, we must have a thorough understanding of these bad habits.

THE BAD HABITS OF ANALYTIC BIOETHICS

Our democratic history and, indeed, important parts of our personal lives speak to the importance of responsibility and individuality in human life. Sociology demands, however, that we reinterpret the notions of individuality that are the foundation of the principles of autonomy and informed consent. Sociology insists that individual behaviors and choices emanate from the norms and customs of their setting and from institutional structures. Take a look at smoking. Although we hold smokers accountable for their behavior, a model of rational individualism cannot explain levels of self-control. Smoking is a matter of probabilities, group dynamics, advertising, capitalist exploitation, and social class. The smoker is also a part of a culture, the object of intense commercialism, and the participant in multiple "spheres of discourse." However, for the purposes of analytic philosophy, the smoker must be reduced to a "person *X* at time *T*." This asocial nature of analytic philosophy is best illustrated by the "trolley problem."

Suppose a trolley is barreling down Powell Street in San Francisco and you are at the switch where the track splits. Ahead of you, tied to the left track, is a thirty-five-year-old woman, a middle manager with two children, who chain smokes. Tied to the right track is another thirty-five-year-old woman, a middle manager with two children, who does not smoke. The trolley cannot be stopped. Which way will you pull the switch?

Note that, besides the stick figures tied to the tracks, the "you" in the moral dilemma is presumed to be an impartial, disembodied, rational person, preferably a trained philosopher certified in trolley problem solving. The point of thought experiments is to isolate relations between key variables, but in the process the real issues are often left out or distorted beyond usefulness. What is absent in the trolley problem is what we think of in our practical lives as "context."

Social context can be introduced to the experiment by endlessly varying the options. Suppose the nonsmoking woman tied to the right track is age sixty-five instead of thirty-five. Or suppose the smoking woman tied to the left track is twenty-five years old and just got pregnant before a moral philosopher burst into her office to drag her off to her theoretical fate on the steel rails at the bottom of Powell Street.

The problem with these stick figures, no matter how you clothe them, is that their experience and complexity is sacrificed to the simplifying principles of analytic philosophy. Conceived with the noble intent to make moral answers concise and to make moral deliberation an objective endeavor, trolley problems lead to the kind of moral dialogue Alasdair MacIntyre criticized in his indictment of American moral commentary and debate, *After Virtue* (1984).

Because only certain kinds of bioethical dilemmas fit into the trolley mode, analytic moral philosophers are forced to practice a form of methodological imperialism, choosing problems that suit their methodological devices, for it is methodology that drives most disciplines and defines the professional identity of practitioners. (This is not merely a habit of philosophers.) Thus, the analytic defense of the necessity of trolley problems, with their stick figures, possible worlds, and phantasmic reality, puts the matter backward. Since that kind of analysis is *defined* as "incisive," as good professional work, then the study of bioethics is constructed to suit the tools in the analytic repertoire, and thick descriptions of reality are abandoned (Geertz 1973). This defense of analytic categorization is familiar; we have heard it from many economists for years.

The simplifying assumptions of neoclassical economics give its concepts their "theoretical power." *Homo sapiens* is reduced to *Homo economicus,* whose only goal in a situation is to rationally maximize whatever most benefits self-interest, especially monetary self-interest (Light 1995). The failure of prevailing economic theories to predict or explain behavior merely leads to elaborating the theories, not to taking noneconomic variables into account. Similarly,

> Thought experiments are one of an array of cognitive techniques used in bioethics to distance and abstract itself from the human settings in which ethical questions are embedded and experienced, reduce their complexity and ambiguity, limit the number and kinds of morally relevant factors to be dealt with, dispel dilemmas and siphon off the emotion, suffering, bewilderment, and tragedy that many medical moral predicaments entail for patients, families, and medical professionals. (Fox and Swazey 1984, 356)

The bad habit of decontextualization is simple to diagnose but, like most bad habits, hard to change. We must provide bioethics with more than better trolley problems, adorned with multiple contingencies. Instead, the trolley problem itself must give way to a more subtle analysis of the meaning of data about cultural preferences, political structures, and clinical situations.

A second bad habit of analytic philosophy is the separation of theory from practice. Moral philosophy in America is often articulated in terms of a generally relevant issue, stripped of the specific institutional contexts that give the issue its meaning and define the options for change. Euthanasia affords a good example of this bad habit. When presented as a general issue, euthanasia admits of huge moral distinctions and simple dogmatic positioning. In practice, the issues of euthanasia are taken up by courts, clinicians, and patients in difficult social contexts where options for treatment and nontreatment are limited and laced with practical ambiguities and consequences. Euthanasia operates in many social spheres, each of which presents a complex vocabulary and extensive institutional history. It is useful to be in the ivory tower to solve problems of symbolic logic, but to solve problems of assisted suicide (especially after the decisions of the ninth and second circuit courts and the trials of Kevorkian; see Annas 1995), one must leave the ivory tower and enter social life. Some moral philosophers have recognized the importance of practice and have begun to address bioethics within a more empirically informed framework (Jonsen 1991; Brody 1993; Caplan 1995), but these are minority correctives to a long analytic tradition that ignored social context. Analytic moral philosophers become naive agents of larger powers by asking the questions and framing the analysis in ways that serve these powers by leaving them assumed and unexamined.

The bad habit of assuming that social engagement is outside the scope of the theoretician is actually not so difficult to kick. The roots of philosophy, both modern and ancient, are rife with theoreticians qua citizens, writing tracts overtly aimed at influencing the media, culture, and policy in intelligent ways. The trend toward speculative abstraction is fairly recent, promulgated by analytic philosophers. Fortunately, there are within the phenomenological and pragmatic philosophical orientations (articulated by John Dewey, Hans Jonas, and others) suggestions for situating philosophy in its biological, scientific, and social context (McGee 1994, 1996; Lachs 1995). The goal of this work is to formulate philosophical reflection in terms of problems in society, rather than transcendent dilemmas. When philosophy begins with an immediate problem, attending to its multiple layers of empirical complexity, it is less able to insist on insular and monodisciplinary reflections that do not translate into policy or action.

A third bad habit is the invocation of "moral intuitions," or beliefs, without appreciating and examining the extent to which the moral "institutions" of bioethicists are shaped by culture, family upbringing, social class, and personal and social injuries. Moral intuition and articles of faith often play a fundamental role in philosophical argument, serving as the anchor or reference point against which the validity of arguments can be tested. Intuitively derived moral philosophy is an enterprise that develops arguments to justify articles of secular faith and what "feels right" for its practitioners. As such, intuitionism is an elaborate tribal ritual of upper middle-class culture.

THE EMPIRICAL CHARACTER OF ETHICAL PROBLEMS

Of course, social scientists are not without sin. Social scientists also develop bad habits; a few even share the bad habits of moral philosophers, stripping people of sociocultural contexts in unreflective ways, letting method determine the mode and/or results of social inquiry. A bad habit more commonly found among social scientists is the reluctance to deal with the reciprocal relationship between data and norms. A richly rendered social science, one that uses critical theories and focuses on the social constructions of reality, a social science that documents the full texture of social action, must be normative. A sociology that acknowledges its normative dimension can help bioethics in important ways. The role of sociologists in bioethics is to analyze the culture of bioethics and to illuminate the social character of bioethical problems (see DeVries 1995). In addition, the sociology of bioethics should participate in a reformulation of norms in terms of the social institutions and problems of bioethics.

Allow us to illustrate what we mean by *reformulation of norms* by examining the "moral" implications of smoking for health insurance. According to the insurance industry and its actuarial concept of fairness (Light 1992), the premiums for smokers (and others who indulge in risky or unhealthy habits) should be higher than nonsmokers because it is unfair for the former to impose part of their higher costs on the latter. Some argue that the premiums should be set to reflect the higher health costs of smokers. Others argue that the premiums should be set to deter policyholders from smoking or to induce smokers to quit. These three policies imply three different methodologies for arriving at an actuarially "fair" rate, and they contain different lines of argument relating fairness to action. Sociologically, the prior question is when, how, and why smokers got singled out and whose agenda this serves (Troyer and Markle 1983). Skiers or cyclists, for example, present a much clearer increase in risk and medical costs within a policy year, but they are not given the same scrutiny as smokers.

After framing the ethical issue in its sociological context, there are empirical questions of whether and how each of the three policies can be accomplished. Suppose, for example, pack-a-day smokers actually turn out to cost less over the course of their lifetimes than nonsmokers. This fact would expose the contrived nature of the moral problem declared by the moral entrepreneurs. Suppose further that those who really run up the premiums are healthy persons who collect decades of Social Security and other benefits and whose long-term chronic disorders run up costs in Medicare and Medicaid that the rest of us are then obligated to pay. Should the moral entrepreneurs not slap a surcharge on precisely the opposite group of people? Otherwise, it would be the long-living, "nonsinning" healthy citizens who end up imposing higher medical costs on smokers, drinkers, and other sinners (Menzel 1990, chap. 4; Morreim 1996). Policies and norms concerning this "sin tax" would then either have to be reformulated so that the data do not matter or reformulated to take account of the data. The retort that only the data have changed, and not the central norm (that risk should be proportionally distributed), misses the point that what really drives the policy here is a social movement or moral crusade (Gusfield 1963). The ethic of actuarial fairness is merely a way of making the crusade philosophical, scholarly, and "objective." Fairness gets its meaning from the social context.

Empirical details cloud the original principle of actuarial fairness until it is not clear what its advocates are talking about. When one thinks of the high costs of smoking, one thinks of lung cancer, heart disease, and other expensive major illnesses that come after years of smoking. But insurance policies are annual contracts, so one can only deal with issues of distributive injustice within a policy year. Separating out the excess costs by age, sex, and years of smoking is a daunting though not impossible task (Hodgson 1992). These costs rise for males in their thirties, peak in their fifties, and then decline to be *less* than nonsmokers in their seventies. The excess costs of women smokers, however, peak in their thirties and decline slowly into old age. One needs also to take into account that it would be unfair to charge as much excess premium to weekend smokers as to daily smokers. Unless such a differentiated schedule of actuarially fair rates is calculated and used, the premiums will be unfair in a different way. And, of course, one assumes that the insurance company will lower the premiums of nonsmokers accordingly rather than use actuarial fairness as a justification for surcharges of pure profit.

Beyond data that help one think through the ethics of a certain practice are the sociocultural contexts of that practice. We argued earlier that analytic philosophy is unusually ill suited to situating problems in subtle contexts of practice and culture. The trolley problem does not allow for contextualization of the kind required for health care risk management. If one's guiding principle is that people are rational, autonomous individuals who should be held accountable for their role in increasing health costs, then those with chronic disorders who manage self-treatment poorly should be taxed when they run up unnecessary costs in acute crisis medicine. Why not slap a surcharge on every diabetic who comes into the emergency room because she did not take her insulin on time? One such incident costs more within a policy year than any policyholder's pack-a-day smoking habit over the same year. Of course, we would hasten to add that this narrow conceptualization of responsibility in risk management leaves out the setting and dynamic forces that result in poorly managed chronic conditions in the first place. One needs to understand the socially and personally constructed character of the philosophical problem and the role of bioethics in it.

Let us turn to the second strategy for discounting smoking, namely, inducing smokers to cease their behavior through incentives or disincentives. Suppose evidence shows that financial disincentives work imperfectly because smoking is embedded in group dynamics and culture (Ennett and Bauman 1993). At that point, the question of whether it is fair to impose surcharges to compel rational, autonomous individuals to give up smoking becomes moot. Suppose some smokers are not trapped in addiction but actually enjoy it. Then what seems to be an act of constructive paternalism to get people to quit would become an act of coercion (Wikler 1978). To what extent would one be substituting one coercion for another: *their* imposition of extra costs on us versus *our* imposition of extra charges on them for their lifestyle choices? Daniel Wikler points out that, even among those with bad habits or addiction, one must recognize second-order volition. Moral reformers paint a picture of people who would otherwise act prudently caught up by "sources of involuntariness" such as ignorance, or being under the sway of external influences, or suffering from difficult circumstances. The reformers aim to liberate these "victims" from such influences and restore their autonomy. But Wikler points out several ways in which this posture imposes the reformer's view of the "victim's" life on the victim so that paternalistic acts become quite coercive.

A further danger is the possibility that one will be co-opted by special interests whose cards are not on the table. Policies that charge higher premiums to smokers and others who have risk-inducing behaviors legitimate risk pooling that insurance companies use more broadly to maximize profits by minimizing the risks they cover (Light 1992). This undermines the social function of health insurance, to provide coverage for people when they get high medical bills and thereby to support, as well, medicine as a social institution. Moreover, sin taxes on behavioral risks presuppose as a telos the vision of an autonomous, rational individual living a risk-free life. This implies a society stripped of much of its richness and texture. One would eliminate all contact sports, penalize women who wait past age thirty-five to bear children, and, in short, remove all risks that make society dynamic.

ON THE SOCIAL CONSTRUCTION OF A MORAL ISSUE

Moral issues are not just "there." Even when they seem obviously timeless and universal, such as "when is killing justified," the fact that they are in the air at a given time and are taken up in certain ways and not others means that they are socially constructed. Figure 1 summarizes six aspects of social construction. In some cases, moral issues come up or are dealt with in certain ways largely because of intellectual or disciplinary forces. That is, they are not so much issues in society at the time as issues in a discipline or a cluster of disciplines. But in many cases, even timeless and universal issues—such as "under what circumstances, if any, is it justified to terminate life"—are framed by the economic, political, religious, and institutional forces of a given historical period. A thoughtful review of those forces and how they affect bioethical work is necessary for careful moral reasoning.

Think of it this way. There are scores, even hundreds, of moral issues lying around. Should people be pouring millions of dollars into distributing millions of tons of toxic substances into the ground to cultivate front-yard lawns? What should we do about the population explosion of pets, about all the cats and dogs that are put to death or left to starve? What are we to make of the ever-increasing proportion of our food that comes to us prepackaged and the subsequent loss of cooking skills and addition of mutagens to the food supply (McGee 1994)? One could go on. The point is that only a few of

Figure 1   The Social Construction of a Moral Issue: Six Issues

Whose issue is it anyway?
Developments and changes (over at least a century)
Attention to the role of class, power, vested interests
Attention to processes of legitimation and institutionalization
Comparative, ironic distance from the current issue
Whose interests are you serving (unintended or not)?

the scores of moral/ethical issues rise to the forefront at a given time and in a given way. Therefore, the politics and social construction of the social problems of our time become a permanent concern. We therefore need to focus on the vested interests, moral entrepreneurs, social movements, and cultural receptivity that result in the rise and fall of social problems. Deviance and normalcy, wrong and right, are not distinct categories but social constructions in a process that has no end (Troyer and Markle 1983).

This is a view understood by Kant, whose third critique examines in detail the meaning of social context, and Mill, whose utilitarianism explores the social rootedness of the good. Nonetheless, quite ironically, it is from a few fashionable passages of Kant's *Metaphysics of Morals* and Mill's *On Liberty* that the strongest defenses, respectively, of universal principlism and individual autonomy derive.

There are a few hints, some useful foci, for examining the social construction of a moral issue. First, it is helpful to understand the developments and changes in the perception of a problem in particular cultural groups over a period of time. This gives critical distance from one's own enterprise. Second, one should pay particular attention to the role of power and interest groups in the development of a moral issue as a moral issue and its differential impact of social classes. The processes of legitimation of an issue and its institutionalization are particularly important; moral philosophers become part of that process and need to be self-critical about it. In the end, one wants to be sure whose interests are being served by the moral deliberations. A good example of this sort of reflexivity is found in the incisive analysis of human genetic interventions by Richard Lewontin and Ruth Hubbard (1996). They have done much to expose the reasons for the radically limited critiques of genetic testing and gene therapy in the literature (see McGee 1997).

ON SOCIAL DIMENSIONS OF ACTION

Having grasped the social and historical construction of a bioethical issue, it is useful to clarify the empirical dimensions of action. Those dimensions, presented in Figure 2, are in an approximate sequence for a social approach to bioethics: knowing, desiring or fearing, starting or trying to start, experiencing, continuing, stopping or trying to, abstaining from the action, and perhaps relapsing. How do people come to know about something, and in what ways do they come to know it? What institutional or cultural frames are involved? What role do resources or deprivations play? What about knowing makes it desirable, or an action to be feared? What are the circumstances and social dynamics under which a person first does or tries something? How is the experience of that action filtered or framed by peers, family, and the social setting? What issues are involved in continuing or discontinuing the behavior? If the behavior is stopped, what conflicting influences are involved in deciding to start

Knowing
Desiring/fearing
Starting (or trying)
Experiencing
Continuing
Stopping (or trying)
Abstaining

**Figure 2   Dimensions
of Action**

again or not? These steps might be thought of as "stations of the habit." There is research literature on each of them. Each involves different dynamics, different influences, and different obstacles. Yet these are dimensions of action not captured by the explorations of the moral actor in the philosophical literature since William James. We suggest that a social methodology for bioethical action begins with these investigations of the dimensions of the problem.

Types and degree of action.   Most actions (including single acts like abortion) are not unitary acts. The dimensions of action intersect with types and degree of the action. It would be useful to organize knowledge from the social sciences here around the morally or philosophically relevant types and degrees, and one needs to think through in each case what they are. In the case of smoking and tobacco consumption, types might be constructed in terms of degree of addiction, degree of polluting others' air, and short-term versus long-term effects. One should note what classifications researchers have used, because they may be informative and open up new avenues of thought about the philosophical issues.

Social and institutional contexts.   How much people know about a given action, when and how they start or continue, which types of actions they take, and other dimensions of the issue all occur in social and institutional contexts. They are summarized in Figure 3.

Anspach (1993), for example, shows how nurses develop different perceptions than do doctors of the "facts" and issues from their constant interaction with infants in NICUs. Her research calls attention to the organizational dynamics by which decisions about terminating treatment are made and the ways in which parents' involvement is managed.

Moral deliberations would be enriched by taking these into account and by considering who else tends to be involved: Who does what to whom under what circumstances? What are the major variations? How do the actions and settings differ by social class? How do the different actors and those acted

Social settings: Who else is involved? Who does what to whom under what circumstances? Variations

Social class; patterns of action by class and actor; reasons for variations

Issues of legality, rule breaking, deviance

Sanctions, stigma, the moral community

Contextual options; being boxed in

Figure 3   Social and Institutional Contexts

upon differ by class, and why? What rules, norms, or laws are being broken, and with what consequences? Finally, what are the contextual options open to actors, and to what extent are they boxed in?

Degree of volition.   To what extent do free will or determinism characterize the behaviors in question? This is a dichotomy that is challenged by empirical evidence about the nature of behavior. The term *free will*, like the term *free markets*, is more ideological than descriptive, representing an abstraction from the actual human experience of thinking about and feeling responsible for one's action. We know of no substantial markets where there are not rules, regulations, and structures. We further suspect there are very few acts that are unshaped by the biological and social structures of personality and temperament, upbringing, and recent social, emotional, economic, and physical situations. Perhaps free will signals a paradigm difference between most of the social sciences on one hand and analytic philosophy, natural law jurisprudence, and much of economics on the other. For example, many courts have ruled against smokers who brought litigation against tobacco companies; these courts hold that smokers are rational beings who exercise free will. But, if this is true, why are tobacco companies spending hundreds of millions of dollars a year advertising in subtle and deliberately manipulative ways that have little or nothing to do with informing rational decision makers? We believe that a method derived from the contextual study common to the social sciences offers a more accurate view of human action.

To that end, we argue that a more subtle and useful way to account for human moral choices can be captured by a scale of volition (Figure 4), with not-so-free will at one end and simple immutable biological causation, like eye color or Down syndrome, at the other end. The point of our scale is merely to demonstrate that the trolley problem and its attendant analytic assumptions about the insularity of moral decision making are in need of redesign in order to better account for personal and social behavior. As John Dewey notes in *Human Nature and Conduct*, one crucial missing dimension of human moral thinking is the construct of habit. Is smoking or drinking a habit, an addiction, or both? Or in some cases one and in other cases the other? Is it a "good"

Personal	Social
"Free" will (relatively speaking)	
Genetic predispositions	Values
Habits	Customs
Needs	Norms
Rituals	Stigmas
Obsession/compulsions	Rules
Addictions	Prescriptions
Genetic determinism	Laws

Figure 4   Scales of Volition

habit or a "bad" habit, and what social construction makes it so? We need a better account of volition and investment in behavior to address such questions and their implications for moral philosophy.

In thinking about some other kinds of "voluntary" behaviors like sexual activity, we need an even stronger category than Dewey's habits, something like "need." A person may have sexual habits, just as he or she may have eating habits, but that is not the same as the "need" to eat or the "need" to have sex. Some might argue there are no such needs, and certainly needs can be culturally and socially shaped. But *Homo sapiens* do a lot of what they do for deep, inarticulate reasons that seem to mitigate against cultural descriptions of short-term best interest. If these reasons are more fundamental than habits but different than addictions, we need in our account of moral action something like "need" as a category.

Interestingly, most behaviors that become habits or addictions begin voluntarily, or at least as voluntarily as a person's social and cultural embeddedness will allow. One might think that after people quit smoking, for example, abstaining and/or relapsing is voluntary too, but considerable evidence indicates that it is much harder not to start again than it was to start in the first place. In this way, initial choice becomes a determinant of subsequent choice. How well can analytic bioethics consider moral issues in the middle categories of this scale, where there is no clear agent, or where responsibility cannot be clearly assigned?

Harm to self and to others.   Finally, how much harm to self or to others is involved in an act or constellation of acts and policies? Harms are often asserted or assumed, but this too is an empirical question, and it needs to be broken down into several categories, as shown in Figure 5. One needs to consider different types of harms—physical, psychological, relational, indirect, and perhaps others—and the degree to which they happen. One needs to

---

Types of harm: physical, psychological, relational
Degrees of harm
Imminency . . . latency of different types of harms
Costs of harms and their distribution to self, to others, to institutions, to society
Sequelae of harms

Figure 5   Morally Relevant Dimensions of Harms to Self and to Others

document and examine short-term, midrange, and long-term harms. Some behaviors have quite different short-term effects from long-term effects. The costs, monetary and otherwise, of these harms needs to be measured or estimated, and the question of who pays what must be addressed. This is especially important and complex in environmental issues. Finally, one wants to look for the sequelae of harms. In all of this there is the need to ask constantly, who is measuring the harms and from what perspective?

These dimensions should encourage those working in bioethics and sociology of medicine to recast the theoretical framework, language, and methods of analytic moral philosophy so that the interpersonal, social, political, historical, and economic contexts of its subject matter become integral to its work. Fox and Swazey (1984, 359–60) are worried that this cannot happen because bioethics is "sealed into itself" with a "mix of naiveté and arrogance." By contrast, our approach marries ethical reflection with rich sociological and ethnographic analysis, beginning with the "brute facts" as experienced by and measured within cultural groups, and culminating with a fulsome account of the goals, values, and possibilities open to those groups. Numerous commentators have noted that sociological analysis provides bioethicists with an array of new tools. Indeed, the study of social groups does much more. Sociologists, we have argued, can contribute to the formation of appropriate ethical standards within the cultures they inhabit, and sociology must play an important role in the articulation and practice of foundational bioethics itself.

REFERENCES

Annas, George. 1995. Medicine, death, and the criminal law. *New England Journal of Medicine* 333(8): 527–30.

Anspach, Renée R. 1993. *Deciding who lives: Fateful choices in the intensive-care nursery.* Berkeley: University of California Press.

Brody, Howard. 1993. *The healer's power.* New York: Cambridge University Press.

Caplan, Arthur. 1995. *Moral matters.* New York: Wiley.

DeVries, Raymond. 1995. Toward a sociology of bioethics. *Qualitative Sociology* 18:119–28.

Dewey, John. 1922. *Human nature and conduct.* New York: H. Holt.

Ennett, Susan T., and Karl E. Bauman. 1993. Peer group structure and adolescent cigarette smoking: A social network analysis. *Journal of Health and Social Behavior* 34:226–36.

Fox, Renée C., and Judith P. Swazey. 1984. Medical morality is not bioethics—Medical ethics in China and the United States. *Perspectives in Biology and Medicine* 35:336–60.

Garfinkel, Harold. 1967. *Studies in ethnomethodology.* Englewood Cliffs, N.J.: Prentice Hall.

Geertz, Clifford. 1973. *The interpretation of cultures.* New York: Basic Books.

Gusfield, Joseph R. 1963. *Symbolic crusade: Status politics and the American temperance movement.* Urbana: University of Illinois Press.

Hastings Center Report. 1996. Dying well in the hospital: The lessons of SUPPORT. 25(6, Suppl.): S1–36.

Hodgson, Thomas A. 1992. Cigarette smoking and lifetime medical expenditures. *Milbank Quarterly* 70:81–126.

Hoffmaster, Barry. 1992. Can ethnography save the life of medical ethics? *Social Science & Medicine* 35:1421–31.

Jonsen, A. R. 1991. Of balloons and bicycles. *Hastings Center Report* 72:14.

Lachs, John. 1995. *The relevance of philosophy to life.* Nashville, Tenn.: Vanderbilt University Press.

Lewontin, Richard, and Ruth Hubbard. 1996. Pitfalls of genetic testing. *New England Journal of Medicine* 334(18): 1192–4.

Light, Donald W. 1992. The practice and ethics of risk-rated health insurance. *Journal of the American Medical Association* 267:2503–8.

———. 1995. *Homo economicus:* Escaping the traps of managed competition. *European Journal of Public Health* 5:145–54.

MacIntyre, Alasdair. 1984. *After virtue.* South Bend, Ind.: University of Notre Dame Press.

Marshall, Patricia A. 1996. The SUPPORT study: Who's talking? *Hastings Center Report* 25(6, suppl.): S9–11.

McGee, Glenn. 1994. Method and social reconstruction: Dewey's *Logic: The theory of inquiry.* *Southern Journal of Philosophy* 32(1): 107–20.

———. 1996. Frontiers in American philosophy. *Transactions* 25:493–6.

———. 1997. *The perfect baby: A pragmatic approach to genetics.* Baltimore: Rowman & Littlefield.

Menzel, Paul T. 1990. *Strong medicine: The ethical rationing of health care.* New York: Oxford University Press.

Morreim, E. Haavi. 1996. Lifestyles of the risky and infamous: From managed care to managed lives. *Hastings Center Report* 25(6): 5–12.

SUPPORT Principal Investigators. 1995. A controlled trial to improve care for seriously ill hospitalized patients. The study to understand prognoses and preferences for outcomes and risks of treatments (SUPPORT). *Journal of the American Medical Association* 274:1591–8.

Troyer, Robert, and Gerald E. Markle. 1983. *Cigarettes: The battle over smoking.* New Brunswick, N.J.: Rutgers University Press.

Wikler, Daniel I. 1978. Persuasion and coercion of health: Ethical issues in government efforts to change lifestyles. *Milbank Memorial Fund Quarterly* 56:303–37.

Zaner, R. M. 1987. *Ethics and the clinical encounter.* Englewood Cliffs, N.J.: Prentice Hall.

Zussman, Robert. 1992. *Intensive care: Medical ethics and the medical profession.* Chicago: University of Chicago Press.

CHAPTER TWO

Medical Publicity before Bioethics: Nineteenth-Century Illustrations of Twentieth-Century Dilemmas

Jonathan B. Imber

The extensive interest in bioethics and bioethical questions by those other than bioethicists speaks to its maturing (that is, institutionalization) as an academic field and professional activity. Bioethics is no longer a marginal enterprise practiced by a few academics; it is an area of interest to the wider society, a regular feature in several media. How did bioethics succeed in capturing the attention of educators and the public? To answer that question, I will develop an argument that concentrates on the peculiarly American dilemma facing medicine today—that is, the question of who speaks for medicine. It is a question that addresses the shaping of public expectations about the role of medicine and the education of physicians in a society caught among competing images of managed care, whether governmental, corporate, or bioethical.

This chapter offers a brief outline of three periods of *publicity* about medical work, with a primary focus on the public controversies created by medical interest in death and dying. The first period, before the rise of scientific medicine, coincides with Auguste Comte's "theological stage," insofar as the speculations about death were also occasions to reason about the fate of the soul. The second period, to which most of this essay is devoted, leaves behind the speculations of the theological elites and replaces them with a social dynamic more familiar to contemporary analysts of public controversies.

During this second period—roughly the one hundred years between 1850 and 1950—medical publicity helped establish the autonomy of medical authority for the public good. The illustrations I use to conduct this examination are drawn from nineteenth-century medical periodicals that contained both "news" about medicine and "information" relevant to its practice. During the first-half of the twentieth century, increasing accommodation of medicine to science worked to suppress, at least temporarily, the widespread public criticisms of the motives of physicians and the goals of medicine.

John Burnham (1982) has called this second period, "American Medicine's Golden Age." Before the Golden Age, significant publicity was created about the rising fortunes of medicine, largely by the efforts of physicians themselves. After the Golden Age—the third period—even more publicity has been created, but this time—our time—physicians are no longer directing the conversation about either their motives or their goals. They have been superseded by a more specialized force of critics known as medical ethicists, or bioethicists.

My interest in the rising importance of medical ethics as the chief mediator between the medical profession and the public began as I was preparing to review a book on the central importance of first-year anatomy instruction on the psychological and professional development of medical students (Hafferty 1991). I came upon an exposé by a recently graduated medical student of Georgetown University, in which she described the disrespectful behavior of male students and professors toward the female cadavers dissected in first-year anatomy, suggesting that such matters were beyond public notice (Fugh-Berman 1992). In earlier periods, the public was quite concerned with the medical uses of the dead. How did this current lack of public attention come about? Answers to this question may help provide one context for understanding the rise and fall of public trust in the medical profession.

Public trust in the corporate enterprise of medicine required an institutional separation between the education of the medical professional and the public notice of the central place of death within that education. Trust, in sociological terms, was founded in the professional assertions of physicians and others that such separation was necessary and appropriate. The new medical-scientific education would enable the physician to confront the public fear of death by identifying that fear with the corporate—that is, professional—promise to find ways to forestall it. Such an education would also insist that the physician rise above that fear by honoring this promise as best as possible. Until the legal and scientific foundations affirming the institutional autonomy of medicine were firmly in place, the profession remained entangled in the public ambivalence about the methods and goals of medical education. After that, something like a vast social amnesia ensued, and only during the past quarter century has it begun to wear off.

"THE SOUL OF THE DECEASED": SACRALIZING THE BODY

The history of medical responsibility in the religious traditions out of Jerusalem and Rome (and the subsequent reformation movements) has consistently emphasized the centrality of the body—its dignity, mystery, and sacred individuality.[1] The medical profession was the mediating institution between these sacred traditions of respect for the body, on the one hand, and the palpable, often painful realities of bodily living, on the other. To illustrate this mediating function of medicine, I present first a report of an autopsy performed in 1533.[2]

According to A. Pena Chavarria and P. G. Shipley (1924), the first recorded autopsy in the new world was conducted on Siamese twin girls on July 19, 1533, in the town of Santo Domingo on the island of Española (Haiti and Santo Domingo). The twins had been born nine days earlier. Postmortem examination was uncommon, and Chavarria and Shipley speculate that the parents' willingness to approve such an examination was possibly the result of the confusion by all concerned about the spiritual status of the twins. Did this monstrous body house two souls or only one? And what did this mean for the rite of baptism? The autopsy revealed that each had her own set of major internal organs (although their livers were conjoined) and that a single naval from without was, in fact, divided into two canals from within.

Confusion about the twins' spiritual or sacred individuality was inherent in theological discussion about the relation of the soul to the body and about where in the body the soul was believed to reside. Tertullian held that the soul was conceived along with the body. Augustine believed that the unborn did not possess a soul until the fifty-eighth day of intrauterine life. Canon law established further that males were animated with a soul on the forty-fifth day and females on the eightieth day. The location of the soul was generally thought to be either in the brain or the heart, but some argued that it resided in the blood. No evidence exists that the liver (the one organ joined together) was regarded as a theologically significant organ. Their deaths did not occur simultaneously, one lingering for a short time after the other expired. The physiological evidence of the twins' separate deaths supported the belief that they were outwardly two individuals, but doubt remained about their inward status, prompting perhaps the call for anatomical study.

The first autopsy in the New World should be interpreted as a symbolic attempt to link the mutilation of the body to newly recognized and theologically informed rational ends. Chavarria and Shipley conclude that "this is the history of perhaps the only *post-mortem* examination ever conducted to study the soul of the deceased" (1924, 302). Seeking to confirm the divine relation of the soul to the body opened the way for acknowledgment of the clinical relation between physiological observation and anatomical discovery. It was precisely the peculiarity of God's creation of Siamese twins that made their dissection theologically relevant, clinically reasonable, and publicly inoffensive. Curiosity about curiosa gave license to investigate and determine what was normal.

If visible death had invisible causes, autopsy was used to display the underlying causes for all physiological events, including death. Faith in the soul was meant to underwrite the search for the causes of its departure from

the body at the time of death. Until the appearance of technologies to prolong a life that would otherwise end naturally, death and the departure of the
soul from the body occurred together. In our time "faith" in the "quality of
life" has been used to justify the search for a recycled soul, now called "personhood." This recycling has permitted a separation, in principle, between
the sacredness of the body and the constantly changing clinical possibilities
for its disposition once it is designated as having no quality or personhood
that is unique and sacred to itself. Of course, the contemporary abortion
debate is one site for struggle over competing definitions of personhood,
whether in the person of the mother or the body of the unborn within her.
But, at the end of life as well, the separation between the sacredness of the
body and the autonomous agency of individuals to determine what they will
do to their bodies reveals as much about the telos of legal rationality as it does
about the technological capacities of modern medicine. This wedge is of his-
toric significance because the rational mutilation of the body, stripped of its
sacred referents, now permits clinical possibilities (for example, organ transplantation, partial-birth abortions, and suicide machines) that threaten the
mediating function of the medical profession. The most concrete threat is the
continuing diminution in trust in the corporate enterprise of medicine.

AFTER RELIGIOUS BUT BEFORE PROFESSIONAL RESPECT
FOR THE DEAD

Christian theological speculations about the appearance, residence, and
departure of the soul made mutilation of the body a matter of what might be
called *sacred rationality*. Even though the soul may depart from the body, a
sacred and sacramental respect for the corpse remains. With the gradual
establishment of laws and practices regarding postmortem examinations and
instructional dissections, medical respect for the corpse was reinforced by the
continued enchantment of the dead body. This enchantment is of two kinds.
The first is simply the familial regard for the corpse, expressed in ceremonies
of burial. The second is the mystery of learning the causes of death itself.
Where no family exists, a disenchanted respect nevertheless remains.
Unclaimed bodies are typically buried in potter's fields, or prior to intern-
ment, given over to medical schools for anatomical study. Different state legislation has evolved for the disposition and uses of unclaimed bodies.[3]

The scientific and rational approach to solving the mystery of death
began its long process of routinization in the formal establishment of medical
schools, both state sponsored and proprietary. In the United States, this
process was marked by periodic public controversy about how medical schools
acquired cadavers for use during anatomical instruction. By the end of the
nineteenth century, autopsy and dissection were considered fundamental to
the progress of medicine. Earlier in the century, religiously led opposition to

medicine typically focused on the philosophy of treatment of diseases rather than on the treatment of corpses.[4] A minister with some knowledge about diagnosis and treatment might recommend his flock to a homeopath over and against a regular physician. The responsibilities assumed by clergy and physicians over the public welfare were not as distinct in 1850 as they were by 1900.[5]

Resistance to anatomical instruction arose indirectly as a result of public fears about grave robbing by so-called resurrectionists, a group not unique to the United States.[6] When a grave is desecrated, the injury is as much to the memory of the deceased as it is to the physical remains. It is not difficult to imagine what the public response must have been like in communities where a corpse had been removed from its final resting place. A small but illustrative literature exists on the practices of resurrectionists, especially in England and the United States.[7] Medical schools across the United States created their own market in anatomical materials, and they were associated with the brazen activities of the suppliers of cadavers described in newspaper reports that periodically appeared.[8]

Massachusetts (in 1831) was among the first states to legalize dissection for the purpose of anatomical instruction, thus making it easier for medical schools to obtain anatomical materials. It took more than fifty years for other states to pass similar statutes. In Maine, for example, in 1869, the New York *Medical Record* reported:

> The application of the physicians of Maine for a law furnishing them with material for dissection, which has been refused by a dozen legislatures, has now taken the shape of a bill which is thought to be unobjectionable. It delivers into the hands of the fraternity the bodies of any persons dying in their city or town, State prison or jail, whose burial must be at the public expense, provided the deceased make no request to be buried, or if his remains are not claimed by friends or kindred. (Vol. 4, 1 April 1869, 71)

The medical community did regard the problem with a certain humor as well. In 1872 the New York *Medical Record* reported the following about the Medical College of Ohio in Cincinnati:

> The College museum has just received a valuable acquisition in the shape of the artistically prepared skeleton of "Old Man Dead," the College Resurrectionist for the past forty years. The skeleton is seated on a tombstone, with spade in hand and pipe in mouth, in perfect self-complacency, apparently over a recent successful "job." (Vol. 7, 15 October 1872, 408)

Reports of grave robbing appeared in places as disparate as Montreal, Philadelphia, North Carolina, and Virginia, as late as 1882. A typical case around this time is illustrated in two reports in the New York *Medical Record* in 1883:

> A Grave Robbery at Camillus, N.Y.—A body was recently stolen from the cemetery at Camillus, N.Y., and taken to Syracuse, where it was left in the dissecting-room of the Syracuse Medical College. The officers found it in this place. It had

not been purchased by the College, as the vender was unknown. (Vol. 23, no. 14, 7 April 1883, 381)

Convicted of Grave-Robbery.—Last spring the grave of Edwin R. Harmon, formerly a prominent resident of Camillus, N.Y., was found to have been opened and the body stolen. The body was subsequently discovered in the dissecting-room of the Syracuse Medical College. Henry Thomson, formerly a medical student and a graduate of Syracuse University, was arrested for robbing the grave. His trial was concluded November 10th, and after remaining out all night, the jury rendered a verdict of guilty. (Vol. 24, no. 20, 17 November 1883, 548)

Unlike Great Britain, where routinization of the supply of cadavers to medical schools had been in place since 1832 and had effectively insulated those who could afford burials from becoming part of that supply, the periodic reports in the United States of "prominent" deceased residents being dug up and handed over to medical schools caused sufficient outrage to demand conviction of the perpetrators, as well as to inspire state legislatures to act to pass anatomical statutes.

The gallows humor about these incidents was evident again in 1884:

The Detroit *Free Press* says: "The Cincinnati *Commercial Gazette* is authority for the intimation that the Ohio medical colleges will not take, hereafter, for dissection, the bodies of persons who have been obviously murdered for the purpose of sale. This will be a heavy sacrifice for the colleges, but it is no more than the community has a right to expect." (*Medical Record*, vol. 25, no. 22, 31 May 1884, 616)

By reporting on such matters in the pages of a medical-scientific journal, an acknowledgment of public conflict as well as professional anxiety was being made. Although the medical profession in some states effectively insulated itself from charges of promoting and abetting the robbing of graves, in other states, physicians, medical schools, and medical societies muddled on in their efforts to disassociate themselves from such charges.

John Blake, former chief, History of Medicine Division, National Library of Medicine, provided the best analytical account of why it took some states much longer than others to establish laws protecting the study of anatomy and thus indirectly protecting burial places from the designs of resurrectionists. Blake recounts the eleven-year struggle of the U.S. Congress to pass an anatomical bill for the District of Columbia, between 1884 and 1895.[9] He argues that efforts to legalize dissection may have been stimulated by press reports like those described in the New York *Medical Record*. He also proposes that nineteenth-century indifference to science by medical schools and the public contributed to the medical profession's inability to demand improvements in the acquisition of cadavers. Instruction in anatomy was not considered a prestigious educational responsibility, and instructors often taught at night, perhaps because they were occupied with other matters during the day and because the nights were cooler than the days. Dissection was deemed scientifically necessary but was poorly taught. Little scientific learning came from it, for either faculty or students. In sum, incorporating the study of anatomy into the scientific study of medicine was a precondition for improving its respectability and enhancing the prestige of those who taught it (Blake 1968).

Blake's review confirms why the efflorescence of anatomy (and pathology) occurred in the first quarter of the twentieth century: As scientific disciplines they finally became essential to the learning and practice of modern medicine. Their link with the quite recent past was finally severed, and the public significance of death was culturally and symbolically transformed. One consequence of this transformation was a cultural repression of the connection between grave robbing and medical education. The public's involuntary revulsion toward this connection was also repressed, and in its place appeared, at least rhetorically, a voluntary and respectful willingness to participate in the greater cause of scientific medicine.

These cultural repressions—forgetting the link between grave robbing and medical education, as well as the transformation of revulsion at such a link into respect for medical-scientific education, erasing even the memories of these memories—also have informed public attitudes toward the practice of animal vivisection. What is remarkable about the cultural enforcement of the scientific respect for the dead human being—which institutionally required concealment of any discourtesy or disrespect toward those donated to the cause of scientific medicine—is that public resistance to the use of animals in medical education (and research) was more vocal and far better organized than the sporadic outcries against and the legislative lethargy about dissection of human cadavers.[10] One obvious explanation for greater public resistance to vivisection is concern with the use of living animals for study and research. William James approached the problem in his reasonable and thoughtful manner: "To taboo vivisection is then the same thing as to give up seeking after a knowledge of physiology; in other words, it is sacrificing human intellectual good, and all that flows from it, to a brute and corporeal good. We live in a world in which it is universally admitted that sacrifice is a universal law—no good comes without some loss" (James 1875, 11).

James anticipated the continuities in cultural discontent between nineteenth-century antivivisectionists and contemporary animal rights activists. His answer to the antivivisectionists of the late-nineteenth century was given as an admonition to medical scientists:

> Our power over animals should not be used simply at our own convenience, but voluntarily limited and sparingly put forth. But the decision when to exert it and when to refrain should rest solely with the investigator himself. If a sweeping prohibitory law were passed, it would of course be a dead letter in a community which boils millions of lobsters alive every year to add a charm to its suppers. By hook or crook, physiologists would operate on living animals in spite of the vigilance of a thousand humane societies; just as the anatomy law was under discussion in England, Sir Astley Cooper told the legislative commit-

tee that if he could not have legally the bodies of outcasts, he should have illegally the bodies of members of parliaments. . . . And this brings us to a point in which we think the Society for the Prevention of Cruelty to Animals may do great good. Let them act morally, through public opinion, and foment, if need be, public dislike of bloody demonstrations in lectures. They will then do good both to animals who are victimized, to the students who demand that their eyes and not their understanding shall work for them, and to the teachers who weakly yield to that demand. Under this hostile pressure, this constant sense of being challenged—which is very different from the sense of being controlled—the vivisector will feel more responsible, more solemn, less wasteful and indifferent. (James 1875, 12–3)

James's conviction that a "hostile pressure" on medicine would be more effective than any governmental control bears witness to the Protestant frame of mind that favored reminders ("this constant sense of being challenged") that would make the vivisector "feel more responsible." His theory of cultural authority is concisely adumbrated here. The vivisector's authority resided first in the person and contingently in the office of investigator or researcher that was occupied by the person.

But in a society where neither church nor state could be relied upon to regulate effectively in the matter of animal vivisection, James acknowledged that "public dislike" of such activities might be more morally persuasive. In effect, he approved of public negotiation about specific activities rather than religious or governmental proscriptions. James sought to balance science and individual conduct with public uncertainty and anxiety about both. The proposal to ban "bloody demonstrations" in 1875 did not eliminate the prospect for even more ruthless cruelties always and just out of public view. Consider the following report thirteen years later in the New York *Medical Record* on the uses of electricity to cause death (see also Hughes 1958):

The law requiring electrical executions of death-sentences will go into effect on January 1st [1889]. The experiments on dogs made last summer by Harold P. Brown, an electrical engineer, were criticised because the weight of the animals killed was less than that of a man, and it was supposed that more current would be required to kill a human being on that account. On Wednesday afternoon Mr. Brown had an opportunity to make a demonstration before Mr. Elbridge T. Gerry, the author of the new law, and the committee appointed by the Medico-legal Society to report on the best means of putting the law into effect. It was sought to find out the amount and character of current that would be required to make death certain and instantaneous. The experiments were made in Mr. Edison's laboratory in Orange [New Jersey]. The first victim was a calf weighing 124 1/2 pounds. The hair was cut on the forehead and on the spine behind the forelegs, and sponge-covered plates, moistened with a solution of sulphate of zinc, were fastened in place. The resistance of the animal was 3,200 ohms. An alternating current of 700 volts was applied for thirty seconds. The animal, however, was killed instantly. It was at once dissected by Drs. Ingram and Bleyer, but the brain, heart, and lungs, were found to be in a normal condition, and the meat was pronounced fit for food. . . . A second calf weighed 145 pounds and had a resistance of 1,300 ohms. The deadly alternating current at 700-volts pressure was applied for five seconds, and produced instant death. To settle permanently the weight-question, a horse weighing 1,230 pounds was next killed by passing the alternating current at 700 volts from one foreleg to the other. . . . The experiments are said to have proved the alternating current to be the most deadly force known to science. (Vol. 34, no. 24, 8 December 1888, 678)

Antivivisection movements do not generally concede to medical science the progress made by particular acts of animal experimentation. Figuring out the most efficient way to execute human beings, by electrocuting calves and a horse, can hardly be described as routine animal experimentation. The dynamic of "public dislike" (that is, public notice and popular protest) responds ex post facto (and unpredictably) to particular events or raises objections routinely in a more organized manner. In either case, James did not anticipate the implications of a suppression of such protest, whether spontaneous or organized.

The suppression of public notice and, to a large degree, of popular protest may be achieved in at least two ways by government and by experts. The archetypal example of governmental suppression of popular notice is the Nazi conduct of human experimentation. But the Nazi case has been used as a benchmark in illustrating and illuminating a second and allegedly more complicated form of suppression of popular notice. Professional expertise still confers authority to determine when medical research is inappropriate. The quite public revelations in the 1960s of "unethical" treatment of human subjects in Britain and the United States prompted a new scrutiny of the design of human experimentation, in other words, greater participation by government and experts in the conduct of medical research. The ubiquitous public confidence in physicians and medicine, which rendered the Nazi case exceptional enough to be ethically irrelevant to the American situation, was shattered in a series of well-publicized exposés, as David Rothman (1991) has described. The rise of bioethics was linked fundamentally to the broader publicity about American medical protocols and governmental infractions of a medical kind. By assuming the mantle of purveyor of justice denied, and thus justifying itself as a surrogate of the public will, bioethics embarked upon a full-scale casuistic refinement of each and every activity related to medical research and practice. The triumph of casuistry in the monastic-like bureaucracies of medicine has amounted to a revolution from within, which continues to the present moment.[11]

PROFESSIONAL RESPECT FOR THE DEAD AND DYING

Respect for the dying and the dead is not a precondition for scientific work and discovery. In recent years debates about the usefulness of data gathered during Nazi medical experimentation demonstrates, however unwittingly, that the ends of medical science are by no means wedded to the means employed to achieve them. The medical profession—insofar as it remains a mediating institution between sacred acknowledgment of the body and scientific uses of it—is constantly tested in how it makes connections between means and ends, creating the many forms of public ambivalence about medical practice in its wake. The culture of medicine (its values and the justifications it gives for its actions) is inseparable from its scientific and theoretical approaches to life itself.

A particularly revealing example of the ambivalence of professional respect for the dead is found in the lives and deaths of the famous nineteenth-century Siamese twins, Chang and Eng Bunker.[12] They were born in 1811 in Bangkok, Siam (the origin of the eponym), were brought to the United States in 1829, and died in North Carolina in 1874. Their lives were widely followed by a public eager to view the living spectacle of two bodies joined together. Their freakishness became their livelihood, but they managed to avoid such hawkers as P. T. Barnum, who is often mistakenly assumed to have made them famous. Both men married and each fathered large families, adding to the public fascination about them.

The Bunkers were as interesting to medical men as they were to the general public (see Bell 1987, 133–5, for an account). From the time they arrived in the United States, they were a subject of medical speculation (The Siamese Brothers 1829). Their novelty was thus encouraged by the profession whose scientific interest could only be fully satisfied once they were dead. Public fascination about their freakishness coincided with medical curiosity about the physical nature of their fusion. By 1874 clergymen in search of the soul (as in the case of the infant twins dissected in 1533) were replaced by a medical profession seeking to solve physiological riddles in the hope of contributing to the slow progress of surgery. Could the Bunkers have been surgically separated? This question dominated the medical discussion about them. The New York *Medical Record* reported:

> Death of the Siamese Twins.—The famous Siamese Twins, Chang and Eng, died at their residence in Surry County, North Carolina on [January 17, 1874]. Chang had an attack of paralysis last fall, which greatly enfeebled his body and clouded his mind. They retired as usual on Friday night, the 16th. Chang was found dead in his bed the next morning, and Eng survived him only about two hours, dying, it is thought, of fright. (Vol. 9, 2 February 1874, 79–80)

Initial speculation about the death of Chang suggested that Eng might have been surgically separated and thus saved. "A dissection of the bodies, which is promised at Philadelphia, will be of interest to every medical man throughout the civilized world" (*Medical Record*, vol. 9, 2 February 1874, 80).

After considerable negotiation with the Bunkers' families and attorney in North Carolina, the twins' bodies were embalmed and moved to Philadelphia. The autopsy took place at the College of Physicians. A first report of the autopsy was made to 101 fellows at a meeting on February 8,

1874. Newspapers caught wind of the meeting, and a subsequent report was made to the fellows and visitors ten days later. The Bunkers' bodies were exhibited to the fellows at the time of the reports. Dr. J. Solis Cohen, who attended the second report, noted that "while the report was being made a twin-apple was handed round—two apples joined together, one larger than the other, and labeled Chang and Eng, in accordance with the relative size of the twins. The passage of this natural vegetable phenomenon at such a time caused considerable merriment" (*Medical Record*, vol. 9, 2 March 1874, 131–2).

Further postmortem examinations confirmed that the Bunkers could not have been safely separated while both were alive because of the special attachment of their livers. With medical interest in their physical status complete, the Bunkers' contribution to medical publicity ended. In certain respects, their public autopsy signaled the first opportunity of the medical profession to establish widespread public attention to its goals.[13] The empire of freak shows that had so neatly dovetailed with medical interest could now be relegated, once and for all, to the margins of proper society. By the turn of the century, professional respectability would not tolerate such exhibitionism, but this exhibitionism was initially good for medical progress. Its unconscious aim was to move the public one step further away from its anxieties about grave robbing in particular and autopsies in general.

A final illustration of significant public attention to the aims of medicine in the second half of the nineteenth century appears in the reports of the shooting and lingering death of President James Garfield in 1881. Garfield's death concentrated public attention on the medical condition of a public leader, like no other in U.S. history. Lincoln's assassination might have achieved such attention, but he died only hours after he was shot. Garfield lived for more than two months after he was wounded. His assassin Charles Guiteau is much better remembered perhaps than Garfield, because after Garfield's death, public attention turned to Guiteau's trial and his plea of insanity. In the field of medical history, the legal struggle to define insanity has proven far more interesting than either Garfield's lingering or the public interest in it (Rosenberg 1968).

Garfield was shot on July 2, 1881, before boarding a train for New York City on his way to deliver an address to his alma mater, Williams College.[14] The assassin fired two times, hitting the president in the side with the second shot. The bullet remained lodged near his spine below the pancreas until his death. Physicians called in immediately to attend to the president were initially of several minds about how to proceed with his treatment. Those doctors, intent upon locating the bullet lodged in Garfield's side, probed with unsterile instruments, thus introducing bacteria into the wound. At his trial, the assassin Guiteau claimed that he had not killed the president, the doctors had. Writing of Garfield's medical care, Dr. T. Burton Smith, the White House physician to former President Ronald Reagan, noted that Garfield's medical care was not inadequate for its day, though, he judges Guiteau's claim as probably correct (Smith 1992).

A wounded and lingering president was the subject of enormous public attention in drawing rooms, churches, and newspapers. An important feature of Garfield's medical care was its publicity. Demand by the public to know more about the condition of his health resulted in the first "medical bulletins" in America. The uncertainty about his recovery produced a cautious optimism almost until the day he died.

For sixty-six days Garfield remained in the White House, suffering the sweltering heat of Washington, D.C. The first primitive air-conditioning in the White House was installed to reduce the heat in his room, in the form of galvanized troughs with suspended sheets of flannel immersed in ice water. The evolution of these technical innovations has obviously progressed, but the way that Garfield's physicians determined to inform the public of his progress established a pattern of professional and public expectation that remains relatively unchanged to the present day. Two times a day, in the morning and the evening, physicians released a statement about the state of Garfield's health as it could be measured (and thus described) in terms of body temperature, pulse rate, and respiration rate.

Something obviously reassuring was achieved in the ritual provision of such information. Prayers for his recovery were conducted, and the intensity of those prayers were often in concert with what were reported to be significant changes in his temperature, pulse, and respiration. These measures were both signs of life and death. The keepers of these measures were physicians whose public visibility was enhanced considerably, given that a president's vital signs were being measured. The national ritual provided a kind of pastoral reassurance while Garfield lingered. Once he was dead, the physicians disappeared. Whatever visibility the medical profession did maintain after Garfield's death was confined to the pages of medical journals, in which assessments were made about the viability of and techniques for removing the bullet from his body, his general medical treatment, and the amount of fees paid to the various physicians who attended to him.

The prolongation of dying, a matter that has achieved national urgency over the past decade, originally gave physicians a public pulpit from which they could galvanize public interest in the work they performed. As lingering unto death has become less a matter of public fascination and more a matter of cultural dread, physicians have receded even more: In the film *Dave* (1992), medical personnel are secreted in the subbasement of the White House where the real president lies comatose, beyond recovery. One hundred years after the lingering death of James Garfield, public interest in the medical control of death has opened new opportunities for retired physicians, Kevorkian being among the most well known at present. The publicity that Kevorkian has attracted is much greater than the attention drawn to the fact that medical ethicists, including the most publicly visible ones, have expressed profound reservations about the Kevorkian approach to euthanasia.

CONCLUSION: BIOETHICS IN THE AGE
OF AGING REPRESSIONS

I have briefly tried to reconstruct a variety of historical events and issues in order to illustrate how the medical profession gradually earned the public trust that until very recently has served well its scientific and professional interests. By the nineteenth century, public fascination with the freakish and the famous was carefully, if not deliberately, cultivated to enhance the presence of physicians in the public mind. This is not to argue that the now standard explanations about the rise of modern scientific medicine are in any way displaced by this examination of medical publicity. The question of medical publicity itself is far more complicated than the selected illustrations suggest.

On the other hand, because the present climate of criticisms about physicians and medicine is also complex, it is important to understand more fully the sources of publicity about medical matters generally. Such publicity is linked to what I would call public expertise, as distinct from other forms of expertise that are rooted in well-established traditions of professional education. Publicists of medical ethics do not train for that capacity; they aspire to it, and if they are industrious, clever, and lucky enough, they become "known" (which is to say, called upon regularly) in the most diffuse forms of media such as television, radio, newspapers, and magazines. A host of lesser "knowns" crowd the corridors of new-class institutions, including various think tanks, special offices of federal agencies, hospitals, universities, and other strategic sites that now afford occasional, if not regular, opportunities for public visibility. Those outside these spheres of public influence on medical ethical matters generally teach or practice medicine in the clinical trenches. We are now able to create a typology that reaches from the older "humanist" physician tradition in medicine to the newer and more aggressive publicist wing now regnant. That older wing, typified in the persona of William Osler (Barondess and Roland 1994), has been displaced by the greater urgency that life and death matters appear to create in the larger society. On the other hand, Arthur Caplan has encouraged bioethicists to participate publicly as much as possible in bioethical matters. As one observer of a national meeting of bioethicists reported, "The challenge, he explained, is for bioethicists to position themselves to be on panels, boards and other decision-making bodies where public policy positions will be established—where the exploding changes in health care that are now underway will be addressed" (Marker 1995, 36–7).

In a letter to the *New York Times* in 1994, R. Alta Charo and Daniel Wikler wrote:

> All that bioethicists can offer is a somewhat less politically or emotionally charged, somewhat more dispassionate evaluation of our options. No doubt you will always be able to find one ethicist who considers a new development

grotesque and another who wants to wait and see. But personal feelings about such innovations, even from respected academics, do not reflect any rigorously derived consensus. We suggest the following pledge be taken by ethicists and the news media alike: No ethicist should be asked for a personal opinion. If asked, no personal opinion should be given. And if given, no personal opinion should be published. With issues so complicated, we cannot afford to let a small group of academics be a self-appointed, secular version of the Committee for the Defense of the Faith. (14 January 1994, A28)

The internal and interdisciplinary "politics" of bioethics is a barely explored social phenomenon. It is not clear who Charo and Wikler are complaining about here, but their own strongly held personal feelings about personal feelings are worth noting. They are not complaining about the public role of the bioethicist but rather about certain bioethicists and about certain ways of being bioethical.

If we focused more on the dynamics of public attention generally, we would know better what the nature of the public demand is for bioethical pontifications and why some individual bioethicists fulfill that demand better than others. The nineteenth-century illustrations offered earlier suggest that the dynamics of publicity always contain a mixture of personal and institutional motivations. Before the institutionalization of scientific method, medical explanation had a theological and speculative edge, which was gradually worn down by a more intricate division of labor of scientific thinking and experimentation. Contemporary criticisms of institutional medicine and science, on the other side of the Golden Age, have been led by various elites within American higher education, including social scientists, legal educators, and philosophers. Nineteenth-century medical publicity sought to put to rest public fears about a medical education that approached death as a technical problem. Twentieth-century medical publicity must deal with a plethora of public fears and is not in the control of any one professional group, least of all physicians.

The decline in corporate trust[15] of physicians and medicine is tied to developments within medicine, especially the extensive division of labor in monitoring and maintaining the health of the American public. The physician is by no means alone any longer at the top of that division of labor. The occupation of medicine is the carrier of an ancient code of conduct infused with religiously inspired demands to equate profession with vocation and conduct with character. But today, physicianhood is divided into too many irreconcilable parts, the latest and most criticized being the "entrepreneurial" doctor—the one who, for instance, sues other physicians for using a patented technique. Admiration for competence substitutes evermore for trust in character, but such admiration does not resolve the more fundamental problem of what devotion to medicine means.

Those at the forefront of identifying these seemingly irreconcilable parts (at first theoretically, and then more practically) have been bioethicists. A leading practitioner of bioethics informed me many years ago that his organization often received phone calls from the anxious and curious about all sorts of medical matters both public and personal. In effect, he was saying that bioethics had succeeded in attracting the attention of the worried well, displacing both physicians and clergymen as clarifiers and consolers. Bioethics is the public relations division of modern medicine, whether physicians (or bioethicists) like it or not. This division of medicine, once exclusively controlled and mediated by physicians, is now tied, in part, to the cultural dynamics of fame and publicity that operate similarly in many social and cultural institutions.

Instead of stripping the halo from the profession, the bioethicist adds another, his or her own, to that of the physician's. Freer to travel, to consult, and to advise, the bioethicist rises above the ordinary profession of medicine caught in the less attractive clinical trenches of "managed care." I do not wish to characterize unfairly the "role" of the bioethicist but, rather, call attention to the need to depict that role in a more straightforwardly sociological manner.

The medical profession is no longer central in the diffusion of its own practices; it has witnessed the transformation of legal (and social) norms by a remarkably small number of bioethical specialists. Bioethicists have been assisted in their task of arguing on behalf of medicine in numerous controversial issues by a *federalizing of emotion*. By federalizing of emotion, I mean in particular a legal mandate from a central government that coordinates and regularizes how medical practice is accomplished. In the United States these mandates—coming from the Supreme Court, state courts, and state and federal legislatures—extend the norm of scientific conduct to that of ethical conduct. Under the pretext of protecting individual autonomy, a more recognizable conformity (among doctors) about what is "normal" human life has emerged and presses evermore on their routine actions at the beginning and end of life.

At present, after the Golden Age of medicine, the public controversies that circulate *around* medicine no longer appear to be essentially tied to medicine or physicians in particular. The federalizing of emotion in bioethics began with abortion, has evolved with organ transplantation, and is consolidating itself over the question of euthanasia. I have written elsewhere about abortion and the medical profession (Imber 1986, 1990). From a sociological perspective, abortion continues to be represented as a contentious public issue in large part because of the present medical division of labor that attends to it. The vast majority of practitioners who are trained to do abortions do not do them. This single empirical fact explains why the abortion clinic has become the national site of a war waged for symbolic territory. The abortion clinic is the price paid for the medical profession's predictable refusal to require its members to negotiate an equitable distribution of the provision of this service among themselves. In this sense, medical provision of abortion is the underside of specialization generally, a fact that makes normative resolution all the more remote—all of this despite the promise of federal protection for the procedure.

A study in the *Annals of Internal Medicine* by L. A. Siminoff and colleagues (1995) reaches the quite unremarkable sociological conclusion that the greatest resistance to organ transplantation exists not among medical professionals but among the public itself. A public familiar with the implications of the criteria for death set forth by the Ad Hoc Committee of the Harvard Medical School to Examine the Definition of Brain Death, as well as the Uniform Anatomical Gift Act, would have been expected to have long ago given up its resistance to the medical uses of dead bodies. But the latest survey suggests otherwise, providing useful empirical confirmation of the fact that even though three-quarters of Americans surveyed *say* they would donate a family member's organs if asked, less than half of those people put into such a position in reality agree to donate another family member's organs. As was true one hundred years ago, the ethical liberalism of medicine finds itself in conflict with public conservatism: In the late 1800s, it was public fear about the use of the dead for medical education; in the late 1900s, it is anxiety about the harvesting of organs. Opinion about organ transplantation conceals anxieties about the practice that come to the surface only when a person is confronted with the reality of approving the use of a loved one's organs. "I don't know of any quick fix" to the problem, Dr. Robert Arnold, one of the authors of the study on resistance to organ transplantation, is quoted as saying in the *New York Times.*

The Harvard criteria, and the federalization of emotion implicit in the Uniform Anatomical Gift Act, were, in their time, in the late 1960s, "quick fixes" to a medical demand to push the limits of medical treatment into new frontiers. A prevailing conviction about this form of medical progress has been that the "technology" surpassed the ethical ability to cope with it. The view that technological progress is somehow always ahead of ethical guidance about its uses is a central piety of the bioethical movement and has probably helped feed the academic as well as public perception that without extensive intervention by courts, no ethical consensus is likely to be achieved. This has relegated the insights offered by the sociology of normative life to a remote corner of the influential industry of bioethical work. A significant cost is paid for the loss of sociological understanding about why people might say one thing and do something else, as with the case of organ transplantation. Regarded by "experts" as ignorance on the part of the public, such resistance to organ transplantation elicits the same incredulity that is expressed by supporters of sex education about efforts to eliminate it in public schools. The mistake in both cases is the assumption that resistance to scientific innovation is by definition socially regressive.

A further paradox arises in the seemingly strong public interest to find ways to end life more conveniently and efficiently. The quite public figure of Kevorkian looms larger than life precisely because he has trumped the medical ethical domain, even though that has not been his explicit intention, since he regards himself entirely as a paternalistic figure who opposes in prin-

ciple allowing anyone other than licensed physicians to perform euthanasia.
He looms larger than any intellectual justification for or against euthanasia
because no social or legal norm is capable of defining what the precise boundary should be between individual will and institutional mandate. Kevorkian
has used publicity to challenge professional indifference, but in so doing he
has also demonstrated the limits to bioethics as an instrument for improving
the public image of professional medicine. This is because bioethics is both
advisor to medicine and in direct competition with it, seeking to give it voice
and be its voice at the same time.

Combined with the push in the courts to federalize emotions about
physician-assisted suicide, the public drama of Kevorkian plays directly into
the hands of those who would claim that the public is worse off with the myr-
iad informal practices that now surround the end of life than it would be with
the complete abolition of laws that formally prohibit it. Having traveled down
a similar road already in *Roe* v. *Wade*, the implications for sociological research
of such "bioethical" matters is immense. What the federalization of emotion
teaches is that informal norms are always with us, regardless of whether the
law supports or prohibits any particular practice.[16]

If the complaint now about assisted suicide is that some people, in the
right circumstances (for example, intensive care units of hospitals), have an
easier time being assisted in their deaths than other people—this being an
example of an unintended consequence of the laws that prohibit the practice—then why will there not be other unintended consequences that will
emerge if the laws are abolished, whether by courts or legislatures?
Interestingly, some of the most powerful public arguments made against nul-
lifying such laws have referred to the vulnerability of certain populations (for
example, older women, the poor) whose cost to the medical system allegedly
outweighs their benefit to society. Federal courts have effected profound
transformations in national sentiment during the past forty years, but sociologists, who have for so long been invested in the liberal trajectories of these
transformations, have ignored the empirical realities that have grown up, as it
were, beneath the principled hopes of federal liberalism. Who could have predicted that the best (or at least, ultimate) protection for the old and the poor
may become a matter of state's rights?

The medical disenchantment of the world has invited a variety of forms
of resistance from disparate sources and has created numerous alliances that
are, at first sight, politically odd. Hospice advocates line up (however uncom-
fortably) with Catholic bishops to oppose physician-assisted suicide. Research
on embryos—reintroduced as an ethically sound activity so long as the distinctions between embryos, fetuses, and newborns are believed to be decisive—has invited suspicions about the federalizing of emotion implicit in the
medical ethical project in late modernity. Far from being an adversarial logic
applied to a wide-range of institutional powers, bioethics has, however innocently or inadvertently, accelerated a process of rationalization. Rather than

speaking truth to power, bioethics seeks to guide that power. The effort to publicize such guidance is, finally, a surrogate for holding that power, without the troublesome (medical) professional problems of accountability. Bioethicists, by virtue of class, status, and party, have been rank apologists for abortion. The rising objections among leading bioethicists against physician-assisted suicide suggests, however late in the day, that even rationalization may have its limits. The public is anxious, and having been fed for so long on a diet of autonomy and professional dominance, it may redirect those anxieties toward bioethicists themselves, as has certainly been the case in abortion. Daniel Callahan (1996) has recognized the costs for a politicization of bioethical disagreements. There is much to learn from the fate of sociology here. The study of resistance to innovation is always closer to the truth of matters than is the wish to paper over the fact that such resistance exists.

Historically, resistance to innovation has been considered a scourge on enlightenment, on the pursuit of knowledge, on the hope of progress. As a result of the federalizing of emotion, the prospect of assisted-suicide clinics alongside abortion clinics is hardly unthinkable anymore. Older resistance to innovation is now complemented by the newer doubt about the ends of medicine. The old resistance and the new doubt, I believe, derive from the consistent uncertainty about how we are taught and untaught to trust others. Such resistance and doubt acknowledge the human condition in which danger, cruelty, and horror remain always on the edge of public view, even as one hundred years of scientific innovation and social progress suggest otherwise. Publicity, like fire or a mob, is the irrational force set loose in a world that otherwise craves order and consistency, and it reminds us, however unconstructively, that the rational boundaries created by institutions are challenged by the anxieties and ambitions of individuals and groups in pursuit of interests regularly and often inconsistent with reason itself.

NOTES

1. The best survey available of these traditions is Numbers and Amundsen (1986).

2. My discussion of this autopsy relies entirely upon Chavarria and Shipley (1924).

3. For a discussion of evolving laws pertaining to the disposition of dead bodies, see Hartwell (1888), Forbes (1898), Jenkins (1913), Jackson (1936), Blake (1955), and Montgomery (1966).

4. See Cassedy (1987). Clergymen were concerned enough about anatomical instruction in medical schools to speak out directly about it. At the annual commencement of Columbia's College of Physicians and Surgeons in 1870, a Reverend Dr. Vinton [possibly John Adams Vinton (1801–1877) or Francis Vinton (1809–1872)] delivered an address entitled "Conception of the Physician" in which "he spoke at length on the kindred nature of the medical and of the clerical professions. He learned that but few medical students were communicants and practical Christians. He also discussed the qualifications of the physicians, and feared that the tendency of anatomical study was to render men inhuman. 'A practiced anatomist cut up a human body as he would a dog.'" (*New York Times*, 3 March 1870, 8:3) Vinton's admonitions were apparently not intended to incite public anxieties about dissection but rather were directed at the character of the faculty and students.

5. Watson (1991) offers ample evidence of the relation between ministering and doctoring in the early formation of professional culture in the United States. If America's separation of church and state was founded in a constitutional resistance to state-established religion, the unity of church and profession emerged as a cultural imperative to retain the religious foundations of public duty, particularly but not only in the higher professions. The history of modern professionalization is the repression of that cultural imperative, especially in its Protestant origins. Bioethics is the post-Protestant, surrogate-Catholic successor to duty and casuistry, respectively.

6. Richardson (1987) depicts the social consequences of the passage of the Anatomy Act of 1832 in Great Britain. In effect, the act allowed for the transfer of dead bodies of paupers to the dissection rooms of medical schools. Before then, only the bodies of executed criminals were made available for dissection, which was widely regarded as a postmortem punishment. The link between punishment and dissection (and thus the strenuous efforts by the working-class poor to avoid a "pauper's funeral") does not appear as compelling in the American case. But, see Waite (1945a). Dylan Thomas dramatized the resurrectionists in Great Britain in *The Doctor and the Devils* (1964).

7. In addition to Richardson (1987), see Packard (1902), Frank (1907), Jacobson (1915), Eliot (1916), Krumbhaar (1922), Howell (1926), Ball (1928), Victor (1940), Heaton (1943), Waite (1945b), Blake (1950), Ladenheim (1950), Edwards (1951), Clark and Cummins, (1962), Montgomery (1966), Fido (1988), Fleetwood (1988), Adams (1990), and Shultz (1992).

8. One example of the public fascination with such brazenness appeared in the *New York Times* (28 February 1867, 5), with the column headline: "Excitement at Buffalo over Medical Subjects." The account continued, "Five dead bodies, two males, two females, and one newborn infant, were found by the Detective Police at the Grand Trunk Railroad depot this afternoon. They were shipped through the American Express Company from Ann Arbor, Mich. The bodies were packed in flour barrels in a nude state and had not been dead over a week. They were not decomposed and bore no marks of violence. The bodies are now being cleansed of flour, and will be exposed for identification to-morrow morning. The city is wild with excitement to know whose relations have been thus desecrated by body snatchers."

9. U.S. Congress, House, *A Bill for the Promotion of Anatomical Science and to Prevent the Desecration of Graves*, 48th Cong., 1st sess., March 3, 1884, H.R. 5650; U.S. Congress, *Congressional Record*, 48th Cong., 1st sess., 15: 1568.

10. Evidence about the behavior of medical students in classes on anatomical instruction during the second half of the nineteenth century and the first quarter of the twentieth century is sparse. Yet, concern about student proprieties was sufficient to move S. Weir Mitchell to remark in 1893: "There are risks to character already active in your lives. When I see men become easily indifferent to the exposures and the pains and suffering of the clinic and the ward, brutal or full of levity when learning the secrets of man's structure in the dissecting-room, then I know that evil has begun which insensibly hardens so many" (Mitchell 1893, 10). An editorial in the *Peninsular Journal of Medicine* in 1874 offered similar sentiments about relations with the public: "The true physician approaches the body of the dead with awe and reverence, that frail tenement of clay whose spirit has passed beyond the boundary of finite knowledge, and impressed with the sacredness of the subject, he will conduct the necessary mutilation with order and decency. If the people receive this impression they will not generally oppose or deny the request for examination, but will gladly avail themselves of the benefit coming directly or indirectly from them" (Editorial 1874).

11. Rothman (1991) does not identify the casuistic approach in bioethics, a specific contribution of Catholic pastoral medicine, recycled from natural law. See Imber (1991b).

12. The most recent accounts of their lives are Hunter (1964) and Wallace and Wallace (1978).

13. Bell (1987, 135) notes without further remark that the College of Physicians broke a fifteen-year relationship with the medical journal responsible for the publication of the College's *Transactions* because of disagreements about who should have control over the publication of the autopsy report. Perhaps the dispute precipitated what was bound to happen sooner or later. Yet it underscores the intensity of public interest in the medical profession and its handling of publicly controversial matters. Another account of the autopsy at the time is given in the *British Medical Journal* (for the full citation, see reference under The Siamese twins 1874).

14. I rely on the following works in reconstructing Garfield's medical case: Balch (1881), Conwell (1881), Ridpath (1882), and Thayer (1882).

15. Corporate "trust," as distinct from trust in specific individuals, was long ago exposed by social critics as an ideological veil for corporate "interest." Marx and Engels lifted the veil by replacing professional "interest" with class interest. See Imber (1991a). Contemporary criticism of professions is often rooted in an ambivalent depiction of their allegedly antiegalitarian, anti-democratic, and elitist character. See Kimball (1992), who argues that the rhetorical claims of eighteenth- and nineteenth-century ministers and lawyers about the meaning of their vocations as professions must not be measured against the late twentieth-century projections backward of "professional dominance" ideologies upon them.

16. Debates about "American exceptionalism" have touched upon nearly every institution in American life. In recent decades, the divide between conservative and liberal legal minds has deepened and has accelerated the tendency to see legal matters in monolithic terms. For a useful, if preliminary, recognition of the problem, see Weyrauch (1996).

REFERENCES

Adams, Norman. 1990 [1972]. *In the dead of the night!: The terrible true story of the Scottish body-snatchers*. Glasgow: Lang Syne.

Balch, William Ralston. 1881. *The life of James Abram Garfield*. Philadelphia: Gorton.

Ball, James Moores. 1928. *The sack-'em-up men, an account of the rise and fall of the modern resurrectionists*. Edinburgh: Oliver and Boyd. [Reprinted as *The body snatchers: Doctors, grave robbers and the law*. New York: Dorset Press, 1989.]

Barondess, Jeremiah A., and Charles G. Roland. 1994. *The persisting Osler—II: Selected transaction of the American Osler Society 1981–1990*. Malabar, Fla.: Krieger.

Bell, Jr., Whitfield J. 1987. *The College of Physicians of Philadelphia: A bicentennial history*. Canton, Mass.: Science History Publications.

Blake, John B. 1950. A note on the "doctors' mob." *Journal of the History of Medicine* 5 (Autumn): 450–2.

———. 1955. The development of American anatomy acts. *Journal of Medical Education* 30 (August).

———. 1968. Anatomy and the Congress. In *Medicine, science, and culture: Historical essays in honor of Owsei Temkin*, edited by Lloyd G. Stevenson and Robert P. Multhauf. Baltimore: Johns Hopkins Press, 169–83.

Burnham, John C. 1982. American medicine's golden age: What happened to it? *Science* 215 (March 19): 1474–9.

Callahan, Daniel. 1996. Bioethics, our crowd, and ideology. *Hastings Center Report* 26(6): 3–4.

Cassedy, James H. 1987. Biting the hand: Medical courtesy, quackery, and the antebellum clergy. *Second Opinion* 5:100–19.

Chavarria, A. Pena, and P. G. Shipley. 1924. The Siamese twins of Española: The first known post-mortem examination in the new world. *Annals of Medical History* 6(3): 297–302.

Clark, Sam L., and Harold Cummins. 1962. Medical education from the ground up or our late resurrection men. *Journal of Medical Education* 37(12): 1291–6.

Conwell, Russell H. 1881. *The life, speeches, and public services of James A. Garfield*. Portland, Maine: George Stinson.

Editorial. 1874. Post mortem examinations. *Peninsular Journal of Medicine* 10 (January): 335.

Edwards, Linden F. 1951. Resurrection riots during the heroic age of anatomy in America. *Bulletin of the History of Medicine* 25(2): 178–84.

Eliot, Llewellin. 1916. Discussion of "A history of bodysnatching, by Frank Baker, M.D." *Washington Medical Annals* 15(4): 247–53.

Fido, Martin. 1988. *Bodysnatchers: A history of the resurrectionists, 1742–1832*. London: Weidenfeld & Nicolson.

Fleetwood, John F. 1988. *The Irish bodysnatchers: A history of body snatching in Ireland*. Dublin: Tomar.

Forbes, W. S. 1898. *History of the anatomy-act of Pennsylvania*. Philadelphia: Philadelphia Medical Pub. Co.

Frank, Mortimer. 1907. Resurrection days. *Interstate Medical Journal* 14(3): 293–310.

Fugh-Berman, Adrianne. 1992. Tales out of medical school. *Nation* 254(2): 1, 54–6.

Hafferty, Frederic W. 1991. *Into the valley: Death and the socialization of medical students.* New Haven, Conn.: Yale University Press.

Hartwell, Edward Mussey. 1888. The study of human anatomy, historically and legally considered. *Johns Hopkins University, Studies from the Biological Laboratory* 2 (July): 65–116.

Heaton, Claude. 1943. Body snatching in New York City. *New York State Journal of Medicine* 43(10): 1861–5.

Howell, W. B. 1926. Some humble workers in the cause of anatomy a hundred years ago. *Annals of Medical History* 8(1): 20–30.

Hughes, Thomas P. 1958. Harold P. Brown and the executioner's current: An incident in the ac-dc controversy. *Business History Review* 32:143–65.

Hunter, Kay. 1964. *Duet for a lifetime.* London: Joseph.

Imber, Jonathan B. 1986. *Abortion and the private practice of medicine.* New Haven, Conn.: Yale University Press.

———. 1990. Abortion policy and medical practice. *Society* 27(5): 27–34.

———. 1991a. Doctor no longer knows best: Changing American attitudes toward medicine and health. In *America at century's end,* edited by Alan Wolfe. Berkeley: University of California Press, 298–317.

———. 1991b. Doctors on trial. Review of *Strangers at the bedside: A history of how law and bioethics transformed medical decision making,* by David J. Rothman. *Times Literary Supplement,* no. 4611 (August 16, 1991): 12.

Jackson, Percival E. 1936. *The law of cadavers and of burial and burial places.* New York: Prentice Hall, 159–66.

Jacobson, Arthur C. 1915. Robert Knox and the "Resurrectionists": A chapter in Scottish anatomy. *Interstate Medical Journal* 22(5): 462–72.

James, William. 1875. Vivisection. In *The works of William James: Essays, comments, and reviews.* Cambridge, Mass.: Harvard University Press, chap 3.

Jenkins, George B. 1913. The legal status of dissecting. *Anatomical Record* 7 (November).

Kimball, Bruce A. 1992. *The "true professional ideal" in America: A history.* Oxford: Blackwell.

Krumbhaar, Edward B. 1922. The early history of anatomy in the United States. *Annals of Medical History* 4(3): 271–86.

Ladenheim, Jules Calvin. 1950. "The doctors' mob" of 1788. *Journal of the History of Medicine* 5 (winter): 23–43.

Marker, Rita. 1995. The Woodstock of bioethics. *Human Life Review* 21(1): 35–52.

Mitchell, S. Weir. 1893. *Two lectures on the conduct of the medical life, addressed to the students of the University of Pennsylvania and the Jefferson Medical College.* Philadelphia: University of Pennsylvania Press.

Montgomery, Horace. 1966. A body snatcher sponsors Pennsylvania's anatomy act. *Journal of the History of Medicine and Allied Sciences* 21(4): 374–93.

Numbers, Ronald L., and Darrel W. Amundsen, eds. 1986. *Caring and curing: Health and medicine in the Western religious traditions.* New York: Macmillan.

Packard, Francis R. 1902. The resurrectionists of London and Edinburgh. *Medical News* 81(2): 64–73.

Richardson, Ruth. 1987. *Death, dissection and the destitute.* London: Routledge & Kegan Paul.

Ridpath, John Clark. 1882. *The life and work of James A. Garfield.* Cincinnati, Ohio: Jones Brothers.

Rosenberg, Charles E. 1968. *The trial of the assassin Guiteau: Psychiatry and law in the gilded age.* Chicago: University of Chicago Press.

Rothman, David J. 1991. *Strangers at the bedside: A history of how law and bioethics transformed medical decision making.* New York: Basic Books.

Shultz, Suzanne M. 1992. *Body snatching: The robbing of graves for the education of physicians in early nineteenth century America.* Jefferson, N.C.: McFarland.

Siminoff, L. A., R. M. Arnold, A. L. Caplan, B. A.Virnig, and D. L. Seltzer. 1995. Public policy governing organ and tissue procurement in the United States: Results from the National Organ and Tissue Procurement Study. *Annals of Internal Medicine* 123(1): 10–17.

Smith, T. Burton. 1992. Assassination medicine. *American Heritage* 43(5): 116–19.

Thayer, William Makepeace. 1882. *From log cabin to the White House: The life of James A. Garfield; Boyhood, youth, manhood, assassination [!] death, funeral.* New York: Hurst.

The Siamese brothers. 1829. *Boston Medical Surgical Journal* 2(29): 459–62.

The Siamese twins. 1874. *British Medical Journal* (March 14): 359–63.

Thomas, Dylan. 1964 [1953]. *The doctor and the devils.* New York: Time Life Books.

Victor, Ralph G. 1940. An indictment for grave robbing at the time of the "doctors' riot," 1788. *Annals of Medical History*, 3d ser., 2(5): 366–70.

Waite, Frederick C. 1945a. Grave robbing in New England. *Bulletin of the Medical Library Association* 33(3): 272–94.

———. 1945b. The development of anatomical laws in the states of New England. *New England Journal of Medicine* 233(24): 716–26.

Wallace, Irving, and Amy Wallace. 1978. *The two: A biography.* New York: Simon & Schuster.

Watson, Patricia Ann. 1991. *The angelical conjunction: The preacher-physicians of colonial New England.* Knoxville: University of Tennessee Press.

Weyrauch, Walter O. 1996. Aspirations and reality in American law. In *Law, morality, and religion: Global perspectives*, edited by Alan Watson. Berkeley, CA: Robbins Collection Publications, 217–26.

CHAPTER THREE

The Triumph of Autonomy in American Bioethics: A Sociological View

Paul Root Wolpe

THE QUESTION

Modern American bioethical thought has been widely criticized for its preoccupation with patient autonomy. Though its roots trace back to theologies and secular philosophies that value other principles as much, or more, than individual autonomy, most human-subject regulation and patient-protection policies, as well as most bioethical debate in the United States, center on the idealized value of maximizing individual autonomy. The use of autonomy as a panacea for ethical problems in medicine is a very recent, and peculiarly American, solution to the problems of modern, technological biomedicine. How did individual autonomy achieve its hallowed place in the American bioethical pantheon? What are the structural and cultural forces that uphold its dominance, even as its weaknesses become more and more apparent? The answers to these questions lie in the unique historical development of American bioethics, and the parallel evolution of the American medical system.

FROM MEDICAL ETHICS TO BIOETHICS

Ethical issues have been an integral part of Western medicine since at least the time of Hippocrates. European history is sprinkled with laws, codes of conduct, and guidelines for moral behavior by physicians. To the modern eye, these codes seem at once contemporary and archaic; though many of the fundamental moral dilemmas have not changed that much over the centuries, the ways physicians think and talk about them have changed considerably. The codes of past centuries seem preoccupied with professional responsibility and privilege; the "paternalistic" model of medicine, as this posture was later named by its critics, saw the physician as both duty holder and decision maker for the patient. The physician was clearly charged with a responsibility to treat patients and to treat them well (Baker 1993). Yet the voice of the patient as an independent moral agent is absent from these discussions. Indeed, the idea of patient autonomy or moral agency appears nowhere in Hippocrates, the prayer of Maimonides, Percival's Ethics, or the early codes of the AMA or the World Medical Association (Veatch 1984). Medical ethics as a field of inquiry debated and defined the duties of physicians toward patients, but exclusively as part of internal professional medical discourse. Outside agents—including the patients themselves—were simply not deemed qualified to participate in the formulation of ethical behavior within the profession.

The eventual shift toward the moral agency of the patient can be considered a first step in the development of *bioethics,* a field distinct from its predecessor, *medical ethics.*[1] The historical roots of modern bioethics were conceived in Nuremberg and its aftermath and gestated by developments such as the dialysis controversies of the early 1960s and early theorists of death and dying in the United States, as well as the seminal work of thinkers such as Joseph Fletcher (1954), Henry Beecher (1966), and Paul Ramsey (1970). Bioethics as a distinct intellectual pursuit, however, was a child of the early 1970s. Born in the wake of public controversies such as the Tuskegee scandal and Christiaan Barnard's first heart transplants, it was quickly institutionalized in bioethics centers such as the Hastings Center, founded in 1969, and Georgetown University's Kennedy Institute, established in 1971, which was the first to incorporate the term *Bioethics* in its title (Reich 1994).[2]

The term *bioethics,* like the field itself, was initially intended to represent a broad-based interdisciplinary field in which no one discipline or discourse was to be dominant. While medicine as an institution grew more powerful through the 1960s, the exclusive jurisdiction of physicians as the arbiters of ethical issues in medicine had begun to erode in subtle ways, through many unrelated but cumulative events. For example, the dialysis dilemmas of the early 1960s brought nonphysicians, for the first time, into the decision-making process of individual treatment allocation; Henry Beecher's exposé of medical research by top physicians in 1966 shocked the profession and public with its demonstration of the medical profession's callous disregard for experimental subjects; and the cultural assault on medicine that began in the social movements of the 1960s—the critique of "patriarchal" medical privilege mounted by feminism and patient rights groups, neo-Marxist attacks on capitalist health systems, public debates over the country's handling of health care services to the poor, deinstitutionalization of the mentally ill, the growing disenchantment with the use of health care dollars, the comparatively sluggish progress of medicine in curing chronic diseases such as cancer, and so on— grew into the "crisis" of medicine that was so often commented upon by the early 1970s.

These assaults created the cultural space that allowed the introduction of the first professional bioethicists, a group of theologians and philosophers who saw themselves as the emerging partners of physicians in solving the new ethical problems of biomedicine.[3] As philosophy in particular had no significant previous association with medicine as a discipline, the new bioethicists may also have foreseen an opportunity to increase general prestige[4] and career advancement through association with an applied realm of great economic and cultural power.[5] The alliance of philosophers and medicine was seen by some almost as a professional salvation, as nicely encapsulated by the title of a 1982 article by Stephen Toulmin, "How Medicine Saved the Life of Ethics." Though ethics as a discipline had been alive in the ivy halls of academe, it was medicine that gave ethics its modern, public voice and gave ethicists a new employment opportunity and a new venue for prestige and career advancement.

While classical medical ethics was an exclusive, inbred dialogue among physicians, bioethics as an institutionalized American discipline emerged largely from the interaction of three intellectual domains: the ongoing ethical inquiry of physicians, primarily as expressed through their specialty journals; jurisprudence, both in court decisions and in the legal debates over their validity and application; and debate and discussion by self-proclaimed bioethicists. Since moral philosophy in the United States was moribund, theologians, especially Protestant theologians (for example, Joe Fletcher, Paul Ramsey, Jim Gustafson, Ralph Potter, and Harmon Smith), were strongly represented among early bioethicists and introduced into its disciplinary matrix themes from their religious tradition (Reich 1993). Yet, within a few short years, bioethics as a discipline became dominated by a new breed of secular moral philosophers.[6] The secularization of bioethics, as we will explore in more detail in the following pages, allowed access to medical venues and governmental policymaking bodies that association with religiously based ideologies would have denied.

THE EMERGENCE OF PRINCIPLISM

To establish a position as the primary disciplinary locus of bioethics—and to gain legitimacy in the eyes of the medical profession—philosophy had to make the case that it had at its disposal a set of tools that could address the practical ethical problems that medicine posed. By the early 1970s, as noted previously, ethics itself was a moribund field of philosophy, having exhausted its preoccupation with metaethical questions (Caplan 1983; Toulmin 1982); nor was the discipline renowned for its practical applicability outside the academy. To the contrary, one of the ongoing criticisms (deserved or not) of modern philosophical ethics, as well as the rest of modern philosophy, was its insularity, arcane language, and technical arguments, which seemingly had little application to the practical problems of moral decision making. Medicine, in contrast, is the quintessentially applied profession. As the cultural authority of physicians over ethical decisions in medicine came under increasing pressure in the 1970s, bioethical philosophers needed to prove they were the rightful heirs to the physicians' jurisdiction over medical ethics. In other words, philosophers had to accomplish the task of turning medical ethics—the realm of physicians—into bioethics, a collaborative endeavor with philosophers at the helm.

Bioethical philosophers had their work cut out for them. The discipline of bioethics in the early 1970s was, as K. Danner Clouser (1993, S10) puts it, "a mixture of religion, whimsy, exhortation, legal precedents, various traditions, philosophies of life, miscellaneous moral rules, and epithets," hardly a propitious start for a field that wanted to influence medical practice. The most notable attempt to remedy this pastiche with a set of coherent principles was undertaken by philosophers at the Kennedy Institute, who tried to systematize bioethics by creating a set of bioethical principles that could be applied to all bioethical cases and that could be used by medical decision makers (that is, physicians) without training in analytic philosophy or phenomenology. "Principlism," as the approach came to be known (often pejoratively), was articulated in Tom Beauchamp and James Childress's (1994) *Principles of Biomedical Ethics*, which originally was published in late 1977 and has become the document in bioethics most resembling a common disciplinary charter. The four principles articulated by Beauchamp and Childress in their book—autonomy, nonmaleficence, beneficence, and justice, the "Georgetown mantra"[7]—promised in their formulation an operationalizable tool for evaluating and adjudicating case-based ethical dilemmas. Though principlism has been assaulted, criticized, or amended by a host of critics ever since (for example, Clouser and Gert 1990; Jonsen and Toulmin 1988), it was quickly adopted as the standard approach to bioethical issues, its seminal contribution is widely acknowledged, and its vocabulary and basic principles remain at the center of bioethical debate (Pellegrino 1993).

Beauchamp and Childress's principlism suggests that the way to apply ethical standards to clinical decisions is not to deduce from high-order theories of ethics or to induce from the minutiae of particular clinical situations but to apply a set of universal ethical principles. Beauchamp and Childress tried to create a balanced set of principles, each of which was to have equal weight when considering bioethical cases, though, of course, certain principles would be more applicable than others in a particular case. Because Beauchamp and Childress intentionally refused to offer a priority weighing or hierarchical ranking of their four principles, a persistent criticism of principlism has been its inability to articulate strategies for deciding between principles when they are in conflict in any particular case or when weighed differently by different parties in a case. Beauchamp and Childress write:

> In stubborn cases of conflict there may be no single right action, because two or
> more morally acceptable actions are unavoidably in conflict and yet have equal
> weight in the circumstances. Here we can give good but not decisive reasons for
> more than one action. (1994, 105)

Beauchamp and Childress deny that the system makes it impossible in general
to distinguish between competing application of principles. They continue:

> True, a relativity of judgment is inevitable, but a relativity of the principles embed-
> ded in the common morality is not. When people reach different conclusions,
> their moral judgments are still subject to justification by good reasons. They are
> not purely arbitrary or subjective judgments. A judgment can be proposed for
> consideration on any basis a person chooses—random selection, emotional reac-
> tion, mystical intuition, etc.—but to propose is not to justify, and one part of jus-
> tification is to test judgments and norms by their coherence with other norms in
> the moral life. . . . We conclude that although flexibility and diversity in judgment
> are ineliminable, judgment generally should be constrained by the demands of
> moral justification, which typically involves appeal to principles. (1994, 105)

By presenting their principles as both "prima facie binding" and yet not hierarchical, they hope to both establish their preeminence in moral guidance
and allow the flexibility of revision and refinement through the particular
profile of applicable principles in any particular case.

This formulation is problematic.[8] Sociologically speaking, abstract principles tend to be poor guides for the micromoral dilemmas facing medicine
on a day-to-day basis. This has led Barry Hoffmaster (1990), for example, to
propose a focus on *quotidian ethics*, the emergent ethics of actual practice, over
principlism. Also, though Beauchamp and Childress try to embed their principles in historical and cultural context, the appeal to universal abstract principles like self-determination easily slights the socially constructed and
historically situated meaning of the term *self-determination* itself. For example,
self-determination in post–World War II America was seen as embedded in
community values; self-determination was actualized from a communal base.
It was not until the late 1960s–early 1970s that self-determination became a
rallying cry for an individual liberty removed from social role and community
value. Similarly, appeal to autonomy may mean different things in different
subcultures; for example, in a subculture such as the Vietnamese Hmong,
autonomous decisions may involve deferring to an elder of the group.

Even more important for our purposes, however, the "principles embedded in the common morality" that Beauchamp and Childress suggest preempt
relativity of judgment are themselves mired in ethically problematic and
socially constructed values. Enormous social pressures create the "common
morality" of a professional realm such as medicine. The background assumptions of the common medical morality, both medico-cultural (for example,
the denial of mortality, heroic care, a secular focus, an individualistic ethos of
etiology and responsibility for illness) and structural (for example, defense of

professional interests, consumer/capitalist medical structures, support by technological and pharmaceutical business interests, structural inequalities of power), should be the subject of ethical inquiry, not the basis on which ethical judgments are weighed. Principles based on a common morality cannot be used to critique that common morality.[9]

LIBERAL INDIVIDUALISM AND PERSONAL AUTONOMY

Beauchamp and Childress suggest that their four basic principles are of equal moral weight and should be applied differentially as particular cases demand. Yet medicine as a profession, and health care as an embedded set of structures and relationships, makes differential weightings of values independent of and prior to particular cases. In fact, this paper will argue, the four principles articulated by Beauchamp and Childress have not been—and can never be—given equal weight in American biomedical culture. For better or for worse (and in opposition to Beauchamp and Childress's model), autonomy has emerged as the most powerful principle in American bioethics, the basis of much theory and most regulation, and has become the "default" principle of applied principlism, the principle to be appealed to when principles conflict.[10]

The conflict between liberal individualism (autonomy) and responsibility to the common good (justice, beneficence) has characterized bioethical thought since its inception, and so has the realization that the struggle was being won by the ethic of individual liberty. In 1984 Robert Veatch argued, in an article entitled "Autonomy's Temporary Triumph," that autonomy was a temporary reaction to paternalism and would soon give way to a more balanced social medical ethic.[11] By 1990 Edmund Pellegrino (1990, 361) was calling the ascendancy of autonomy over the traditionally primary value of beneficence "the most radical reorientation in the long history of the Hippocratic tradition" and declared it "well-nigh irreversible." Some scholars (including Childress himself) have lamented that this reliance on autonomy leads to bad judgments and asks autonomy to do the work of other principles (Childress, Callahan, Ackerman), while others have defended it and even argued for yet more or deeper autonomy (Batholeme, Engelhardt, Katz, Veatch). Indisputably, however, patient autonomy has become the central and most powerful principle in ethical decision making in American medicine.

There is no inherent reason that autonomy must become the primary ethical principle in a medical tradition. American medical history itself only developed an autonomy-based ethic since the late 1960s. Similarly, in many religious systems of medical ethics (for example, Freedman 1996), in other indigenous healing systems (Gallagher and Subedi 1995), in other Westernized societies (for example, Otsuka 1977; Surbone 1992), and even in many American subcultures (Blackhall et al. 1995), other principles and formulations have been given priority. Renée Fox and Judith Swazey (1984, 342)

list the moral virtues expected of physicians in China—and neither patient
nor practitioner autonomy is among them. The Chinese demand of their
practitioners more socially based values, such as a spirit of self-sacrifice,
patience, modesty, self-examination, self-criticism, and frankness about one's
limitations and mistakes. Even in the United Kingdom, from whence we
derive the common law on which our valuing of autonomy is partially based,
the courts have often valued other principles, such as physicians' professional
standards, over patient autonomy (Kirby 1995). America stands almost
alone—Canada may be the sole rival—in elevating autonomy to such dominance in medical decision making.

A host of structural and cultural forces, internal and external to medicine, have selected for autonomy in the United States and have suppressed
the moral valence of competing principles.[12] While there are far more factors
contributing to this trend than can be covered in a chapter of this size, it is
instructive to sample a few to see how deeply embedded autonomy is in the
American medical ethos.

Intrinsic Factors

There are reasons intrinsic to the principles themselves that mitigate
against their equal weighting in clinical biomedicine. Let us take as an example the principle of nonmaleficence. It is predicated on Hippocrates' maxim
Primum non nocere, "First, do no harm," which has been elevated over time to
the primordial axiom of Hippocratic medical ethics. The idea of not inflicting
harm is almost universally accepted as a basis of ethical medical practice. Yet
its value as a guiding principle is compromised both by the nature of biomedical therapeutics and the modern abstraction of the concept of harm.
Biomedicine's current armamentarium can be quite harsh in its side effects
and iatrogenic harms: Chemotherapies attack the body's rapidly dividing
cells, leaving patients weak, hairless, and sterile; burn treatments are excruci-
ating; psychopharmaceuticals can leave patients with devastating side effects
such as tardive dyskinesia; surgeries can result in a host of undesirable sequelae; rehabilitation from spinal cord injuries can seem as cruel as the
injuries themselves. The harm of disease and the harm of treatment thus
become conflated in the minds of the average patient, who cannot imagine
one without the other.

The medical community does not consider these as "harms" because
they have defined harms to refer only to ends, not means. If the medical culture judges the outcome (being alive) as being preferable to the harm (even
if the patient disagrees with medical judgment), the patient has not, by definition, been unjustifiably harmed by medicine. Some proximate harm (for
example, a needle stick) has always been a part of medical therapeutics, but
the stakes have risen in modern biomedicine. Modern biomedicine has
tended to cast treatment in terms of violent conflict, as a "battle with disease,"

and, as in any battle, even the winning side suffers casualties. Physicians are joined in this effort by the powerful "arms" suppliers in that battle, biotechnology and pharmaceutical companies, who want to encourage the continued use of their products, whatever the proximate harms (see May 1983, on "physician as fighter").

At the same time, the concept of harm has been inflated in medical decision making to include subjective harms such as psychological and social harms, and so almost any medical decision can be justified on the basis that not to proceed will cause psychological harms to the patient.[13] These parallel tendencies so compromise the principle of nonmaleficence that it clearly can no longer serve the Hippocratic purpose of being the primary principle of (bio)medical ethics.

Similar problems confront the other principles. Beneficence, still a powerful underlying justification for medicine, promotes the right of individuals to obtain treatment and the duty of society to care for them, but these are relatively uncontroversial issues. Beneficence, however, also demands the provision of the best treatment for a particular patient. Some of the most intractable social problems in bioethics, such as assisted suicide and heroic measures in damaged neonates, for example, revolve around the debate over what is in the best interests of the patient. Is it in the best interests of a patient to remove unbearable suffering by helping the patient die or to keep the patient alive despite the pain? Which is "beneficent"? While beneficence can override autonomy—we will restrain a person at risk of harming himself or herself or others—Beauchamp and Childress recognize the difficulty in granting beneficence an equal footing with autonomy in the modern medical model, or even asserting the obligation of professional beneficence when it clashes with autonomy rights:

> Whether respect for the autonomy of patients should have priority over professional beneficence has become a central problem in biomedical ethics. For proponents of autonomy rights for patients, the physician's obligations to the patient of disclosure, seeking consent, confidentiality, and privacy are established primarily (and perhaps exclusively) by the principle of respect for autonomy. Others, by contrast, ground such obligations on the professional's obligatory beneficence. The physician's primary obligation is to act for the patient's medical benefit, not to promote autonomous decision making. However, autonomy rights have become so influential that it is today difficult to find clear affirmations of traditional models of medical beneficence. (1994, 272)

Beneficence is the principle most likely to come into direct conflict with autonomy in daily practice. Yet those who preach beneficence over autonomy are accused of "paternalism," a highly pejorative appellation in the present social climate. Critics of this account of beneficence argue that acting "for the patient's benefit," without clear, autonomous communication by the patient of what that "benefit" means to him or her, is both empirically impossible and morally objectionable (Veatch 1995). It is no wonder that

Beauchamp and Childress find so few supporters of the traditional model of medical beneficence.

Justice, the final principle, is in fact, the principle most likely to infringe on, if not overrule, autonomy. In pursuing fairness in health care distribution, justice can limit autonomous choice; for example, human organs are (purportedly) distributed without consideration of class or race,[14] which infringes on my autonomous choice of a transplant. Unlike autonomy, however, principles of justice are less easily detached from underlying ethical theories, and so competing theories of justice apply the principle differently. Deciding how to justly distribute organs is a complicated matter; giving people the right to refuse to donate or receive them is easy. When the two conflict, the easy path is often taken. The American system is without universal health coverage or an equitable distribution of medical resources or personnel in part because such laws are resisted with claims of threats to individual autonomy. As Albert Jonsen (1993) puts it, the issue of justice is banal on the level of the individual patient, and the country is unwilling to deal with it on the level of the medical system.

Pursuit of autonomy has become dominant in the American model of medical decision making in part because its application is comparatively straightforward and uncontroversial. Even if we agree on the importance of principles of nonmaleficence, beneficence, or justice, their application is complicated and their meaning in any particular case can be disputed. It is just such confusion that led to the inconclusiveness of the right-to-health-care debate in the 1970s. Autonomy allows for a much clearer path of action: Once we agree on the primary importance of letting the patient decide, finding a way to apply ideals of autonomy in the clinical setting becomes a technical problem.[15]

Autonomy in Regulation and Policy

A related issue that reinforces the power of autonomy is the relative ease of codifying and implementing principles of autonomy in regulation and policy. Daniel Callahan (1993) has argued that as bioethics developed, cultural discomfort with public discussions of ethics (in particular, religiously based ethics) moved the country away from a public moral language toward a more neutral language of rights. The course the United States chose was regulation, it being, as Callahan writes, "the way we in the United States typically deal with controversial issues" (1993, S8). However, regulation itself may not be as American as the creation of forums for discussion and dispute. The creation of oversight committees, institutional review boards (IRBs), state and federal regulatory commissions, presidential panels, and so on has become a cottage industry in formulating bioethical policy in the United States, as have ethics committees, bioethics conferences, media panels, television documentaries, and other less formal means for debating bioethical dilemmas.

The principles of nonmaleficence and beneficence are both easy to write into codes, but once there almost impossible to implement. As noted before, standards of nonmaleficence and beneficence are notoriously slippery, and clinical application of the principles to situation-specific problems is usually relegated to the realm of clinical decision making and professional judgment. For example, the attempt to legislate beneficence/nonmaleficence through President Reagan's Baby Doe regulations, whereby health care personnel were to report cases of damaged neonates who were denied treatment, was a spectacular failure and was rescinded.

On the other hand, issues of justice, especially distributive justice, once legislated, can be clearly defined (for example, quotas). Such legislation in bioethical issues, however, tends to be generalized under laws of nondiscrimination and equal access and so apply more to institutional or governmental health care policies than to the microprocesses of clinical medicine. Yet even on the broader level of policy, when justice and autonomy seem to conflict, American culture has been progressively favoring autonomy. President Clinton's health care plan, for example, was defeated in large part because opponents played on public fears of diminished individual autonomy.

Of the four principles, only autonomy is easily codified into a set of rules and regulations pertaining to day-to-day clinical health care. The strong American tradition of privacy rights and personal liberties has elevated "the patient's right to decide" as the rallying cry of both bioethical theory and of medical jurisprudence. America is the most rights-centered society on Earth, and so it is not surprising that medical decision making so often gets recast in terms of personal rights (Annas 1993).

To handle complex bioethical issues, courts must "technicalize" them, reduce them to medicolegal principles that can be legislated (Fox 1990). Broad ethical problems in clinical research and, to a slightly lesser extent in clinical medicine, are often solved by creating "autonomy enhancers"—which in most cases means lengthier and more explicit informed consent forms. The informed consent form, the regulatory mechanism of autonomy, has become the guarantor of autonomy in the clinic and the panacea for ethical problems in research. Rather than disallowing an experimental treatment, for example, an oversight body may decide instead to allow it as long as there is full disclosure of its risks, an example of Childress's (1995) argument that autonomy is often asked to do the work of other principles (in this case, most likely, nonmaleficence).

The dominance of the autonomy principle in jurisprudence is illustrated by the recent Ninth Circuit Court decision to strike down a law that prevented physician-assisted suicide in the terminally ill (*Washington* v. *Glucksberg* 1997). Since the late 1960s, there has been a steady progression toward more and more autonomous decision making at the end of life. In the 1970s, American physicians were still arguing about whether patients must be told about terminal diagnoses; by the 1980s, the country was grappling with the right to disconnect life supports in brain-dead patients; by the late 1980s, it was a right to die with dignity when death was imminent; and in the late 1990s, it is the right to assisted suicide when illness gives way to despair. The Ninth Circuit Court's 1996 land-mark decision allowing limited types of physician-based suicide is based squarely on the shoulders of patient autonomy, as these excerpts indicate:[16]

> In deciding right-to-die cases, we are guided by the Court's approach to the abortion cases. Casey in particular provides a powerful precedent, for in that case the Court had the opportunity to evaluate its past decisions and to deter-mine whether to adhere to its original judgment. Although Casey was influenced by the doctrine of *stare decisis*, the fundamental message of that case lies in its statements regarding the type of issue that confronts us here: "These matters, involving the most intimate and personal choices a person may make in a life-time, choices central to personal dignity and autonomy, are central to the liberty protected by the Fourteenth Amendment" (Casey, 112 S.Ct. at 2807).
>
> Like the decision of whether or not to have an abortion, the decision how and when to die is one of "the most intimate and personal choices a person may make in a lifetime," a choice "central to personal dignity and autonomy." A com-petent terminally ill adult, having lived nearly the full measure of his life, has a strong liberty interest in choosing a dignified and humane death rather than being reduced at the end of his existence to a childlike state of helplessness, dia-pered, sedated, incontinent. How a person dies not only determines the nature of the final period of his existence, but in many cases, the enduring memories held by those who love him.
>
> The legislature finds that adult persons have the fundamental right to con-trol the decisions relating to the rendering of their own medical care, including the decision to have life-sustaining procedures withheld or withdrawn in instances of terminal condition. The legislature further finds that modern med-ical technology has made possible the artificial prolongation of human life beyond natural limits. The legislature further finds that, in the interest of pro-tecting individual autonomy, such prolongation of life for persons with a termi-nal condition may cause loss of patient dignity, and unnecessary pain and suffering, while providing nothing medically necessary or beneficial to the patient. RCW 70.122.010. [FN74]

Though this decision is not typical, there is virtually no appeal in it to the state's interest in maintaining life or the duty not to kill. The triumph of autonomy makes such arguments sound both regressive and repressive. Whether this decision is an anomaly or represents the legal trend of the future, only time will tell.

The Secularization of Bioethics

Jonsen (1991) has argued that America was founded on a combination of Calvinist and Catholic puritanical moralism, which led to a belief in an immutable order of divine providence and moral truths. This "moral funda-mentalism," as Jonsen calls it, still rears its head in the religious right, but the country has repudiated it in policy. What we are left with, Jonsen suggests, is a "secular fundamentalism" of deeply held moral principles shorn of religious rationale. Bioethics, Jonsen argues, began in the hands of theologians informed by moral fundamentalism[17] and quickly fell into the hands of those who had come from philosophical schools of moral skepticism, leading to probabilistic and relativistic positions. Callahan (1990, 2) has written of the gravity of this transition:

> The most striking change over the past two decades or so has been the secularization of bioethics. The field has moved from one dominated by religious and medical traditions to one increasingly shaped by philosophical and legal concepts. The consequence has been a model of public discourse that emphasizes secular themes: universal rights, individual self-direction, procedural justice, and a systematic denial of either a common good or a transcendent individual good.

Though the bioethicists of the 1970s began the process of secularizing bioethics, Jonsen argues, they were strongly influenced by its moralistic origins and so still needed to work from some set of principles. Jonsen argues that principlism therefore became the "peculiarly American approach to ethical analysis" where "autonomy, beneficence, nonmaleficence and justice became the bioethicists' distant echoes of the Calvinist's Decalogue" (Jonsen 1991, 127).

Whether or not one agrees with Jonsen's analysis, principlism has functioned, for a time, as the secular equivalent to the Calvinist decalogue. In fact, implicit within principlism are a number of latent theological assumptions (Fox 1994). However, principlism necessarily stresses different duties and values than explicitly religiously derived codifications. Western religion traditionally subordinates the priority of the self to higher values of community and the sacred; religious voices have consequently been less willing to uncritically accept autonomy and liberal individualism as the dominant bioethical values. This conflict is not new or limited to bioethics. Religious values often conflict with secular values over other issues of autonomy such as abortion, prayer in public schools, or sexual behaviors. Yet religious voices tend to be absent in American policy formation when compared with other countries, both because of concerns about church-state separation and because of America's religious pluralism. If secularization is the American response to religious pluralism, how then can a country with strong religious beliefs and institutions, but a weak religious voice in policy formation, make policies about traditionally "religious" questions such as when life is worth living or the acceptability of assisted reproductive technologies? As Fox puts it:

> [Secularization in American bioethics] is also an instrumental, political, and moral response to a basic societal question that the whole phenomenon of American Bioethics poses: How can, and should, an advanced modern, highly individualistic, pluralistic, and religiously resonant society, like the United States, founded on the precept of governance "under law," rather than "under

men," and the sacredly secular principles of separation of church and state and freedom of belief, try to achieve collective and binding consensus about the kinds of bioethical issues that are now in the public domain? (1990, 209)

Philosophers, perhaps rightly, recognized that bioethics could not emerge as a field without the secularization attendant to professionalization. Neither the medical profession nor those who formulate policy would have sanctioned a sectarian ethic as a definitive moral voice. The paradox of our church-state separation is that it ultimately denies the religious voice a role in the process of policy formation. In the absence of unified moral communities, pluralism is translated into a radical individualism where all moral voices have equal valence. Autonomy as a guiding principle of American public life is meant, in part, to ensure freedom of religion and religious expression, but, ironically, it tends to silence the religious voice in policy formation, which is often the strongest voice in defending other values, such as justice.

Rituals of Trust: Informed Consent

"Practically every development in medicine in the post–World War II period distanced the physician and the hospital from the patient and the community, disrupting personal connection and severing the bonds of trust" says David Rothman in *Strangers at the Bedside* (1991). The "strangers" of the title are a new breed of physicians who are ensconced in clinical and academic institutions that physically isolate them from their patients (and whose high salaries socially isolate them from their patients as well). The overall transition of the locus of health care from the community-based primary care practitioner to institutional management (first through hospitals and clinics and more recently through managed care) has shifted the patient-physician interaction from a generalized exchange in an organic setting (the community) to a restricted (market) exchange in a bureaucratic setting (Betz and O'Connel 1983). Where "organic" trust is scarce, rituals of trust naturally emerge.

Informed consent is the modern clinical ritual of trust. Informed consent involves the physician trusting the patient with what used to be privileged professional information (risks, procedures to be used, the exact nature of the problem) and the patient returning the trust by allowing the physician to invade his or her bodily integrity despite the knowledge of risks. This formalistic ritual becomes increasingly necessary where informal bonds of trust have eroded. Some evidence of this may be the little-noted fact that informed consent rituals were first articulated most fully in human-subject *research* and only later in the clinical setting. By the mid-twentieth century, research was moving away from the use of individual patients in clinical settings and beginning to use large, anonymous subject populations where the subjects were not likely to know the researcher. Principle One of the Nuremberg Code, written in 1947, states that subjects' consent in medical research must be voluntary, competent, informed, and comprehending. In clinical medicine, on the other hand, cases that involved patient consent were considered by the courts primarily under the laws of battery or malpractice until the *Salgo* v. *Leland Stanford Jr., University, Board of Trustees* case in 1957, where the term *informed consent* is first written into law, hinting at its modern implications almost ten years after the Nuremberg Code.[18] It was *Salgo* that finally shifted patient consent in clinical settings from being beneficence-based (doing surgery without patient consent "hurts" the patient) to autonomy-based (a patient has a right to self-determination through informed, comprehensive consent).

Medical research in the nineteenth century was primarily done by physicians on their own patients in their clinics or on their colleagues' patients who were hospitalized. There was no clear theoretical or practical differentiation made between standard practice and experimental therapy. As modern epidemiological methods developed, however, researchers started looking for subject pools in orphanages, the army, insane asylums, and state hospitals. It makes sense that the informed consent ritual should develop first in these settings, where the researcher often does not know the patient and interpersonal trust has no basis. In clinical medicine, the trust between physician and patient is (presumably) greater. Informed consent and lawsuits attendant to perceived violations of informed consent have become more important as structural barriers to trust have grown, including greater use of managed care, increased reliance on tertiary care providers and institutions, and heightened mobility of the American public. All these developments lead to increasingly transitory relationships between patients and practitioners.

Despite the calls of some medical reformers to reform medical education and teach physicians a more patient-based style of medicine, barriers to trust cannot be overcome by simply "humanizing" medical exchanges. Solutions based solely on changing medical curricula are destined to fail. As M. Betz and L. O'Connel (1983, 86) note, "Trust is a structural product, and not merely a function of the communication skills of exchange partners." The structural impediments to trust have resulted in a consumer orientation to medicine, and where caveat emptor reigns, the public will insist on good package labeling. In a world where medicine has become a good to be consumed and where patients are customers to be wooed, informed consent becomes the disclosure of contents on the back of the box. Informed consent involves discussion of the nature of a procedure, its risks and benefits, and alternative treatments, and it is enacted through the modern ritual of free assent, the signing of a contract. The contract model reciprocally reinforces the primacy of autonomy by tying medicine to other ritualized signings in modern society—loans, rentals, licensing—where two parties are exercising their free right to exchange goods and services. Give someone the right not to sign something, and then their signing it becomes a clear symbol of the exercise of autonomous choice. Autonomy can thus be upheld and dispensed in a ritual that reinforces the freedom of medical decision making without disturbing its underlying structural impediments.

Autonomy and Medical Authority

The elevation of patient autonomy to primary status in the medical encounter may seem, at first, contrary to the received sociological wisdom about medicine as a sovereign profession. Medicine is the quintessentially insular and exclusive profession, so it would not seem likely that physicians would welcome the emergence of strong standards of patient autonomy and decision making. In fact, the incursion of governmental regulation into informed-consent issues in both medical research and clinical care was initially resisted (Katz 1984; Rothman 1991). Yet, the resistance was surprisingly short-lived, and by 1982 it was clear that medical decision making was being made collectively rather than paternalistically, and the normative questions were being framed largely by outsiders, not by physicians. If the medical profession made a virtually unimpeded march to the pinnacle of professional power and authority, as Paul Starr (1982) has suggested, why would they not fiercely resist the emerging movement toward patient autonomy, which, by definition, infringes on their authority in the clinical encounter?

It was clear by the 1970s that medicine as practiced since World War II was under assault and its ethical bases were not a sufficient response to the attacks. Protestations of medicine's beneficence were countered by claims, especially among feminists, of its paternalism. Medicine's claim to nonmaleficence was countered by new terms like iatrogenic illness, most notably and popularly in the work of Ivan Illich (1975). Justice as the primary ethical underpinning of medicine was not attractive to physicians for two reasons. On a national level it would mean medical reform on a large scale, and physicians could not be sure they would retain control over that effort.[19] In the clinical encounter it would force physicians to become the gatekeepers of medical care (Pellegrino 1993), the "rationers" of care, a position that physicians still resist.

Furthermore, patient autonomy is not as corrosive of professional privilege in the clinical encounter as it first appears. Autonomy tends to be a negative right (in that a person has the right to refuse treatment) rather than a positive right (a person cannot generally demand a particular treatment). Physicians are still the translators and filterers of information to their patients, patients still generally defer to physician recommendations, and physicians remain the medical experts we turn to as a society for definitions of disease.[20] In addition, physicians often conceive of informed consent as a matter of beneficence, not patient autonomy; for example, professional journals and meetings often portray informed consent as a technique to increase patient satisfaction and clinical outcomes (for example, Peters 1994). Informed consent is therefore subsumed under the rubric of beneficent medical practice and retains its aura of professional power and authority. Informed patient decision making also tends to shift the sense of responsibility for bad outcomes partially onto the shoulders of the patient, a desirable shift in an age of malpractice suits. In fact, as Charles Bosk (1992) points out, genetic counselors take this trend to its logical conclusion, using the principle of autonomous decision making to abandon participation in the process of patient decision making altogether.

The focus on patient autonomy also benefits physicians by minimizing the tendency for government regulation of the content of medical care. If patients make individual, informed decisions about their care, presumably with knowledge of the risks and potential benefits, then the government itself can assume a lesser role in monitoring and regulating the content of care. Government bodies join other regulating bodies, like IRBs, in using the rituals of autonomy to avoid scrutinizing the content of clinical care—or proposed research methodologies—for more fundamental ethical problems. Bioethics, established medicine, and the government all conspire to speak in economic terms about patient responsibility and the patient as "consumer" and thereby avoid their responsibility for reform or critique of the assumptions underlying health care (Fox 1994).

Supporting ideals of patient autonomy holds other advantages for the medical profession. It is not, in the final analysis, patients or regulators who threaten physician privilege but administrators, both in hospitals and in managed care companies. Eliot Friedson (1984) predicted in the early 1980s that managed care would redistribute physician authority but would not erode the overall authority of physicians; some physicians would become the employees, but only of other physicians, as HMOs would be controlled by physicians. At the time, Friedson could not imagine that physicians, or society, would allow the erosion of physician authority over the content of care. Such erosion is now clearly taking place. While seeming to scrupulously avoid the content of medical decision making, the creation of funding strategies and capitation schemes limits medical options and the authority of the physician to act in the best interests of the patient. In the final irony, it is the strong voice of patients, patient advocacy groups, and employers, along with their lawsuits, rather than the authority of the physician, that is forcing managed care companies to pay for the treatments patients want. Remarkably, patient autonomy has become the physician's ally in battling the erosion of physician autonomy in managed care.

THE TRIUMPH OF AUTONOMY?

The triumph of autonomy in American medicine has not happened in isolation, of course. "The right to individual liberty" is a long-standing and mythologized American value. One could easily write a modern history of America by tracing the theme of individual liberty, especially as it has been translated into "rights." Medical disputes have played an important role in the public debates over individual liberties: The struggle over abortion, end-of-life care, refusal of medical treatment, and so on almost always evolve into rights-based arguments about autonomous decision making. Nor should the triumph of autonomy be overstated. Concern for other principles result in FDA oversight laws, IRB requirements, taxation and allocation, and other important safeguards. The triumph of autonomy is one of balance and historical trend; autonomy has become progressively more important over time and especially in clinical medicine.

Yet there is some evidence that autonomy's dominance may be eroding. The inherent problems of idealized autonomy, structural and ideological, have become clearer. Champions of autonomy have often assumed that, given the appropriate risk-benefit analysis, decisions can in some absolute sense be "free." Yet the idea of "free choice" is itself socially constructed and situated. Even at our historical moment, with its emphasis on individual autonomy, multiple constraints conspire to undermine the ideal of individual freedom necessary for truly autonomous decisions. Physicians remain the gatekeepers to most medical information in any particular clinical situation and filter that information through their own biases in any presentation of options and risks. Even if consent could truly be "informed," the nature of serious disease itself is coercive, as decisions must be made from within the cloak of fear and desperation that accompanies serious illness. The constellation of structural factors that can add a coercive element to decision making is almost endless; the power and prestige of the medical profession influences people toward physician recommendations, even as the erosion of trust makes them wary of physician motivations; families or communities often manipulate or coerce their members into medical decisions; class, race, education, cultural, and religious factors can limit patient options, understandings, and perceptions of medical possibilities; life circumstances, such as the need to get back to a job that will not tolerate long medical absences, coerce patients to make certain types of decisions.

Changes in medical technology and the organization of medical care have also begun to challenge the priority value of autonomy. Managed care is chipping away at physician and patient autonomy alike, though there is evidence that, as the market becomes saturated and competition more fierce, consumer desires will become a bigger factor in the managed care marketplace. New medical technologies, such as preimplantation germ-line genetic engineering, have forced society to begin to ask where the limits of personal autonomy lie. Ironically, the same questions are being raised in the oldest of technologies as well; feminists, who tend to be militant about women's autonomous choices over their own reproductive health, are split over whether autonomy should be limited when African women want female circumcision or infibulation (Schwartz 1994). Communitarians have also been vocal in attacking autonomy, critiquing liberalism for neglecting community, one's obligation and responsibility to others, the value of political life, and rights-based individualized justice (Buchanan 1989). Veatch, an early advocate of patient autonomy, has taken an interesting and somewhat paradoxical approach that reinforces autonomy while pairing it with more communal values. Veatch has argued that medical practitioners cannot share and understand the autonomous needs of their patients unless they share similar values and background. Patients should therefore be matched with physicians that are more like themselves—similar in ethnic, religious, and moral backgrounds, part of their patients' community (Veatch 1995). Here autonomous decision making has brought us full circle back to community values.

In the final analysis, it is almost certainly not the debate between autonomy and justice—or any of Beauchamp and Childress's other principles—that will characterize the future of bioethical reasoning. Principlism itself emerged in a particular time and historical context, giving the fledging field of bioethics a shared language and method for conceptualizing problems. In the future, new categories will be formulated that transcend or make irrelevant the language of principlism. Such a reformulation is already starting. For example, the direct conflict of principles of autonomy and justice in American feminist attitudes toward (mostly African) females who choose circumcision as their "ethnic heritage" break easy models of the "balance of principles" and suggest that new ways must be found to conceptualize difficult bioethical dilemmas. Susan Wolf (1994), as a further example, has argued that the empirical studies of clinical bioethics since the early 1980s, as well as the rise of pragmatism in determining health care ethics and law, render Beauchamp and Childress's theoretical categories obsolete. She notes, for example, that despite the centrality of respect for autonomy, empirical studies show that a sizable number of people do not want to make decisions for themselves. Similarly, recent studies show that significant ethnic and religious subpopulations of the United States do not share a fetish for individualized autonomous decision making, believing instead in the primacy of the family in making important medical decisions (Blackhall et al. 1995). These social forces, and others, are working to temper the reliance on autonomy and will lay the foundation for a postprinciple bioethics.

Modern interpretations of religious categories of ethics, and secular principles like Beachamp and Childress's, emerge from particular historical moments and are culturally bound to the societies that produce them. The sociological critique of bioethics is important in understanding the socially situated and therefore socially constructed nature of bioethical reasoning, and so stands as a corrective and a caution to the development of bioethical policy. Fortunately, bioethics has become a field with a certain cachet today, and social scientists are beginning to make larger contributions to the field. Those contributions can stand both as an intellectual critique and a resource for making more enlightened guidelines for patient protection in modern health care.

NOTES

1. The terminological distinction is mine; many people use *medical ethics* also to refer to modern bioethics. However, I think the distinction is useful.

2. The full name for the Kennedy Institute when it opened in 1971 was The Joseph and Rose Kennedy Institute for the Study of Human Reproduction and Bioethics (Reich 1994).

3. I use the term *biomedicine* to differentiate the dominant medical system, based on the work of the medical-scientific-industrial complex and perpetuated in the educational and licensing systems of the major medical schools and state boards, from other parallel American medical systems such as folk medicine, "alternative" medical techniques, and competing foreign and domestic theoretically driven systems such as chiropractic, Christian Science, or Ayurvedic medicine.

4. The advancement of professional prestige was more problematic, for within academic philosophy there was little prestige in being a bioethicist.

5. It should be noted that these new bioethicists did not simply impose themselves on physicians or medicine; they were invited by physicians to participate in medical decision making as physicians began to confront allocation decisions, which included judgments of social worth—that they did not feel qualified to make—such as who deserved to get scarce dialysis resources.

6. A scattering of others also saw challenges and opportunities in the emerging field, including social scientists, nurses, and other allied medical professionals. However, their numbers were small compared to physicians, philosophers, and legal scholars. An argument can be made that the clergy, especially through the Catholic Church, was also an influential part of the early establishment of bioethics.

7. I do not have the space here to go into depth about the meanings and the controversies over the meanings of these terms individually. Their use in the bioethical debates about which I write will become clear over the course of this discussion. The interested reader is referred to Beauchamp and Childress (1994) for a complete discussion of definitions.

8. Beauchamp and Childress themselves recognize many of the problematic issues of principlism, and in the fourth edition of their textbook (Beauchamp and Childress 1994), they add new opening chapters that seem to move away from the deductive, singular approach of their earlier formulation to one that looks more at common practice (Emanuel 1995).

9. Emanuel (1995) suggests that Beauchamp and Childress's introduction of the idea of a "common morality theory" in their fourth edition is a move away from their earlier justification in utilitarian and deontological ethical theories, which have been much criticized, and toward a more constructivist view of ethics.

10. *Autonomy* in the context of this article will refer, unless otherwise indicated, to patient autonomy, not the professional autonomy of physicians. It is patient autonomy that is held up as a principle of medical ethics by Beauchamp and Childress.

11. Veatch's article was part of a special issue on the problems and potentials of autonomy, and many other authors made similar criticisms of the overreliance on autonomy. Most agreed that autonomy's dominance would soon give way to more communal values.

12. Some early critics of Beauchamp and Childress proposed competing or supplemental principles in their critiques of Beauchamp and Childress's principlism. By now, however, bioethics as a discipline has in effect moved past principlism, as competing moral theories and skeptical philosophical challenges to overarching moral values have been proffered (though principlism still has its defenders, cf. Lustig 1992). This development, however, only reinforces the reliance on autonomy, which becomes the operative principle for bioethical decision making in an era of competing moral philosophies.

13. For example, "psychological harm" to the mother or patient is routinely cited as the medical justification for abortion, cosmetic surgery, and other controversial procedures.

14. I write "purportedly" due to suspicions that the rich and prominent—Mickey Mantle, Governor Casey of Pennsylvania—get privileged treatment and because of data that shows, for example, that African Americans wait longer than white Americans for transplants—such as an average of nine months longer for a kidney transplant (Gaston et al. 1993).

15. In practice, ensuring and exercising autonomy is not simple at all—there are disagreements and contradictions in the arguments about how to maximize autonomy among

minors, the mentally ill, and other vulnerable populations; in the coercive influences of class, medical setting; and social environment, and in the limits set by insurance reimbursements, for example. The final section of the paper revisits this issue.

16. The subsequent Second Circuit Court decision in New York, also concerning physician-assisted suicide, emphasized issues of equal protection over autonomy. Since this article went to press, the Supreme Court overturned the lower court decisions and determined that there was no constitutional right to assisted suicide, and therefore states presumably have the right to ban or to allow it as they choose.

17. As noted before, American bioethics can point to religious origins; for example, Fletcher was an Episcopal theologian, Ramsey wrote from the point of view of Christian ethics, Childress himself is a minister, and Beauchamp is also religiously trained. It is very likely, however, that these authors, as well as other religiously trained bioethicists, would strongly object to Jonsen's characterization of them as "moral fundamentalists."

18. This point should not be overstated. A large amount of case law before *Salgo* established the need for patient consent before procedures, and there were some scattered cases that somewhat presaged *Salgo;* also, what Judge Bray meant by "informed consent" in the *Salgo* decision is itself far from clear (Katz 1984). Still, unlike *Salgo,* the vast majority of prior decisions did not articulate modern components of informed consent, such as the physician's duty to disclose certain types of information (Faden and Beauchamp 1986). For example, as late as 1955, in the case of *Hunt* v. *Bradshaw,* the Tennessee Supreme Court was still affirming that failure to tell a patient of the risks of surgery was not actionable if the physician exercised reasonable care and diligence in the surgery itself (Katz 1984). Such decisions were virtually ended by *Salgo.*

19. Recent developments in health care have proved them correct. The major changes in health care delivery, both nationally and in the industry through managed care, are being made primarily by nonphysicians and erode physician control of even traditionally medical decisions such as therapeutic recommendations.

20. I do not mean here to underestimate the role of nonphysician practitioners in this dynamic. Pursuit of both professional autonomy and patient autonomy has certainly contributed to the erosion of physician authority in relation to other practitioners, such as nurse-practitioners and those who practice nonestablishment medicine. It is notable that physicians have fought against the threat of competing practitioners and internal threats by dissenting physicians far more vigorously than they have resisted increased patient autonomy (Wolpe 1990, 1994).

REFERENCES

Annas, George J. 1993. *Standard of care: The law of American bioethics.* New York: Oxford University Press.

Baker, R. 1993: History of medical ethics. In *Encyclopedia of the history of medicine,* edited by W. Bynum and R. Porter. London: Routledge.

Beauchamp, Tom L., and James F. Childress. 1994. *Principles of biomedical ethics.* 4th ed. New York: Oxford University Press.

Beecher, Henry K. 1966. Ethics and clinical research. *New England Journal of Medicine* 74: 1354–60.

Betz, M., and L. O'Connel. 1983. Changing doctor-patient relationships and the rise in concern for accountability. *Social Problems* 31: 84–95.

Blackhall, Leslie J., et al. 1995. Ethnicity and attitudes toward patient autonomy. *Journal of the American Medical Association* 274(10): 820–5.

Bosk, Charles L. 1992. *All God's mistakes: Genetic counseling in a pediatric hospital.* Chicago: University of Chicago Press.

Buchanan, Allen E. 1989. Assessing the communitarian critique of liberalism. *Ethics* 99: 852–82.

Callahan, Daniel. 1990. Religion and the secularization of bioethics. *Hastings Center Report* (July–August): 2–4.

———. 1993. Why America accepted bioethics. *Hastings Center Report* (November–December, suppl.): S8-9.

Caplan, Arthur L. 1983. Can applied ethics be effective in health care and should it strive to be? *Ethics* 93: 311–19.

Childress, James. 1995. Looking to the future of informed consent. Talk given at Informed Consent in Health Care: Who Really Decides? Sponsored by the Center for Bioethics, University of Pennsylvania, Philadelphia.

Clouser, K. Danner. 1993. Bioethics and philosophy. *Hastings Center Report* (November-December, suppl.): S10–11.

Clouser, K. D., and B. Gert. 1990. A critique of principlism. *Journal of Medicine and Philosophy* 15:219–36.

Emanuel, Ezekiel J. 1995. The beginning of the end of principlism. *Hastings Center Report* 25:37–8.

Faden, Ruth R., and Tom L. Beauchamp. 1986. *A history and theory of informed consent.* New York: Oxford University Press.

Fletcher, J. 1954. *Morals and medicine.* Princeton, N.J.: Princeton University Press.

Fox, Renée C. 1990. The evolution of American bioethics: A sociological perspective. In *Social science perspectives on medical ethics,* edited by George Weisz. Philadelphia: University of Pennsylvania Press, 201–20.

———. 1994. The entry of U.S. bioethics into the 1990s. In *A matter of principles? Ferment in U.S. bioethics,* edited by Edwin R. DuBose, Ron Hamel, and Lawrence O'Connell. Valley Forge, Penn.: Trinity Press, 21–71.

Fox, Renée C., and Judith P. Swazey. 1984. Medical morality is not bioethics-medical ethics in China and the United States. *Perspectives in Biology and Medicine* 27:336–60.

Freedman, Benjamin. 1996. *Duty and healing: Foundations of a Jewish bioethic.* Internet: http://www.mcgill.ca/CTRG/bfreed/

Friedson, Eliot. 1984. The changing nature of professional control. *Annual Review of Sociology* 10:1–20.

Gallagher, Eugene B., and Janardan Subedi. 1995. *Global perspectives on health care.* Englewood Cliffs, N.J.: Prentice Hall.

Gaston, R., et al. 1993. Racial equity in renal transplantation: The disparate impact of HLA based allocation. *Journal of the American Medical Association* 270:1352–6.

Hoffmaster, Barry. 1990. Morality and the social sciences. In *Social science perspectives on medical ethics,* edited by George Weisz. Philadelphia: University of Pennsylvania Press, 241–60.

Illich, Ivan. 1975. *Medical nemesis: The expropriation of health.* London: Calder & Boyars.

Jonsen, Albert R. 1991. American moralism and the origin of bioethics in the United States. *Journal of Medicine and Philosophy* 16:113–30.

———. 1993. The birth of bioethics. *Hastings Center Report* 23:S1–4.

Jonsen, Albert R., and Stephen Toulmin. 1988. *The abuse of casuistry.* Berkeley: University of California Press.

Katz, Jay. 1984. *The silent world of doctor and patient.* London: Collier Macmillan.

Kirby, M. 1995. Patient rights—Why the Australian courts have rejected "Bolam." *Journal of Medical Ethics* 21:5–8.

Lustig, B. Andrew. 1992. The method of "Principlism": A critique of the critique. *Journal of Medicine and Philosophy* 17:487–510.

May, William. 1983. *The physician's covenant.* Philadelphia: Westminster Press.

Otsuka, Yasuo. 1977. A short history of bioethics in Japan. *Japanese Studies in the History of Science* 16:17–22.

Pellegrino, Edmund D. 1990. The relationship of autonomy and integrity in medical ethics. *Bulletin of PAHO* 24:361–71.

———. 1993. The metamorphosis of medical ethics. *Journal of the American Medical Association* 269:1158–62.

Peters, Robert. 1994. Matching physician practice style to patient informational issues and decision making preferences. *Archives of Family Medicine* 3:760–4.

Ramsey, P. 1970. *The patient as person.* New Haven, Conn.: Yale University Press.

Reich, W.T. 1993. How bioethics got its name. *Hastings Center Report* (November-December): S6–7.

———. 1994. The word "bioethics": Its birth and the legacies of those who shaped it. *Kennedy Institute of Ethics Journal* 4:319–35.

Rothman, David J. 1991. *Strangers at the bedside: A history of how law and bioethics transformed medical decision making.* New York: Basic Books.

Schwartz, Robert. 1994. Multiculturalism, medicine, and the limits of autonomy: The practice of female circumcision. *Cambridge Quarterly of Healthcare Ethics* 3:431–41.

Starr, Paul. 1982. *The social transformation of American medicine.* New York: Basic Books.

Surbone, A. 1992. Truth telling to the patient. *Journal of the American Medical Association* 268:1661–2.

Toulmin, Stephen. 1982. How medicine saved the life of ethics. *Perspectives in Biology and Medicine* 25(4): 736–50.

Veatch, Robert M. 1984. Autonomy's temporary triumph. *Hastings Center Report* (October): 38–42.

———. 1995. Abandoning informed consent. *Hastings Center Report* (March-April): 5–12.

Washington v. *Glucksberg.* 1997. 65 U.S.L.W. 4669.

Wolf, Susan M. 1994. Shifting paradigms in bioethics and health law: The rise of a new pragmatism. *American Journal of Law and Medicine* 20:395–414.

Wolpe, Paul R. 1990. The holistic heresy: Strategies of ideological control in the medical profession. *Social Science and Medicine* 31:913–23.

———. 1994. The dynamics of heresy in a profession. *Social Science and Medicine* 39:1133–48.

====CHAPTER FOUR====

Bioethics and the Coming
of the Corporation to Medicine

Jeanne Guillemin

Ethics institutes and programs in the United States grew from only several in the early 1970s to more than 150 by 1993. Although bioethics purported to support the autonomy of physicians, its inherent conservatism failed to alert doctors to the modern commercialization of health care and its negative impact on physician authority and patients' rights. The postwar combination of heroic medicine, centralized hospital bureaucracies, and medical science all worked to encourage a capitalistic absorption of the health care market.

In 1969 the opening of the Institute of Society, Ethics, and the Life Sciences—later famous as the Hastings Center—marked the beginning of the successful field of bioethics. The center's founder, philosopher Daniel Callahan, had been executive editor of *Commonweal* and was already a significant spokesman for the new postwar generation of Catholic intellectuals. Discontented with the 1968 papal encyclical against artificial contraception (*Humanae Vitae*), Callahan was looking for a secular forum for exploring moral issues (Walters 1985). He found it by joining forces with psychiatrist Willard Gaylin to create an independent center located just outside New York City, securing crucial access to funding sources, medical centers, and the media.

Following suit, in 1971 Dutch-born physician André Helligers secured funding for the Joseph and Rose Kennedy Institute for the Study of Human Reproduction and Bioethics at Georgetown University. Helligers, like Callahan, was Catholic and opposed to the church's position in the encyclical. He recruited an ecumenical group of philosophers and theologians to the institute. Yet at both settings, and at the Hastings Center in particular, secularism ruled.

This institutionalized rejection of Catholic dogma was a victory for enlightenment values that, in various modes, already dominated American philosophy. According to Reinhold Niebuhr (1969), analytic schools of thought had already imposed a secular framework on Christian ethics. The absolute (as in the absolute authority of the Church) was rejected in favor of the pragmatic. The transcendental (as in explanations of the meaning of life or of ultimate good and evil) was put aside in favor of rational processes as the means of ameliorating human circumstances. Reason was equated with virtue, impulse with the root of all evil, and the individual was prized over the community. As Niebuhr argued, American ethics developed in close conformity with the dominant bourgeois culture so that the Christian ideal of love, for example, was transformed into "the counsel of prudent mutuality so dear and necessary to a complex commercial civilization" (1969, 9).

The conformity between American cultural values and the development of bioethics was noted in retrospect by Callahan himself:

> Politically America has always been a liberal society, as manifested by the market system economically and by a great emphasis on individual freedom in our cultural and political institutions. Bioethics came along with the kind of intellectual agenda that was wholly compatible with that of liberalism. (1993, 8)

The liberalism referred to by Callahan harkens to America's well-entrenched libertarian tradition, wherein a primary value is put on individual rights and autonomy and Calvinist-derived understandings of virtue and redemption through autonomous rational action prevail (see Jonsen 1991).

This and other enlightenment legacies have the potential of promoting social change, as in Rawlsian philosophy (Rawls 1971), when the concept of social justice prevails, or, as in the work of Robert Nozick (1974), when the argument for libertarian values is universalized. American bioethics, however, was conservative from the outset, shunning social perspectives and concentrating on the professional dilemmas of physicians.

For philosophers the choice of physicians as clientele was providential. The American investment in medicine and health care was on the upswing, from 7 percent of the GDP (gross domestic product) in 1970 to 14 percent in 1995. In 1970 there were just over 308,487 physicians in the United States, with a ratio of 151 per 100,000 people. In 1992 the number of physicians was 627,723, with a ratio of 242 per 100,000. During this time bioethicists filled many new institutional niches and created more of their own. Although the Hastings Center remains the nation's most prestigious bioethics institute, 152 other centers and programs are now active in the United States (Nolen and Coutts 1993).

The majority of these enterprises were created between 1983 and 1991, when the normative base for physician-patient relations was fast shifting from a government-private mix to a more commercial foundation. A little more than half of these ethics centers (eighty) are located at medical schools and serve medical students, professionals, and teaching hospital staff.

The other bioethics establishments range from a few independent centers to government-sponsored programs (for example, at veterans' facilities). Some, like the Christian Medical and Dental Society (started in 1931 in Texas) go back to the time when medical professionals were formulating their own ethical codes. Still others promoted the humanities as a means of understanding medical dilemmas and only later identified themselves as ethics institutes. Some, such as the Agricultural Ethics Institute at the University of Iowa, have extended into environmental issues. Attached to a medical school or not, bioethics ventures are primarily professional ventures seeking professional clientele. The exception is Health Decisions, a volunteer citizen movement that started in Oregon in the late 1980s and now exists in twelve other states.

THE CONSERVATISM OF ETHICS

The phenomenal success of bioethics, particularly in medical schools, occurred because philosophers offered a legitimate, essentially conservative rationale for physician autonomy, one that embellished the physician's role as an autonomous moral agent who could and should deny the larger world of competing authorities.

> The way that bioethics has defined individualism, the centrality that it has accorded to this value-complex, the degree to which it has played down a social perspective on personal and communal moral life, its parsimonious insistence on a cost-containing framework of analysis, and the extent to which its rationality and methodology have distanced it from the phenomenological reality, and the human complexity of lived-in medical ethical situations, have converged to form a gestalt that is congruent with other fundamentals of a conservative outlook. (Fox 1980, 210; see also Fox and Swazey 1984)

The conceptual narrowness of the ethics enterprise assisted the physician in avoiding the onus of the social, which for decades in medicine has been associated with the threat of socialism and even of socialized medicine (Merton 1957, 28–9). Such apprehensions are more than linguistic. In a nation that prizes pragmatic action, the recognition of a social order of problems fairly dictates broad-based solutions that threaten the individual. The problems that bioethics ignored were, among others, the bureaucratic structure of hospital organization, the capitalist expansion of medical-industrial complex, disparities of income and life chances between rich and poor, and gender inequities, as if these more sociologically defined areas were without important moral dimensions or consequence for practicing physicians.

While philosophers were staking out new turf, particularly at hospitals and medical schools, they resisted competition from other academic quarters, from sociologists in particular but also from historians and economists. Lawyers, as technical experts rather than intellectuals, frequently appeared at bioethics conferences to address specific case issues with the same rationalist, temporizing approach as modern ethics.

The important question about bioethics is exactly how its perspective ultimately failed American medicine. By its specialized "blinders," as Max Weber would have said, the field deflected the attention of its clientele, primarily physicians but also the general public, from the two most crucial developments in modern health care. The first of these developments was the rampant depersonalization of patient care in hospital settings. The second development was the free-market takeover of health care, via corporate mergers and the national expansion of HMOs (health maintenance organizations). The invention of large successful for-profit chains like Humana and Columbia demonstrated clearly what every student of sociology knows: Bureaucratic rationality is a template for capitalist expansion (Weber 1958, 230–1).

The first development was necessary to the second in that the physician-patient relationship had to become standardized before medical services could become commodities on the national market. The sum effect of these two developments, the degradation of patient care and the commercialization of medicine, has been to compromise the moral autonomy of American physicians, who are now prey to market forces, while diminishing the rights of patients, whose health care has become goods for sale in the marketplace.

VALUE COMPATIBILITY AND THE "CLOAKED ECONOMY"

The shortsightedness of the bioethics vision presents a paradox, for ethicists have consistently advocated physician autonomy *and* made the rights of patients the subject of many forums. Part of the explanation lies in the very compatibility referred to by Callahan between libertarian values, bioethics, and commerce. Having allied themselves in principle with the free market, neither physicians nor bioethicists focused on the expansion of commerce into hospital care as a problem. Not acquainted with Weber on predatory "high capitalism," they apparently saw no distinction between individual enterprise (starting an ethics center or setting up a joint practice) and the workings of corporate industry. Instead, the perceived threat was from government. Both physicians and ethicists were most concerned with intrusions on physician autonomy from institutional review boards, research on human-subject regulations, brain-death criteria, Baby Doe regulations, and a host of other legal pressures. As a result of government regulations, the rights of patients and human subjects emerged as challenges to physician authority that were then recoded as ethical dilemmas.

Another reason for the success of bioethics, also related to its conservatism, was the problem of the "cloaked economics" of public and private moneys in postwar American medicine. Modern, hospital-affiliated doctors (in contrast to the old-fashioned private practitioners) learned to compartmentalize their mission of healing from the cash nexus. Physician control over diagnosis and therapy was supposed to be executed in a kind of sacred realm, as if these decisions generated no costs or charges. It was not supposed to matter if a patient was covered by Medicaid or private insurance, or was an indigent. A surgeon removing a gallbladder was not supposed to be thinking about how much, or if, the patient would pay for the procedure or how much the operating room cost. Consonant with this elevation of medical practice to a sacred, one might say, priestly art, the corporate economics of health care—namely, the combination of public and private reimbursement that underwrote physicians' wealth and status—were supposed to keep money external to the physician-patient relationship. Hospital administrators did their part by keeping patient billing, salaries, and the expense of running the physical plant within their jurisdiction.

Bioethics perpetuated this obfuscation of the economic realities of medicine. For years, major cases in medical ethics floated in moral ether, without economic import. The judgment to give renal dialysis to one patient or another—say, the young mother of four or the derelict sixty-year-old man—was framed as a matter of triage, or fairness, but not as participation in a burgeoning market for new medical technology. A neonatologist's overtreatment of a critically ill newborn was configured as an issue of patient advocacy, rather than a conflict of interest for a hospital-salaried specialist. While billions of dollars were being poured into organ transplantations and its enormous technical and organizational superstructure, bioethicists provided "as if" scenarios to help physicians reflect yet again on young mothers and derelicts.

Eventually, when government raised the issue of cost containment, ethicists incorporated the term solely for its regulatory effect. They continued to avoid broader fiscal facts, such as the profits being reaped out of the GDP by medical technology industries and insurance companies and, not the least important, the handsome rewards physicians were receiving for their work. A physician's average income in 1987 was $80,000, in the upper 5 percent of American workers; in 1993 it was $174,000, in the upper 3 percent. This money was not earned in a vacuum. Besides incorporating their practices and buying diagnostic equipment and laboratories, American physicians have been aggressively courted by industry, accepting sample products, going to meetings paid for by pharmaceutical and supply manufacturers, editing medical journals underwritten by industry, and owning stock in such companies, even sitting on their boards. In this invisible part of medical economics, the physician is as agentic as when treating patients (see Rodwin 1993). Yet, from the point of view of American bioethics, this domain lay beyond moral criticism.

The original circumstances that favored bioethics are different from the present reality of American health care. The question of the future of bioethics can only be answered by examining the past social context in which its practitioners prospered.

MEDICAL HEROISM, SCIENCE, AND BUREAUCRACY

American medicine is historically reactive. It rebounds, at times slowly and often selectively, to social and cultural upheavals, to scientific innovations, and to the changing needs of different populations of patients and practitioners. At present the trend seems almost textbook Weber, with capitalism overtaking both science and medicine and subverting their rational aims to its own.

If we go back to the 1950s, we can trace three main antecedents to the present commercialism in health care. First is the role of physician as medical hero. Second is government support of medical science. Third is the centralization of American hospital care.

Fundamental to American culture are the Calvinist-derived values—individualism, the need for redemptive action, the identification of worldly gain with virtue and of poverty with sin, the contrasting modalities of bodily abstinence, rational action, and righteous anger—that also inform American schools of philosophy and bioethics (Walters 1985). Since pioneer days these values were the mainspring of our culture's violence, legal and illegal, as well as our appreciation of efficiency and heroic action.

In medicine these cultural values are expressed in the rational control of mind over body expected of practitioners and also patients. Historically, physicians in particular have been expected to repress their emotions as a sign of manly strength as well as required professional demeanor. Nurses might cry, but not doctors (see Chambliss 1996).

The tradition of "detached but passionate concern" evolved within a male subculture profoundly influenced by military experience and definitions of valor. In American history, technical and organizational advances in military medicine (many of them, such as anesthesia and penicillin, developed during wars) have frequently been transferred to civilian medical services as if they were an army on the home front.

Following World War II, the equation of medical, hospital-based science with an army was reflected in "the war on cancer," "the fight against polio," and the March of Dimes. In clinical practice, the developing concept of heroic intervention made the physician, the surgeon in particular, a kind of warrior, the ruggedly individualistic risk taker—in common hospital parlance, "the gunslinger," or the John Wayne who triumphed by aggressive action and technical skill. Much later Susan Sontag (1978), drawing on her experience as a cancer patient, would write about the use of military metaphors in diagnosis and therapy: Death was the enemy; the patient's body was the battleground; the physician the warrior armed with modern technology. The idea that physicians can conquer death reflects both the high value placed on individualism (which cannot contemplate its own end without horror) and the inviolate authority of the physician. But the loner image of the physician was an illusion (see also May 1983).

Militarism in medicine made heroes of physicians, but it found its organizational realization in the central hospital, which united science and medicine for efficient treatment. Government support, via a variation on statist capitalism, fueled the growth of hospitals and the many commercial ventures in medical technology and insurance. Science was an important part of the campaign. In the 1950s American physicians, equipped with penicillin and sulfa drugs developed for the troops, had never had better therapies at their command. They would have many more. The politically contentious U.S. Congress, again finding common ground in medicine, created the National Institutes of Health in 1946 and then increased its funding. Its budget went from $52 million in 1950 to $430 million in 1960 to $1.6 billion in 1968.

In the 1950s the high status of physicians was such that the notion of the patient as a person was then "more honored in the breach than the observance" (Merton 1957, 25). At that time the innovative work being done in medical ethics was largely limited to dialogues among academic philosophers and theologians. In 1954 Joseph Fletcher published *Morals and Medicine*, which articulated a Protestant response to Catholic moral tradition. Fletcher represented the individual patient as having the right to veracity, to control sexual reproduction, and to control the circumstances of dying. The work both reflected old Calvinist values and was ahead of its time in pitting the autonomy of the ordinary citizen against both physician paternalism and Catholic dogma.

GOVERNMENT AND CENTRALIZED HOSPITALS

The civil rights movement of the 1960s has been cited as the root source of medical ethics (Rothman 1990, 197). It raised the general issue of autonomy for African Americans that later translated to legal restraints on human-subject research and to the promotion of patients' rights. Medical authority (including scientific experimentation on humans) was ultimately challenged because political authority throughout the country was challenged. New norms were conveyed to other disenfranchised groups, other minorities, women, and the disabled; the liberation of these populations ultimately rebounded on physicians. The representation of minorities and women among physicians—and, I might add, among philosophers—was minimal.

Political consciousness certainly did change in the 1960s and 1970s, but a *Zeitgeist* explanation of the origins of bioethics downplays the structural influence of the federal government on the treatment of patients and the beginning of limitations on physician autonomy. To begin, increased government support for science after the war required physicians to be more accountable to human subjects. Government influence expanded with the increased direct funding of patient care, which started with veterans and grew after 1963 with Medicare and Medicaid.

By 1966, when Henry Beecher published his landmark article "Ethics and Clinical Research," it was already clear that physicians receiving medical science support from the government would have to prove themselves responsible to democratic values and pay the regulatory piper. In 1962 Senator Estes Kefauver had held investigatory hearings on physicians administering experimental drugs without informing patients. In his piece Beecher enumerated twenty similar instances of published research (winnowed from fifty) in which subjects were subjected to the risk of harm without their knowledge. Ethicists then and since have attributed this malfeasance to role conflict between the scientist in relentless pursuit of truth and the physician who cares for the patient.

The unhappy reality behind Beecher's article, though, was that American science and medicine were fast turning into a joint conglomeration of bigger and more centralized institutions within which physician-patient relations were becoming normatively depersonalized. This centralization of hospitals, financed by research moneys and new public reimbursements for patient care, was the government's other significant influence on the treatment of patients.

In the 1950s the government supported the building of hospitals and expansion of medical schools as if it were waging a war for modern medicine. Throughout the 1960s the established institutions continued to expand. Medical schools in particular took over multiple urban hospitals and created research institutes for applied technologies. The rationale, as it always is in mergers and centralization, was that any organization housed under a single roof was more efficient. In this new context, the role of the physician shifted in conformity to what Paul Starr described as "the new structure of power" (1982, 277). "Physician-chiefs" acquired enormous authority and control of hospital resources. Younger physicians were educated in an atmosphere of intense technical and professional competition that promoted medical specialization (as more scientific than general medicine) and acute care intervention (as more heroic). Meanwhile, community and non-acute care hospitals (for example, maternity facilities) were shutting down by the hundreds.

By 1970, for the first time, American medicine was widely held to be "in a crisis" of a fiscal sort (Starr 1982, 381). Although the crisis was defined as economic, due to rising hospital costs, the government and media did most of the complaining. Other sectors were not complaining. The links between well-funded science, medical schools, and new medical industries had been forged, without financial restraints. Physicians, most hospitals, and industries were unworried. Private insurers, because they could select more healthy customers and increase rates, had no great problem. Even the government refrained from radical cost-cutting action.

The crisis was real, but it had more to do with the multiple interactional constraints imposed by the central hospital. The centralization of hospital care was part of a general American trend to consolidate service institutions. Supermarkets put little grocery stores out of business, large schools closed little red schoolhouses, and shopping malls shut down Main Street businesses. The operative word was and is *volume*. More people would come and buy more things that have been bought cheaper on a large scale. The principle appeared to work because central hospitals emerged as the standard-bearers of modern medicine and American medicine became defined as hospital care. Yet in this context, physician relations with patients had to suffer. In the name of rational efficiency, science, and heroism, patients became cases and diseases.

In addition, as more physicians did their major work in hospitals, they left behind the autonomy of private practice for prestige, security, and higher volumes of patients. But they also exposed themselves as practitioners to rational criteria for performance, to a more public scrutiny, and to potential legal redress. Even those affiliated with smaller hospitals or not affiliated at all organized themselves in small-group practices as tax and legal havens. The problem, as we know now about malpractice suits, was not physician mistakes or the failures of technology, but relational—that is, how well the patients and families *thought* they were getting along with the practitioner. Patients were looking for empathy, but doctors, already trained to be emotionally detached, now had bureaucratic rationality and science defining interaction in the workplace. To step out of the heroic rational role, to express feeling, constituted deviance.

But there was another, deeper problem than the unfriendly relations between physicians and patients. A hospital is not a supermarket. Although it has all the characteristics of a bureaucracy, its function of imposing rational order on the chaos of human disease and death is unique. It is also an impossible goal. Our experiences of mortality have nothing rational about them, and less in American culture than in other more pacific ones. The American hospital serves, indeed, it survives, on populations that drive recklessly, abuse drugs and alcohol, smoke cigarettes, and kill in righteous anger. It is within our libertarian tradition to resist regulation of what we do with our bodies. Nonetheless, round the clock, hospitals confront and struggle with human finitude, using routine not to handle customers but to meet the onrush of human casualties.

At its best, a hospital complements what an individual physician does with his or her skills. Yet in the central hospital, the need for the individual physician is diminished, and teamwork takes over. Increased volumes of patients and a greater percentage of severely ill patients demanded the presence of other professionals. The rotation of hospital staff both orders and diffuses elite physician contact with the sick and dying. In the teaching hospital model, the routine relegation of surveillance to those lower in the hierarchy—fellows, nurses, and medical residents—protects the higher-status consulting physicians from prolonged contact with patients. The work of relating with families also falls to those lower in status (see Anspach 1993; Chambliss 1996).

By the 1970s observant physicians knew that medical science was producing not victories but "halfway technologies." Treatment for the virtually incurable physical ailments of an aged industrial population (diseases of the major organs, cancers, strokes) was primitive, a mixture of surgeries and mechanical support. Physicians' own relation to science was also increasingly problematic, in that they were often on the receiving end of drugs and technical procedures invented by laboratory scientists, rather than being themselves the innovators. Medical uncertainty, always a problem in medicine, became amplified by the fact that the medical marketplace was open to an unending proliferation of new goods. Physicians, expected to know what every innovation accomplished, relied on each other at conferences and meetings to find out. Meanwhile, real progress was taking place in basic science, in the laboratories of chemists, physicists, and biologists at major medical centers who were investigating the structure of DNA. This, too, would come to physicians as received wisdom. Physicians, in sum, were not the masters of science or applied technology, and this—along with teamwork—was a blow to their authority. Physicians also sensed that hospital organization was insufficient to the miseries of dying and the mysteries of death. In that epoch, though, the polarities of reason as virtue and emotion as vice were endemic to the organizational structure.

For a physician in the 1970s, bioethics offered another kind of rationality, a concomitant to if not a relief from medical science and bureaucratic routine. Emotions, life, and love, like sociology, were excluded areas of inquiry, but the personal experiences of medical cases were legitimated.

In 1970 the theologian Paul Ramsay published his brilliant book *The Patient as Person,* the first and perhaps the last truly passionate argument made for a mutually respectful relationship (a "covenant") between physician and patient. The potential of that work would not be developed. Instead, ethics became a discourse between male philosophers and their male clients: physicians whose authority was being shaken, although not yet seriously, by bureaucracy, technology, and demographic change. Bioethicists, especially those at independent institutes or only ancillary to hospitals, identified with physicians as autonomous moral actors and sought to put themselves "in their shoes" (Walters 1985, 12).

Relative to the present, male philosophers and physicians at that time brooked few challenges to their authority. Funding for medical science was still ample and reimbursements for services secure. Physicians were in charge of most hospitals, and many still saw private patients. Hospital administrators had barely made their entrance, nor had women physicians. At this time, 1970, 95 percent of the physician population was male, and faculties at the major medical schools were virtually all men. Ninety-one percent of all medical students were also male. The same gender imbalance characterized academic philosophy and theology. The physician lament, to which bioethicists lent willing ears, was for a freedom idealized from private practice and experienced in the first flush of miracle drugs and hospital expansion.

THE FURTHER SEPARATION OF PHYSICIAN AND PATIENT

For the next two decades, the heroic intervention model prevailed in hospitals. Despite continued cries of economic crisis from the government, health costs during the 1980s continued to rise because the government had neither the means nor the will to restrain the free-market economy. Meanwhile, heroic, hospital-based medicine did more to erode the moral agency of the physician than any government regulation, for two reasons:

1. Its practitioners refused to admit the changing needs of the population. The continued increase of an older population, the AIDS epidemic, the rise in medical problems specifically related to poverty—all these demanded a revision of professional norms, for example, from aggressive intervention to palliative and preventive models of action.
2. Physicians were complacent about the organization of their fortress, the central hospital. They did not realize that its administrative weight would grow as a matter of bureaucratic self-perpetuation. According to the Bureau of the Census, between 1970 and 1991, the number of health care administrators in the United States increased by 697 percent, while the number of total health care personnel increased by 129 percent. The average American hospital has fifty staff members just for billing. About a quarter of a typical hospital's budget goes to administrative costs.

In the context of the central hospital, the loss of physician authority was compounded by a shift away from physician expertise to organizational efficiency. Historically, medicine has not based its legitimacy on claims of organizational efficiency, for the rationalization of its technique was sufficient to the claim that the service was "as efficient as necessary" (Abbott 1988, 194–5). Andrew Abbott goes on to write, "It is clear that efficiency becomes a central legitimacy claim only when science, broadly understood as rational expertise, is not available." In modern hospital care, however, it is not that physician expertise is unavailable, only that it is subsumed in a competing structure. Only the physician can order treatment for the patient, but the efficient implementation of that treatment depends on the system.

Starting in the early 1970s, the claim of rational efficiency in medicine was on its way to becoming fully organizational. That is, hospital service, not medical technique, became its newest and most efficient representation. In 1973, deploring the waste of human life in accidents, advocates for emergency care were successful in persuading Congress to fund the training of paramedics and underwrite the purchase or use of ambulances, airplanes, and helicopters in thousands of communities across the country. The war in Vietnam, like the war in Korea, had made us experts on saving the wounded, and those lessons applied to civilian life. The television program *M*A*S*H** gave us the new media image of physicians. They were military men but irreverent, stuck with a bad job but stoic and committed to teamwork. Emergency medical service was born and with it intensive care units (ICUs).

The "quick save," though, was no magic bullet, as the Karen Quinlan case in 1975 demonstrated. The public learned that mechanical ventilation and intravenous feeding in an ICU could support "a persistent vegetative state" and also that hospital administrators and physicians were ill equipped to deal with the legal and emotional repercussions of new lifesaving technology. As became the pattern, the ethical perspective on this tragedy emphasized the physician's dilemma. When, put grossly, should the plug be pulled?

The Quinlan case did nothing to spur critical evaluation of routine heroic intervention. To the contrary, the growth of ICUs, initially located only in central hospitals, emerged as yet another institutional elaboration on the theme of heroic rescue. Like emergency care, intensive care aimed to rescue those in peril, whether postoperatively, from accidents, from heart or general medical failure, or from premature birth or birth trauma.

Unlike emergency care, the ICU was wedded to progressive science and medical specialization. The selection of the worst medical cases made it predictable that medical expertise would often fail, but that the victories, against the odds, would be dramatic. Further, the ICU was based on a division of labor heavily reliant on junior staff, physicians and nurses who lacked the status of senior specialists and buffered them from the battle. More important, by organization and case selection, the ICU took the depersonalization of patient care to its limits. It imposed complete bureaucratic order on the most vulnerable, least autonomous human beings imaginable. Critically ill patients, immobile and silent, were segregated in special environments, akin to moonscapes, where multiple technologies were interposed between them and the medical staff. If, as Michel Foucault (1973) suggests, the patient on the operating table is analogous to the autopsied corpse, the ICU patient is analogous to the corpse in a casket.

Nonetheless, the ICU was a success because it addressed our cultural values and, like emergency care, maximized access in a way that seemed not only equitable but also, at times, the redress of ills caused by poverty. It served patients whose illness was a function of a violent or destructive lifestyle, of a delay in seeking medical attention, of poverty, or simply of age. Defined as progressive treatment, it spread from central hospitals to smaller ones at lower levels of capacity and staffing, where satellite units could then participate in the transfer of patients to or from the central unit. The neonatal intensive care unit (NICU) was the perfection of this organizational invention (Guillemin and Holmstrom 1991; Guillemin 1994), regionally incorporating obstetric units as well as delivery room facilities within the same hospital.

By the early 1980s the medical bank was about to break. Per capita spending on health care doubled between 1963 and 1982. Americans were spending more out of pocket than Canadians or Europeans with socialized medicine, but their health status was worse (Fuchs and Hahn 1990). The

growing contrast between rich and poor, between affluent Whites and economically disadvantaged minorities, was part of the problem, which began to
be reflected in disparities between private hospitals serving middle-class-
income populations and public hospitals serving the lower classes.

In both settings, however, costs rose. Private insurers raised deductibles
and co-payments, limited coverage, and rejected clients with preexisting conditions, especially AIDS. States pruned their Medicaid rolls and, in Oregon,
set priorities on treatment categories. Finally, in the 1980s the government
imposed limits on hospital care, using DRGs (diagnostic related groups) to
standardize patient treatment. Although the burden fell on patients whose
well-being was subject to the hospital budget, DRGs constituted the most
severe restraint on physician decision making in the history of corporate
American medicine.

Yet the revolution in medical norms came not from government or the
medical profession but from commerce. In the late 1970s large industries,
such as Kaiser in California and 3M in Minnesota, had taken the lead in
developing HMOs as alternative prevention-oriented health plans for
employees. The logic that prevention is cheaper has never been well tested
(Huntington and Connell 1994), but HMOs cut costs in part by reorganizing physician care. They put physicians on fixed salaries and limited access
to specialists. In 1978 HMOs insured only 3 percent of the U.S. population.
By 1997 they covered more than half and, with aggressive policies for wholesale purchase of goods and services, were still expanding. One of their
major targets is the elderly. California-based Secure Horizons, for example,
absorbs Medicare contracts and, by cost cutting on services and procedures,
makes a profit.

Along with HMO expansion, major hospitals are merging in yet another
round of centralization. Only this time, they must be cost conscious about
what technologies they will offer and how to balance expensive specialist versus lower-cost generalist services. To the end of capturing patient markets,
community-based clinics are being incorporated as satellites of central facilities. American hospitals will probably always offer NICUs, hip replacements,
and coronary bypasses, but not everyone will be a customer. Approximately
38.9 million Americans are uninsured, many of them minorities and the
young, and millions of others of all backgrounds are underinsured.

THE FUTURE OF MEDICAL ETHICS

The past of bioethics was secure because it was linked to an established elite.
Its future is probably secure now that it is entrenched in institutional settings.
Still, questions remain about who its clientele will be and what the field has to
teach them. The majority of American physicians are white, male, and over
forty years old. They will probably always be interested in rational frameworks

that presume their moral authority. However, if they are clinicians, they cannot help but notice that the people they work with and the patients they treat have changed.

Women, for example, now comprise 40 percent of all medical school students, almost 20 percent of practicing physicians, and 24 percent of medical school faculty. The significant presence of women in the profession raises the issue of whether, as happened in secretarial work, teaching, and nursing, their entrance feminizes and devalues the occupation. In any event, women are not the physician elites of thirty years ago. In financial terms, the salaries of female physicians are around 60 percent of those of male physicians, and women are overrepresented in the lower echelons of medical school positions, which may be attributed to their younger age range and responsibilities for children. They are also overrepresented in specialties that have lower status, such as pediatrics, family medicine, obstetrics, and radiology, and are marginal to the high-technology ventures of hospital care. They are only 14 percent of the membership of the American Medical Association. By virtue of their choice of specialties, which lend themselves to the prevention model, more female physicians than male ones may be represented among the salaried employees of HMOs and in a position of limited autonomy.

In fact, younger physicians of both sexes and varying races and ethnicities are being required to integrate themselves into a more commercial medical context. The focus on applied or clinical ethics in medical school curricula, which account for much of the recent increase in programs, reflects this reality and the need to find new norms of behavior. To wit, the definition offered by Terry Perlin (who surveyed the area), clinical ethics is "a field that combines efforts at finding the optimal approach to patient care with a serious concern for the feelings and viewpoints of patients, families, and providers" (1992, 11).

Clinical ethics reflects the felt need to mediate the goals of organizational efficiency and, though its programs may fleetingly refer to goals of beneficence or distributive justice, their aim is to teach how to manage interaction so that disruptive conflict can be avoided. What do you do if you find out that a medical colleague is guilty of malpractice? Is it worth it to become a whistle-blower? How do you explain to a weakened patient that the allotted time for a hospital stay is up? Is it worth it to make a special application for extra days? An already disabled child may be the victim of abuse by the mother's boyfriend. Should you inquire further? An operation must be done on a homosexual who has not been tested for HIV. Should you request the test? The moral autonomy of the clinician in these and other cases is doubly fictional; the real choices are between a certain sensitivity of phrasing and a brashness that could provoke a lawsuit against the hospital.

Is such a level of problem solving worthy of being called bioethics? Callahan, perhaps bemoaning the passing of the entrepreneurial phase of bioethics, thinks not:

Bioethicists have, on the whole, become good team players, useful to help with moral puzzles now and then and trustworthy not to probe basic premises too deeply. Unless one is willing to persistently carry out such probes, the idea of a loyal opposition carries no weight. (1996, 19)

Apparently, the bourgeois "counsel of prudent mutuality" that Niebuhr referred to finds its apotheosis in a clinical ethics fitted to modern health-care settings. But how can this be? Behind the rationality of clinical ethics and the corporate takeover of medicine rampages the chaos of our mortality, which is not negotiable. Hospitals are still the most important loci of medical care, and they struggle constantly with emergency and intensive care and with violence, urban and suburban. AIDS continues to eviscerate whole generations of young people. Are hospital staffs prepared to witness interminable suffering and senseless death? Or has it evolved that, since professionals take the status of their clients, unlucky droves of younger physicians and nurses will be serving in the trenches of medical care, while elite older physicians still play golf on Wednesday? Perhaps we should take it seriously that the most popular show on television in 1995 was *ER*, a drama set in a hospital emergency room. The thematic tension in the show comes from the young staff's valiant attempt to repress emotions in the face of unending gore and terrible human anguish. Yet most episodes focus on how staff members feel about each other, rather than about patients, who are slung about like sides of beef. The question remains whether a sense of empathy for vulnerable patients is possible in the speeded-up context of modern medicine.

Consider also the bleak outcome of SUPPORT (Study to Understand Prognoses and Preferences for Outcomes and Risks of Treatment), a $28 million, eight-year study of how physicians handle the wishes of terminally ill patients (SUPPORT 1995). Full-time trained nurses were placed in five teaching hospitals to facilitate communication between physicians and patients gravely ill with multiple-organ failure, colon or lung cancer, heart failure, emphysema, and other diseases.

The hope was that the pain of such patients, who account for 40 percent of all hospital deaths, would be diminished and that their wishes concerning the withdrawal of care would be heeded. But the project reported failure. Half the patients experienced moderate or severe pain at least half the time in their last three days of life. In four cases out of five, physicians misunderstood patients' preferences concerning resuscitation. A physician who participated in the study reported that he was not surprised by the results because "the drive of the system is to provide life-extending versus comfort care."

The inadequacy of this response cannot easily be redressed by bioethics courses or, for that matter, by sociological treatises. Both disciplines, secular to the core, prize reason over feeling and have avoided the deeper questions of good and evil and the meaning of life. Weber himself wrote bleakly (and with the presumption that men are heroic) concerning the rationalized "disenchantment of the world":

> To the person who cannot bear the fate of the times like a man, one must say: may he rather return silently, without the usual publicity build-up of renegades, but simply and plainly. The arms of the old churches are opened widely and compassionately for him. (1958, 155)

Religious transcendence, though, is not simply there for the taking, although the market for spiritualism is thriving. The cultural legacy of the Enlightenment, including that nagging mind-body dichotomy, can hardly be cast off at will. Instead, we have to reimagine health care.

The interactive experience, which Elliot Mishler (1984) and Howard Waitzkin (1991) have shown is crucial to analysis of health care, is also crucial to its reform, if one can imagine the personalization of professional-patient relations, the grounding of the concept of covenant. Suppose a physician sits with a sick patient in a hospital room and reads poetry out loud, so they both share a deep reflection. Suppose in a large public hospital, Spanish-speaking family and friends invade a patient's room, surround her, surround the doctor and nurse, who speak back to them in Spanish. Suppose a group of residents meets on its own to talk about death, for which they have hardly any words, and so they talk about *M*A*S*H* and the Bible. Suppose volunteer citizen groups like Health Decisions mobilize politically against the commercialization of health care.

Suppose physicians confront legislators with new laws for protecting patients in HMOs and for protecting physician authority to defy policies that harm patients. These acts are possible; they have been done, not in the name of religion but out of a sense of the communality of human experience. Everyone is disabled sometime, as Irving Zola used to say, as a child or with illness or age, so why pretend invulnerability? Everyone dies sooner or later. Why leave dying to the dehumanized "drive of the system"?

It is clear that, unless our professional disciplines and our culture can infuse rationality with emotion, no really deep insights into our lives and deaths are possible and we risk an awful dehumanization. Yet the integration of reason with feeling entails more than the postmodern pitting of the subjective against the objective. Rather, it means finding where in our traditions—in religion and history, in art and music and poetry, in family and friendship, in children, in letters in the attic—we can pose the frailty of our individual limited life ventures against the larger sweep of time and still find hope in the present and in each other. Even the intellectual Weber, expressing trepidation for the fate of the Jews, knew how to quote with empathy from the beautiful, centuries-old watchman's song of Isaiah, to hear in that voice the seeker confronting the cyclical forces of history:

He calleth to me out of the Seir, Watchman, what of the night? The watchman said, The morning cometh, and also the night: if ye will enquire, enquire ye: return, come.

In the meantime, in modern America, entrepreneurs in the corporate health world, including bioethicists, must struggle with that redoubtable oxymoron, "business ethics."

REFERENCES

Abbott, Andrew. 1988. *The system of professions. An essay on the division of expert labor.* Chicago: University of Chicago Press.

Anspach, Renée. 1993. *Deciding who lives: Fateful choices in the intensive care nursery.* Berkeley: University of California Press.

Beecher, Henry E. 1966. Ethics and clinical research. *New England Journal of Medicine* 274:1354–60.

Callahan, Daniel. 1993. Why America accepted bioethics. *Hastings Center Report* (November-December, suppl.): S8–9.

———. 1996. Calling scientific ideology into account. *Society* 33(4):14–19.

Chambliss, Daniel. 1996. *Beyond caring: Hospitals, nurses and the social organization of ethics.* Chicago: University of Chicago Press.

Fletcher, Joseph F. 1954. *Morals and medicine; The moral problems of: The patient's right to know the truth, contraception, artificial insemination, sterilization, euthanasia.* Princeton, N.J.: Princeton University Press.

Foucault, Michel. 1973. *The birth of the clinic. An archaeology of medical perception.* New York: Random House.

Fox, Renée C. 1980. The evolution of medical uncertainty. *Millbank Memorial Fund Quarterly* 58:2–47.

Fox, Renée C., and Judith Swazey. 1984. Medical morality is not bioethics—Medical ethics in China and the United States. *Perspectives in Biology and Medicine* 27:337–60.

Fuchs, Victor R., and Thomas S. Hahn. 1990. How does Canada do it? A comparison of expenditures for physicians' services in the United States and Canada. *New England Journal of Medicine* 323:884–90.

Guillemin, Jeanne. 1994. Experiment and illusion in reproductive medicine. *Human Nature* 5:1–22.

Guillemin, Jeanne Harley, and Lynda Lytle Holmstrom. 1991. *Mixed blessings. Intensive care for newborns.* New York: Oxford University Press.

Huntington, Jane, and Frederick Connell. 1994. For every dollar spent—the cost-savings argument for prenatal care. *New England Journal of Medicine* 331:1303–7.

Jonsen, Albert R. 1991. American moralism and the origin of bioethics in the United States. *Journal of Medicine and Philosophy* 16:113–30.

May, William. 1983. *The physician's covenant.* Philadelphia: Westminster Press.

Merton, Robert K. 1957. Introduction. In *The student physician. Introductory studies in the sociology of medical education,* edited by Robert K. Merton, George Reader, and Patricia Kendall. Cambridge, Mass.: Harvard University Press.

Mishler, Elliot G. 1984. *The discourse of medicine: Dialectics of medical interviews.* Norwood, N.J.: Ablex.

Niebuhr, Reinhold. 1969. *An interpretation of Christian ethics.* New York: Harper.

Nolen, Anita L., and Mary Carrington Coutts. 1993. *International directory of bioethics organizations.* Washington, D.C.: Kennedy Institute of Ethics.

Nozick, Robert. 1974. *State and utopia.* Cambridge, Mass.: Harvard University Press.

Perlin, Terry M. 1992. *Clinical medical ethics: Cases in practice.* Boston: Little, Brown.

Ramsay, Paul. 1970. *The patient as person: Explorations in medical ethics.* New Haven, Conn.: Yale University Press.

Rawls, John A. 1971. *Theory of justice.* Cambridge, Mass.: Harvard University Press.

Rodwin, Marc. 1993. *Medicine, money, and morals: Physicians' conflicts of interest.* New York: Oxford University Press.

Rothman, David J. 1990. Human experimentation and the origins of bioethics in the United States. In *Social Science Perspectives on Medical Ethics,* edited by George Weisz. Boston: Kluwer Academic, 185–200.

Sontag, Susan. 1978. *Illness as metaphor.* New York: Farrar, Straus, & Giroux.

Starr, Paul. 1982. *The social transformation of American medicine.* New York: Basic Books.

SUPPORT Principle Investigators. 1995. A controlled trial to improve care for seriously ill hospital patients. *Journal of the American Medical Association* 272:1591–8.

Waitzkin, Howard. 1991. *The politics of medical encounters. How patients and doctors deal with social problems.* New Haven, Conn.: Yale University Press.

Walters, Leroy. 1985. Religion and the renaissance of medical ethics in the United States. In *Theology and bioethics. Exploring the foundations and frontiers,* edited by Earl E. Shelp. Boston: Reidel, 3–16.

Weber, Max. 1958. *From Max Weber: Essays in sociology,* edited by H. H. Gerth and C. Wright Mills. New York: Oxford University Press.

CHAPTER FIVE

How the Atomic Energy Commission Discovered "Informed Consent"

Jonathan D. Moreno and Valerie Hurt[1]

THE PRESIDENT'S ADVISORY COMMITTEE ON HUMAN RADIATION EXPERIMENTS

On October 3, 1995, President Clinton released the final report of the Advisory Committee on Human Radiation Experiments. The committee—composed of fourteen private citizens, including experts in bioethics, health law, radiation oncology, nuclear medicine, epidemiology, and biology—examined thousands of documents and heard testimony from hundreds of witnesses in order to uncover and evaluate human-subject research involving ionizing radiation that was sponsored by the federal government between 1944 and 1974. The committee was created by Clinton in response to a number of reports of government-sponsored radiation experiments, including the injection of plutonium into eighteen hospital patients to gather metabolic data during and shortly after World War II. These experiments seem to have occurred without any intent to benefit or to obtain consent from these patients. The reports of these experiments raised questions about the government's role in several other, possibly unethical, human radiation experiments.

Many of the documents that proved important to the committee's work were made available to the public for the first time, as part of a massive declassification effort ordered by the Clinton administration. Thus, the committee was engaged in the first post–cold war assessment of the ethics of research with human subjects by the U.S. government.

By the time the committee finished its work, thousands of federally sponsored experiments involving ionizing radiation were identified. The committee charge was to examine and judge these experiments by discovering the ethical standards applicable at the time of the experiments, determining whether these standards were violated, and comparing the conduct of these experiments with today's human research requirements.

Although the first charge (discovering the ethical standards applicable at the time) may appear straightforward, in fact this proved to be a very challenging problem of historical reconstruction and interpretation. In this paper we explain why this proved so difficult in one particular case, that of the postwar Atomic Energy Commission (AEC), and what conclusions we as staff members were finally able to draw and commend to the committee. We have chosen to focus on the AEC because, in an historical revelation of great interest to the bioethics community, a 1947 AEC document used the term *informed consent* ten years earlier than what had been thought to be the first documented mention of it (in the legal case of *Salgo* v. *Leland Stanford Jr. University* 1957). Some of our observations in this paper go beyond the committee's official conclusions, and we now write in our capacities as private scholars rather than as federal advisory committee staff members.

Today's federal research standards require that informed consent be obtained from all research subjects, including healthy subjects and patient-subjects. Patient-subjects are permitted to participate in research designed purely to advance scientific understanding without prospectively offering any direct medical benefit to them, as long as they are informed of this fact. In the case of children, permission must be obtained from parents or a legal guardian and assent must be sought from any child capable of offering it. There are also special protections for fetuses and prisoners.

CHALLENGING THE CONVENTIONAL WISDOM ABOUT THE HISTORY OF FEDERAL REQUIREMENTS

As scholars have noted, however, these standards were not applied to all human subjects in the past. Patient-subjects, those who were both ill and subjects of research, were often experimented on without their consent.[2] When the committee was founded in 1994, conventional wisdom asserted that few ethical standards were promulgated by the government during the 1940s and 1950s. The need for voluntary consent from subjects of research was thought to have been seldom considered by government officials, if at all. Two known exceptions were the National Institutes of Health's Clinical Center healthy-volunteer program, which required consent from its inception in 1953, and the army's infectious disease program, which also used healthy subjects and operated under a long tradition of voluntary participation that began with Walter Reed's yellow fever experiments at the turn of the century. Apart from these exceptions, when the Advisory Committee began its work, it was generally believed that the government had not developed substantial standards for the ethical conduct of research with human subjects.

The evidence uncovered by the Advisory Committee disputes this view and suggests that parts of the government had articulated substantial standards for government-sponsored research with human subjects as early as 1947. This was the same year that an international military tribunal judging the doctors who conducted experiments on humans in Nazi Germany promulgated the Nuremberg Code, a ten-point document considered today to be among the cornerstones of modern medical ethics.[3] Moreover, some of the documents dating from this period pay special attention to the responsibilities owed patient-subjects. The Nuremberg Code is often criticized for failing to distinguish patient-subjects from "healthy" or "normal" volunteers.[4] It remains unclear if these standards were adequately disseminated, although existing evidence strongly suggests they were not.

In this paper we present and evaluate evidence from one government agency, the AEC, of the early concern expressed by several government officials for the protection of human subjects and the government's responsibility in maintaining that protection. High officials in the AEC, including the first general manager, Carroll Wilson, articulated and communicated requirements for consent and therapeutic intent that surpass even today's standards. These requirements appeared in internal memoranda and in several letters to AEC contract researchers. Although these documents are inconclusive and the requirements articulated in them were not translated into comprehensive policies for AEC-sponsored research in the 1940s and 1950s, they present a far more sophisticated concern for the welfare of human research subjects than previously recognized. Records of the AEC's early attempts to establish standards for the use of patient-subjects in biomedical research may be too sparse to give a clear picture of the legal standards that should be used to judge government-sponsored research during this time, but they nevertheless provide a valuable look at some early conceptions of the government's responsibility for human subjects of research.

THE AEC AND IONIZING RADIATION RESEARCH

The AEC opened its doors in January 1947, taking over most atomic energy–related activities from the Department of Defense and the Manhattan Project. As the government entity most involved in the development and use of atomic energy, the AEC was uniquely situated to establish and promote policies for radiation-related research with human subjects. The AEC was the primary supplier of radioisotopes used in research during the 1940s and into the 1950s. Documents from this period show that the civilian staff of the AEC, sensitive to the ongoing debate over civilian versus military control of atomic energy, recognized its simultaneous responsibility to provide access to the new technology of ionizing radiation to researchers while maintaining careful control of radioisotope use to prevent human harm. In the shadow of Hiroshima,

Nagasaki, and the 1946 nuclear bomb tests in the Bikini atoll, the AEC moved quickly and cautiously in its dual role of promoter and protector in the field of atomic energy.

AEC General Manager Wilson was appointed acting administrative director for the AEC in November 1946 and succeeded to the general manager's position in January 1947 (Lilienthal 1964, 150). Wilson assisted David Lilienthal, former head of the Tennessee Valley Authority and the first chairman of the AEC, during the drafting of the Atcheson–Lilienthal plan for the future disposition of atomic energy. Prior to working with Lilienthal, Wilson served as an assistant to Vannevar Bush, the president's science advisor during World War II. Lilienthal came into the AEC project with a strongly hands-off and delegatory approach to management, and Wilson's job was to implement this approach in the AEC's vast responsibility for production, promotion, and regulatory control of atomic energy. Wilson's workload that first year was enormous, making the attention he gave to the conduct of medical research with human subjects all the more noteworthy.

As the AEC took over the biomedical program of the Manhattan Project, it contemplated a significant expansion in the clinical use of radioisotopes. The AEC's role in this expansion was multifold: It supervised and regulated the manufacture, distribution, and use of all radioisotopes in the United States and in some other countries. The AEC's activities included oversight for both private and public researchers, including those at AEC-sponsored laboratories and other government facilities, such as the National Institutes of Health and the Department of Defense. Frequently the AEC supplied radioisotopes produced in its own reactors, such as Oak Ridge, although occasionally researchers obtained radioisotopes from nonfederal facilities, such as the cyclotron at the University of California. The AEC maintained oversight of these other arrangements through the review and approval process conducted by the Isotopes Distribution Division.

The radioisotope distribution program involved an extensive screening and approval process designed to ensure safe handling of the radioisotopes and prevent injury to workers, research subjects, and the public.[5] Among its outreach efforts, the AEC initially offered radioisotopes to cancer researchers at no charge and later changed this offering to an 80-percent discount until the program was discontinued in 1961, after the use of radioisotopes had become an accepted and necessary part of medical practice.[6] Regulation of non–AEC funded researchers was an unprecedented exercise of government control over essentially private activity, justified, no doubt, by the unusual nature and risk of the product being supplied by the government. The aim of this regulatory process was aimed mainly at concerns for safety and risk to the research subject, not at ensuring the subject's voluntary participation or potential medical benefit. In contrast, the AEC's exercise of control over its funded research program included clear concerns for subject consent and therapeutic intent.

USING HUMAN SUBJECTS

In December 1946, immediately prior to the AEC's assumption of control, the Manhattan Project suspended plans to continue human studies until the AEC set standards for human testing and approved the proposed research (Nichols 1946). The Manhattan Project–sponsored research included the first seventeen of the infamous plutonium injections into hospital patients (Advisory Committee on Human Radiation Experiments 1995, chap. 5).

In January 1947 the AEC's Interim Medical Advisory Committee, which was to supervise the proposed biomedical program, recommended resumption of clinical testing with human subjects (Warren 1947). In response to this recommendation, the AEC general counsel's office convened a meeting with Stafford Warren, formerly the medical director of the Manhattan Project and the chairman of the Interim Medical Advisory Committee, and Major B. M. Brundage, the chief of the AEC's medical division. In this meeting, an interim authorization for a program of "clinical testing" with radioisotopes was granted, pending approval by the full commission. In the record of the meeting, it is made clear that this authorization included the condition that

> it be susceptible of proof that any individual patient, prior to treatment, was in an understanding state of mind and that the nature of the treatment and possible risk involved be explained very clearly and that the patient express his willingness to receive treatment. (Burling 1947)

Although a written patient "release" was also suggested by the legal staff, it was rejected on Warren's request. Instead, all agreed that at least two physicians would "certify in writing" that the patient had received an explanation and had agreed to the experimental "treatment" (see Burling 1947).

A month after this meeting, in April 1947, Carroll Wilson wrote to Warren, who was also dean of the medical school at the University of California at Los Angeles, indicating the commission's formal approval of the proposed research program and describing the standards to be employed in clinical research with human subjects. First among the conditions Wilson described was the expectation that it have some "therapeutic effect" for the patient involved. Wilson (1947a) wrote, "Treatment (which may involve clinical testing) will be administered to a patient only when there is expectation that it may have therapeutic effect." As in the March agreement made by Warren, Brundage, and the general counsel's office, Wilson (1947a) added that it was

> to be susceptible of proof from official records, that, prior to treatment, each individual patient, being in an understanding state of mind, was clearly informed of the nature of the treatment and its possible effects, and expressed his willingness to receive the treatment.

To take the "therapeutic effect" requirement first, it is unclear from Wilson's letter if he intended "therapeutic effect" to mean benefit for the patient only or to include benefit for science without the prospect of medical benefit to the patient. In light of the reality of the practice of medical research and the fact that significant progress is made with patients who themselves receive no benefit from their participation in research, a requirement for therapeutic benefit may seem unreasonable and in fact surpasses the requirements in place today. Alternatively, Wilson may have meant to exclude only research that offered no genuine prospect of advancing the care of the subject or medical science generally, an interpretation consistent with today's ethical standards.

Yet, whether Wilson intended to exclude human testing designed only to advance science is questionable. Wilson was not a physician or a scientist engaged in the practice of medical research. Setting rules for human research was a minor part of his work at the AEC, and he was probably given little information on the practice of medical research before issuing this order. There is reason to believe he lacked clear understanding of research practice. A fair argument may be made that he set parameters for research on the basis of commonsense considerations of right and wrong—namely, people should not be used as test subjects or put at risk without some prospect of benefit.

Echoing this idea at military discussions on proposed research with human subjects during 1947 and 1948 was Shields Warren, a physician formerly on the faculty of Harvard Medical School. In his role as the director of the AEC's Division of Biology and Medicine, the home of the AEC's biomedical research program, Warren demonstrated the caution that characterized the AEC's approach to research with human subjects. Despite the urgent demands of defense planners, he argued vociferously against the use of human subjects in high-exposure radiation experiments related to a proposed nuclear energy–propelled aircraft. Warren commented: "I am very much opposed to human experimentation when it isn't good for the individual concerned and when there is any other way of solving the problem."[7]

Still, the AEC engaged in a great number of human experiments, many of which offered no prospect of therapeutic benefit. The second requirement set by Wilson in his April 1947 letter, the requirement for the subject's oral consent, offered a more realistic and enforceable restriction on medical research and demonstrated a consideration of human subjects unprecedented at the time. AEC recognition of the unique concerns raised by using people as a means without their consent is further demonstrated in an October 1947 internal memorandum addressing the practice of radioisotope tracer research. This research generally offered no prospect of therapeutic benefit to the patient-subject. Among the "cons" of this research, the memorandum notes:

1. Moral, ethical, and medico-legal objections to the administration of radioactive material without the patient's knowledge or consent.
2. There is perhaps a greater responsibility if a federal agency condones human guinea pig experimentation. (Memorandum 1947)

The reference to "human guinea pig experimentation" is not qualified in the memorandum, nor is it clear if it refers to all human subjects or only those engaged in nontherapeutic research. What it shows, however, is that the AEC staff had some understanding that patient consent to research participation was an ethical component of research, particularly when that research is funded by the government.

Wilson's rejection of a proposed written-consent requirement suggests a deference to the professional autonomy of physicians seen in other parts of his letter. Wilson states that the AEC-sponsored program was to continue on condition that "the decisions as to the advisability of treatment will be made by the doctor concerned" (Memorandum 1947). Further, Wilson added,

> The Commission does not intend to influence in any way the exercise of judgment by the doctor as to the administration of any particular treatment authorized under the approved program. . . . it seemed evident to me that the doctors would not allow their judgment on this matter to be influenced by anyone. (Memorandum 1947)

The "approved program" in this case was the program outlined by Stafford Warren and his Interim Medical Advisory Committee in January 1947. From a relatively small program of isolated human testing at only a few institutions during the Manhattan Project era, the committee planned a larger program to include at least twelve institutions in a variety of research projects (Marsden 1947). Wilson's statement suggests an underlying territorial debate about which division of the AEC would control the operation of the sponsored medical research program but also reveals the weight accorded physicians in clinical research at this time. Wilson apparently understood the tradition that physicians ought to make treatment decisions unencumbered by bureaucratic interference and sought to preserve that tradition insofar as he could simultaneously protect citizens from unethical exposure to radiation through government-sponsored clinical experiments.

HOW THE AEC SAW ITS ROLE
IN RESEARCH REQUIREMENTS

When considered in the context of the AEC's takeover of the Manhattan Project's biomedical program, Wilson's requirement for therapeutic benefit and consent become clearer. The AEC was a civilian agency assuming responsibility for an emerging technology many believed was better left under military control. As it began its work, the AEC classified many reports of the Manhattan-era plutonium injections for fear of lawsuits and bad publicity (Advisory Committee on Human Radiation Experiments 1995, chap. 5). For example, in March 1947 a declassification officer warned against publication of some human studies:

It is unlikely that these tests were made without the consent of the subjects, but no statement is made to that effect . . . Unless, of course, the legal aspects are covered by the necessary documents, the experimenters and the employing agencies, including the U.S., have been laid open to a devastating lawsuit which would, through its attendant publicity, have far reaching results. (CH-3607 n.d.)

Brundage, who with Stafford Warren and the AEC legal office had developed the standards for the resumption of clinical research articulated by Wilson in April 1947, concurred in the classification order, citing the "medical legal aspects in the use of plutonium in human beings" (Brundage 1947).

In part to avoid the fears raised by these previous experiments, the AEC leadership may have developed a compromise position to permit research with consenting human subjects on the assumption that such research, when designed to help the participant subject, was acceptable. By way of contrast, the use of human subjects as a mere means to scientific inquiry was not acceptable, regardless of the apparent need of the research.

Unfortunately, very little evidence is available from which to discern definitively Wilson's intentions at the time he drafted the April 1947 letter or subsequent statements by him and others about the conditions for AEC-sponsored biomedical research. These statements did not appear in a form that many commonly recognize as "policy," such as regulations or official orders. Moreover, there is little evidence that Wilson's statements were disseminated to most AEC-sponsored researchers or non-AEC researchers working with AEC-supplied radioisotopes. In light of these facts, the Advisory Committee concluded that "it is not clear that conditions stated by individual officials [such as Wilson] rise to a level that all would be comfortable calling policies." (Advisory Committee on Human Radiation Experiments 1995, 215). Consequently, our discussion of these statements can only suggest *possible* explanations for the appearance of these statements.

With that said, some evidence shows that the consent standard outlined by Wilson may have had some limited effect, even if hard evidence of implementation of the therapeutic benefit requirement standard does not appear. In the medical records of the patient given the eighteenth plutonium injection, which was conducted at the University of California in June 1947 under AEC auspices, a notation appeared stating that the patient, who was "fully oriented and in sane mind," agreed to the procedure after its experimental nature was "explained" to him.[8] This experiment offered no prospect of medical benefit to the patient.

The implementation of the consent provision for one patient shows some effort to follow consent standards set by the AEC at a time when few physician-researchers obtained patient consent for experimental interventions (Advisory Committee on Human Radiation Experiments 1995, chap. 2; see also Rothman 1991). Unique among federal funders of biomedical research, the AEC's requirement for subject consent may be understood as

arising from three-factors: (1) concern about the uncertain effect of radioisotopes on the human body, (2) the special aura surrounding radiation, especially after Hiroshima and Nagasaki, and (3) the special role played by the
government as a sponsor of research in this new arena.

DISCOVERING "INFORMED CONSENT"

Throughout 1947 the AEC continued to refine conditions for research with
human subjects. In June 1947 the AEC convened an independent, blue-
ribbon Medical Board of Review, composed of distinguished physicians and
scientists, many of whom were not intimately involved in the work of the
Manhattan Project. The AEC was a new agency, and the advisers were needed
to help set a course for its biomedical research projects. At its three-day meeting, the Medical Board of Review considered the substance and procedure for
future AEC-sponsored research, including the conditions under which
human experiments would proceed.

The conditions set by the medical board were communicated by
Wilson in response to the inquiry of an AEC-sponsored researcher. Robert
Stone was a University of California researcher heavily involved in
Manhattan Project human experiments, including three of the plutonium
injections at the University of Chicago (Advisory Committee on Human
Radiation Experiments 1995, 241–2). Stone continued to work with the AEC
through the 1940s and 1950s and asked to have reports of his research
declassified for publication. In denying this request, Wilson advised Stone of
the current formulation of the AEC's policy for research with human subjects, as drafted by the medical board in June 1947 and endorsed by the
Advisory Committee on Biology and Medicine that fall. In a November 1947
letter to Stone, Wilson noted that the Medical Board of Review, in approving "the position taken by the medical staff of the AEC," indicated without
further qualification that no "substance known to be, or suspected of being,
poisonous or harmful" should be used in human subjects unless all of the
following conditions were met:

a. that a reasonable hope exists that the administration of such a substance will
   improve the condition of the patient,
b. that the patient give his complete and *informed consent* in writing, and that the
   responsible next of kin give in writing a similarly complete and informed consent, revocable at any time during the course of such treatment. (Wilson 1947b,
   emphasis added)

These conditions go far past the requirements Wilson communicated to
Stafford Warren and constitute a powerful standard that far exceeds the current requirements for participation in medical experiments. The requirement
for direct medical benefit to the patient adds credence to the idea that Wilson

intended his April 1947 requirements to exclude research that used human subjects as a mere means to advance medical science.

Moreover, the Medical Board of Review's requirement for "informed consent," drafted originally in June 1947, predates by two months the Nuremberg Code and by ten years the California judiciary's articulation of the term in a medical malpractice case, the incident to which most scholars attributed the earliest known use of the phrase.[9] By requiring written informed consent from the subject and the subject's next of kin, the medical board substantially expanded Wilson's April 1947 requirements and implied that deference to physician autonomy would not trump the documentation of subject consent. On the whole, this severe consent requirement substantially surpasses today's consent requirements, poses practical difficulties, and is of questionable ethical status, given that individuals alone have the right to control their bodies.

Following this letter to Stone, Wilson wrote of his response to Alan Gregg, the chair of the AEC's Advisory Committee on Biology and Medicine. Wilson assured Gregg that the conditions articulated by the Medical Board of Review and detailed to Stone would "inform him [Stone] as to the conditions that must be met in future experiments" (Wilson 1947c). There is little evidence that Wilson communicated these standards to other researchers and they did not appear in the public version of the Medical Board of Review's report. Nonetheless, that the medical board and Wilson, with the approval of the Advisory Committee on Biology and Medicine, articulated such a serious and extensive set of conditions reflects a remarkable consideration of the ethical standards for research with human subjects.

The Medical Board of Review's statement was drafted in light of the AEC's multiple hats and unique position. As a government body involved with militarily classified research and simultaneously engaged in a process of promoting a new technology for public use, the AEC often faced competing goals, such as medical progress and patient's rights. Recognizing this, the drafters of the medical board's statement of the standards for human research observed:

> Were it not for the extreme value and pressure for securing reliable information on the limits of human tolerance of radioactive substances there would be no need for explicit reference to this subject [human testing] . . . we believe that since secrecy must of necessity mark much of the medical research supported by the federally-sponsored AEC, particular care must be taken in all matters that under other circumstances would be open to investigation and publicity. (Wilson 1947b)

Thus, when faced with a great medical need to understand the potential harm to individuals from exposure to radiation behind the shield of national security, the AEC's medical leaders did not shrink from responsibility or attempt to justify unethical practices in the name of the public good. Nor did they ignore the possibility that unethical conduct might occur under the umbrella of deference to physician autonomy. Rather, the AEC's medical leaders sought to identify what constitutes unethical practice and make clear that such practice was unacceptable in secret or in public. They identified standards for the ethical conduct of research with human subjects where previously none were articulated by government officials or on so broad a scale. Their refusal to allow research outside ethical norms, given the opportunity afforded by the classified nature of some research, demonstrates a remarkable commitment to protection of human subjects.

AFTERMATH: IMPLEMENTATION AND ENFORCEMENT

We must not forget that little evidence suggests the requirements stated by the Medical Board of Review were widely implemented. Although the AEC sponsored a great amount of research through the 1950s and 1960s, it is doubtful that the requirements of these 1947 policies were widely enforced. Failure to enforce the policies may have been partly because the requirements included provisions that did not fit into the practice of medical research, like the ban on research offering no direct medical benefit, and that were of questionable ethical status, like the requirement for written informed consent from the next of kin for all subjects.

Through 1948 and 1949, the AEC relaxed some of the apparently strict restrictions. For example, a draft document of the conditions for radioisotope experiments at "AEC establishments," developed in 1948 in response to a request from Shields Warren, the director of the Division of Biology and Medicine, permits experiments that "contribute to knowledge on radiation protection" without offering any direct medical benefit to the subject (Experimental use 1948). This standard reflects the recognition that much medical research lacks potential benefit to the subject. The document categorically distinguished between healthy (called "normal volunteer") subjects and patient-subjects but required "full knowledge" and consent from both groups. A special note was made that patient-subjects be of "sound mind." Written consent was not required of any subjects, however.

Further evidence of the AEC's limited efforts to enforce consent requirements appears in a 1951 letter responding to an inquiry about existing policies for human experimentation from Los Alamos National Laboratory (Redman 1951). Shields Warren cited the conditions articulated by the Medical Board of Review in Wilson's November 1947 letter to Robert Stone and advised, though did not require, compliance with the conditions enumerated (Warren 1951). Five years later, in 1956, Los Alamos again inquired about the current policy for the use of humans in tracer experiments (Shipman 1956). The Division of Biology and Medicine again informed its laboratory that human experiments were to be conducted on the condition that the subjects are "bona fide volunteers and fully informed as to the procedure involved" (Dunham 1956). Additionally, a 1959 letter from AEC researcher Robert Stone indicates that patients given radioactive iodine when the use of such material was not an "accepted medical procedure" were required to sign a consent form "at the request of the AEC" (Stone 1959).

The AEC distributed hundreds of thousands of radioisotopes for medical research to thousands of investigators around the country and abroad. In 1948 the AEC articulated a consent requirement applicable to some patient subjects.[10] In a somewhat circular description of "instances in which the disease from which a patient is suffering permits the administration of larger doses for investigative purposes," the AEC permitted experimentation on the condition that the subject consented to the procedure (see Lough 1949, 5–6). The Isotope Distribution Program's requirements were compiled into a formal guide to the "Medical Use of Radioisotopes" in 1956. Perhaps reflecting the language employed by the National Institutes of Health's Clinical Center research program, this guide makes reference to a consent requirement for "normal subjects" only.

GET IT IN WRITING?

Although evidence of consent requirements and procedures during the late 1940s and 1950s seems remarkable in light of contemporary scholarship, it should be added that the written forms used to certify patient consent during this time were not as elaborate as the documents we today think of as "consent forms." They were generally modeled upon the surgical releases commonly used in all hospitals at the time. For example, in 1950 new patients to the AEC-sponsored Oak Ridge Institute for Nuclear Studies, a hospital devoted to research with radiation, were informed in a patient information packet that all treatment at the hospital was "experimental" but were required to sign a "Waiver and Release" that did not describe the treatment but included a lengthy release from the patient for any claims against the hospital.[11]

In another example, a University of California form for patient signature entitled "Information for Patients Receiving Radio-iodine" advised only that radio-iodine is "like x-rays," which "have been used for treatment of certain thyroid diseases," and that "while the use of radio-iodine is still experimental, we believe it will be more satisfactory than x-rays" (Wells 1955). While perhaps less legalistic than the Oak Ridge forms, the California forms are arguably coercive and lack the explanatory text we typically think of today as necessary to genuinely inform a prospective subject of the risks and benefits of participation in research. Thus, while contemporary consent forms certainly continue to have as at least part of their purpose an attempt to protect the institution and its officers from liability, the intervening years have made a significant difference in the amount and nature of the content of these forms, content that holds out some prospect of helping the subject understand the proposed research.

GOVERNMENT'S ROLE: RECONSIDERING THE RECORD

Despite the contemporary criticism of the consent practices and procedures of AEC researchers in the 1940s and 1950s, early AEC efforts to develop a policy for the use of human subjects in research reveals a far stronger consideration of ethics in medicine than were previously believed to have obtained in the period immediately following World War II, particularly in the federal government. It also shows that the leaders of the AEC recognized the unique responsibility of government to its citizens when it sponsors medical research: The government must ensure that individual rights are not casually subjugated to the public good.

Indeed, if the documents give cause for concern about the conduct of any specific societal group, it is that of physician-investigators. On numerous occasions, in the AEC story we have related and elsewhere, researchers who were also doctors of medicine proved to be jealous guardians of their professional prerogatives. Often they operated from sound principles of professional autonomy and concern for the well-being of those in their care, but they were not always able to perceive when medical progress and personal liberty could conflict, nor were they always clear about the limitations of the research imperative. These influential physicians also proved adept at limiting the ability of government officials to intrude into their self-regulated sphere.

Professional resistance to external regulation may have contributed to a lapse of institutional memory concerning the early AEC discussions. In 1984 a court found that a U.S. Public Health Service (PHS) decision not to inform Navajo uranium miners about their risks was "consistent with the medical ethical and legal standards of the 1940s and 1950s. It was not until the 1964 and 1965 period that federal guidelines were established for the conduct of federally-funded research projects."[12] As we now know, the court's assertion was inaccurate. In a related and tragic irony, the AEC determined early in its history that the mining did not fall within its jurisdiction. Were it not for this determination, the principles of the Wilson letters might well have applied to the PHS observational research of lung cancer among the miners.

The AECs early efforts to come to terms with the rights of human subjects and to give meaning to its formula, "informed consent," prefigure the debates and discussions that have come to characterize the field of bioethics. Although it may indeed turn out to be the case that the AEC was the first to use the term *informed consent,* its subsequent career required that it be reinvented by those who followed.

NOTES

1. The authors worked on the staff of the Advisory Committee on Human Radiation Experiments. The enclosed views are those of the authors and do not represent the views of the Advisory Committee. The findings, recommendations, and analysis of the Advisory Committee are expressed in the "Final Report of the Advisory Committee on Human Radiation Experiments," available from Oxford University Press (New York) under the title *The Human Radiation Experiments* (1996).

We are grateful to Jon Merz for his comments on an earlier draft and to Dillan Siegler for her assistance in preparing the final draft.

2. Many scholarly studies examine the history of experimentation on humans. See Annas and Grodin (1992); Faden and Beauchamp (1986); Katz (1972); Rothman (1991).

3. See *United States* v. *Karl Brandt et al.* (1949); Faden and Beauchamp (1986, 153–6).

4. Numerous scholars have called the Nuremberg Code unhelpful and unresponsive to the medical community for its failure to recognize the healthy subject/patient-subject distinction. It is commonly perceived as an anomaly that gave little direction to American physicians. See Katz (1993, 28). Among other cornerstones in modern medical ethics, the first to recognize the distinction between healthy subjects and patient-subjects was the Declaration of Helsinki, a 1964 document promulgated by the World Medical Association. See Faden and Beauchamp (1986, 156–7).

5. This is documented in "Availability of Radioactive Isotopes: Announcements from Headquarters, Manhattan Project, Washington, D.C." (1946); Isotopes Branch (1946b); Isotopes Branch (1946a); Atomic Energy Commission Isotopes Division (1949). See also Advisory Committee on Human Radiation Experiments (1995, chap. 6).

6. See: Atomic Energy Commission Isotopes Division (1949); Aebersold (1954).

7. See Atomic Energy Commission (1950). Unfortunately, Warren was not so scrupulous concerning an observational study of the effects of radiation exposure upon uranium miners, as he blocked release of information about its hazards on at least one occasion. Warren is in many respects a tragic figure of this period who struggled deeply with conflicting demands. See Proctor (1995, 44).

8. Precisely what was explained to the patient remains unknown, although the format of the notation suggests it was meant to comply with Wilson's requirements. See Advisory Committee on Human Radiation Experiments (1995, 257). Note also that documentation of consent has not been found for the only other radioisotope injections at the University of California under AEC auspices. One involved the injection of americium into a teenage boy with cancer, and the other involved injection of zirconium into a middle-aged woman with ovarian cancer. Neither injection offered the prospect of medical benefit to the patient. See Advisory Committee on Human Radiation Experiments (1995, 256–8).

9. See *Salgo* v. *Leland Stanford, Jr. University Board of Trustees* (1957). *P.2d* 317:170.

10. See Lough (1949). These requirements were subsequently published in a publicly distributed document. See Atomic Energy Commission Isotopes Division (1949).

11. See Oak Ridge Institute for Nuclear Studies (n.d.). The form states that the hospital has described the "character and find of treatment."

12. See *Begay* v. *United States*, 591 F.Supp. 991, 997–998 (D. Ariz. 1984).

REFERENCES

Aebersold, Paul C. 1954. Letter to T. H. Johnson, Director, Division of Research. ACHRE, no. TEX-101294–A-4 (November 2).

Advisory Committee on Human Radiation Experiments. 1995. *Final report of the Advisory Committee on Human Radiation Experiments.* Washington, D.C.: U.S. Printing Office.

Annas, George J., and Michael Grodin, eds. 1992. *The Nazi doctors and the Nuremburg Code: Human rights in human experimentation.* New York: Oxford University Press.

Atomic Energy Commission. 1950. Transcript of meeting of Advisory Committee on Biology and Medicine. ACHRE, no. DOE-012795–C-1 (November 10).

Atomic Energy Commission Isotopes Division. 1949. Supplement no. 1 to catalogue and price list no. 3, July 1949. ACHRE, no. DOD-122794–A-1 (September).

Availability of radioactive isotopes: Announcements from headquarters, Manhattan Project, Washington, D.C. 1946. *Science* 103:697–705.

Begay v. *United States.* 591 F.Supp. 991, 997–998 (D. Ariz. 1984).

Brundage, Major B. M. 1947. Memorandum to declassification section. ACHRE, no. DOE-113094–B-4 (March 19).

Burling, John L. 1947. Memorandum to Edwin Huddleson, deputy general counsel, Atomic Energy Commission. ACHRE, no. DOE-051094–A-468 (March 7).

CH-3607. Excerpts from statements of reviewers. n.d. ACHRE, no. DOE-113094–B-4.

Dunham, Charles. 1956. Letter to Thomas Shipman. ACHRE, no. DOE-091994–B-2 (July 5).

The experimental use of radioactive materials in human subjects at Atomic Energy Commission establishments. 1948. ACHRE, no. DOE-051094–A-267 (March 29).

Faden, Ruth, and Tom L. Beauchamp. 1986. *A history and theory of informed consent.* New York: Oxford University Press.

Isotopes Branch. 1946a. Agreement and conditions for order and receipt of radioactive materials. ACHRE, no. NARA-082294–A-31. Oak Ridge, Tenn.: Research Division, Manhattan District.

———. 1946b. Details of isotope procurement. ACHRE, no. NARA-082294–A-31. Oak Ridge, Tenn.: Research Division, Manhattan District.

Katz, Jay. 1972. *Experimentation with human beings: The authority of the investigator, subjects, professions, and state in the human experimentation process.* New York: Sage.

———. 1993. Human experimentation and human rights. *St. Louis University Law Journal* 38:7–54.

Lilienthal, David E. 1964. *The journals of David E. Lilienthal: 1945 to 1950.* New York: Harper & Row.

Lough, S. Allan. 1949. Minutes of 22–23 March 1948 meeting of the Subcommittee on Human Applications as discussed in the minutes of the 13 March 1949 meeting, sent to H. L. Friedell, G. Failla, J. G. Hamilton, and A. H. Holland. ACHRE, no. DOE-101194–A-13 (July 19).

Marsden, E. H. 1947. Memorandum to R.C. Armstrong: Comments on report of the 23–24 January 1947 [*sic*] of the Interim Medical Committee, U.S. Atomic Energy Commission.

Memorandum to the Advisory Committee on Biology and Medicine. 1947. ACHRE, no. DOE-051094–A-50 (October 8).

Nichols, Colonel K. D. 1946. Letter to the area engineer, California area. ACHRE, no. DOE-112094–B-2 (December 24).

Oak Ridge Institute for Nuclear Studies. n.d. Application forms for admission to the medical division of the hospital and waiver release forms. ACHRE, no. DOE-121494–C-3.

Proctor, Robert N. 1995. *Cancer wars.* New York: Basic Books.

Redman, Leslie. 1951. Letter to Alberto Thomson, chief, Technical Information Service, Division of Biology and Medicine, Atomic Energy Commission. ACHRE, no. 051094–A-609 (January 12).

Rothman, David J. 1991. *Strangers at the bedside: A history of how law and bioethics transformed medical decision making.* New York: Basic Books.

Salgo v. *Leland Stanford Jr. University Board of Trustees.* 1957. P.2d 317:170.

Shipman, Thomas. 1956. Letter to Charles Dunham, Director, Division of Biology and Medicine, Atomic Energy Commission. ACHRE, no. DOE-091994–B-1 (June 18).

Stone, Robert S. 1959. Letter to John Adams, chief of staff, Department of Neurosurgery: Consent forms for patients receiving radioactive isotopes. San Francisco: University of California, Special Collection Accession, no. AR 86–2 (April 14).

United States v. *Karl Brandt et al.* 1949. The medical case, trials of war criminals before the Nuremburg military tribunals under control council law no. 10. Washington, D.C.: U.S. Printing Office.

Warren, Shields. 1951. Letter to Leslie Redman. ACHRE, no. DOE-051094–A-603 (March 5).

Warren, Stafford L. 1947. Report of the 23–24 January 1947 Meeting of the Interim Medical Committee of the United States Atomic Energy Commission. ACHRE, no. UCL-111094–A-26.

Wells, Paul O. 1955. Forms from Earl Miller, University of California, San Francisco, attached to a letter to Elmer A. Lodmell, chief, Radiological Service, Walter Reed Army Hospital. ACHRE, no. DOD-012295–A (January 14).

Wilson, Carroll L. 1947a. Letter to Stafford Warren, dean of the Medical School, University of California, Los Angeles. ACHRE, no. DOE-051094–A-439 (April 30).

———. 1947b. Letter to Robert Stone. ACHRE, no. DOE-052295–A-1 (November 5).

———. 1947c. Letter to Alan Gregg. ACHRE, no. DOE-052295–A-1 (November 5).

CHAPTER SIX

Institutional Ethics Committees: Sociological Oxymoron, Empirical Black Box

Charles L. Bosk and Joel Frader

Despite the collective belief that medical practice rests on solid scientific grounds, change in medicine typically comes about in a haphazard, complex fashion. New practices often constitute reactions to external social, political, and economic forces, rather than adoption of technical advances. Certainly, the major restructuring of health-care practices begun in the late 1980s and early 1990s—*integrated networks* brought about through mergers and acquisitions with promised efficiencies of scale; *managed care*, with its purported elimination of wasteful, inefficient, and unnecessary care; cost savings through health maintenance organizations, which supposedly flow from prevention rather than more expensive rescue—all provide examples of changes based on theory rather than systematically established grounds. Other wholesale changes in practice follow changes in fashion among leaders in health care professions prior to concrete demonstration of benefit. Examples in medicine include the introduction of coronary care units (Bloom and Peterson 1973), the use of fetal monitoring (Hess 1980; Nelson et al. 1996), and radical surgical treatment for breast cancer (Fisher et al. 1985).

This process—transformations in practice absent persuasive evidence of efficacy—is now being repeated with the institutionalization of what Renée Fox (1989) has called the "bioethics movement." We refer here to the establishment of small groups in hospitals, nursing homes, and the like, known as hospital or institutional ethics committees (IECs), to respond to moral issues and to clinical ethics consultation (CEC) services. The fact that IECs and CEC are the mechanisms to resolve multiple tensions and conundrums in delivering modern care is in itself not surprising, as each adopts well-worn structural responses to problems of social control. In most health care settings, CEC uses familiar methods modeled on medical practice (La Puma and Schiedermayer 1991) to deal with patient, family, or staff behavior that deviates from the expected or from what authorities prefer. In many ways, IECs simply extend long-established patterns of peer and community oversight and provide a mechanism for educating those in the institution and for generating institutional policy (Ross 1986). In other ways, IECs and CEC are a novel response to the exquisitely difficult, painful existential dilemmas of contemporary medical care.

INSTITUTIONAL ETHICS COMMITTEES: HISTORICAL BACKGROUND AND CONTEXT

Since the late 1960s, responding to the memory of Nazi medical experiments and the more recent scandalous behavior of researchers in the United States, the federal government has required institutions that receive federal research support to have in place an institutional review board (IRB). These committees, according to federal regulations, must include at least seven members, including a scientist, a practicing physician, a nurse, and one community "representative." The IRB's stated role is to ensure that proposed experimentation falls safely within both professional and community norms for acceptable conduct. Operationally, this often means a limited review in practice. IRBs focus on the risk-benefit ratio of proposed research and the extent to which consent forms are both understandable and complete. IRB review is completely forward looking and relies on an honor system; there is rarely, if ever, surveillance to assess compliance. Nonetheless, since their introduction, IRBs have provided review of research protocols. In doing so, these committees expanded the circle of those who can legitimately participate in the collective oversight of biomedical and behavioral research.[1]

In this light the emergence of IECs seems little more than an extension of an organizational innovation into a new domain. But, of course, matters are more complicated than they appear. Thinking of IECs as a linear development of earlier forms of professional oversight and control misses much of what is new in this organizational form and certainly misses the important ways that IECs differ from IRBs. Most significantly, it discounts the fact that IRBs were largely the product of federal mandates, which regulated their membership, their functions, and, even to a degree, their procedures. IECs, as we will soon see, grew in a much more free-form way, with no requirements for representation, no clear delimited tasks, no set procedures, and no formal mandate for coming into being (Cransford and Doudera 1984). Institutions were compelled to have IRBs if they wished to retain federal support; there was no similar incentive to encourage recalcitrant institutions into developing IECs. The recent requirement of the Joint Commission on the Accreditation of Health Care Organizations that institutions seeking accreditation have a mechanism for resolving problems in clinical ethics is silent on what that process should be. If IECs are the proper mechanism, how they should then be structured and function or, more to the heart of the matter, what standards or processes the IEC should adopt for reaching substantive closure on moral matters is unspecified.

Origins are difficult to trace with precision. How beginnings are located, what counts as an institutional antecedent to IECs, and what forerunners are ignored tell us more about the intent of the analyst than it informs us about IECs. If the analyst tells the story in such a way that IECs are seen as an extension of earlier organizational forms, then one can expect a Whig history of medical ethics. Each moment is a monument in the march of progress that allows greater weight to be put on ethical values at the bedside. On the other hand, if the account emphasizes the work necessary to impose these strange and new questions into alien and uninviting territory, then one will hear a tale in which bioethicists and those concerned with a more broad, holistic view of medical action are courageous reformers, expanding human liberties in domains hostile and resistant to such expansion. There is a substantial validity to both accounts, making it a difficult narrative problem to tell both at the same time.

This explanatory difficulty aside, to explain and analyze the rise of IECs, it is necessary to begin somewhere. Three early developments are worthy of mention.[2] As Renée Fox and Judith Swazey (1974) reported, citizens' committees in Seattle formed to allocate scarce kidneys among the multiple potential recipients faced many ethical dilemmas and can be seen as a forerunner of current committees. However, it is worth noting that such committees faced enormous pressures trying to reach consensus, never articulated standards for decision making, and eventually disbanded, an outcome perhaps helped along by considerable adverse publicity. An important feature of all these groups was the sharp focus on case-by-case decisions. The committees functioned, in effect, as clinical consultants. As with most such clinical activity, neither the social rules that structured the consultation nor the philosophical and social values assumptions that shaped the decisions were explicit.

Next, there were the controversies surrounding nontreatment in neonatal intensive care, stimulated by the report of Raymond Duff and A. G. M. Campbell (1973) at Yale–New Haven Hospital. These authors revealed their private troubles and decision making as a way to force a public reevaluation of the operating procedures and underlying presuppositions that tended to support more, or excessive, treatment rather than permit the deaths of patients with poor prognoses. At Yale then, there were no ethics committees, but there was merely public recognition of the need for them. At about that time, others had begun to suggest that ethically focused intrainstitutional groups might begin to confront the growing disjunction between capacity and rationale for life-extending treatment. The publication in 1971 of *The Medico-Moral Guide* of the Catholic Bishops (of Canada) recommended the formation of medico-moral committees in Catholic health care facilities. Although the guide identified the absence of sufficient personnel trained in theology and ethics and the lack of involvement of hospital personnel as potential problems, hoped-for benefits from committee formation included education of staff and the widening of the moral dialogue about the proper mission of modern health-care institutions. In 1976 a lawyer and a pediatrician (Robertson and Fost 1976) suggested committees might help address some of the ethical and legal questions that treatment-limitation practices raised. There was, then, a call from several quarters to pay special attention to ethical problems in the domain of health care, especially in regard to the increasing frequency of dilemmas consequent to advancing medical technology.

Arguably, the single biggest impetus to the formation of ethics committees came in 1976 when the Supreme Court of New Jersey, in the Quinlan case, adopted a proposal in the literature by Karen Teel (1975). The court suggested that hospitals form ethics committees to keep disputes, such as the one before them, out of the courts. Three features of this landmark decision are worth noting:

1. The New Jersey court was silent about how these committees should be organized and how their deliberations would prevent litigation.
2. The court distorted Teel's recommendation and, in so doing, created some confusion about whether the committees were to concern themselves with medical matters, such as prognosis and futility, or with morals.
3. It is unclear how committee arbitration squares with the right, articulated by the Quinlan court, of individuals or their surrogates to make private medical decisions. Nonetheless, here was a court in a widely publicized case calling for a major change in how ethical dilemmas were managed.

The judicial call for peer review lifted the question of limiting life-sustaining treatment from the exclusive purview of the physician-patient relationship but left unclear the justification and best method(s) for such interventions. Similar conceptual and procedural confusion prevailed during and after 1982–1985, a period of somewhat frenetic federal regulatory initiatives and congressional action invoking infant-care review committees to oversee treatment in cases of "handicapped" newborns. These developments followed in the wake of the Baby Doe case from Bloomington, Indiana. More recent legislation (in Maryland) and proposed regulation (New York state) requiring ethics committees to have some sort of consultative role in morally problematic cases have not settled a host of legal and philosophical questions of where IECs (should) fit in. As instruments of social control, the effectiveness of ethics committees seems to have been somewhat constrained by questions about the lawful and moral grounds for groups of strangers to intervene in medical decisions typically negotiated among patients, their loved ones, their surrogates, and treating professionals (Lo 1987; Fleetwood et al. 1989).

ETHICS CONSULTATION: HISTORICAL BACKGROUND

The foregoing actually tracks much of the development of CEC, in that a large fraction of the consultative practice in medical ethics first occurred, at least in any formalized sense, through and by ethics committees. There is no easy separation of the origins of either. But there was another avenue of approach leading to CEC: the incorporation of theologians, philosophers, and occasionally others from the humanities (including sociologists) into clinical teaching programs in medical schools and some residency (especially family practice) programs, in the 1960s and 1970s (Fletcher et al. 1989; Rothenberg 1989). To the extent that these "moral experts" became confidants and advice givers to clinicians' grappling with real cases, rather than individuals who used the material presented on rounds to illustrate the general value and validity of ethical analysis, CEC was emerging in situ.

The appearance of nonclinicians, who some clinicians came to rely on, seems to have touched one or more sensitive nerves, leading to a contentious debate about what sorts of individuals might legitimately claim the mantle of consultant (Zaner 1993). We need not rehash that debate, but we should note that the question of how much clinical knowledge and skill CEC requires remains unsettled. Of course, how much and what sorts of knowledge and skill such a consultant ought to have (for example, philosophical, theological, mediation, legal, interactional, and small-group behavior) is an equally unresolved question, though these areas seem not to have created as much heat. That having been said, at least one prominent critic (Scofield 1993) claims that the very idea of *anyone* aspiring to the title of ethics consultant so offends our (political) tradition of individual liberty in a pluralistic society that we should quash any attempt to legitimize the role. These important questions—of what collection of characteristics constitute, and whether or how our society might endorse, the establishment of a new, historically complex profession (in the sense of having decidedly heterogeneous origins)—stand before us in the late 1990s. Indeed, one of us (CLB) sits on a blue-ribbon panel under the sponsorship of the Society for Health and Human Values and the Society for Bioethics Consultation, which is funded by the Greenwall Foundation, to deliberate on this very set of questions.[3]

PROBLEMATIC SOCIAL FEATURES OF ETHICS CONSULTATION

By Committee

In their way, ethics committees are an illustration of a sociological principle of Simmel—that of negative solidarity. It is relatively easy for groups to come together to identify what is wrong—in this case, inadequate attention paid to the ethical dimension of clinical care. Agreement often dissolves, however, when members of the group begin to pose remedies. Because our focus here is on the matter of the clinical consultative role of IECs, we will note some of the problems of committees relative to the consultative function. Among the issues are the following: the membership of the IEC, the kind of authority consultative activities ought to be regarded as having, and the procedures for organizing consultative activities.

Membership. Each institution has its own procedures for establishing membership on ethics committees. In some, the committees are open to volunteers. While this may ensure a certain level of motivation, we might wonder about how self-selection operates here. Who volunteers to be an ethical watchdog in an institution, and why? Of course, other means of selection are just as suspect. Appointment by administration raises questions of independence and of whose interest the committee serves. Election—given the gravity of the tasks—appears unseemly. Further, no method of selection does much to ensure that committee members possess the requisite expertise and knowledge base.[4]

The hospital is a complex formal organization; it is not clear who in the ranks should serve on ethics committees. Presumably, the more inclusive a committee, the better its chances of expressing a consensus, assuming we accept, as Jonathan Moreno (1995) argues, the importance of consensual agreement. But, there are many ways to be inclusive. Some ethics committees have top administrators and even members of the board of trustees. Their presence may send a message about the importance of ethics in or to the institution, but surely their participation can also inhibit the free flow of ideas. Many ethics committees include hospital legal counsel. To the extent that such attorneys can help clarify the inevitable questions of law that arise in ethically troublesome cases, hospital counsel can help the process work more efficiently. However, because the fiduciary responsibility of the hospital's legal staff is to advocate for positions protecting the hospital's interests, as opposed to the interests of individual employees or professional staff or the interests of patients and their loved ones, potential exists for (unacknowledged) conflict of interest to mar moral discourse. In addition, the well-known tendency of legal opinions to quiet if not quash discussion, given physicians' pervasive fear of litigation, may also undermine ideal moral problem solving.

How many physicians and how many nurses does a committee need? Which classes of workers do we include, and in what proportions? Do we seek out clinically essential people from the shop floor, such as respiratory therapists who deal with many of the patients whose right-to-die questions vex modern medicine? What of patient representation? Is it necessary or somehow beside the point? Is community participation as (symbolically) necessary here as it is with IRBs, or do the different missions of the two bodies signal different needs with regard to input by nonhospital personnel? This multitude of questions is not an idle listing of potential problems. Membership indicates who can speak and whose opinions are counted or discounted. Membership may determine even which issues are seen as legitimate ethical concerns and which are not. After all, both Renée Anspach (1993) and Daniel Chambliss (1996) have argued that a great many issues interpreted as ethical problems are merely structural disagreements among workers unequal in power, in different ranks, with different core tasks, and with disparate role-bound moralities. In this view, the label *ethical* legitimates a disagreement that the organizational actor with greater rank and authority could otherwise dismiss. To sharpen this point, we note that ethical problems within hospitalized care have arisen coincident in time with greater militancy among nurses to have their professional authority and expertise acknowledged. So, saying that a hospital has an ethics committee tells us very little unless we know as well who serves on the committee and under what authority.

Authority for and of consultation. It is worth recalling that part of the rationale of the Quinlan court's advocacy for ethics committees was to create an alternative arena, besides the courts, for resolving these dilemmas. To the extent that IECs are seen as carrying the authority of quasi-legal bodies, substituting for more formal (and expensive) procedures in the judicial system, one needs to worry about two probable consequences. First, as noted previously, invocations of "the law" in medical contexts tend to preempt more wide-ranging considerations, specifically those of moral import, which of course leads to missing the point of almost any kind of CEC. Thus, having an underlying legal motive for consultation both gives the process more clout than it might otherwise have and undermines the substantive ethics discourse. Second, as some have noted (Lo 1987; Fleetwood and Unger 1994), committee processes in hospitals typically do not entail the procedural safeguards—*due process* to use the legal system's term—that formal court proceedings typically include (see later).

But again, the social ramifications of authorizing IEC intervention are complex. The IEC can become, intentionally or otherwise, a mechanism for "cooling the mark out," just as an IRB can be (Levine 1983). Patients and their families now have another layer between them and a public complaint should they and their caregivers have a disagreement about what constitutes appropriate treatment. Thus, IECs may keep cases out of court, but this is not necessarily the same as having autonomy respected, ethical action ensured, or justice done. IECs may actually make it easier for physicians to override the wishes of patients and their families. A division of labor occurs: Hospital physicians can focus on technical matters and take care of the patient's physiological demands; everything else can be "reduced" to ethics by physicians uncomfortable or ill equipped to deal with interpersonal or moral subtleties and then turfed to a specialized committee.[5] A couple of examples have been published by one group. Each case involved a child who physicians felt had received "enough" treatment. In the first instance, physicians concluded that it would not be appropriate to again use intensive care for a profoundly mentally disabled child with seizures and recurrent pneumonia (Paris et al. 1990). The child's mother disagreed and requested mechanical ventilation and other therapy that would sustain the child's life. The physicians took the case to the IEC, which supported and agreed to back them and the institution in a court action. In the second instance, a child had developed severe acute respiratory failure and failed conventional therapy (Paris et al. 1993). The physicians agreed to a trial of extracorporeal membrane oxygenation (ECMO) as a last-ditch effort to permit recovery. However, as they embarked on the use of ECMO, they told the family that the treatment would be time limited. As the allotted time expired, not only without lung recovery but with other organ system failure developing as well, the family requested that ECMO be continued. Again, the physicians took the case to the IEC, claiming they had no obligation to provide "futile" treatment. The IEC again supported the physicians. If one can get beyond what is the "right" thing to do in these cases, it is not difficult to see how one could view them as instances where a powerful group of (mostly) professionals, the IEC, simply chose to support one value system (invested in efficient use of medical resources and a particular view of the quality of life) over another (invested in the value of biological human life itself and the particular lives of the unfortunate children, regardless of their mental state) held by those with much less institutional and social power, families of patients.

Procedures for organizing consultations.   As we have already noted, keeping ethics cases in an IEC and out of the court also means giving up the legal system's elaborate protections for aggrieved parties. Committees are not bound to use specific rationales to arrive at decisions, need not observe any particular rules of evidence, nor need to announce or justify their decisions in any detail. Of course, we have no empirical evidence that such a lack of rules matters, and there are, naturally, advantages to hospital-based, rather than judicial, procedures. An IEC (or individual consultant) may have the ability to be sensitive to situational nuance, to act swiftly, and to bring to bear clinical experience that judges lack; committees can be informal, nonintimidating, and flexible. These qualities, if realized, do seem to suggest IECs can be a good substitute for moving into the courts.

But, as long as IECs operate behind closed doors, as Bernard Lo (1987) has pointed out, there is no way to tell whether they provide concrete advantages over more accountable processes, like those in the court system. In a very peculiar way, IECs reverse a trend in contemporary U.S. society toward more open systems with greater equality at the very same time that they seem to instantiate them. The very absence of any procedural standards makes it very difficult for outsiders to know how to evaluate the claim that the decision reached in a given case was endorsed by the IEC.

Individual ethics committees may or may not be clear on any of the following issues: who has the right to initiate a CEC; who has the right to appear before an ethics committee engaged in a consultation; how the group arrives at its decisions; how decisions are communicated (orally, in writing, in the medical record) and to whom (professionals only, patients and families as well as professionals). Not only are the internal workings of the ethics committee vexed, there are similarly tangled issues of the committee's relation to the hospital and larger environment.

Other issues include but are not limited to the confidentiality of deliberation—are committee findings and recommendations discoverable in malpractice actions? In addition, one can ask how proactive versus how reactive should committees be. That is, should all cases of a certain type receive prospective oversight or retrospective oversight, or should the IEC become involved in a case only when asked to comment on a specific concern. The Baby Doe law and regulations raise this issue fairly starkly. Should every neonatal case in which physicians and/or families considered forgoing treatment be brought to an infant care review committee? Perhaps IEC investigation should occur only with those cases typically thought of in terms of "handicapping conditions," such as those involving chromosomal abnormalities like Down syndrome (trisomy 21), or recognized clinical associations (syndromes) without a clear genetic basis. In fact, states (the only parties directly affected by the federal law) and hospitals have responded in a wide variety of ways. In some places, IEC involvement is mandated in various types of cases; elsewhere, the IEC only becomes involved if asked by a party in a particular case. In some places, case review is inclusive but only occurs retrospectively—that is, after clinical judgments have been arrived at and a disposition made.

Different modes of committee organization reflect different organizational understandings of what ethics committees are supposed to do and on whose behalf they are supposed to do it. If access to case consultation by a committee is limited only to physicians, or does not allow patient or family testimony, and conveys its opinions through letters to physicians that do not become part of the medical record, this reflects a very different understanding of organizational mission than a process whereby anyone can refer a case, in which all are allowed to give testimony and all recommendations appear as a note in the hospital chart. Herein lies a major problem. If ethics committees increase legal liability by revealing disputes about the proper standard of care, then we might expect that use of them would be at best reluctant. On the other hand, when heeding the recommendations of committees is optional, members may well ask what the point of committee involvement might be. The proper balance between consent and coercion has yet to be found. It is one thing to put ethics committees in place; it is clearly quite another to ensure that they are taken seriously.

By Individual Consultant

The general concerns about consultation by committee also apply to consultations by individuals (or small teams of committee members). We can consider qualifications rather than membership, as well as matters of authority for consultation and the procedures to be followed.

Qualifications. As previously stated, precisely who qualifies as a consultant has by no means been settled. The necessary background, in terms of formal education or mastery of a body of knowledge and set of skills, remains controversial. Looking beyond formal characteristics of the consultant, of course, we should not ignore social status. There are in this area, as with other aspects of the actual doing of clinical ethics, few data to help us understand, for example, whether physician-ethicists versus nurse-ethicists versus philosopher-ethicists versus lawyer-ethicists (and so on) are especially "successful" (never mind how one might try to determine that) in helping resolve ethics disputes or in educating the public or institutional staff members about major issues in health care ethics. One can reasonably infer from the literature on consultation (as we do from our own experience, see Frader 1992) that physicians prefer to deal with physician-ethicists and nurses favor nurse-ethicists or specially organized nursing ethics committees. What this means—that is, whether it represents more than occupational solidarity or simply suggests that occupationally similar consultants communicate best with those with matching backgrounds—remains unclear. Skepticism about the inherent superiority (however defined) of one sort of consultant over another seems in order.

Authority.   Regarding the authority of consultants to do their work, the issues may be somewhat more sharply focused than with a committee. After all, one of the advantages of having a committee is the opportunity to diffuse responsibility across statuses, across occupations, and sometimes across employers (that is, some on the IEC work for themselves, others for the hospital, others for a university, others may not be employed at all). If all the ethical weight of a situation falls on a single individual, how much more need we be concerned about whether that person reports directly to an administrator, an ethics committee, or some sort of clinical authority? Does it matter if the consultant is compensated by the hospital or through his or her faculty position at the affiliated university? Does it matter if the consultative activity results in a charge to the patient? These questions raise an additional level of concern, beyond the institutional bylaws or state legislation or regulations that support consultative activity, about agency. If the consultant is salaried by the hospital or the hospital pays for his or her "piece-work," it seems legitimate to ask about the consultants' loyalties, as we would ask about the participation of hospital legal counsel on the ethics committee. There is an assumption in much of the CEC literature that consultants are "patient advocates," a mantle claimed by just about everyone these days, but the basis for that role seems both ideologically and structurally unclear in most instances.

Procedures.   Rather than asking various parties to appear before a committee in a hearing-like setting, typically individual consultants or small teams go to the clinical setting to meet with interested parties. Assuming this is possible in a place ensuring reasonable privacy, it may offer a sociological and political advantage of, at least, appearing to accommodate to the needs of those directly involved. But there is, of course, a prior set of questions. Who will the consultant seek out, and how will the consult approach such individuals? If the person or persons requesting consultation has qualms about the reaction of others, especially the attending physician, the requestor(s) may not want to discuss the consultation directly and openly. Most institutions require that the attending physician be notified of a CEC involving her or his patient, and some institutions still require attending physician approval/acceptance of the consultation. But that doesn't settle the question of *who* should notify attendings and whether the identity of the requestor must be disclosed.

These tensions also involve other aspects of consultative process. If, as is often the case, it appears that disputes can be managed by better communication among the involved parties and that a meeting or meetings of such individuals could be helpful, the consultant has to help overcome fears and other resistance to getting people together and then manage or mediate the discussion session. No matter what else, such procedures differ substantially from the quasi-judicial process often invoked in consultation by IECs, clearly call for different skills by those charged to lead in the matter, and have different sorts of implications for institutional social interaction during and after a consultation.

SOCIOLOGICAL INTEREST IN ETHICS CONSULTATION

Two features of CEC are immediately interesting.[6] First is the relative neglect of this development by sociologists. For some time now, sociologists have written critically of how health care professionals have used their expertise to narrow patient's options, disattend patient or family preferences, and in general overwhelm the will of sick persons and their loved ones. Unfortunately, the medical practice that we essentialize in this manner may not accurately reflect the current world of hospital practice. Little attention has been paid to whether changes in recent years—like the use of ethics committees and consulting ethicists and new legal rules (for example, the Patient Self-Determination Act, PSDA), which in theory provide a more muscular version of informed consent regarding such things as do-not-resuscitate orders—alter the traditional conception of the dominant professional and the compliant patient.[7]

There has been a remarkable increase in what might be termed the *epidemiology of ethics*—health services–type research conducted about the impact, if any, of advance medical directives, in accord with the PSDA or hospital policy, and whether the preferences of elderly or dying patients for end-of-life care are known or used by health care professionals or potential surrogates (Uhlmann et al. 1988; Zweibel and Cassel 1989; McCrary and Botkin 1989; Tomlinson et al. 1990; Danis et al. 1991; Sehgal et al. 1992; Stelter et al. 1992; Hare et al. 1992). There have also been surveys of "users" of CEC that address satisfaction with the process (La Puma 1987; La Puma et al. 1988; Perkins and Saathoff 1988; La Puma et al. 1992; McClung et al. 1996). Regrettably, none of this research ought properly be called sociological. The empirical studies typically have been done by insiders who are often some of the same individuals who lobbied for or against the policy changes and/or implemented them. The sociological studies that have looked at how ethics enter the world of the hospital bedside all precede the institutionalization of the ethics function in roles or committees (for examples, see Zussman 1992, Anspach 1993, Fox and Swazey 1992, Bosk 1992; for a general discussion of these works and the relation of ethnographies of medical practice and bioethics, see Chambliss 1996, Frank 1995, Crigger 1995, or DeVries 1995).[8]

The absence of research here is particularly noteworthy in light of the joint commission regulations that, as we have noted, spurred the development of IECs. The fact that those regulations require only that hospitals have in place a "process" for dispute resolution surely created a situation where the variety of responses might shed some interesting light on the relationship between institutional structure and mission and the way institutions "handle" ethics. This lack of empirical attention is all the more surprising given the penchant of sociology to investigate the unintended consequences of planned social change and the divergence of organizational blueprints from everyday operations.

In addition, the process by which a new professional segment achieves legitimacy, successfully claims turf, and defines its domain of competence is of continuing interest to students of the professions.[9] Alternatively, the competition between scientific-technological rationales for action and humanistic models informed by philosophic or religious systems is fundamental to sociologists of culture, as is the construction of ethical authority. After all, there is little gainsaying that as a formal organizational actor in the modern hospital, the professional ethicist, whether in the guise of ethics committee or individual consultant, is a rather recently created role, the very existence of which challenges some of the clinical power and authority assumed by the attending physician in the context of the physician-patient relationship.

At the same time, the sociological literature suggests that the ethical authority these new actors claim to have is a poor substitute for the authority of science. Historically, moral authority is a type presumptively in retreat in a technologically complex, bureaucratic, and secular world. Why is it reappearing now, especially in that most modern of postmodern organizations—the tertiary care medical center? There is an empirical puzzle here that embarrasses our theories. So what is going on? How did this new (yet very old-fashioned looking) form of power and authority arise? Who are these "beeper" ethicists at the bedside, and why do others seek their advice? At the very least, the rationales by which authority is claimed, the domains in which these claims are accepted, and those in which it is resisted deserve our attention.

No better topic would seem to exist for looking at these issues than the institutionalization of ethical consultation. Here individual experts or committees either invade or are invited into the private space of the physician-patient relationship to discuss what course of action best satisfies the demands of morality as well as the question of how well—if at all—the demands of morality, professional customs and standards, and legal requirements can be harmonized. Phrasing the issue this way, of course, poses a problem. In writing of ethical consultation in problematic circumstances, or of bioethics more generally, there is a tendency to write as if all ethical problems are the result of conflict between physician and patient over what is the proper course of action. It is a convenient shorthand to write this way. The empirical world is of course more complex. Some conflicts and their attendant requests for consultation are intraprofessional—different specialty groups of physicians disagree among themselves about what proper action is; some are intrafamilial—brothers and sisters, children and parents argue over the bedside about who knows best what the patient, now unable to articulate a preference, really wanted; some are inter-professional—professional actors (for example, doctors and nurses) each with their own definition of professional mission disagree. Ethical disputes in the hospital do not even require two parties locked in a disagreement. A single individual, uncertain about the course of action, may clearly see the branches of the decision tree, feel lost in the ethical forest, and then request a consultation. Here there is a meeting for resolving conflict, but the conflict is intrapsychic. Finally it is worth noting that more than a few ethical troubles are created because the three spheres of morality, professional custom, and law are in conflict with one another.

So, whether for its theoretic or empirical attractions, one would think sociologists would be tripping all over themselves either explaining how ethical authority is socially constructed or superintending its deconstruction. One would think, to borrow David Rothman's evocative phrase, that we would insert ourselves and our analytic capabilities among all those other "strangers at the bedside." This has not happened.[10]

Perhaps because it has not, what empirical literature we have on IECs and their consultation function or the activities of individual consultants comes largely from those involved in their implementation. This literature stresses that most of those who have used consultative services have found the experience helpful, were satisfied with the results, and would request consultation again.[11] Of course, this does not tell us anything about the content of these consultations, the cases where consultation was appropriate but resisted (that is, satisfaction may be an artifact of self-selection) or even what exactly it was that created a "satisfying" consultation or "helpful" advice. The banality of this literature, which mimics social science in method and interpretation, is startling until one realizes that this is more an exhortatory than an informational literature. It exists to underscore that ethics committees are effective, deserve institutional resources, improve the quality of care, serve physician interests, and threaten no one. And all this may be so, but it would be nice to have some sociological discussion of the phenomenon.

SOCIOLOGICALLY, ETHICS CONSULTATION MAY NOT BE SUCH A GOOD IDEA[12]

Until we have better data, we need to think about CEC theoretically. When we do so, a number of issues appear. All of them point to the inappropriateness of using IECs for ethical consultation. (Most of these remarks apply to individual ethics consultants as well, depending of course on the details of who is doing the consultation. To the extent that individual consultants are fellow clinicians, nurses, or physicians from within the organization, only the lack of a committee meeting itself makes any difference.) What is surprising is that whereas almost all these objections have been raised, occasionally forcefully, they have not been taken more seriously, and more has not been done either to see if the potential dangers occur or to guard against them. All speak to the difficulty of receiving an unbiased, independent reading of a case that is situated within an ongoing organizational context. (Of course, this assumes that what one wants is unbiased and independent and further suggests that medical consultations, such as those done by hematologists or infectious-disease subspecialists have this quality. Both assumptions can be questioned.) The very fact that some of these difficulties are both obvious and public yet disattended raises questions about whose interests IECs are designed to serve.

First, members of IECs, like members of most committees in most formal organizations, will have other roles to play in the organization. In most cases, these other roles are more important than voluntary committee service, which is more often than not uncompensated and unrewarding. Just because work is uncompensated and unrewarded does not mean workers will be slipshod. The fact that institutions can get their members to take on such thankless tasks seriously and work so hard at them is somewhat mysterious to us, all the more so when we are the ones donating the effort, losing the sleep, and struggling with issues that are unlikely to make us friends. Yet since IECs depend to a certain extent on exploited labor, the question always hangs in the air: How much effort is this worth? What is the personal price individuals are willing to pay to gear their ethical convictions into the world of cases that do not involve their patients?

With IECs, institutions can play upon the fact that those who toil in them with an interest in ethics are in the position of missionaries—they are bringing the word to colleagues who have not yet received it. Their own critique of care and their own sense of what is needed commits them to their work. The hospital, greedy organization that it is, can play upon these commitments and receive in turn a tremendous amount of unpaid labor. And here may lay the rub. As long as much of the labor is unpaid, it is devalued. Yet if the organization somehow were compelled to pay for the labor, it might decide it did not need it after all, but thank you anyway.

So ethicist is a role added to a primary-role system, which itself is coming under scrutiny to be more productive. In those other, more primary roles, committee members are likely to have dealings with the same colleagues whose ethical problems are now before them. In most situations, this is not a problem. Physicians understand that an ethics case consultation is not a trial, for they themselves may have initiated the consultation. Mature professionals recognize the difference between receiving advice and being judged.

Yet case consultations are not abstract affairs—they are not about words on a page or concepts in the abstract; they involve people in what is often a very closed world. Questions meant innocently to elicit information can bruise egos. Recommendations meant to resolve a stalemate can appear as an insult to one's judgment. The very fact that a dispute has reached an impasse such that those involved in it need avail themselves of a formally established procedure for dispute resolution can in itself be seen as an indictment of one's competence in the clinical arts or, worse, that one's behavior is seen by some as "unethical" and therefore a potential source of embarrassment. So, in the closed world of the tertiary care hospital, a world in which committee members may have very complex relations with those colleagues on whose case they are now consulting, an independent judgment unpolluted by all the other connections among co-workers in the organization should not be a taken-for-granted outcome. This one may be junior to that one and dependent on him or her for referrals. Or this one may be a rival with that one and wish for nothing so much as an occasion for public embarrassment. Committee members may have a variety of complex relations—friends, competitors, professional collaborators. In a word, they are colleagues. And when this consultation is over, when service on the committee is ended, they will continue to be colleagues coexisting in the same workspace.

The work of ethics committees then depends on individuals placed in dual relationships. This is of course true of other oversight committees in academic institutions, but it is a defect in them as well. Dual relationships are recognized by many professional codes of ethics as improper and banned. Committee members can recuse themselves if in their judgment the dual relationship poses a problem, but this places the burden on the individual member. It does not recognize how a complex structure of ongoing work relationships embeds the consultations of the hospital ethics committee in a continuous web of social interaction, most of which has nothing to do with this consultation but might be deeply affected by its outcome.[13]

If the image of the dual relationship seems overdrawn, perhaps we can appropriate another analogy to make the same point. In their fashion, ethics committee members are in a structural position similar to that of floor managers in industry.[14] The ethical standards and legal requirements for action can be thought of as management directives. The impasses, disputes, quandaries, and questions that come to committees for consultation can be thought of as problems on the line. The floor manager's job is to apply management's directives to line workers. This is not done without significant tension, compromise, and heartache, according to the ethnographers of the industrial workplace. Like the floor managers, members of the IEC are in the middle, subject to various and multitudinous forces—the pushes and pulls, strains and squeezes—which make it so hard to steer between the rocks and hard places of social life. It may also be the case that the farther members of IECs are from the everyday work of the hospital shop floor, the more devalued their consultative advice, suggestions, and recommendations are—just as industrial floor managers find their influence with workers wanes the closer they get to management. Moreover, just as floor managers are seen as ineffectual allies by workers when they are too distant from management to affect its directives, so may IEC members seem ineffective to those with whom they consult since committee members are constrained by legal rules and moral customs and are relatively powerless to change them. Further, to the degree their advice appears to suggest change in the handling of the case, they may, like floor managers who are punctilious about management's rules, be perceived as meddlers who do not have the interests of the workers at heart.

And, of course, suspicions and bad feelings may run in the other direction as well. In fact, they are much more likely to run that way. Behind almost every ethical problem that requires consultation, there is also a tangled social situation. Whether it involves the conflict of patients' families among themselves or with staff, or of staff among themselves, the kinds of situations that beget consultations are stressful.[15] In fact, if one just looks at those areas where health care is most problematic, it is hard to see how it could be otherwise. In many situations, consultation is a signal of a process stymied either by conflicted wills or deep moral qualms. In cases where families have conflict within themselves or with staff, there is bound to be some distrust of the hospital and its staff. Beyond that, the members of the ethics committee are likely to be strangers to families but not to hospital staff. There may be the sense that the consultation is just a charade to uphold the rationales, logic, and action that the family has had such problems with anyway. Procedurally, neither informality nor formality is likely to calm fears about fairness. Informality may lead to a sense of not being taken seriously, whereas formality can be seen to stack the deck in favor of organizational insiders who know the institution's ways. The point here is that if family members are allowed to present their story (some ethics committees do not allow this), when they look around the room they will see people who dress like, sound like, and look like the other staff who have given them such trouble. In such circumstances they may not feel like they have been given a fair hearing.[16]

Such feelings do indeed point to a real problem with CEC—how does the consultant or committee provide a hearing within the walls of the organization, yet provide and appear to provide an independent and even-handed reading of the situation?[17] This appearance of fairness is further compromised when CECs concern matters that have some bearing on the hospital and its standing. For example, in the late 1980s, surgeons at the University of Chicago began considering liver transplantation in children, using lobes from a living donor (the child's parent). The impetus was the shortage of cadaveric organs and the recognition that as many as a third of patients awaiting a liver die before an organ becomes available. This was the first such undertaking in the United States. Ethicists at the university began meeting with the involved surgeons and developed a proposal subsequently submitted to and accepted by the institution's IRB. The group displayed its reasoning in a report (Singer et al. 1989) that received widespread attention. A similar situation involved the University of Pittsburgh and its attempt to develop additional organ sources through the use of non–heart beating (that is, non–brain dead) organ donors (Frader 1993).

There was nothing egregiously wrong with the procedures or the justifications given by the committees approving them. Neither is at issue. Rather, the problem is the propriety of a committee ruling on a procedure in which so much is at stake institutionally. In cases of innovative medical action, where so much publicity is generated from being first, is there not tremendous pressure on organization members not to stand in the way? If all the boats rise with the tide, if organizational prestige is transferable to members of that organization, then there is something unrealistic about asking committee members to be the ethical arbiters of innovation. This is all the more so in tertiary care hospitals with their emphasis on research, innovations, and the clinical frontier.

In addition, the same point may cut the other way. Just as committee members may be chary of acting to slow innovation that promotes the good name of the institution, we may expect them to be equally chary of situations that could bring negative publicity to the institution. So, in cases where the chance of media spectacle is high and where attending physicians have decided that this game is not worth the candle, ethics committees may agree. Life is short. Committee members have other, more weighty responsibilities. The path of least resistance in such cases might be particularly attractive. How often consideration of the organization's good name comes into play is an empirical question, as are questions of how often such considerations skew decision making. Frequencies may be less important here than appearance. What is critical is that given their stake in the organization, ethics consultants and committee members have difficulty in making the claim that they are disinterested in that good name.

An additional problem presents itself when hospitals have very specific missions, besides the more general one of providing health care. For example, when hospitals are affiliated with religious communities, do IECs and consultants then have the additional responsibility of framing their reasoning in terms consistent with that religion's ethical standards? Are the ethics of a Catholic or Jewish hospital different from those of the larger, multicultural, pluralistic society of which they are a part (Loewy 1994)? If so, how far should these ethics apply to patients who are not members of the faithful? In public hospitals, what role do distributional questions play in weighing individual cases? In proprietary hospitals, are there specific obligations to consider shareholders' profits? In general, this may be seen as a problem of deciding how "universal" versus how "particularistic" CECs are intended to be. Denying the legitimacy of particularism seems an infringement on the prerogatives of individual organizations to chart their own destiny. Accepting it seems to deny patients the autonomy that CECs are intended to protect. On the other hand, affirming universalism appears to pretend an ethical certainty that we do not possess. Denying it accepts arbitrary choices and impositions of power that CECs would seem charged to avoid.

Finally, as Joel Frader (1992) has pointed out, there is something rather sociologically and politically naive in assuming that a committee ensures a decision representative of the community's will. The power inequities that characterize decision making outside the committee do not disappear simply by forming a committee. There is no guarantee that the more senior, the more powerful in the committee (or in the often less structured process used by individual consultants), will not dominate decision making. That is, disinterested decision making may be hostage to multiple considerations extraneous to the ethics of the case. Nurses may be dominated by physicians. Assistant professors may feel hostage to senior colleagues. This, like so many of the issues we have raised, is an empirical question; and like so many of the difficulties we have raised, it requires data before any judgment can be made.

CONCLUSION

As critics of health care, social scientists are a notoriously hard lot to please. For years they criticized mental hospitals as repressive places that stripped patients of their dignity, social identity, and civil rights while providing precious little in the way of therapy (see Goffman 1961 for the classic statement). When, partly in response to this critique, patients were deinstitutionalized, the critique was turned on its head, and social scientists found that patients in the community were degraded by the poor conditions in which they lived, harmed by overmedication, and deprived of dignity, social worth, and autonomy.

For years social scientists critiqued a fee-for-service system that was said to provide powerful incentives for unnecessary treatment, to create fee barriers limiting access to necessary care, and to undermine the professional integrity of physicians overly aware of their economic self-interest (see Freidson 1970 for the classic statement). Now, when, in part as a response to this critique, managed-care regimes have been instituted, we have turned this critique on its head. Prepaid capitated health care is said to discourage needed services, to create barriers of access because of the reluctance to enroll those who are in less than perfect health or have actuarial risks, and to undermine the professional integrity of physicians overly aware of their self-interest (Rodwin 1993 provides a useful overview).

For years social scientists critiqued physicians for their policies of information control. Physicians were said to control tightly what information was passed to patients, to magnify clinical uncertainty, and in general to limit autonomy by preventing patients and their family access to necessary information (Quint 1967; Davis 1963; Glaser and Strauss 1965, 1967, 1968; Strauss 1970). Often such policies were justified as a way of minimizing the emotional distress associated with illness. In operation they were said to frustrate patients' ability to provide informed consent for treatment. With more muscular notions of patients' rights and informed consent, physicians' practices changed. Now they were criticized for overwhelming patients with technical information, not providing enough emotional support to patients, and limiting their role responsibilities to the narrowest possible technical domain. No sooner than the suggestions of critics of health care are implemented, then those same critics carp at the unintended consequences of the planned social change. Under such conditions we might expect that those who, with the best of intentions, try to improve the quality of health care through ethics consultation may experience substantial frustration.

We have identified the sociological currents that run through CECs—the next step is for social scientists to begin watching CECs work, attending to these sociological dimensions. Only then will we discover how CECs extend, limit, or otherwise redirect medical power.

NOTES

1. This is not the place to assess how well IRBs have succeeded at the tasks assigned them. Suffice it to say that, almost simultaneously with the establishment of federal standards, there was the establishment of a research literature that looked critically at the operation of IRBs. Early examples included Barber et al. (1973) and Gray (1975). It is worth noting that there has been little addition to that literature since those early days. We really don't have much idea whether contemporary IRBs in fact do what they were set up to accomplish.

At the same time, to document compliance with federal regulations, the administrative functions of both hospital and university research needed to be expanded. This was matched by the formation and growth of the federal Office for the Protection from Research Risk (OPRR) to oversee the IRB function and a similar office in the Food and Drug Administration to oversee that agency's rules about the investigation of drugs and devices. In 1979 a nongovernmental agency, the Hastings Center, introduced *IRB*, a journal that serves as a forum for the discussion of intellectual and administrative issues regarding human research subjects.

2. A recent treatise by Moreno (1995), a philosopher, on efforts to achieve consensus in bioethics provides a more comprehensive, if also idiosyncratic, historical account of the rise of ethics committees. Moreno notes that committees, beginning in the 1920s and 1930s, often deliberated on which mentally handicapped persons would have sterilization procedures. Somewhat later, small committees stood in judgment over which women would have abortions prior to the *Roe* v. *Wade* decision by the U.S. Supreme Court.

3. When asking CLB to serve on this panel, whose official title is the SHHV-SBC Task Force on Standards for Bioethics Consultation, the task force co-director who issued the invitation made it clear that it was CLB's lack of involvement in and knowledge about ethics consultation that made him an attractive potential member. The co-director was looking for an "outsider who knew something about professionalization." Given that so many fit this description, CLB was flattered to be asked. It should probably be mentioned as well that the other of us (JF), though not a task force member, drafted the original submission to the foundation pointing out the need for such a panel.

4. A peculiar feature of this point is that it is valid, even though as we will argue in the text, it is difficult to specify exactly what the content of that expertise is or what the nature of those skills are. In any case, it is not so clear that the purpose of the hospital ethics committee is to provide an expert opinion. When opinions are called for, when advice is sought, its expertness in these cases might not be its most important quality. Again, we will deal with this point in the text as well.

5. Anspach (1993) has pointed out how physicians psychologize dissent among the families of children in neonatal intensive care units. Parents who disagree—rather than being seen as having their reasons, their values, and their life-plans—are seen as disturbed, subjects for psychological services. Bosk (1992) found that genetic counselors were used in much the same way. Emotional and ethical work were split off from the more technical aspects of doctoring. This work was then turfed to genetic counselors. But Anspach and Bosk both did their fieldwork before the current institutionalization of ethics in the hospital. We are suggesting that the ethics committee may now be used in much the same way.

6. Many of these points apply to ethics consultation when done by individuals in the role of ethicist, as well as when they are functioning in committees. Others—those specifically about committee dynamics—do not.

7. Our caution here refers primarily to recently published results of the SUPPORT project. That research carefully documented the lack of impact on end-of-life medical decisions in tertiary intensive care units despite detailed feedback to clinicians about the preferences and experience, especially pain and suffering, of the critically ill patients.

8. As noted before, there is an interesting contrast here to the response of sociologists to informed consent regulations. Here researchers first documented processes that made the case for

fuller communication and then began almost immediately looking at the impact of new regulations. We might wonder why one change generated a response among researchers while the other did not.

9. This point is worth belaboring with some theory. The process is sociologically interesting whichever metaphorical perspective one adopts for looking at professionals. Whether describing a Hughesian "struggle for license and mandate"; a Bucherian and Straussian "shared community of identity and fate"; a Sarfitti–Larsonian "project"; a Parsonsian adoption of "fiduciary responsibility"; an Abbotian "jurisdictional struggle"; or a Freidsonian "professional dominance"—the empirical phenomenon of a new area of responsibility in partly the same old and partly new hands is a phenomenon of intrinsic empirical interest. The fact that one both so visible and so adaptable to one's favorite propositions about professions is at the same time so ignored is difficult to explain.

10. We will not speculate much here about why this has not occurred, however tempted we are. We cannot resist the opportunity to suggest that one reason for our lack of interest may itself be a latent consequence of a sociological tendency to think in terms of the manifest and the latent. Actually, these days we use other terms not so loaded with the connotations of a discarded functionalism. We write of the implicit and the explicit, the tacit and the taken for granted, the public and the private, the revealed and the hidden, the surface and the deep structure, the *parole* and the *langue*—whatever. However we label the dichotomy, the underlying conceptual operations are the same—scratch surface explanations deep enough and we find self-interest. It may be that we sociologists have not looked at the new occupation of ethicist and the new practices of ethical consultation because we are already certain of their meaning—they are and can be nothing more than an attempt to preserve professional power by internalizing a critique and thereby disarming it. In this line of thinking, IECs are simply a way of silencing resistance and challenges to medical authority by taking charge of the dispute process and professionalizing it. In this light, it is again worth noting the number of physician-ethicists who claim that medical ethicists who consult must also be physicians.

11. It is worth noting here that in another context, Wertz, Sorenson, and Heeren (1988) were puzzled by their inability to discover any dissatisfaction in patient surveys of genetic counselors. It may be that dissatisfaction is hard to elicit—although this is a conclusion that rings false to us, subjected as we are to regular student evaluations. An alternative explanation is that satisfaction or dissatisfaction is relative to expectations. So, if expectations are sufficiently negative and if nothing untoward results, then users of a service may report satisfaction. The point to be stressed is that satisfaction does not stand alone with some pristine meaning. Rather, we need to know as well why an encounter was satisfying and what was satisfying about it. For example, we are satisfied with our dentist every time we go and do not need a root canal. This satisfaction has little to do with the service rendered and is clearly inappropriate as a proxy measure for that service's quality.

12. It is only fair to inform the reader that one of the authors (JF) actually engages in the practice of clinical ethics consultation and has been a member of the board of directors of the national organization promoting such activity. The reader will have to decide if or how this confuses the picture sketched herein.

13. One might object that this is really an empirical, not a theoretical, point. Rather than cast general aspersions, we should give specific examples. Of course, specific examples require just that kind of research that we argued is so necessary. Our own experience in academic environments suggests that it is possible for other agendas to temper ethical commitments, to avoid confrontation, or to build alliances and trust.

14. Right here we are engaging in a rather straightforward Hughesian analysis of the workplace, trying to find the dilemmas of high-status work in a less exalted workplace.

15. Once again, we must note that there is a tendency to think about ethics problems as representing conflict, an inability of the parties involved to reach a moral consensus. Though convenient, such language obscures that even when there is agreement among the parties, even when they have reached consensus, an ethics consult may be needed. The parties may need to reassure each other that what they wish today is both morally acceptable and socially feasible. The image of moral conflict among the parties has the defect of suggesting that one is right (and hence ethical and moral) while the other is wrong (and hence, at least in this instance, a moral reprobate). It ignores the way ethical conflict involves opposing rights that then need to be balanced, mediated, or compromised. A second problem of the notion of ethical conflict with resolution by committee deliberation is that it reinforces an adversarial, judicial perspective and a language of rights. Neither is the only way nor may either be the best way to think about ethical issues. Finally, an image of ethics prob-

lems as conflict on the shop floor overlooks how much that parties agree to may be nonetheless ethically problematic.

Two interrelated phenomena are at work in the conflict imagery. First, there is a tendency to ethicize problems related to social structure. This transforms issues of power and authority—and more recently, economics—into issues of principle—generally, autonomy, beneficence, nonmalfeasance, and justice. This is a particularly effective strategy for those with lesser power. It is a strategy of empowerment that helps level the playing field.

Second, once structural problems have been turned into ethical problems, there is a social tendency to turn them into legal ones. This move places an emphasis on contending parties, formal rules of procedure (including what things to count as evidence for propositions), and then justifications for action in terms of principles. The emphasis here becomes not just this case but all cases that could arise in the future and would be like this case. The legalism may be extremely ad hoc—that is, difficult consultations create the need for procedures that may fall into disuse until the next difficult or controversial case, at which point the procedures may be revised.

16. What is at issue here is not the actual fairness or the reasonableness of consultative advice (if in fact such advice and recommendations are even communicated to families). Both may be impeccable, as may be the motivations and intent of committee members. What is at issue is, when those from lay culture contend with those from the professional culture of the hospital, nothing short of total acquiescence of those in authority can convince the family that they really were taken seriously.

17. We have here used the circumlocution "provide and appear to provide" since both are so important to the appearance of justice. We have no doubt that committees make their best efforts to render the best judgments possible. But with the growing divide between professional culture and lay culture, with the professionalization of the ethics function, and with the bureaucratization and routinization of ethical conflicts, it seems quite possible that, however just the actual reasoning of committees or consultants, the appearance of justice will be wanting.

REFERENCES

Anspach, Renee R. 1993. *Deciding who lives: Fateful choices in the intensive-care nursery.* Berkeley: University of California Press.

Barber, Bernard, et al. 1973. *Research on human subjects: Problems of social control in medical experimentation.* New York: Sage.

Bloom, Bernard S., and Osler L. Peterson. 1973. End results, cost and productivity of coronary-care units. *New England Journal of Medicine* 288: 72–8.

Bosk, Charles L. 1992. *All God's mistakes: Genetic counseling in a pediatric hospital.* Chicago: University of Chicago Press.

Chambliss, Daniel F. 1993. Is bioethics irrelevant? *Contemporary Sociology* 22(5): 649–52.

———. 1996. *Beyond caring: Hospitals, nurses, and the social organization of ethics.* Chicago: University of Chicago Press.

Cransford, Ronald E., and A. Edward Doudera. 1984. The emergence of institutional ethics committees. *Law Medicine & Health Care* 12(1): 13–20.

Crigger, Bette Jane. 1995. Bioethnography: Fieldwork in the lands of medical ethics. *Medical Anthropology Quarterly,* n.s., 9(3): 400–17.

Danis, Marion, Leslie I. Southerland, Joanne M. Garrett, et al. 1991. A prospective study of advance directives for life-sustaining care. *New England Journal of Medicine* 324: 882–8.

Davis, Fred. 1963. *Passage through crisis: Polio victims and their families.* Indianapolis: Bobbs-Merrill.

DeVries, Raymond G. 1995. Toward a sociology of bioethics. *Qualitative Sociology* 18(1): 119–28.

Duff, Raymond S., and A. G. M. Campbell. 1973. Moral and ethical dilemmas in the special-care nursery. *New England Journal of Medicine* 289(17): 890–4.

Fisher, Bernard, Madeline Bauer, Richard Margolesse, et al. 1985. Five-year results of a randomized clinical trial comparing total mastectomy and segmental mastectomy with or without radiation in the treatment of breast cancer. *New England Journal of Medicine* 312: 665–73.

Fleetwood, Janet E., Robert M. Arnold, and Richard J. Baron. 1989. Giving answers or raising questions? The problematic role of institutional ethics committees. *Journal of Medical Ethics* 15: 137–42.

Fleetwood, Janet, and Stephanie S. Unger. 1994. Institutional ethics committees and the shield of immunity. *Annals of Internal Medicine* 120: 320–5.

Fletcher, John C., Norman Quist, and Albert R. Jonsen. 1989. Ethics consultation in health care: Rationale and history. In *Ethics Consultation in Health Care*, edited by John C. Fletcher, Norman Quist, and Albert R. Jonsen. Ann Arbor, Mich.: Health Administration Press.

Fox, Renée C. 1989. The sociology of bioethics. In *The sociology of medicine: A participant observer's view.* Englewood Cliffs, N.J.: Prentice Hall.

Fox, Renée C., and Judith P. Swazey. 1974. *The courage to fail: A social view of organ transplantation and dialysis.* Chicago: University of Chicago Press.

———. 1992. *Spare parts: Organ replacement in American society.* New York: Oxford University Press.

Frader, Joel E. 1992. Political and interpersonal aspects of ethics consultation. *Theoretical Medicine* 13: 31–44.

———. 1993. Non-heart-beating organ donation: Personal and institutional conflicts of interest. *Kennedy Institute of Ethics Journal* 3(2): 189–98.

Frank, Arthur W. 1995. *The wounded storyteller: Body, illness, and ethics.* Chicago: University of Chicago Press.

Freidson, Eliot. 1970. *Profession of medicine: A study of the sociology of applied knowledge.* New York: Harper & Row.

Glaser, Barney G., and Anselm L. Strauss. 1965. *Awareness of dying.* Chicago: Aldine.

———. 1967. *The discovery of grounded theory; Strategies for qualitative research.* Chicago: Aldine.

———. 1968. *Time for dying.* Chicago: Aldine.

Goffman, Erving. 1961. *Asylums, essays on the social situation of mental patients and other inmates.* Garden City, N.Y.: Anchor Books.

Gray, Bradford H. 1975. *Human subjects in medical experimentation: A sociological study of the conduct and regulation of clinical research.* New York: Wiley.

Hare, Jan, Clara Pratt, and Carrie Nelson. 1992. Agreement between patients and their self-selected surrogates on difficult medical decisions. *Archives of Internal Medicine* 152: 1049–54.

Hess, Orvan W. 1980. Impact of electronic fetal monitoring on obstetric management. *Journal of the American Medical Association* 244: 682–6.

La Puma, John. 1987. Consultations in clinical ethics—issues and questions in 27 cases. *Western Journal of Medicine* 146: 633–7.

La Puma, John, and David L. Schiedermayer. 1991. Ethics consultation: Skills, roles, and training. *Annals of Internal Medicine* 114: 155–60.

La Puma, John, Carol B. Stocking, Marc D. Silverstein, et al. 1988. An ethics consultation service in a teaching hospital: Utilization and evaluation. *Journal of the American Medical Association* 260: 808–11.

La Puma, John, Carol B. Stocking, Cheryl M. Darling, and Mark Siegler. 1992. Community hospital ethics consultation: Evaluation and comparison with a university hospital service. *American Journal of Medicine* 92: 346–51.

Levine, Murray. 1983. IRB review as a "cooling out device." *IRB: A Review of Human Subjects* 5(4): 8–9.

Lo, Bernard. 1987. Behind closed doors: Promises and pitfalls of ethics committees. *New England Journal of Medicine* 317: 46–50.

Loewy, Erich. 1994. Institutional morality, authority, and ethics committees: How far should respect for institutional morality go? *Cambridge Quarterly of Healthcare Ethics* 3(4): 578–84.

McClung, John A., Russel S. Kamer, Margaret DeLuca, and Harlan J. Barber. 1996. Evaluation of a medical ethics consultation service: Opinions of patients and health care providers. *American Journal of Medicine* 100: 456–60.

McCrary, S. Van, and Jeffery R. Botkin. 1989. Hospital policy on advance directives: Do institutions ask patients about living wills? *Journal of the American Medical Association* 262: 2411–4.

Moreno, Jonathan D. 1995. *Deciding together: Bioethics and moral consensus.* New York: Oxford University Press.

Nelson, Karin B., James M. Dambrosia, Tricia Y. Ting, and Judith K. Grether. 1996. Uncertain value of electronic fetal monitoring in predicting cerebral palsy. *New England Journal of Medicine* 334: 613–18.

Paris, John J., Robert K. Crone, and Frank Reardon. 1990. Physicians' refusal of requested treatment: The case of Baby L. *New England Journal of Medicine* 322: 1012–5.

Paris, John J., Michael D. Schreiber, Mindy Statter, et al. 1993. Beyond autonomy—physicians' refusal to use life-prolonging extracorporeal membrane oxygenation. *New England Journal of Medicine* 329: 354–7.

Perkins, Henry S., and Bonnie S. Saathoff. 1988. Impact of medical ethics consultations on physicians: An exploratory study. *American Journal of Medicine* 85: 761–5.

Quint, Jeanne C. 1967. *The nurse and the dying patient.* New York: Macmillan.

Robertson, John A., and Norman Fost. 1976. Passive euthanasia of defective newborns: Legal considerations. *Journal of Pediatrics* 88: 883–7.

Rodwin, Marc A. 1993. *Medicine, money, and morals: Physicians' conflicts of interest.* New York: Oxford University Press.

Ross, Judith Wilson. 1986. *Handbook for hospital ethics committees.* Chicago: American Hospital Publishing.

Rothenberg, Leslie Steven. 1989. Clinical ethicists and hospital ethics consultants: The nature of the "clinical" role. In *Ethics consultation in health care,* edited by John C. Fletcher, Norman Quist, and Albert R. Jonsen. Ann Arbor, Mich.: Health Administration Press.

Scofield, Giles R. 1993. Ethics consultation: The least dangerous profession? *Cambridge Quarterly of Healthcare Ethics* 2: 417–26.

Sehgal, Aswini, Alison Galbraith, Margaret Chesney, et al. 1992. How strictly do dialysis patients want their advance directives followed? *Journal of the American Medical Association* 267: 59–63.

Singer, Peter A., Mark Siegler, Peter F. Whitington, et al. 1989. Ethics of liver transplantation with living donors. *New England Journal of Medicine* 321: 620–2.

Stelter, Keith L., Barbara A. Elliott, and Candace A. Bruno. 1992. Living will completion in older adults. *Archives of Internal Medicine* 152: 954–9.

Strauss, Anselm L., ed. 1970. *Where medicine fails.* Chicago: Aldine.

Teel, Karen. 1975. The physician's dilemma: A doctor's view: What the law should be. *Baylor Law Review* 27 (winter): 6, 8–10.

Tomlinson, Tom, Kenneth Howe, Mark Notman, and Diane Rossmiller. 1990. An empirical study of proxy consent for elderly persons. *Gerontologist* 30: 54–64.

Uhlmann, Richard F., Robert A. Pearlman, and Kevin C. Cain. 1988. Physicians' and spouses' predictions of elderly patients' resuscitation preferences. *Journal of Gerontology* 43: M115–21.

Wertz, Dorothy C., James R. Sorenson, and Timothy C. Heeren. 1988. "Can't get no (dis)satisfaction": Professional satisfaction with professional-client encounters. *Work and Occupations* 15: 36–54.

Zaner, Richard M. 1993. Voices and time: The venture of clinical ethics. *Journal of Medicine and Philosophy* 18: 9–31.

Zussman, Robert. 1992. *Intensive care: Medical ethics and the medical profession.* Chicago: University of Chicago Press.

Zweibel, Nancy R., and Christine K. Cassel. 1989. Treatment choices at the end of life: A comparison of decisions by older patients and their physician-selected proxies. *Gerontologist* 29: 615–21.

CHAPTER SEVEN

The Social Construction of Euthanasia and Medical Ethics in the Netherlands

Rob Houtepen[1]

Most writings on medical ethics assume that everyone knows what it means to discuss a moral issue. Concerning euthanasia, for example, participants in the debate distinguish between moral, medical, and social aspects of the issue. Whether respect for a person's autonomy implies any obligation to assist, upon request, in the shortening of that person's life is discussed as a moral issue. Whether someone's ailment may be deemed to be incurable is considered to be a medical issue. Whether enough resources are available to provide sufficient care for terminal patients is treated as a social issue. Enlightened discussions of euthanasia allow for the interplay of such aspects and include legal and religious considerations (Kimsma and van Leeuwen 1993).

Such distinctions correspond to a division of labor among professional disciplines. Each of the relevant professional disciplines deals with a specific aspect of the problem. Ethicists give solutions for ethical issues, physicians provide us with the medical facts and figures, and political theorists deal with social issues. The contributions of the various disciplines should of course be integrated so that the problem as a whole can be solved in a neat way.

The history of medical ethics shows, however, that it is by no means clear what counts as the moral, medical, or social aspect of a problematic issue. Moreover, it is often unclear which discipline has the authority to speak on ethical issues. To borrow a concept from the sociologist Gusfield, one might say that a number of disciplines share the "ownership" of the problem:

> The ability to create and influence the public definition of a problem is what I refer to as "ownership." . . . At any time in a historical period there is a recognition that specific public issues are the legitimate province of specific persons,

roles, and offices that can command public attention, trust, and influence. They have credibility while others who attempt to capture public attention do not. (Gusfield 1981, 10)

The metaphor of property ownership indicates that ownership is not entirely secure. There is potential competition among professional disciplines for the ownership of a problem. If the balance of power is altered, the definition of the public issue involved will change as well. As long as we remain safely within the confines of the "paradigm" of one professional discipline, we may be sure of the nature of the issue involved and of the kind of arguments relevant to its discussion. In the broader public arena, however, the definition of a problem is a problem in itself, and the force of arguments may be evaluated on grounds that go beyond the disciplines concerned.

In this article the euthanasia debate in the Netherlands is analyzed from this sociological perspective. The focus is on the struggle for the definition of the problem, with an eye on the specific contributions of different disciplines and on their influence over the outcome. I do not restrict myself to an assessment of the relative power and appeal of certain professional groups and perspectives, rather I show that within the process of the development of the debate on euthanasia, the participants themselves evolved. The debate was not confined to the issue of euthanasia. In the end the nature of medical ethics itself was at stake. The question was not merely what the best "solution" would be to the problem of euthanasia, defined as a moral issue. Neither was the issue merely one of the relative force of moral considerations weighed against medicolegal considerations. The debate over euthanasia in the Netherlands was also over the implications of defining euthanasia as a *moral* issue. This is a question regarding the substance of ethics. Thus, at least in the Netherlands, the discipline of medical ethics was substantially changed by the euthanasia debate.

Following Latour (1987), I argue that the dichotomy of facts and values—that is, the medical and the moral aspects of ethical issues in medicine—can be studied as the outcome of a struggle. What counts as a moral argument and what does not is decided by social interaction, not ethics textbooks. The degree to which euthanasia is an ethical issue, or alternatively a sociomedical issue, is open for debate. The nature of bioethics itself is at stake in such debates.

The early years of the Dutch euthanasia debate were selected as a case study for several reasons. The debate was public, and the intensity and continuity of the debate were high. The debate—dynamic in character, especially in its early years—took place in several arenas with different sorts of participants: medicine, politics, religion, law, and philosophy, with the mass media enabling comparisons of different contexts. Key concepts such as autonomy, quality of life, respect for life, and the proper goals of medicine were involved. This period also marks the breakthrough of social involvement with many dimensions of medicine. Physicians were increasingly challenged to account publicly in such matters as ethics, costs, and success. In this period the idea of medical ethics as a distinct branch of the academic enterprise took hold. What the nature of this specific enterprise was, and who were the ones to perform its tasks, were still open questions.

I limited my collection of data in two ways. First, my research ends in 1975. In 1975 the Supreme Court (ruling in the Postma case), the Royal Dutch Society of Physicians (KNMG), and the main advisory body of the government concerning health care issues (*Gezondheidsraad*) had taken largely similar positions in the issue of euthanasia. We know retrospectively that the nature of the debate has not shifted radically since that time.

Second, my aim in this article is not to give a complete reconstruction of the public debate. My focus is on the contributions that could be expected to be involved with the definition of medical ethics. My prime sources have been monographs on euthanasia and medical ethics and all the articles about euthanasia that appeared in medical journals and journals generally discussing ethical, religious, legal, and philosophical issues. The debate among academic professionals is my main focus.

To cover several dimensions of a struggle for the definition of the problem, I ask five questions:

1. What is the definition of the actions involved?
2. Who are considered to be relevant actors?
3. What are considered to be relevant arguments?
4. How is the moral dimension of the issue defined?
5. What are the scope and role attributed to ethics?

Using these questions, we can trace a development in three partially overlapping phases. In the first phase, roughly until 1970, the concept of medical ethics primarily refers to a code of conduct for physicians. The concept of euthanasia refers to a broad category of actions, and euthanasia is debated on a small scale, as an issue that physicians should agree on. In the second phase, from 1969 onward, issues in medical ethics are regarded as social issues. Concerning euthanasia, many alternatives are provided by many participants in a broad debate about how social guidelines should take shape. Under the heading of "ethics," a wide variety of claims is offered, often implying a radical redefinition of the medical profession. The nature of the issues involved and the possible outcome of the debate were essentially contested. From 1973 onward, in the third phase, the question of euthanasia was largely settled in a framework provided by lawyers. This settlement involved a social definition of the responsibilities of the physician toward the patient. This recently developed "ethic of informed consent" functioned as a new, publicly defined code of conduct. Though making them publicly accountable for their actions, it provided physicians with sufficient clarity about their responsibilities and sufficient professional autonomy. The concept of medical ethics acquired two quite distinct meanings. On the one hand, it referred to the content and the vocabulary of the new public rules of conduct for physicians. In this sense of the word, many participants could raise claims and try to influence those public rules. On the other hand, ethics came to refer to a specialized discipline, which addressed questions regarding the margins and the foundation of the public rules, such as the exact nature and the limits of the concept of autonomy. These specialists addressed the "leftovers" from the public debate.

PHYSICIANS IN NEED OF GUIDELINES

In the 1960s, the euthanasia issue and medical ethics were firmly in the hands of physicians. The concept of *medical ethics* referred to a set of specific do's and don'ts for physicians. At the one hundredth anniversary of the Royal Dutch Society of Physicians (KNMG) in 1949, the question of the nature of medical ethics had specifically been stated and firmly answered: It was a code of conduct for physicians (Roelink 1970, 387). This code was recorded in the KNMG manual on "medical ethics and code of conduct" (KNMG 1959). The manual delivered a straightforward answer to the question whether certain actions were allowed. Concerning euthanasia, the guidelines followed the principle of "absolute respect for human life," as outlined by the World Medical Association:

> The meaning of this is that he [the physician] himself may never take a point of view other than aiming to preserve life. He will never for example, for a suffering human being, perform an action which aims to shorten life in order "to his judgment" to limit the suffering. Neither will he be justified to withhold the necessary care for the preservation of life, because he would consider this to result in an augmentation of suffering. (KNMG 1959, 14)

The physician was explicitly forbidden to make any kind of judgment concerning the meaning of suffering or life itself. Desperate patients should be protected against themselves.

A premonition of the turning tide was the keynote lecture by the psychiatrist Rümke at the annual KNMG meeting in 1959. He was asked to speak on the subject "Do we die on time?" (Rümke 1959). Rümke thought the growing concern expressed by this question was a result of new resuscitation techniques and, to a lesser degree, the development of geriatrics. This set a theme that gradually became more prominent in the 1960s: Old principles and rules were challenged by new technological possibilities. In debates in 1959 and 1960, the issue was raised whether stopping or not starting a reanimation procedure should be considered an act of euthanasia, that is, whether it was assisted suicide. Langemeijer, attorney general of the Dutch Supreme Court, argued that stopping the procedures would not fall under the articles of

Dutch law prohibiting euthanasia and assistance to suicide "because such reanimation as a means to restore to a life, that is at all humane, is hopeless" (Langemeijer 1960). He also argued that the law on assisted suicide would not apply in a case of refusal of treatment by a patient, even if "one might consider this [refusal] immoral on solid grounds" (p. 190). The participants in the debate agreed that, in many cases, the personal conscience of the physician would have to be decisive.

In the 1960s, resuscitation remained the occasion to raise issues of medical ethics concerning the prolongation of life and the acceptance of death. A prominent physician, den Otter, noted that many colleagues expressed a need for a new code of medical ethics, offering guidelines to deal with "the problems surrounding the artificial prolongation of life," resulting from new technological possibilities (den Otter 1963). Den Otter opposed the idea of a new code because "it is my conviction that there is no need at all for new formulations in medical ethics and even less necessity for discussions with worried and concerned theologians, philosophers and lawyers. On the contrary: it is my opinion that the initiative should come from medicine itself" (p. 183). He appealed to the best traditions of the professional ethics. Concerning the influence of the family of the patient in these issues, consensus occurred in the debate among physicians and lawyers that the physician should discuss the case with the family but need not give the family any say in the decision. Concerning the will of the patient in matters of reanimation, the medical orthodoxy was aptly formulated by the physician Stolte: "Let us put first that properly, the doctor is the agent of his patient. The sick person, who has entrusted himself to the doctor, delegates to him, be it implicitly or explicitly, a number of decisions which he will have to make on behalf of the patient" (1960, 84).

Most participants in the debate on ethical aspects of reanimation remarked that it touched fundamental existential questions such as the meaning of life and the acceptance of death. The physicians and lawyers involved, however, limited themselves to passing remarks on these subjects. It was the Catholic moral theologian Sporken (on his way to becoming one of the first and most influential medical ethicists in the Netherlands) who defined such issues as the heart of the matter. In a series of articles for the journal of the Dutch Association of Catholic Physicians, he drew on the deliberations of a discussion group on medical ethics, consisting of Catholic physicians and (theological) ethicists: "In the discussion of ethical questions concerning reanimation and the prolongation of life, the core question turns out to be more and more: can life, such as it will more or less certainly be the final result of treatment, be acceptable, livable and meaningful?" (Sporken 1965b, 382). In this context Sporken raised considerations such as the purpose of medical action, the balance of benefits and suffering, the subjective possibilities for the patient to give meaning to his or her life, the tasks possibly left for a patient to fulfill in life, and the interests of the community in a person's life.

According to Sporken the fundamental principle remained an absolute respect for the life of the patient. The concept of "life," however, need not merely be interpreted biologically. It could and should be qualified in terms of meaning. Sporken also argued for a "shift from the battle against disease and death towards the acceptance of death" (1965a, 282). He expressed concern that the physician's own fear of suffering and death would provide an unconscious motive for a forced effort to prolong the patient's life.

Thus, issues were raised that went beyond the framework of traditional medical ethics. There were signs that some physicians were responsive to the idea that such wider issues could not adequately be dealt with by the profession alone. In 1968, for example, it was noted in several articles that the development of the technique of heart transplantation, including the demand for donors, would give rise to questions concerning the moment of death and the need to prolong medical treatment. The physician van Osch called for a joint committee of physicians and other disciplines—among which he mentioned philosophers, ethicists, and lawyers—to address such questions (van Osch 1968). In 1970 Roelink, secretary general of the KNMG, admitted that the KNMG code of conduct had more to do with etiquette than with ethics. Asked to give an historical overview of the treatment of ethical issues within the KNMG, he argued that such a task was difficult, since "'real' medical ethics is actually a problem of recent years only" (Roelink 1970, 386). The overview claimed that, in the annals of the KNMG, ethics was mainly invoked when the interests of physicians were at stake.

From within the medical profession, however, attempts were made to adapt the traditional framework to the new circumstances. A major event in this context was the 1968 appearance of an edited volume on *Recent Medical Ethical Thought*, as part of an authoritative series of medical textbooks (Kortbeek 1968). Eight out of ten authors were physicians, one was a lawyer, and one a theological ethicist. Four out of eleven chapters were dedicated to end-of-life decisions. By present standards many of these contributions contain a curious mixture. On the one hand, there are various acknowledgments that the issues involved in these decisions, raised by new technical possibilities, surpass the sphere of medical authority. On the other hand, the framework for the presentation of these issues is seen entirely as a dilemma for physicians with a paternalist concern for their patients. Thus, the author of the chapter on "Prolongation and Shortening of Life," the physician Jongsma, acknowledges a patient's "right to die" (Jongsma 1968, 137). The gist of his treatment of the issue, however, is better captured by his final note: "In the great responsibility of the physician and the duty to salvage his patient from his miserable suffering, also lies his greatest personal freedom" (p. 138). In the chapter on reanimation, the physician Stolte argues that the responsibility of the patient should play a more prominent role, but careful consultation among colleagues and permanent discussion within the profession as a whole remain the best guarantee for proper procedure (Stolte 1968, 144). A chapter on

"The Right to Die," by the geriatrician Schreuder, ends in a plea for "person-al ethics" and "individual morality" of the physician, above "rules of conduct" for the profession as a whole (Schreuder 1968, 155–6). Under the heading "Euthanasia,"'Marlet, a psychiatrist, discusses a wide variety of end-of-life deci-sions, including "euthanasia in a narrow sense," also identified as "direct euthanasia" (Marlet 1968). Influenced by ethicist Sporken, Marlet claims: "What fundamentally matters is not which set of norms he [the physician] dis-poses of, but the ethical attitude to life from which he approaches the human questions" (1968, 185). Marlet elaborated on this in terms of the ethos of the community as a whole toward life and death, which should "largely deter-mine" the physician's ethos. This stance, which was rather atypical for a physi-cian at the time, was embedded in the more usual appeals to personal conscience and the personal relationship with the patient.

Concerned outsiders did not necessarily put as much trust in the capac-ity of the medical profession to develop the framework to cope with the new moral issues. In a review of "Recent Medical Ethical Thought" for the jour-nal of Catholic physicians, for example, the philosopher Tellegen (1969) directly challenged the entire framework of traditional medical ethics: its tak-ing the exclusive point of view of the physician, its focus on the one-to-one relationship of physician and patient, its emphasis of a paternalistic relation-ship of trust between both, its method of deductive application of general principles to individual cases, its fixation on fixed rules of conduct and its elitist stress on the unity of medical services. Tellegen's central argument was that the revolutionary changes in society and culture as a whole and the vast increase in medical power necessitated a radical shift in medical ethics instead of merely updating traditional principles in order to deal with the changing circumstances.

The undisputed catalyst of the professional debate on medical ethics and the public debate on euthanasia, however, was the enormous public success of the publication in 1969 of a monograph by the popular Dutch psychiatrist and philosopher Jan Hendrik van den Berg, advocating radical views in favor of euthanasia, both active and passive. In *Medical Power and Medical Ethics,* van den Berg argues for a revision of the ground rules of medical ethics, in view of the immense increase of technical power in medicine. The old ground rules pre-scribed the physician to "preserve, save and prolong human life, wherever and whenever he could" (van den Berg 1969, 19). According to van den Berg, this made sense in a situation where therapeutic potential was actually very limited. Armed with the new technical power, the new ground rule of medical ethics should be: "The physician is under obligation to preserve, save and prolong human life, where and when it is meaningful" (p. 47). In particular, two ele-ments of his plea caused much controversy. First, he made an outright plea for active euthanasia and illustrated this with shocking photographs of disabled patients. Second, he called for a "small committee" in each hospital and nurs-ing home to decide on such matters. Van den Berg excuses himself for his proposals, arguing that he strived for openness and regulation in a domain which had hitherto been characterized by covert action on subjective grounds. He advocates "in principle, to each and at any time" the principle of informed consent as a right of the patient and an obligation for the physician, provided the patient is disposed of the right mentality to cope with such complete openness (p. 35). Also, he argues that "it is indeed unnecessary to break down a meaningful existence to the last stone, before the right originates to die at last. Such right holds at any moment" (p. 45).

Many commentators evoked the memory of the Nazi euthanasia program to denounce van den Berg's proposal. The controversy surrounding the book, however, provided the impetus for many authors to engage in a debate on euthanasia and medical ethics. Until 1969 nearly all the (few) publications on euthanasia and related issues appeared in medical journals. In the following years the amount and variety of contributions to the debate and of sources in which they appeared increased considerably. It is also remarkable that, although denouncing van den Berg's propositions, most authors proved receptive to the idea that technical developments within medicine might necessitate an alteration of the very ground rule of medical ethics. Such reasoning from facts to normative principles would have been deemed a "naturalistic" fallacy by orthodox ethicists.

Van den Berg's attack on traditional medical ethics in matters of life and death was joined by several other mavericks operating on the periphery of the medical profession. An article by the psychiatrist van den Hoofdakker in a popular philosophical journal sparked much controversy. Under the title "The Stronghold of Pedants," a clear appeal to the general spirit of debunking of authorities in those years, he denounced the castelike stance of the medical profession and its paternalism toward patients (van den Hoofdakker 1969). The popular physician-lawyer Schuurmans Stekhoven claimed that the medical profession was involved in something of a conspiracy of silence regarding the "twilight area" of decerebrated "things" that were kept alive (Schuurmans Stekhoven 1969b). Invoking "human rights," among which are a right to self-determination and a right to die, he claimed that in many instances artificial prolongation of life, legally speaking, was a matter of "maltreatment" and "abuse of power" (Schuurmans Stekhoven 1969a).

Thus, at the end of the 1960s traditional medical ethics was severely challenged, especially regarding questions of life and death. It did not go without a struggle. In the intensive debate in the early 1970s, which is described in more detail in the next section, many physicians expected relief from a revision of the medical ethics code. The KNMG installed a committee to this effect. This effort did not succeed, but this fact should certainly not be attributed to a lack of effort on the part of physicians, eager to receive an updated set of guidelines for medical decisions at the end of life. Such attempts to restore the medical code, however, took place in a context far different from the one in the 1960s.

The debate on euthanasia and medical ethics in the 1960s can be characterized on the basis of the questions outlined earlier. The object of the debate was a broad set of actions: not merely "direct" and "active" euthanasia, but all decisions to act or not to act that would result in hastened death of the patient. The morality and legitimacy of all these decisions was at stake. However, already discernible was a tendency to reserve the term *euthanasia* for direct and active interventions. Linked to the issue of reanimation, nontreatment decisions were most prominent in the debate. The majority of the participants in the debate were physicians, and the prime arena was formed by medical journals. Occasionally, there were contributions by lawyers and, especially in the journals for Protestant and Catholic physicians, by ethicists. The latter parties, however, presented no challenge to the idea that the medical profession itself should try to find acceptable answers to the new questions. All the participants agreed that the availability of new techniques, which threatened to create a possibly prolonged "twilight zone" between genuine life and certified death, necessitated a rethinking of time-honored rules. As to the concept of death, both more limited "medical" observations and more general "philosophical" reflections were apparently deemed relevant by all parties involved. There was wide agreement that some concept of *terminal care*, as opposed to an unrestricted commitment to the prolongation of life, was called for in medical ethics. Also, the concept of *patient's rights* was increasingly invoked by physicians and lawyers. Regarding hard cases, however, refuge was invariably taken in the personal consciousness of the physician and the personal relationship with the patient.

The moral dimension of the debate revolved around the extent to which one might put limitations on the primary obligation to preserve the patient's life. The debate moved toward a general recognition of an obligation to stop futile ("meaningless") medical actions. In 1969 the definition of medical ethics was still uncertain. To many physicians the preferable option would be to modify some of the ground rules of the medical ethics code, while preserving its professional character. Flanked by lawyers, with their concept of "rights," and by philosophers and ethicists, with notions such as "meaning," other physicians became receptive to ideas that would make medical ethics dependent on the social development of ideas. At the threshold of the 1970s, the fate of medical ethics was undecided.

SHIFTING PERSPECTIVES ON EUTHANASIA AND MEDICAL ETHICS

In the second period, voices that had been peripheral dominated the professional debate on euthanasia and its consequences for medical ethics. The main arena of this debate was *Medisch Contact*, the journal of the KNMG. Normally a journal by and for physicians, it opened its columns to a wide variety of authors on euthanasia and medical ethics. A lawyer was "glad that M.C. [*Medisch Contact*] has put this subject on the agenda and that it is prepared to give the floor to others than physicians" (de Bruyn 1969, 814). Early in 1969 the prominent neurologist Prick opened the debate with a short article, which proved to contain most of future orthodoxy (Prick 1969a). He argued that traditional medical deontology on preserving life was untenable in view of present technical possibilities. A redefinition of the tasks of the physician at the end of life should focus on three points:

1. *Preserving life as long as it was meaningful.* This involved judgments on the acceptability of the "life situation" of the patient and on the prospects for "spiritual recovery" (p. 83). Discontinuing "extraordinary means," involving complicated technical instruments and special experience and efforts, would not be a matter of euthanasia since the patient could not survive without the extraordinary means. Chronic patients should be allowed to determine whether their life would continue to be meaningful. Refusal of treatment should be respected, provided the patient's decision was based on true freedom and was not determined by passing moods of depression.

2. *Alleviating the suffering.* The remedying of pain, even if it results in a shortening of life, should be accepted. Since the risk of death is coincidental, euthanasia is not involved.

3. *Guiding the dying process.* Every patient has a right to die. The physician should beware not to fall back into "tormenting industriousness" (p. 85). Decisions on the moment of death should not be influenced by the possibility of organ donation.

Apparently, Prick was still somewhat uneasy with the firmness of his stance and concerned with the impression it would make on the outside world: "If need be, one must accept the complications of extra-ordinary means, if stopping the equipment would give bystanders the idea that we disposed of life and death of the victim" (p. 84). This held "even if we are, morally speaking, totally justified."

Prick's article raised so much attention that it was reprinted in several other journals. A number of writers defended the principle of "absolute respect for human life" and expressed their worries that a slippery slope was entered if one allowed the physician to decide whether extraordinary means might be discontinued. This standpoint, which could be defended with referral to the latest edition of the code of medical ethics, was deemed by others to be "extreme." Prick stated, "We cannot accept an unaltered and rigid medical ethics" (1969b, 505). A lawyer argued that the possible consequences of new medical techniques were such that the responsibility "is no longer bearable by physicians alone. It will have to be shared by ethicists, religious leaders, psychologists, etc., and actually by all who feel responsible for human life, in order to prevent, as well as possible, misuse of the possibilities that now happen to exist" (de Bruyn 1969, 814).

The prominent Catholic ethicist Sporken was ready to share this responsibility. In an influential monograph on medical ethics and in several articles in physicians' journals, he added two new elements to his continuing argument for the acceptance of death. First, he agreed with van den Berg that "the true interests of the patient provide the point of departure and the fundamental norm for medical action. Therefore, it is also my opinion that the physician-patient relationship must be characterized by dialogue and discussion, in which the final and decisive word belongs to the patient" (Sporken 1969b, 1432). It must be noted, however, that this recognition of patient autonomy was hidden in two sentences in one article and did not at first play any recognizable role in Sporken's position on euthanasia. In the course of 1970, Sporken did start to speak, with very little emphasis, of "the fundamental right for every human being to die his own death" (1970d, 673). Second, and more influentially, he did not categorically condemn active euthanasia anymore, arguing that no fundamental, rational, and moral difference existed between passive and active euthanasia (Sporken 1969b, 1433). This did not diminish the importance of emotional differences, nor should it entail a plea for legalization of active euthanasia. The latter could only be acceptable in extraordinary cases, where a terminal patient was "through" with his or her life but confronted with a final period of dehumanizing suffering. Active euthanasia should remain limited to highly individualized decisions in the context of a personal relationship with the patient in extreme cases, "where general ethical norms no longer offered a real solution" (Sporken 1969a, 17). According to Sporken this meant that legalization would be premature, since "law follows ethics and concerning euthanasia we are not through with ethics yet" (p. 16).

Sporken set very high stakes for the "medical-ethical duty to provide terminal care" and the right of patients to receive such care; to him these formed the necessary context for euthanasia. True terminal care dealt with feelings of anxiety, loneliness, and grief. This could only be done by engaging in real dialogue and the building of an honest and personal relationship with the dying person (Sporken 1970c, 164–5). In practice, Sporken noticed, physicians and others were often unable to provide such care: "It seems to me that the impotence to provide true terminal care, which we all share, concentrates itself in the impotence of the physician and his refusal to start terminal care by giving an honest answer to the sick person about his condition" (p. 167).

Sporken argued that "medical ethics aims to be a critical reflection on the medical ethos, the attempt to penetrate the concept of humanity that manifests itself in the concrete norms of the ethos, critically testing this on its authenticity" (1969b, 1434). In matters of life and death, individual ethics had to draw on social ethics, both in medicine and in culture as a whole. Therefore, "the medical ethics of the future necessarily has to be culture criticism" (p. 1434). Ethics should no longer claim to offer dogmatic or timeless principles. Ethics should move along with the evolution of culture, reflecting on the changes (Sporken 1969c, 9). "True-to-life ethics can only originate and exist in the reality of life itself and will therefore necessarily be just as dynamic and even experimental in character as life" (Sporken 1970b, 410). On the other hand, Sporken complained about the reluctance of physicians to acknowledge the intrinsically social and ethical character of medicine itself:

> Propositions such as "a multidisciplinary approach of problems" and "dialogue with non-physicians" are praiseworthy, but in my opinion false, inasmuch they leave medical thinking alone and then draw up certain ethical norms for medical thinking from the outside, under pressure from "laypersons," who demand justification from the physician for his actions. Medical science and medical practice should shift the center of gravity of their attention to the personalist and social, including ethical, aspects of medical action itself. (Sporken 1970a, 420; 1970c, 163)

Thus, the prime protagonist of the specifically "ethical" perspective on matters of medical ethics raised far-reaching claims, using a wide variety of arguments. Sporken expressed convictions that were common among ethicists and philosophers. The philosopher Tellegen proclaimed the demise of an "old ethics," in which individual cases were brought under timeless general principles (Tellegen 1970, 383). Medical ethics was not merely confronted with rapid developments in techniques, opinions, and behavior: "The new ethics will itself be characterized by development. The opening of perspectives will become the criterion of responsible action—to me, to our group, to mankind . . ." (p. 384). The growing cooperation and mutual dependence of physicians and others called for a shift from microethics to macroethics: "The increase of interdependence of people calls for a growth in awareness and involvement of all, for further democratization, as it is called. This also goes for the physician-patient relationship. Because we people can only handle today's task when as many participants as possible actively share in this work" (p. 385).

The desire for a broad debate concerning medical ethics was not welcomed by all participants. In a review of van den Berg's book, the aforementioned physician-lawyer Schuurmans Stekhoven complained of the fact that van den Berg deliberately addressed the wider public:

> But I could only give a negative answer to the question whether it is ethically just, or even defensible, to discuss this [active euthanasia] in a booklet, which, bypassing the doctors in attendance, is specifically addressed to the patients, nay specifically addresses itself to them with the encouragement to decide for themselves whether to die in a dignified or an undignified way. (Schuurmans Stekhoven 1969b, 1360)

Concerning resuscitation, Schuurmans Stekhoven also argued against the primacy of ethical deliberations concerning the futility of medical action: "Essentially, the problem of stopping resuscitation is primarily a question of legal administrative death registration . . . Concerning the determination of the border between life and death, law is much more important than ethics" (p. 1360). He even claimed that the fundamental irrationality of philosophy and moral theology contributed to "the feeling of desperation that creeps upon every physician confronted by the 'life-death' problems that have artificially become unstuck by the 'attainments' of modern medicine"

(Schuurmans Stekhoven 1969c, 1517–18). At several other occasions physicians expressed their concern that medical-ethical questions concerning issues of life and death were discussed by physicians in publications for a larger public (Huyckx 1969, 2154; Bax 1971, 1853).

Lawyers weighed in with reminders to physicians to give a public account of their ethical stance. In a review of van den Berg's book, the future dean of health care lawyers, Leenen, objected that van den Berg relegated too much decision power to physicians (Leenen 1969, 353). Regarding euthanasia, he argued that the power of decision of both patients and doctors should be subjected to social control. Leading circles within the KNMG recognized that a dialogue with the outside world on medical ethics, specifically questions of life and death, was inevitable. That physicians by now could not settle matters within their own circle had become clear when the KNMG's Permanent Committee on Medical Ethics officially declared that, in view of the complexity of the issues and the differences of opinion among physicians, they could not produce a revised edition of the *Manual on Medical Ethics*. This fact was sufficient to define the situation as "the crisis in medical ethics" (Metz 1970, 330). The KNMG decided to devote its annual meeting of 1970 to the subject. In a preview of this meeting in its magazine *Medisch Contact*, the editor reflected that physicians had to acknowledge that "the ethic of the physician, in connection with his present medical capacities, will more and more become a social rather than an individual matter" (van Mechelen 1970, 274).

At this KNMG meeting, with Sporken and the KNMG chairman van der Drift as speakers, physicians were confronted with quite revolutionary views. As a prime example of the problems in medical ethics, van der Drift referred to the principle of respect for life. Due to the technical developments in medicine, this principle had now become a mere starting point in the search for answers to certain moral problems, instead of providing the definite solution. Speaking on behalf of the executive committee, van der Drift remarked that reflection on the apparent evolutionary and timebound character of medical ethics had led to the conclusion that "the study of ethical aspects of medical subjects is now better served by designating the problems and offering matter for thought, than by putting forward propositions which in the past have often been considered to be certainties" (van der Drift 1970, 413). In the opinion of the executive committee of the KNMG, physicians were no longer considered to be the sole or prime experts on medical ethics:

> This position implies the recognition that to all the groups of people, who together form the national community, should be ascribed just as much moral consciousness regarding medical issues. Between these different groups of the population may not be presumed an order of rank based on expertise or involvement with the subject of medical ethics. The sole or greater expertise in medical-ethical issues of physicians, that was mostly alleged in the past, has somewhat alienated them from the society which they as a profession wish to serve, because of the rapids in the present period of time. (p. 414)

Even concerning the traditional sanctimony of medical ethics, the individual relationship of trust between physician and patient, the rules of conduct should be subjected to certain forms of social control: "Where there is a matter of social-ethical influences on the formulation of rules of conduct, it will have to be acknowledged that representatives of society deserve a certain amount of influence" (p. 414). Van der Drift remarked that by now the issue of abortion had been defined by the public at large as a matter of the right of self-determination of the pregnant woman. This mere fact was consequential: "This autonomous development of the ethical experience of laypersons regarding medical subjects, points to the involvement of the patient as an unignorable factor in the study of medical-ethical problems" (p. 415). In response to the rhetorical question "What is left?" van der Drift proposed as the founding principle of medical ethics: "the essential interest of the patient, as an individual or a group" (p. 415). The rising influence of other professional disciplines should be a reason for physicians to "want to discuss with everyone whom, because of his expertise, can contribute to a better understanding of this miraculous phenomenon called 'human being.' This applies specifically where the moral aspect of medical action regarding questions of life and death is concerned" (p. 415).

Van der Drift argued that the uncertainties, brought about by the rapid scientific and social developments, meant that medical ethics was now fundamentally pluriform in nature. Therefore, there would be no new official manual on medical ethics and rule of conduct, and the Permanent Committee to that effect was disbanded. "Starting from the right to existence of a pluriform medical ethics and the desirability of a multi-disciplinary study of the issues at stake," a looser working party formed by interest groups within the KNMG would invite experts to write "capita selecta" on specific issues (p. 416). Those should be collected in a loose leaf KNMG publication, which could permanently be updated.

Essentially, van der Drift's argument was that the patient's trust in the physician, which was the cornerstone of medical ethics and medical practice, was now better served by openness than by seclusion in ethical matters. To that effect his final appeal to his colleagues read: "The time is over that medical ethics could give the appearance of being a secret doctrine, belonging to the essentials of the secret of physicians as a group" (p. 417). Thus, the interests of the physicians themselves to conduct proper practice necessitated a recognition of public influence and patient autonomy.

At the same memorable occasion, Sporken delivered his by then-familiar message concerning the intrinsic ethical character of medicine and the medical-ethical duty to provide terminal care:

> Summarizing the recent evolution of medical ethics, . . . distancing itself from a code of conduct for doctors, medical ethics is engaged more and more with medical action itself. At the beginning, the relationship of physician and patient

is central in this effort . . . showing the patient more explicitly in his totality as a human being, i.e. in his physical, personal and social situation of existence. (Sporken 1970a, 419)

In this argument, Sporken gave extensive attention to the reasons for the inability of physicians to provide proper terminal care: "The explanation for this impotence must, in my opinion, primarily be sought in the impotence to announce the truth on dying, to follow up on this conversation and to give meaning to the inevitable reality of death" (p. 422). Sporken specified what was at stake in the latter aspect as "the help to the patient to reach self-realization in his dying" (p. 423). Thus, Sporken's claims, on behalf of ethics, involved a holistic view of the patient as well as a social determination of the responsibility of the physician.

Although historical words were spoken at this widely publicized KNMG meeting, only few physicians were present (Wennen 1970, 629). Apparently, the debate on medical ethics in professional journals had not necessarily drawn much attention from rank-and-file physicians. Also, the only publicized reaction to the meeting attacked many elements of the lectures: the abandonment of the ethical code, the influence of society on the physician-patient relationship, and Sporken's "ideology" of meaning and self-realization (van Meurs 1970, 566–7). Sporken himself was, apparently, uneasy with his status and role as an ethicist in medical circles. He explicitly characterized himself as a layman and excused himself for that (Sporken 1970a, 418). Also, he complained that physicians perceived that ethicists "are still the people 'who know how to behave,' a sort of 'professional inventors of norms': To make it a little more easy for myself and possibly also for you, I would like to state explicitly beforehand: it is not the task of the ethicist to draw up norms on behalf of his discipline, which should then hold for medical action" (Sporken 1970d, 669). In the end "the task of the ethicist is to make himself superfluous as soon as possible" (p. 669).

Other "ethicists" were not as modest as Sporken. The philosopher Klever was the only nonphysician in a working party on medical ethics of the Dutch Humanist Society. In an extra edition on medical ethics of the humanist magazine *Rekenschap*, Klever argued that, notwithstanding the rapid changes in values and norms, ethics still had to deal with fundamental principles: "It is the task of medical ethics to reflect systematically on the fundamental principles of medical action and to attempt to clarify these conceptually and in their connection" (Klever 1970, 3). This meant that "alongside the professional code of the doctor, there is a place for a special medical ethics, though only as a specification of the general principles in such a way that they are relevant to the medical sector" (p. 7). The leading principle is autonomy: "Therefore, medical ethics must be *personalist*, i.e. place the rights, wishes and interests of the person at the center" (p. 10). According to Klever, autonomy should also be the leading principle in matters of life and death: "First I want to state that to each human being, an autonomous existence implicates: *the unshirkable and unalienable right to self-determination concerning the arrangement, prolongation or termination of one's life"* (p. 10).

In a later article in the leading Dutch philosophical journal, Klever (1972) drew the consequences of his line of argument, applied to euthanasia. He preferred to use this concept in the broader sense of any good death, interpreted by Klever as any self-directed death. This would make euthanasia, in any sense of the word, a private matter: "The human being himself should die his own death, in the form that he chooses. Therefore, euthanasia lies entirely at the personal level of one's own death (which by no means excludes the relevance of intersubjective factors)" (p. 303). Whether the final act was performed by a physician or not was merely a technical matter, with the physician in a purely executive role:

> In all circumstances it is usual to have one's decisions discharged by others, mostly specialists. If one wants to be transported through air, one trusts oneself to the captain of an airplane. The sick have themselves operated by a competent surgeon. Ethically speaking, there seems to be no objection to trust someone else with the execution of a suicide-decision, or rather of the artificial design of one's death. Why not "farm out" here as well? (p. 303)

Such radical views concerning the subjection of medical ethics to social norms, regarding euthanasia, were also advocated by the lawyer Ekelmans:

> Following the footsteps of the "trias politica-doctrine" I perceive the tasks of the physician to be executive (and advisory). To him, society has entrusted the monopoly to provide medical care. Society must, from its convictions, therefore prescribe the physician how he ought to act at the borderline of life and death and in protection of human life, not voluntary but obligatory. In these matters, neither the individual physician has to decide, nor physicians as a group according to the ruling convictions of the group, but the person himself, observing the rules to be ordained by society. (1971, 795)

Ekelmans expressed this view in an article, in which he ventured very radical opinions concerning the end of life:

> It seems to me that, as soon as it is finally impossible for a human being to live as a human being in reciprocal real social communication with others, the remaining life, which is only human in origin, can no longer make a claim to protection and will no longer need it. This human substratum or preparation then has a right to die totally (and immediately), if only to prevent further deterioration and dehumanization, which is an aspect of respect for human life as well. (p. 793)

Ekelmans even introduced the relevance of a population policy in the contemporary euthanasia discussion: "Thus, the progress of science in regard to the beginning/production of life and the (unlimited) prolongation of the lifespan, will irrevocably imply a compulsory regulation of human reproduction and the termination of human life, even if not defect" (p. 793). It is noteworthy that nowhere in his argument does Ekelmans use legal arguments or explicitly speak as a lawyer.

Ekelmans was by no means the only author linking the euthanasia debate to issues of population policy and allocation of resources. Others compared the costly efforts to prolong individual life in the rich countries of the first world with the millions dying from poverty and relatively "simple" diseases in third world countries. The humanist magazine *Rekenschap* published a translation of an article by the Polish philosopher Kolakowski (1972), defending respect for individual life against pleas for population policy. The ethicist Heering denounced economic motives but gave weight to considerations concerning the availability of a sufficient amount of caregivers to care for the elderly (1971, 859). The Protestant minister Krop argued that "a purposeful population policy not only implies a conscious regulation of birth, but also a call for conscious termination of life" (1971, 1035).

Sporken found support for his culture-based view of medical ethics in a discussion group of prominent Catholic physicians, ethicists, and lawyers (Wellen 1971, 62–6; Sporken 1971, 232–6; Sporken 1972b, 30–3; Manacker 1973, 490–6): Instead of being merely a professional code, "medical ethics is more and more regarded as part of the general ethics, including social ethics, and consists of critical reflection on the ethos concerning health care, as it exists in a specific pattern of culture (for example, the western European and Christian one)" (Wellen 1971, 63). This means that "of course, medical responsibility is social responsibility. . . . So far the physician was mainly geared towards the individual relation, but now he gets more attention for the social consequences and therefore the social responsibility of his actions" (p. 63). The final consequence of this view was that "politics, especially if interpreted as action encouraging the good arrangement of society, is really the highest form of ethics" (p. 64). This conception of medical ethics was linked to a broader view of the tasks of a physician: "If special areas are indicated with a special term, in casu medical ethics, there is often a corresponding reality. But is this a recommendable reality? Isn't there specifically a danger that the physician deals with an abstraction, that the individual is lifted out of his social context and regarded merely as an individual, whereby the really personal does not receive enough attention?" (p. 63).

In a 1971 volume of *Medisch Contact*, a number of articles entailed such pleas for a broadening of medical ethics concerning euthanasia. The ethicist Heering (1971) deliberated on the criteria for the worthiness of protection of human life. He tried to define the essence of humanity, invoking notions such as "a minimum ability to communicate" and "interhuman solidarity." The Protestant minister Krop noted that the euthanasia debate "means that in medical circles there have rightly arisen doubts as to the status of the medical profession as 'applied science,' enabling her practitioners to keep aloof from anthropological presuppositions and social implications" (Krop 1971, 1033). Krop argued that enabling voluntary euthanasia would not violate the patient's trust in the physician, but rather enhance this trust (p. 1034).

The KNMG itself persisted in its policy of stimulating and broadening the debate on medical ethics. Roelink (1971), secretary general of the KNMG and secretary of its ethical committee, reported that the latter now made a strict distinction between issues of etiquette and decency and issues concerning the foundations of medical ethics. Explicitly, the committee directed its activities in the latter domain toward all workers in health care and invited contributions from all interested persons, whether they were active in health care or not. In a contribution entitled "The Socialization of Medical Ethics," another member of the committee, the sociologist Dekker, added that the committee accepted "the fact that our so-called 'medical ethics' apparently becomes dynamic and multiform" and the ensuing "divergence of opinions" as a given (Dekker 1972, 263). The committee thought that health care as a whole should be subjected to critical ethical reflection, including aspects of politics, policy, power, and human relations:

> On the one hand there is a need for more control and accountability of action in health care, on the other hand more attention should be directed towards societal structures and processes that influence health and the ethical aspects of health care itself. The committee hopes to stimulate this discussion in the Netherlands, a discussion which should preferably be held together with other disciplines and the patients/consumers. (p. 266)

Thus, from 1969 onward the debate on euthanasia and medical ethics presented physicians with the challenge of radical claims concerning the very purpose and the framework of their profession. Such claims were uttered by representatives from different professions and by some of the leading representatives of physicians themselves. Philosophers and ethicists, although few in number, succeeded in raising the stakes of the debate over medical ethics by stressing the cultural and existential dimensions. There was no consensus about what might count as a moral argument and what was involved in delineating the issue of euthanasia as an issue of medical ethics. The nature and scope of medical ethics were contested.

The second phase of the debate did bring some consensus. Euthanasia was deemed to be a public issue, and physicians were expected to enact society's norms. Euthanasia was treated by most as a very broad issue, involving questions about cultural attitudes toward death, the meaning of life, the goals of medicine, and the personal relationship between physician and patient.

SETTLING MATTERS BY REDEFINITION

Thus far, the debate had largely been waged by individuals. From 1972 onward institutional groups and government commissions began to enter the fray. Early in 1972 the governing committee of the largest Protestant church, the Dutch Reformed Church, unanimously accepted a remarkably liberal working document on euthanasia. It contained no unconditional rejection of active euthanasia and conditionally legitimized passive euthanasia:

> To live, in the biblical sense of the word, presupposes the possibility of communication. Where it is certain, after thorough medical investigation, that this possibility is blocked with no expectation of recovery, the border to the no man's land between life and death is crossed. . . . It should therefore be considered ethically justified to stop medical treatment in this case, since prolongation offers no prospect of any result. (Nederlands-Hervormde-Kerk 1972, 34–5)

This position was argued in terms of the Christian view on the meaning of life.

Lawyers had already started framing an alternative for the ethical and religious vocabulary of meaning. In her dissertation on *Medico-Legal Aspects of the End of Human Life*, van Till (1970) claimed authority for society on matters that were once considered the proper domain of physicians. Treating the matter of death criteria, van Till notes: "[This] seems to be a purely medico-technical question, but only becomes so after the cultural community in which the question arises has decided what a living human being is and according to which kind of criterion shall be judged when this human life ends or is ended" (van Till 1970, 10). In general she claims that most of the decisions in this domain are partly extramedical. Van Till insists that the legal system, representing social norms, must ensure that such matters are dealt with in an equal and objective way (p. 10). The medicolegal approach also strengthens the position of the patient by defining the relation between physician and patient as a contractual relationship where all patients have a set of rights. Van Till even argues "for the recognition of a new personal right: *the right to an undisturbed dying process*" (p. 26). From this, she deduces a right to euthanasia for patients in a terminal phase: "Apart from the question whether it may be allowed to a physician to let a person die earlier than inevitable, the question arises whether the patient in such circumstances . . . has a proper *right* that such medical behavior is applied to him . . . in my opinion this question should be answered affirmatively" (pp. 105–6).

Such legal claims may have sounded equally unfamiliar, disturbing and threatening to physicians' ears as similar claims made in the name of "ethics." But, given a recognition of the primacy of patient demands and society's norms, the medicolegal approach had more comfort to offer than "ethics." First, the lawyers suggested that a clear framework for decision making might be agreed on instead of the eternal ethical doubts, reservations, and vagueness. Second, the juridical approach promised to deliver physicians from a range of ethical dilemmas. Concerning the conflict between the norms of respect for life and the right to die, for example, van Till (1970) remarked that the utterance of the patient's wish "means that the person involved *himself* has made the choice in this conflict of norms. . . . Therefore, there is no longer a necessity for the physician to choose in this conflict" (p. 96). Third, the juridical way guaranteed a unique, firm, and clear position to the physician. Thus, after van

Till established that many authors left open the question of whether euthanasia should be regarded as a medical action, she firmly pleaded for definition of euthanasia as an action restricted to physicians (p. 107).

Given the legal questions that swirl around euthanasia, it is remarkable that in the early 1970s careful legal reasoning was nearly absent in the professional debate. Lawyers had contributed to discussions in medical and other journals, but they did so in a personal capacity. It was not until 1972 that articles with a specifically juridical point of view appeared. Enlarging upon van Till's work, Ekelmans (who earlier contributed several "personal" articles) speculated on the grounds for exemption from prosecution. He found one in the existence of a "state of emergency," arising from the obligation for the physician to "uphold a legal good which, given the circumstances, is more important, bears more weight" than the prohibition of euthanasia (Ekelmans 1972, 1099). In a lecture to nurses, the lawyer Rang emphatically reaffirmed that "if euthanasia is ever to be juridically justified, it will have to be a medical action by a physician, or a refraining from a medical action, by a physician" (Rang 1972, 22). At the same occasion, the ethicist Sporken explicitly left open the question who, if anyone at all, might be allowed to perform euthanasia: "This means that a bystander can deliver his cooperation to the termination of the dying process, provided the patient *himself truly* asks this and the one who helps has such a *relation* with the patient that he can follow this decision in his conscience" (Sporken 1972c, 32).

Lawyers were working behind the scenes of the professional debate, exercising more influence than ethicists. In 1970 the Secretary of Health created a committee on euthanasia within the official government advisory body, the Health Council. Its task was phrased and interpreted in terms of "problems in medical ethics" (*Gezondheidsraad* 1973, 3, 7). Among its sixteen members were six lawyers and one ethicist. In its unanimous report in 1973, the committee pointed out that, given the pluriformity of values concerning this issue in society, it would not be possible to conceive a general and durable set of norms which would be accepted by the population as a whole. It was possible, however, to devise a set of practical rules based on some widely accepted general principles: respect for human life and recognition of the rights of the individual and the interests of the community. This approach suggested that physicians were to act according to general rules, articulated not by their profession but in the public domain. According to this medico-legal approach, these rules would not deal with questions concerning the value of human life. The relative value of a human life was now considered a private matter:

> In the past, many felt that some authority (the government, the church, the academically trained expert), based on some better insight, could determine what contributed to someone's well being, better than the individual himself. Nowadays the conviction has taken hold that each individual has enough insight in what is in his interest and therefore has a certain degree of right to make a choice and contribute to a decision concerning his well being. (p. 13)

This led to the conclusion that "a patient has the right to refuse medical treatment (by means of a valid declaration of his will)" (p. 25). Physicians who respected the patient's rights might count on exemption from punishment for euthanasia, if their actions conformed to common medical practice:

> To be able to appeal to justifiable grounds or reasons for exemption from punishment—to the discretion of the judge—a physician who breaks the law [on euthanasia] because he feels a conflict of duties, will have to make it plausible that he has complied with what was stated earlier, i.e.: A physician will always be obliged to act "according to his best knowledge and competence," "always primarily in the interest of the patient" and in consideration of his valid will and rights. Action or refraining from action by a physician will not be allowed and will be reproachable if, without convincing and decisive arguments, his action or refraining from action is not in accordance with what is legally prescribed, or also with what is customary under the circumstances among physicians, or with fixed national or international rules or guidelines for physicians. (p. 25)

Thus, in a proposition recognizing *patient* autonomy, physicians received a large amount of *professional* autonomy. The ideas of the health committee were clearly articulated in early 1973 in an article by van Till. She outlined a set of criteria that became the guiding principles of Dutch euthanasia practice: incurable disease, unbearable suffering, no other solution possible, backed by a second (medical) opinion, and in the interest and in agreement of the patient (van Till 1973). These principles became formal after their use in the widely publicized "Leeuwarden euthanasia process" and their acceptance by the court (see *Redactie* 1973, 373).

The report of the Health Council precipitated a shift in the meaning of medical ethics. Inspired by a juridical point of view, it stressed patient rights and defined the relationship between physician and patient as a contractual one (thereby settling the issue of judgments on the meaning or value of a patient's life); it delineated the professional autonomy of physicians in a legally defined social context (opening the way for "legitimate" performance of active euthanasia by physicians on grounds of an emergency situation caused by a conflict of duties). Thus, the definition of medical ethics moved back to a code of conduct. The new code of conduct went beyond mere etiquette— more parties were involved, and it was explicitly dynamic, open to change— but, *as a whole*, the resolution of the euthanasia question along these lines made a new "medical ethics" acceptable to physicians.

The executive committee of the KNMG swiftly embraced the report of the Health Council (Leuftink 1973, 587–8). With regard to active euthanasia, it stressed that the physician remained the responsible person, recognizing the necessity of consultations with colleagues and others involved, guided by social norms (p. 588). The editor of the authoritative volume on medical ethics, the physician Kortbeek, endorsed the Health Council's point of view that questions regarding the meaning of existence were a matter for the patient only (Kortbeek 1973, 440). One of the reasons for physicians to involve themselves in the settlement of the euthanasia issue was that they had apparently been caught by surprise by the earlier jurisprudence on abortion: "To cling rigidly to old points of view [regarding euthanasia], based on traditional 'black-or-white points of view' creates the risk that the world enforces new 'rules of the game' upon us, as has happened regarding abortion, without appreciating the value of norms" (Heering and Heering 1973, 843). This fear was also expressed by the KNMG's committee on euthanasia: "It is forseeable that the vision regarding euthanasia will change. We will have to be conscious of that and deliberate on this beforehand, to avoid . . . that an ethic will be forced upon us. Didn't many physicians get this feeling when abortion was allowed by the government on a very broad indication?" (KNMG-*werkgroep-euthanasie* 1975, 14). This fear provided a strong motivation for physicians to take initiative in the public settlement of euthanasia in order to protect their professional autonomy.

From 1973 onward, physician contributions to the euthanasia debate took a medicolegal tone. When asked to write a special editorial for the prime scientific medical journal *NtvG*, the prominent physician-professor Meyler solved questions of meaning by relegating them to patient autonomy: "The physician should make all efforts to prolong life, only if life has meaning in the eyes of the patient" (Meyler 1973, 554). In the ensuing discussion, the focus gradually shifted from the "euthanasia, yes or no" perspective toward a "euthanasia, under which conditions" perspective. After specifying the conditions to be included in a liberal euthanasia law, Postma-van Boven and Postma, both physicians, made it clear that a juridical definition of the situation had priority over the medical definition: "If there is to be no change of law, we need a juridical examiner rather than a medical examiner" (Postma-van Boven and Postma 1973, 1133).

The acceptance of the medicolegal settlement of euthanasia among physicians became especially apparent with the publication in 1975 of the final discussion report of the KNMG committee on euthanasia (KNMG-*werkgroep-euthanasie* 1975, 7–16). The report contained an explicit recognition of the public sovereignty regarding euthanasia and medical ethics: "Concerning the ethic regarding euthanasia, the community will have to make decisions on a multi-disciplinary basis" (p. 15). It endorsed the contract model of the relationship between physician and patient, and it recognized the patient's right to refuse treatment and the physician's duty to tell the truth (p. 13). Against this background the committee formulated a set of criteria for correct procedure by physicians, both regarding passive and active euthanasia. It acknowledged that the values and norms involved would alter as an effect of social developments: "Historically, society has always determined physicians' norms and thus our own norms will change in the future" (p. 14).

Where did this turn toward legal and social definitions leave the ethicists? The KNMG committee on euthanasia devoted a number of paragraphs of their report to the relationship between physicians and other experts. They did not include ethicists, nor did they in any way refer to medical ethics as a specific form of expertise. The competence on issues of meaning was exclusively divided among the patient and the physician (p. 11). In the face of the evolving consensus, the Catholic ethicist Beemer warned against the reduced "ethical" vocabulary of the euthanasia debate and defended the "broad" character of the issue:

> The ethical involvement with the problem [of euthanasia] threatens to become abstract, because it overlooks the societal appreciation for old age as well as other marginal groups and it does not draw into the reflections on meaningful life the disturbing question what the life of an older person is worth to society. It works with concepts such as person, freedom and happiness without subjecting them to criticism. (1973, 89)

In a review of one of Sporken's books, a fellow ethicist accused him of individualizing and medicalizing the issue of euthanasia (*Vox Theologica* 1973, 101). On the whole, however, ethicists found very little support for their claims regarding the broad nature of the issue of euthanasia and the primacy of questions of meaning.

In the course of 1974, other expectations of ethics started to be voiced. The clinical chemist BenGershôm complained about the vagueness of most of the key concepts in the debate on euthanasia (1974, 579). He suggested that physicians should be schooled in philosophy, specifically logic and analytic philosophy, before a fruitful ethical discussion on euthanasia could be held. The physician Iemhoff (1975) complained about the lack of distinction among the level of existing norms and values, the level of morals, and the level of systematic reflection on morals, the level of ethics. He argued: "It is the specific task of the ethicist to withhold himself from a moral judgment. . . . An ethical analysis should, in my opinion, have the same artificiality as (other) scientific research and should uphold the same distance towards the everyday opinions on man and the world and morals" (p. 363).

In this third phase of the debate, the term *euthanasia* still denoted a broad range of issues, but the real debate was about active euthanasia. Lawyers came to the fore and largely defined the terms under which the issue would be resolved:

1. A recognition of the public character of the issue
2. Patient autonomy as the primary principle
3. A recognition of the autonomous and indispensable role of the physician, including the possibility of a conflict of duties

Within this framework, the focus of the debate shifted toward the proper *procedure* to be followed by physicians. Accountability to the patient and to the society were now regarded as indispensable to such procedure. The physician Kortbeek noted that the most important new element resulting from the developments concerning euthanasia was the creation of a practice of deliberation between the patient and others and the doctor (Kortbeek 1973, 440).

In this phase, "medical ethics" regarding euthanasia became a new kind of code of conduct for physicians. Unlike the period before the 1970s, the framework was publicly—that is, legally—defined. Thus, under the heading of "(medical) ethics" went both the outline of a "medicolegal settlement" and the plea for a broad cultural debate.

CONCLUSION

An explanation of the Dutch euthanasia debate of the early 1970s can be given in terms of a struggle among professionals for the definition of euthanasia as a public problem (Gusfield 1981). Physicians, who were hitherto "owners" of medical ethics, saw themselves confronted with radical claims to yield control of their activities and to hold themselves publicly accountable. Ethicists joined in this choir, specializing in questions of meaning and other fundamental questions with no certain outcome. Lawyers, on the other hand, promised to deliver a clean handling of public accountability: a procedural solution to matters of autonomy and possible conflict. In the end, physicians gave up a limited amount of autonomy, settling for guidelines that gave them enough working space within relatively clear boundaries. Fundamental issues raised by the early ethicists no longer needed to be addressed, since they were relegated to the patient's wish. The "ownership" of euthanasia, while nominally acknowledged to rest in the hands of "society," was now shared by physicians and lawyers.

Such a description of the euthanasia debate might still leave the impression that it involved a struggle on the ownership of a previously definable issue, euthanasia, within a previously definable arena, medical ethics. The very substance of medical ethics was at stake in the euthanasia debate in the early 1970s in the Netherlands. There was a fundamental uncertainty about what should be the core of medical ethics and who could define it. Our present familiarity with the settlement reached by 1975 can lead us to overlook the revolutionary challenge to the concept of "medical ethics" that preceded it and about the multidimensional character of the settlement.

Consider the influence of professionals and professional groups. First, there was a remarkable variety of contributions. Even in the physicians' journals, authors from many disciplines and professions participated in the debate. Eventually, the debate was framed by a coalition of physicians and lawyers, a fact most clearly expressed in the report of the Health Council. A "settlement" was reached "behind the scenes" of the debate. In this settlement the lawyers represented the social norms that physicians acknowledged as the foundation of medical ethics. The legal framework ensured that euthanasia remained within the competence of physicians and gave physicians a sufficient amount of certainty. Physicians had learned from the regulation of abortion, which many felt to be forced on them, that they had to negotiate to protect their autonomy.

Looking at the arguments used in the debate, we find differences in the definition of the appropriate work of medical ethics. The discussion of euthanasia in the Netherlands included the following issues: the threat of a lack of societal means to care for (elderly) chronic and terminal patients, the need for a population policy, the numerous comparisons between the importance of euthanasia and terminal care on the one hand and hunger in the Third World or the Vietnam war on the other hand, Klever's radical defense of patient autonomy and the obligation of the physician to be of assistance to a patient's death wish and van den Berg's plea for small committees with authority to decide upon active euthanasia, also in cases of incompetent patients. Several participants, among whom several "ethicists," argued that the focus of debate should not be the morality of certain definable actions, but rather the morality of our attitudes toward life and death and toward weak social groups such as the aged and the disabled. This corresponded with pleas to give issues of "meaning" a central role in the debate. Such pleas were common in the late 1960s and early 1970s. By the middle 1970s, they became less frequent. They were not honored in the "medicolegal settlement" where issues of meaning were relegated to the authority of the patient.

Another noteworthy development was that, from the early 1970s, the "personal conscience" of the physician was no longer invoked as the final touchstone. It was in fact seldom mentioned. In the earlier days the concept of morality encompassed both medical ethics, in the sense of a strict code of conduct, and personal conscience. In later days it was acknowledged that there could be differences in moral judgment and that these differences should be explicit and public. The possibility of moral pluralism was built into the ethical framework and taken out of the hands of individual physicians.

Most evident in my analysis is the development of medical ethics from a static code of conduct by and for physicians, toward a multidisciplinary application of dynamic social norms. In the euthanasia debate of the early 1970s, there was a fundamental uncertainty about the nature of medical ethics and what one should expect from ethicists. This uncertainty must be understood in the context of uncertainties concerning the relationships between physician and patient and physician and society, arising from cultural, social, and demographic developments. The use of legal norms to resolve the ethical dilemma of euthanasia gave primacy to the contract model of the physician-patient relationship, preserving both patient and professional autonomy. The proper exercise of euthanasia came to be considered a matter of proper procedure. Lawyers provided the framework of what was later to be called "informed consent." To ethics in the broad sense of the word, and thereby to "ethicists," remained the domain of the examination of individual and cultural values, which to some was fundamental and to others was marginal. By the mid-seventies the first pleas could be detected for a concept of ethics that was new to medical ethics: conceptual analysis by experts schooled in philosophy and logic.

My analysis suggests that medical ethics is best understood as a "heterogeneous network," first described in Latour's sociology of science (Latour 1987). The primary focus of research on medical ethics should be the configuration of scientific, technical, moral, personal, social, and cultural "aspects." For example, does "the morality of euthanasia" refer to the question of whether certain acts are allowed or may be omitted, or to the responsibilities of physicians, or to the control of individual citizens over lethal chemical substances, or to cultural attitudes toward suffering and dying, or to any other definition of the issue? The answer to this (long) question lies in a proper understanding of the configuration of all these aspects. Defining the issue at stake as a moral, medical, legal, or social issue, does not involve the choice of one aspect to the exclusion of others, but rather the use of one aspect to define the configuration as a whole. Intellectually, therefore, the term *medical ethics* should primarily be understood to refer to this heterogeneous network, not to any one aspect of it.

In "normal" circumstances we use the term *medical ethics* unproblematically. But changes in our attitude toward death, in the division of labor in health care, or in the public availability of drugs might completely change our present concept of medical ethics. The Dutch debate on euthanasia in the early 1970s is special in the sense that a fundamental uncertainty in many aspects of medical practice made visible links that are normally invisible because of their stability. Under stable circumstances, a veil of terminology and professional demarcation hides the dynamic and constructed character of medical ethics. The Dutch case reminds us that the social definition of medical ethics involves forces other than moral argumentation and actors other than ethicists. This case study shows us the contingency, not only of medical morality concerning euthanasia, but of medical ethics itself.

NOTE

1. This article owes its existence to the encouragements of Guy Widdershoven and Raymond de Vries. Olga Haveman has offered invaluable assistance in the collection of data and in the earlier stages of interpretation.

REFERENCES

Bax, H. R. 1971. Tenzij een wonder gebeurt. *NtvG* 115:1853.

Beemer, T. 1973. De maatschappelijke waardering van de ouderdom, ofwel: Het euthanasie-debat als tijdspassering. *Vox Theologica* 43:74–89.

BenGershôm, E. 1974. Nadenken over medische ethiek: Maar hoe? *MC* 29:578–80.

Berger, P., and T. Luckmann. 1966. *The social construction of reality: A treatise in the sociology of knowledge.* Garden City, N.Y.: Doubleday.

de Bruyn, A. J. 1969. De medische ethiek met betrekking tot de nieuwste ontwikkelingen in de geneeskunde. *MC* 24:814.

Dekker, E. 1972. De vermaatschappelijking van de medische ethiek. *MC* 27:263–6.

den Otter, P. G. 1963. Reanimatie. *Soteria: orgaan van de protestants-christelijke artsenorganisatie in Nederland* 7:182–6.

Ekelmans, J. 1971. De mondige sterveling. *MC* 26:791–5.

———, J. 1972. Juridische aspecten van euthanasie. *NtvG* 116:1096–1102.

———, J. 1973. Het euthanasievraagstuk. *MC* 28:866.

Gezondheidsraad. 1973. *Advies inzake euthanasie.* Den Haag: Ministerie van Volksgezondheid en Milieuhygiëne.

Gusfield, J. R. 1981. *The culture of public problems.* Chicago: University of Chicago Press.

Heering, H. J. 1971. De grenzen van het menselijke bestaan; Medisch-ethische overwegingen. *MC* 26:859–862.

Heering, M. J., and H. J. Heering. 1973. Stervensverlangen—stervensbegeleiding—euthanasie. *MC* 28:841–4.

Huyckx, F. J. A. 1969. Medische macht en medische ethiek. *NtvG* 113:2154.

Iemhoff, W. G. J. 1975. Ethiek en moraal. *MC* 30:363–6.

Jongsma, M. W. 1968. Verlenging en verkorting van het leven. In *Recent medisch-ethisch denken 1,* edited by L. Kortbeek. Leiden: Stafleu.

Kimsma, G. K., and E. van Leeuwen. 1993. Dutch euthanasia: Background, practice, and present justifications. *Cambridge Quarterly of Healthcare Ethics* 2:19–35.

Klever, W. N. A. 1970. Algemene beschouwingen over de beginselen van de medische ethiek. *Rekenschap* 17:3–11.

———. 1972. Euthanasie. Ethische beschouwingen over het menselijk sterven. *ANTW* 64:297–304.

KNMG. 1959. *Medische ethiek en gedragsleer.* Utrecht.

KNMG-werkgroep-euthanasie. 1975. Discussienota van de werkgroep euthanasie. *MC* 30:7–16.

Kolakowski, L. 1972. Het doden van gehandicapte kinderen als het fundamentele probleem van de filosofie. *Rekenschap* 19:9–15.

Kortbeek, L. 1968. *Recent medisch-ethisch denken 1.* Leiden: Stafleu.

———. 1973. Euthanasie bij zwakzinnige kinderen. *Metamedica* 52:438–42.

Krop, M. A. 1971. Het recht op de dood. *MC* 26:1033–5.

Langemeijer, P. M. G. E. 1960. Reanimatie. *MC* 15:188–91.

Latour, B. 1987. *Science in action.* Cambridge, Mass.: Harvard University Press.

Leenen, H. J. J. 1969. Moderne visies op de medische ethiek. *Katholiek Artsenblad* 48:349–55.

Leuftink, D. A. E. 1973. Het euthanasie-vraagstuk. *MC* 28:587–8.

Manacker, D. W. 1973. Medische ethiek in impasse. *Metamedica* 52:490–6.

Marlet, J. J. C. 1968. Euthanasie. In *Recent medisch-ethisch denken 1,* edited by L. Kortbeek. Leiden: Stafleu.

Metz, W. 1970. Over de crisis in de medische ethiek. *MC* 25:330–2.

Meyler, L. 1973. Euthanasie. *NtvG* 117:553–5.

Nederlands-Hervormde-Kerk. 1972. *Euthanasie.* s'Gravenhage.

Postma-van Boven, G. E., and A. Postma. 1973. Euthanasie. *NtvG* 117:1133–4.

Prick, J. J. 1969a. De medische ethiek met betrekking tot de nieuwste ontwikkelingen in de geneeskunde. *MC* 24:83–85.

———. 1969b. Collega Prick antwoordt Mr. Goudsmit. *MC* 24:504–5.

Rang, D. J. F. 1972. Juridische vragen rondom de euthanasie. In Schreuder, Rang, and Sporken 1972, pp. 18–25.

Redactie. 1973. De rechter en euthanasie. *MC* 28:373.

Roelink, H. 1970. De Koninklijke Nederlandse Maatschappij tot Bevordering der Geneeskunst en de Medische Ethiek. *Metamedica* 49:385–95.

———. 1971. Medische ethiek en gezondheidszorg. *MC* 26:1123–5.

Rümke, H. C. 1959. De docter en het probleem van de dood. *MC* 14:2097–3002.

Schreuder, D. T. R. 1968. Het recht om te sterven. In *Recent medisch-ethisch denken 1*, edited by L. Kortbeek. Leiden: Stafleu.

Schreuder, J. T. R., J. F. Rang, and P. Sporken. 1972. *Leven tot (w)elke prijs?* Lochem: De Tijdstroom.

Schuurmans Stekhoven, W. 1969a. Tussen leven en dood. *Intermediair* 31(10):17, 19, 27.

———. 1969b. Arts en wet. *NtvG* 113:1358–60.

———. 1969c. Ethanasie. *NtvG* 113:1517–8.

Sporken, C. P. 1965a. Sterven als levensopgave. *R.K. Artsenblad* 44:277–83.

———. 1965b. Medische ethiek en levensverlenging. *R.K. Artsenblad* 44:375–89.

———. 1969a. Euthanasie: Ingrijpen in het stervensproces? *Katholiek Artsenblad* 48:11–7.

———. 1969b. Medische ethiek als Cultuurkritiek. *MC* 24:1431–4.

———. 1969c. *Voorlopige diagnose. Inleiding tot een medische ethiek.* Bilthoven: Ambo.

———. 1970a. Stervensbegeleiding: Medisch-ethische plicht? *MC* 25:418–24.

———. 1970b. Vijftig jaar medische ethiek in het Katholieke Artsenblad. *Metamedica* 49:395–411.

———. 1970c. Stervensbegeleiding: Medisch-ethische plicht? *Theologie en Pastoraat* 66:161–70.

———. 1970d. Medisch-ethische vragen in verband met aesthesie. *MC* 25:669–73.

———. 1971. Medische ethiek andermaal in discussie. *Metamedica* 50:232–6.

———. 1972a. *De laatste levensfase. Stervenshulp en euthanasie.* Bilthoven: Ambo.

———. 1972b. Medische ethiek in discussie III: Individu en maatschappij. *Metamedica* 51:30–3.

———. 1972c. Levenshulp, stervenshulp en euthanasie. In Schreuder, Rang, and Sporken 1972.

Stolte, J. B. 1960. Reanimatie en de grenzen van kunstmatige levensverlenging. *R.K. Artsenblad* 39:84–8.

———. 1968. Kunstmatige verlenging van het leven. In *Recent medisch-ethisch denken 1*, edited by L. Kortbeek. Leiden: Stafleu.

Tellegen, F. P. A. 1969. Enkele reflexies op "Recent medisch ethisch denken I." *Katholiek Artsenblad* 48:282–91.

———. 1970. Ethiek in de cultuuromslag: Ter inleiding. *Metamedica* 49:382–5.

van den Berg, J. H. 1969. *Medische macht en medische ethiek.* Nijkerk: Callenbach.

van der Drift, L. 1970. Medische ethiek anno. *MC* 25:413–7.

van den Hoofdakker, R. 1969. *Het bolwerk van de beterweters: Over de medische ethiek en de status quo.* Amsterdam: Van Gennep.

van Mechelen, J. J. 1970. De komende algemene vergadering. Vraagstuk van de ethiek. *MC* 25:273–4.

van Meurs, J. H. 1970. De maatschappij en de ethiek. *MC* 25:566–7.

van Osch, H. F. C. M. 1968. Over het ogenblik van sterven en over orgaantransplantatie. *R.K. Artsenblad* 47:290–4.

van Till-d'Aulnis de Bourouill, H. A. H. 1970. *Medisch-juridische aspecten van het einde van het menselijk leven.* Deventer: Kluwer.

———. 1973. Jurist en euthanasie. *MC* 28:46–50.

Vox Theologica. 1973. Boekbespreking. *Vox Theologica* 43:101–2.

Wellen, D. J. 1971. Van de conferentietafel. *Metamedica* 50:62–6.

Wennen, E. 1970. Medische ethiek. *MC* 25:629.

CHAPTER EIGHT

International Research in Bioethics: The Challenges of Cross-Cultural Interpretation

Dorothy C. Wertz[1]

Bioethicists around the world have a common vocabulary. Of course, the field of bioethics takes very different forms outside North America, but bioethicists often use English words, coined in the United States, to define ethical concerns. One way to make plain the social shape of bioethics and to explore the influence of the United States on the field is to examine one area of bioethical concern in several nations. The emerging field of medical genetics affords an ideal setting for such research because it cross-cuts almost every problem found in bioethics and is found in all developed and many developing nations.

Few social scientists have attempted international or cross-cultural research in professional ethics, perhaps because of the logistical difficulty of approaching professionals in different nations. At a minimum a researcher would need the help of at least one well-established professional in each nation or culture. Other reasons for the paucity of research in this area include (1) ethnocentrism in the researcher's own culture and the other cultures to be studied; (2) difficulty in translating some ethical concepts common to English-speaking or Western European cultures, such as autonomy, privacy, and nondirectiveness, which are less familiar elsewhere; and (3) differences in the definition of a profession or specialty in different nations.

In medicine, professionals in the more technologically advanced nations may say, in effect, "We have nothing to learn from the ethical views of other nations," as if technological sophistication somehow conferred ethical sophistication on practitioners. This was in fact the response we received when we first presented a proposal for a government contract to study ethics and genetics cross-culturally. At the same time, professionals in non-Western nations or developing nations may say, "We are so unique or our social/economic situation is so difficult that we must have a unique response to ethical problems, and we think that outsiders cannot assess our responses fairly." This was the response when the European Society of Human Genetics recently censured China for requiring premarital steril- ization of persons with mental retardation; the Chinese claimed that for- eigners had no understanding of China's needs, human values, and culture.

A uniform sample selection of professionals may be next to impossi- ble. For example, most nations have no certifying boards or examinations in medical genetics. In some nations, such as Poland, midwives do much of the genetic counseling. In others, such as the United Kingdom and South Africa, "genetic nurses" play a role. In Hungary, the United States, Germany, and many other nations, Ph.D.s do much of the diagnosis and counseling. In the United States and Canada, master's-level, board-certified genetic counselors play a major role. In defining a professional specialty for study, it may be more appropriate to delimit the sample from the patient point of view and to study whomever is providing services, rather than applying uniform criteria of training or degrees that will inevitably omit many providers.

But, despite these inherent difficulties in cross-cultural ethics surveys, several researchers have conducted them. Darryl Macer (1994) surveyed attitudes toward biotechnology, gene therapy, genetic testing and abortion, and new reproductive technologies among the public, university students, and high school teachers in ten nations, with 6000 responses to a six-page survey. Therese Marteau and her colleagues (1994) surveyed geneticists, obstetricians, and pregnant women in the United Kingdom, Germany, and Portugal with regard to attitudes toward genetic disabilities, prenatal diag- nosis, and abortion, using some of the case vignettes from the international survey described here. In her study the views of the three groups in each nation paralleled each other, and Germans were more reluctant to abort than respondents in other nations.

In what follows I concentrate on the methodological and conceptual difficulties inherent in international or cross-cultural research, to help future researchers and to highlight the way society shapes ethical questions and solutions. I speak from my own experience with two major surveys on geneticists' ethical views. The first, in 1985–1986, surveyed 1098 geneticists in nineteen nations (including the United States), using fourteen case vignettes that described ethical problems commonly occurring in the prac- tice of medical genetics, including disclosure of sensitive information, non- paternity, sex selection, new reproductive options, and directiveness in counseling. In all, 682 (62 percent) geneticists responded. Results appeared in a book (Wertz and Fletcher 1989a), with a chapter written by a geneticist in each participating nation, and in medical and bioethics journals (Wertz et al. 1990; Wertz and Fletcher 1989b). The second survey, in 1993–1994, was more ambitious, with 4594 geneticists in thirty-seven nations, including all of North America and Western Europe, most of Latin America, China, India, Israel, Japan, Thailand, Turkey, Australia, Russia, the Czech Republic, Hungary, and Poland. Although the fifty-page questionnaire was too long by most social science standards, 2903 persons (63 percent) responded, ranging from 16 percent in Cuba to 100 percent in Greece. Anything over 50 percent is usually considered an excellent response for a physician survey in the United States, since physicians are notoriously difficult to survey. The results of the survey appear elsewhere. This paper concentrates on the research experience itself.

Although bioethicists speak of principles, action-guides, and the ethics of relationships, bioethics does not stand apart from society. Its very embeddedness in society fleshes out and subtly changes the more abstract principles and sheds light on the culture itself. The research process illustrates the larger issues of relationships between bioethics and culture.

METHODS OF ADMINISTRATION

In each country (except the United States, where we mailed the surveys directly), we asked a well-known geneticist (often the president of the national professional association) to distribute and collect the questionnaires. This person was responsible for identifying all practicing medical geneticists or genetic counselors who had completed their training (our criteria for selection) and for writing a cover letter to his or her colleagues. In the smaller countries, such as Switzerland or Norway, where our colleague might be able to identify each of perhaps five or ten respondents through sociodemographic data in the responses, we gave respondents the opportunity of sending their questionnaires directly to us in the United States. This was important because in some countries junior professionals may be reluctant to diverge openly from the opinions of their seniors. In some countries, where the average physician may earn less than $5000 a year, our in-country colleagues showed an avid interest in trying to identify the occasional individual who earned $75,000–100,000. (This meant that we had to remove age, income, and years in practice when we supplied our colleagues with raw data for further analysis.)

Despite the problems involved in distributing surveys through a colleague in each nation, we believe that this approach produced a higher response rate than distributing surveys directly. Our subsequent experience with a two-page questionnaire (on a closely related subject) mailed directly to members of genetics societies showed that the two-page direct-mailed survey produced a lower response rate (45 percent) than the fifty-page survey (63 percent) distributed by a colleague within each nation, despite the fact that the two-page survey was accompanied by a cover letter from a well-known person in each culture area (Latin America, Europe, Canada).

We field-tested both the 1985 and 1993 surveys in the United States. Before finalizing the questionnaires, we distributed them to our international colleagues for comments and suggestions. This led to many changes. Initially, each question consisted of a case vignette (for example, genetic tests, done for another purpose, show that a husband is not the biological father of a child), followed by a checklist of possible choices of action (tell him, don't tell him, tell the mother alone, and so on), followed by a list of possible reasons for the choice of action (for example, preserving family unity, preventing harm to the child, the husband's right to know). We had hoped to avoid the truly massive task of coding and organizing "write-in" responses, which we had undertaken in the 1985 survey. In the end it was impossible to avoid inclusion of qualitative responses. The French objected to our checklists of reasons (though not to the checklists of actions) on grounds that they were "boring" and said that no one would answer the questionnaire. The Germans, on the other hand, loved the checklists of reasons and were disappointed when we ultimately omitted them. They claimed that Germans liked lists and would not take the time to write in their own reasons. (They were right. The German questionnaires had very few and brief write-in comments. The French wrote voluminously and quoted Diderot, Rousseau, and Voltaire.) In the end we abandoned the "checklist approach" to moral reasoning because we decided that it was putting the words of Western culture into people's mouths. The only way to find out why people would choose a course of action was to let them say it in their own language and then have it translated. (We left the choices of action in the form of checklists, there being only a limited number of actions available to medical professionals.)

There were trade-offs in giving up checklists. The lists were originally constructed to provide measurable scales (for example, for belief in patient autonomy or for positive or negative feelings about disability) that could be compared among countries and that could be used in regression analyses. The qualitative responses, even when assigned numeric codes as a shorthand, cannot be used as quantitative scales or in multivariate analyses. Coding and managing qualitative responses to over 2900 questionnaires was a truly massive task, requiring almost two years. The amount of data far exceeds that manageable by computer programs, such as Ethnograph or Nudist, that are designed for this type of research.

Our best alternative was to devise our own codebook and enter the reasons into the overall SPSSX (Statistical Package for the Social Sciences) data set so that we could make some general comparisons between countries. We then entered a sample of the reasons themselves into a database for retrieval in future writing. Although this required much effort, we now have a very rich data set of moral reasoning in a variety of nations.

Our colleagues asked for other changes in the questionnaire. Some genetic disorders, such as Huntington disease and cystic fibrosis, are virtually unknown in Asia, though geneticists read about them in the course of their training. These disorders figure prominently in Western ethical discussions and have no counterparts that we could use as examples in Asia. We knew that we were being ethnocentric in using them as examples in the case vignettes, but they appeared in clinical practice in thirty-three of the thirty-seven countries, and we wanted to have uniform questions across all countries. India, China, and Thailand had no objections. Our Japanese colleague, however, argued that Japanese geneticists, with no experience of either disorder, would not give thoughtful answers, and he wished to substitute sensorineural deafness, which was his specialty. After lengthy discussions with Japanese colleagues in the United States, we decided to stick with the original Western diseases. Deafness is not comparable to Huntington disease, which appears in middle age and leads to progressive mental and motor deterioration, ending in death after about ten years, or to cystic fibrosis, a disorder of the lungs and pancreas with a median life expectancy of twenty-nine years. No one could suggest a Japanese equivalent for either disorder. There were other questions that did not apply in some parts of the world, especially questions about methods of payment for genetics services. We did not ask about private health insurance, as this is nonexistent in many nations. Alternatives were "national public health insurance" or payment by "patient out-of-pocket." In many countries the latter term is simply not applicable. Geneticists in many nations also found questions about possible refusals of employment or insurance on genetic grounds strange; they seemed to think that this could happen only in the United States. Examples of other situations that some respondents said were impossible in their countries were a single woman who decides to become a mother (impossible in China), a couple with five sons who want a girl (also impossible in China, because no one has five children), a commercial DNA bank (impossible almost everywhere at present, but coming in the future), a school system that asks whether a child has had genetic tests (possible in France, but not in Germany), a bus driver who could become unemployed if his employer learns he is at high risk of heart attack (impossible in Western Europe, where disability laws would protect him). We retained all these items in the questionnaire as applicable in the United States and some other countries, in some cases providing the option of "not applicable in my country."

The 1985–1986 survey was entirely in English. English is now the international language of science and medicine. The 1993–1994 survey, which had more economic support, was translated into Chinese, Czech,

French, German, Hebrew, Hungarian, Japanese, Polish, Portuguese, Spanish, Russian, Thai, and Turkish, by our geneticist colleagues in the various nations. Each translation was checked by an American geneticist or scientist who was a native speaker. In all cases, there were mistakes that needed correction. Some translations underwent correction on four separate occasions. Mexico was responsible for a generic Spanish translation used in Spain and throughout Latin America, except Chile, which chose to circulate the questionnaire in English. Some Latin American countries differed in preferences for formal or informal modes of address (our Mexican colleague had chosen the informal). Brazil was responsible for the Portuguese translation, but our colleague in Portugal decided in advance to circulate the questionnaire in English because she claimed all Portuguese geneticists were fluent in English. Our colleagues in Belgium, Denmark, Finland, Greece, India, Italy, the Netherlands, Norway, Sweden, and Switzerland also decided to use the English version. In Egypt our colleague feared that government censors would suppress an Arabic version because issues related to prenatal diagnosis and abortion are difficult to discuss openly. She circulated the English version by hand rather than by mail. An attempt to include Saudi Arabia in the study failed because colleagues there said the issues could not be discussed, even though geneticists might face them in practice.

We asked our colleagues to do a three-wave mailing: survey, follow-up postcard, and survey. Each survey was accompanied by a postcard to be returned to our colleague separately from the questionnaire, giving the respondent's name and indicating that he or she had returned the questionnaire, so that our colleague would not need to send further mailings. In some nations, such as Germany, colleagues took the initiative of telephone follow-up. In Peru our colleague delivered and collected the surveys in person. In Turkey and west China, a small financial incentive ($25, to be donated to the professional association) was necessary to ensure a good response rate. Payment ultimately became necessary in the United States as well, to boost the response rate from 46 percent to 70 percent. The United States (and the genetic counselors' association in Canada) also required a fourth mailing, with a greatly shortened version of the questionnaire, and a telephone reminder. In contrast some countries actually lengthened their questionnaires. We offered our colleagues in every country the opportunity of adding several questions relevant to their own situation. India added 10 questions on sex selection (in addition to 6 questions already in the questionnaire), the Netherlands added 3 questions on cystic fibrosis carrier screening (in addition to 11 questions in the questionnaire), and South Africa added 3 questions on use of interpreters. Germany added 113 questions on the effects of the experience of the Third Reich and on nondirectiveness in counseling, producing a bound volume the size of a small telephone book, yet the Germans had a response rate of 61 percent.

From the foregoing description, it becomes apparent that methods of administration will not be uniform in a multination survey, regardless of the researcher's intent. No matter how carefully one instructs colleagues, some will inevitably take different initiatives that become apparent only later. In many cases, these initiatives are probably necessary to ensure a decent response rate in that particular culture. The alternative—sending a member of the U.S. research team to each country—would be prohibitively expensive and might not produce a better response.

After we circulated preliminary results at international meetings, some professionals felt that their colleagues' sample selections had been too narrow or that an additional mailing could increase the response rate. Accordingly, we organized a fourth mailing in Argentina, Belgium, Canada, and Cuba. This approach carries the disadvantage of lapsed time (perhaps a year after the initial survey), but it is perhaps more important that professionals in each country feel satisfied with their representation, especially if the results are to be reported in international journals.

ADVANTAGES AND DISADVANTAGES OF USING QUESTIONNAIRES

Questionnaire surveys are rarely used outside North America. This leads to both advantages and disadvantages for the survey researcher. The advantage is that unlike U.S. physicians, who may receive up to several surveys a week from commercial companies, often accompanied by prepayments for responding, most health care providers elsewhere have rarely, or more likely never, received a survey of any kind. Unlike U.S. physicians, who often throw surveys away without looking at them, providers in other countries may be more likely to take a survey seriously. The disadvantage of approaching people who are unfamiliar with surveys is that some respondents will answer without much thought. For example, sizable percentages in some developing nations, such as Cuba and Mexico, said that they would tell patients about options that were not even available in their countries, such as preimplantation diagnosis (a technologically sophisticated procedure involving in vitro fertilization, which is still in the research stage in the United States) or "surrogate motherhood." Although some of the more "extreme" responses (for example, a majority in Russia advising pregnant women to have abortions if prenatal diagnosis indicated that the child would be obese) may have resulted from a previous lack of discussion of ethical issues in professional circles, unfamiliarity with the survey method itself may also contribute. Ideally, a researcher should be able to follow up a questionnaire survey with telephone interviews of a random sample. Practically speaking, this is impossible in the countries where it might be most useful because of the condition of telecommunications. Our international colleagues hope that further discussion of the issues, based on the results of our previous surveys, will lead to more thoughtful responses in the future.

Besides the survey of genetics professionals, we are conducting a survey of genetics patients' ethical views in the United States, Canada, France, and Germany, using questionnaires. Our colleagues in France and Germany have found it much easier to conduct patient surveys than we have in North America. They do not have to go through institutional review boards (IRBs) in order to conduct anonymous surveys. Their patients do not have to sign informed consent forms before taking such surveys, and they do not have master's-level genetic counselors who are protective of their patients. Our European colleagues were able to collect one hundred surveys a month with almost no effort on the part of staff and with only a few clinics participating. Most patients not only responded but also wrote "thank you" on the questionnaires for being asked about their opinions. In contrast it has taken us two-and-one-half years in the United States and Canada to collect 350 questionnaires, even with thirty clinics initially offering to participate. Some clinics are still going through IRB review after two years. In other clinics, genetic counselors felt that the questionnaires were too intrusive, that patients did not read sufficiently well to understand them, or that distributing them would take too much staff time. Perhaps one-third to one-half of North American patients have declined to participate despite monetary compensation for their time. (No compensation was offered in Europe.) We suspect that the differences in response rates are due to the manner of distribution and the requirement of signing a lengthy consent form. Patients in the United States, unlike physicians, have not been oversurveyed, and those who have responded have often said they were grateful for an opportunity to express their thoughts.

RESULTS

Most respondents seemed to accept the overall selection of issues in the questionnaire. When, at the end, they had a chance to comment on the questionnaire itself, a total of only 2 percent said that it was culture-bound, United States–oriented, centered on high-tech society, or ignored third world reality. Only 1 percent complained of language difficulties or lack of clarity. A few (less than 1 percent) said that the case vignettes were too hypothetical, that the choices of answers provided were manipulative and directive, or that they might answer differently if they took it another time.

We were pleased to note that almost all professional respondents to the 1993–1994 survey knew how to distinguish an ethical problem from a technical problem. This is an important distinction of which many students entering college ethics classes in the United States are unaware. In the

1985 survey we included careful directions for answering the "why would you choose this course of action?" sections, lest respondents say things like "I would repeat the test and if the result was greater than *X*, I would do the following additional tests," which is not an *ethical* reason. We provided a case example and suggested that ethical reasons might include "refusal to lie, obligation to make the truth known, responsibility to society at large, or to avoid causing harm." In some countries, most notably Japan, our "suggested examples" came back to us verbatim as responses to many of the cases. In 1993 we decided to prevent any temptation to use our words. Therefore, we did not present a sample case and took the risk of receiving technical responses. Most people used ethical language in responding to the second survey, suggesting that most know how to distinguish ethical from technical problems.

Some ethical concepts that form the keystone of biomedical ethics in North America and Western Europe, however, do not affect practice elsewhere to the same extent and in fact may be understood only with difficulty. The overriding principle in English-speaking nations is patient autonomy, or respect for persons. This includes the right to information, the right to decide, the right to self-determination, respect in the provider-patient relationship, and, by implication, truth telling and nondirective counseling on the part of the health care provider. This concept emerged during the Enlightenment in the eighteenth century and underlies the writings of Thomas Jefferson and the U.S. Constitution. In the American colonies and later the United States, there was always an implicit right to medical self-determination (de Tocqueville 1835; Walters and Wertz 1989). Genetic counseling, a profession that emerged in the United States after World War II, took this right to an extreme, partly because it focused largely on education rather than treatment and an educational interaction gives more equality to the "patient" (or client) than a treatment-oriented interaction, and partly because counselors wanted to avoid the "eugenic advice" of the 1930s when they discussed reproductive alternatives. Thus, genetic counseling adopted the "nondirective" approach of presenting information and helping clients work through to their own decisions (Sorenson et al. 1981; Reed 1974). Telling clients what to do, or giving purposely slanted information so that they will come to what the counselor thinks is the "right" decision, is considered unacceptable in English-speaking nations. Elsewhere, however, physicians find the concept of nondirectiveness difficult to understand. In most nations medicine follows a paternalistic tradition of doing (or advising) whatever the physician thinks best for the patient. The principle of nonmaleficence ("do no harm") outweighs the principle of autonomy in many nations. Thus, outside North America and Western Europe, the majority of geneticists think that giving purposely slanted information after a prenatal diagnosis is the most ethical approach because it will prevent harm to parents and/or fetus. Only if the geneticist does not know what he or she thinks is right in a situation (or perhaps does not want to take the trouble to think about the most ethical approach) does the patient get to decide, untrammeled by advice. The language used expresses this difference in approach. In English, respondents say "the patient has a *right* to decide" or "has a *right* to know." In Spanish or Chinese (for example), the phrase is "the patient *ought* to decide" (because I can't, it's too difficult), "*has* to decide," or even "has a *duty* to decide." This is a fundamentally different approach from investing inalienable rights in the patient.

When trying to export concepts such as autonomy and nondirectiveness, health care providers need to remember that the Enlightenment was a northern and western European phenomenon that did not fully permeate some European countries, including Spain (and by extension, Latin America). It is difficult to convey these concepts to Latin Americans today. There is no standard translation for the phrase "try to be unbiased," which appeared as one choice of answer on our questionnaire. It may be translated as "neutral" or "objective," but neither really carries the weight of the English phrase. The Spanish word often used for "counseling" (*consejo*) means "to give advice." (*Asesoramiento,* which means "to provide information and offer supportive counseling," is often passed over as too long to use.) German has only one word for counseling, *beraten,* which also means "advise." Thus, although more geneticists in Germany than in some other continental European nations claimed that they would "be as unbiased as possible," responses to a special set of questions added by our German colleague to assess interpretations of nondirectiveness suggest that being unbiased included telling the client what the counselor would do if in the client's situation, along with other approaches generally *not* considered nondirective in North America. One can only wonder how much the language itself contributed to the interpretation of counseling.

Another concept that many respondents found difficult to understand outside the English-speaking world was anonymity. In countries where few surveys were conducted, many did not believe that responses would be truly anonymous. Despite the printed instructions, "Do not write your name on the questionnaire," some questionnaires arrived complete with names. Some people, who were not sure whether they had returned the questionnaire, wrote and asked us to find their questionnaires in order to be sure. They believed that we had somehow placed identifying marks on each questionnaire. People simply could not believe that anyone would do a survey without wanting to know how particular individuals had responded. On the other hand, some respondents in France and in Spanish-speaking countries were upset when "age" was inadvertently translated as "date of birth," a mistake that I would urge researchers to avoid. In some countries, it is easy to identify a fellow professional simply by knowing the birth date, which may be on identity cards or in professional association records. In supplying raw data to colleagues in other nations, we had to remove some of the sociodemographic data, because in some cases our colleagues showed an avid interest in identifying individuals who had unusual responses or who made "too much" money.

The concept of patient privacy is also a product of the Enlightenment that is unknown in most of the world outside North America and Western Europe. Privacy differs from confidentiality. Confidentiality, or the "keeping of secrets," is a universal concept. Secrets fall into several categories. These include (1) *natural secrets*, which are so horrible that they should never be spread abroad (for example, Oedipus marrying his mother). Many respondents probably thought that a genetic test, done for another purpose, unexpectedly showing that a man was not the father of a child was a natural secret. (2) *Committed secrets* are those that the respondent has personally promised never to tell. (3) *Role-related secrets* apply to sacred knowledge, to information revealed in the confessional, and, because in many cultures medicine originated as a sacred calling, to information passed from patient to physician. Respondents described this as "the medical secret."

Privacy goes beyond confidentiality by establishing a space around the individual, which becomes the individual's property. According to John Locke (1977), "Every man has a property in his own person." Privacy began in seventeenth-century bourgeois culture, with the individual ownership of many objects and of private living space, including, for perhaps the first time, bedrooms with separate entrances (Schama 1987). (A tour of Versailles, or any other European palace, will demonstrate that even royalty did not have this concept of privacy. There were no hallways. People had to walk through many other people's bedrooms to get to their own.) Privacy has perhaps reached its extreme in the English-speaking world, with much attention to "genetic privacy" (for example, ownership of one's DNA samples) in ethics and law. By contrast, the Chinese have no word for privacy. In most of the world (outside North America and Europe), respondents did not consider privacy important. Answers to one of our cases were revealing. The case described a patient newly diagnosed with a genetic condition. His diagnosis meant that his siblings and children were at 50 percent risk of developing the same disorder, but he refused to allow the health care provider to tell them about their risks. We asked providers whether they would (1) respect the patient's desire for confidentiality; (2) tell relatives about their risks, but *only if they ask*; (3) tell relatives even if they do not ask; (4) send the information to the patient's referring physician who would decide what to do. Respondents were directed to choose *one* answer only. To our surprise, respondents in many countries chose answers 1, 2, and 4 simultaneously. Their explanations indicated that they did not consider these choices contradictory. Many stated that they were preserving patient confidentiality as long as they did not tell nonrelatives and did not tell relatives who did not ask. Telling relatives who asked, even though this expressly contradicted the patient's wishes, was not seen as a breach of confidentiality. Similarly, in many parts of the world, respondents thought that spouses and relatives should have automatic access to patient information. This reflects an overall cultural approach that assumes that everybody knows everybody else's business in most spheres of life. North American discussions of individual ownership of banked DNA (or even of individual rights to control uses of anonymized DNA) may appear somewhat strange elsewhere.

On the other hand, some concepts found elsewhere are rarely mentioned in the English-speaking world. Notable among these is patient responsibility, which appeared prominently in comments almost everywhere except the United States, Canada, the United Kingdom, and Australia. In these four countries, responsibility appears to pertain mainly to the health care provider.

In Latin countries the father's rights over his children may stem solely from the act of generation and may be considered absolute. That the father might be separated from the mother and might have no intention of seeing the child made no difference. Some respondents thought that as progenitor he had automatic rights to know genetic information about a fetus and also to play a role in deciding the fate of that fetus. Such "biological thinking" is comparatively rare in English-speaking nations.

The word *eugenics* almost never appeared in North American or European reasoning, except as an example of unspeakable evil, having been totally discredited by the Nazis' actions. In China, however, *eugenics* is not only a good word but is also actually regarded as an ethical "principle" to be followed. (Use of the term *principle* was interesting since Confucianism, which underlies modern Chinese culture, is based entirely on hierarchies and is an "ethics without principles.") For most Chinese geneticists, eugenics was the primary goal of genetics, stated as such without hesitation. Although many in other developing nations expressed similar sentiments to those of the Chinese, they used the term *prevention*, which they regarded as different from eugenics. In many cases, however, the terms appeared synonymous.

Otherwise, "politically correct" language appeared limited to the United States and, to much lesser extent, other English-speaking nations. Political correctness almost always requires additional words (for example, "child with cystic fibrosis" instead of "CF child") or less loaded synonyms (for example, "genetic disorder" or "genetic condition" instead of "genetic disease"). English, which as a Germanic-Romance hybrid has more words than other languages, usually has an acceptable synonym. In other languages, however, there may be only one word to describe a situation. Under these circumstances no one thinks of replacing a term that in English would be politically incorrect, nor does the existing term carry the same negative connotations as would be found in English. Thus, in French the words *handicappé* and *mongolisme* are common parlance in genetics and are not considered demeaning to those with disabilities. *Defective, malformed,* and *diseased* appear in the literature, apparently without protest. "Person-first" language ("child with _____") is never used. We might begin to ask ourselves whether political correctness is merely a luxury for those whose languages have ample synonyms or whether the existence of only one description in some other languages has in fact damaged public perceptions of disability. Both statements may be true, but we have not yet looked for possible relationships between respondents' views on disability and the connotations of the language commonly used to describe it. In any case, our questionnaires, which were carefully devised to use politically correct language suggested by consumers and people with disabilities, immediately lost most of this political correctness on translation. This was perhaps inevitable.

We developed a codebook for analyzing the write-in comments (see Table 1). In the 1985 survey the codes were based on five moral principles commonly found in textbooks on medical ethics (Beauchamp and Childress 1994): autonomy (respect for persons), nonmaleficence (avoidance or mitigation of harm), beneficence (a positive performance of good works), justice, and strict monetary utilitarianism (cost-benefit analysis), plus a set of codes for "nonmoral reasons," such as "my supervisor won't allow this." Most respondents did not name actual principles. Instead, they used what Tom Beauchamp and James Childress (1994) call "action-guides," a shorthand, practical statement that is usually based on a principle. As we built up the codebook inductively, we categorized and clustered the actual responses from a random sample of questionnaires into ninety-eight short statements, under the headings of the five principles listed above. As we continued to read the rest of the questionnaires, we added to and revised some of the original codes. The codebook remained under development until the final questionnaire was coded. The 1985 codebook appeared in several publications (Wertz and Fletcher 1989a, 1989b, 1991). We then summed up the total number of responses under each heading. Not surprisingly, in the 1985 survey autonomy accounted for the majority (59 percent) of responses. The United States, Canada, United Kingdom, Sweden, and Australia were the most autonomy-oriented, whereas Hungary, Norway, India, and France were the least. Beneficence accounted for few answers (11 percent), as did justice (5 percent).

Caroline Whitbeck, a feminist philosopher of science, suggested that principle-based bioethics was outdated and proposed an analysis based on needs and relationships. It was too late to recode the entire 1985 data set, but we experimented with reorganizing the ninety-eight action-guides under the following five headings: rights and obligations (reciprocal relationships), needs and responsibilities (reciprocal relationships), deserts

TABLE 1   Codebook for Moral Reasoning

Choice of action depends on patient characteristics   (reflects attention to differences between patients of different backgrounds)
   Age
   Sex
   Education
   Income
   Religious belief, ethnicity, culture
   Other patient characteristics
Perceptions of disability
   Disability as a burden/undesirable—"wrongful birth"
   Disability is socially caused
   Disability can be overcome, child can be adopted
Deserts (special "extras" owed to people because of prior injustice or prior good work)
   Minorities
   Women (special mention of position of women in family or society)
   People with disabilities
   Other deserts
Autonomy   (the ethical conviction that individuals should be treated as autonomous agents, e.g., unconditional right to self-determination, choice, informed consent, autonomy, own decision, use of available technical options, right to refuse, full disclosure, right to referral, right to abortion)
   Patient (or parents, if a child)
   Spouse/partner
   Relatives at risk
   Geneticist or physician (right to refuse to perform a procedure or to withhold
      information), or employer
   Counselor should be nondirective, support whatever decision clients make
   Patient requests should be respected, whether they are right or wrong
Ethical conviction that there is a responsibility or obligation to protect the autonomy of the person even though it may be diminished   (e.g., person is vulnerable, incapacitated, has knowledge that is incommensurate with the geneticist's knowledge, or geneticist has knowledge of patient's secrets or diagnosis; includes answers mentioning dignity of or respect for other party)
   Patient
   Child
   Explicitly acknowledges that autonomy is diminished
Right to know   (entitled or deserve to know; reasonable request; includes the right *not* to know)
   Patient (parents if a minor)
   Spouse/partner
   Relatives at risk
   Professional colleagues or third parties (insurers, employers, school)
Need to know
   Optimal choices, or decisions are *based upon use* of medical/genetic information by
      patient, relatives, geneticist, referring physician, or third parties
   May change mind about abortion or other actions after receiving test results
Truth telling   (rule-oriented; use for Kantian arguments)
   Honesty, obligation to tell truth
   Refusal to lie

TABLE 1   (*Cont.*)

Right to privacy or confidentiality
  Patient
  Child or adolescent
  Relatives at risk
  Physician-patient relationship (trust, confidentiality)
Prevent or minimize physical or moral harm or risk of harm   (moral harm–deceit)
  Duty to warn third parties, including relatives, of harm—including harm from new
    or experimental procedures
  Responsibility to give advice, direction, guidance, education
  Do no harm (includes harm to third parties or relatives)
  To patient (includes burden of disease on parents)
  To fetus or child (*harm other than abortion*)
  To future children, including *prevention of birth defects* (includes helping patient
    have a normal child)
  Oppose abortion
  Oppose abortion of normal fetus
  Preserve family unity, resolve conflict through discussion
  Truth telling to avoid harm
  Truth telling as a source of harm
  No benefit gained from truth telling (no need to know)
  Potential misuse of information by third parties
  Avoid social stigmatization, discrimination in the workplace or elsewhere
  Harm through regulations or government intervention
  Viability, or life begins at birth; respect for nature
Patient responsibility
  Patient's responsibility: "duty to know," whether they want to or not, and to use
    information; general patient responsibility
  Patient is irresponsible
  Harm to society if sex ratio upset, sex discrimination
  Parent's request serves no useful purpose
  Do not set a precedent that will harm the moral order (slippery slope
    argument)
  Removal of guilt or anxiety now, help with present problems
  Physician's responsibility to provide health care for family, society
  The "Golden Rule" of Christian tradition: Do unto others as you would have
    others do unto you
  Benefits outweigh possible harm
  Means of truth telling so as to maximize good (means of telling truth, support,
    counseling, referrals)
  Parental responsibilities to care for children with disabilities
Prepare for the future
  Family planning, making informed reproductive choices
  Prepare patient for the future, including help coping with stresses of disease or
    abortion
  Child will be in normal range, despite genetic diagnosis
Improvement of life, society
  Future generations
  Health care, education; respect for science
  Insurance coverage
  Workers' health (includes responsibility of factory to worker)

TABLE 1   (*Cont.*)

Working conditions

Social unity, respect for diversity

Protection of persons through regulation or licensing of labs and providers (ensure proper level of service, quality control) to prevent misuse; general need for laws; use of laws to prevent fetal abuse; disability laws; compulsory sterilization laws

Common good, public health, public safety

Population limitation

Maintain balanced sex ratio

Eugenic arguments—cost to society

Fairness

Equal access

Entitlement to full insurance coverage

Right to medical care that is affordable

Fairness or unfairness; they deserve or don't deserve the service

Interests of the fetus ought to be treated equally with those of living persons at some point

Allocation of resources

Use resources wisely; don't waste resources

Appropriate or inappropriate use of technology—medical indication or no medical indication

All available services should be provided on request

Gaining acceptance (historical evolution)/accepted by community

Utility

Efficiency or utility

Cost-benefit analysis

Protection of economic interest of third parties, including taxpayers

They have a right to whatever service they can pay for out-of-pocket

Medicine (or genetics) should not be a business

Nonmoral answers

Compromise (stated as such by respondent) includes referral to another center, disclosure to another physician rather than patients, consult with ethics committee; do nothing because no action will make a difference

Fear of lawsuit

Logistically or technically difficult, accurate or inaccurate, correct or incorrect, advances in technology will solve ethical dilemma

Law, regulations, supervisor, institution forbids/requires, permits

Not accepted, controversial

I do not accept or approve of this

This is not a geneticist's problem; should be dealt with by another professional

The Bible (or equivalent in my religion) tells me so

Situation unrealistic; I have never seen this in my practice

I approve of this or am neutral

Missing

Relationships   (see National Society of Genetic Counselors code for 1–4)

None

With self

With patient/client

With colleagues

TABLE 1   (*Cont.*)

With society, institutional third parties
With own sense of professional integrity
With patient's family
Patient intrafamilial
Patient, marital
No answer
Consequences mentioned
Yes
No
No answer
Basis for comment
Principle or rule-based (refers to a principle such as autonomy, or to the
   categorical imperative)
Action rule-guided
Experience based (refers to another case; the "casuistry factor")
None of the above
No answer
Culture-bound v. universal
Culture-bound (refers to specific practices, *regulations,* situation in own country,
   e.g., entrepreneurial medicine in the United States)
Universal (refers to practices applicable across cultures)
No answer

---

and justice (reciprocal), good of the health care system, and good of society. The ninety-eight action-guides fit into this revised schema without too much difficulty, though we probably would have coded some questionnaires differently if we had started with a relationship-based analysis. Around the world, more responses fell under needs and responsibilities (48 percent) than under the legal language of rights and obligations (45 percent), though the reverse was the case in the United States (44 percent versus 49 percent). Despite Carol Gilligan's (1982) hypothesis that women are more likely than men to structure their moral reasoning in terms of needs and responsibilities, our 1985 survey found few significant gender differences, possibly because only 35 percent of respondents were women (compared with 65 percent in 1995) and most had been socialized into the profession by men. The 1994 survey found far more differences (Wertz 1997). Respondents not only differ by gender but also by profession. Master's-level genetic counselors, for example, differed from physicians on 60 percent of questions. Female physicians differed from male physicians on almost half the questions, around the world, but the *direction* of difference varied by geographic area. Few answers fell under deserts and justice, good of the health care system, or good of society.

In the codebook for the 1993–1994 survey, we deleted some codes that were rarely used in 1985 and added some that reflected areas of growing concern within the past ten years, such as attention to differences among patients with different ethnic backgrounds or personal characteristics, perceptions of disability, and the position of women. Table 1 represents the 1993–1994 codebook. Like the 1985 codebook, the 1993 codebook was a living entity. We continued to add to codes as needed. In 1993 respondents brought up the following new codes, not present in 1985: patient responsibility; patient irresponsibility; respect for science; protection of persons through laws to prevent fetal abuse, disability laws, or compulsory sterilization laws; protection of economic interests of the taxpayers; do nothing because no action will make a difference; this is not a geneticist's problem and should be dealt with by another professional; life begins at birth; and respect for nature. Most of these new codes (except for economic interests of taxpayers and "this is not a geneticist's problem") came from outside the United States. "Respect for nature" and "do nothing" rarely if ever appeared in the comments of U.S. respondents. In some cases we had to make a code do "double duty," as we had allowed for only 98 codes. In any future survey we would allow for up to 998 codes (three columns of data), expecting to end up with a total of perhaps 150.

The codebook of ninety-eight reasons developed for the provider survey also covered most of the reasons given by patients. We allowed space for more reasons, but added only thirteen. Among the reasons patients gave that were not given by any of the over 2900 geneticists were "conciliation and reconciliation—everybody should discuss this together and come to agreement," "profitmaking by geneticists," "leave it in God's hands—do not interfere," "coercion to have prenatal diagnosis," "protect patient's financial status," and "threat to democracy." Patient (or perhaps "client" or "consumer," the politically correct terms in the United States) culture may prove to be considerably different from professional culture.

We plan to analyze the data in several ways. First, we will cluster most of the ninety-eight codes under the major headings in Table 1 and will add up total responses under each heading, using the SPSSX multiresponse procedure. We will look at responses by country and by sociodemographic variables such as gender of respondent. We will then reorganize the ninety-eight headings according to relationship theory, using the five headings described earlier (rights-obligations, and so on), and will perform the same analysis to see whether subgroups reason differently.

In both the 1985 and 1993–1994 surveys, we coded the qualitative data for consequentialism in thinking. Did respondents mention a possible consequence of their actions? In 1985, in 39 percent of responses, they did, ranging from 29 percent in Japan to 83 percent in Norway. In 1985 we also recorded the number of reasons that a respondent gave. Women gave more reasons than men, but otherwise the data were uninformative. We also coded whose welfare appeared most important (for example, patient, family unit, child or fetus, geneticist, or society). Most respondents (72 percent) gave primacy to the patient's welfare, followed by family (15 percent). In 1985 we also coded for conflicts expressed in the reasoning (for example, client-family, client-geneticist, parent-child or fetus, individual-society). In 74 percent of responses, there was no mention of conflict. In 1994 we decided not to record the number of reasons because this might reflect only fluency in English in those nations that chose not to use translations. We also abandoned the idea of coding for conflicts or for whose welfare was most important because these efforts had given us little information about cultural differences. Instead, in 1994 we coded for the possible presence of relationships in a respondent's reasoning. Our reason for doing so stemmed from the new Code of Ethics of the National Society of Genetic Counselors (1992). This code is based entirely on the counselor's relationships—with self, patient or client, colleagues, and society. To this list we added the geneticist's relationship with a personal sense of professional integrity and with patient's family, the patient's own intrafamilial relationships, and the patient's relationship with spouse or partner. Because we had once again allowed too few columns, we had to add relationship to institutional third parties to the code for relationship with society. Interestingly, most comments neither mentioned nor implied a relationship of any kind. This does not mean that geneticists do not feel close to their clients, only that they do not seem to refer to relationships in describing the basis of their ethical reasoning. This phenomenon deserves further investigation, both by observation of counseling sessions and by interviews, to see why relationships are not brought into ethics.

In 1994 we recorded the basis of each response: (1) principle or rule (explicit mention of autonomy or categorical imperative); (2) action-guide (a less formal, more practical statement, ultimately based on a principle); or (3) personal experience with a similar case. Our choices were based on Albert Jonsen's article "Balloons and Bicycles" (1991), in which he argues that the view of an ethical dilemma from a hot-air balloon would give a broad picture such as that provided by a principles approach, whereas the view of the same dilemma from a person on the ground would give a close-up picture of personal experience. Jonsen argued that both views were essential to ethical reasoning. Most of our respondents reasoned from a middle ground: action-guides (Beauchamp and Childress 1994). Few reasoned from personal experience, although in response to specific questions after each case vignette from one-third to two-thirds said they had had similar cases. They apparently chose not to use their experience to justify their actions. More referred to formal principles, such as autonomy, than referred to experience. This is another area of moral reasoning that needs further research.

Finally, in 1993–1994 we coded for whether a response was culture-bound (referred to specific practices, regulations, or cultural/economic situation in the respondent's own country) or universal (implied that the respondent's choice of action was applicable across cultures). Most responses were coded as universal, including all of those from the United

States. There were few cases where respondents spoke of the legal, social, or economic situation in their country as a causative or limiting factor (with the exception of China). This may have been a result of limited writing space in the questionnaires, which varied according to the translation and which was not under our control. It may also have resulted from our initial directions to respondents to try to answer as if they were not bound by policies or regulations. In any future surveys this information would be better gathered by asking in a separate question, following each of the ethical problems most open to cultural influence: "To what extent was your response influenced by the cultural/religious/economic situation in your country?" For questions about counseling after prenatal diagnosis reveals a fetus with a genetic condition, most geneticists are aware of the religious, cultural, and legal climate surrounding abortion; it would be interesting to gauge the extent to which they feel this climate affects their practice.

In the future, cross-cultural discussion of ethics may lead to greater similarities among professionals. In 1993–1994, contrary to our expectations, most geneticists had *not* received part of their training abroad. In the future, more will travel to other countries for training. Master's-level genetic counselors and genetic nurses, mostly women, will appear in more countries. If their training follows models developed in the United States, there may be more attention to client autonomy and privacy. The diffusion of ethical concepts is likely to be from North America and Europe to other nations, rather than vice versa. This is not to say that North America has nothing to learn from other cultures; the concept of the family as a unit that shares both genes and genetic information—a concept found in other parts of the world—is uniquely relevant to genetics. Nevertheless, North Americans in the survey tended to see themselves as the ethical center of the world to a greater extent than respondents elsewhere. North Americans expressed their answers in universal terms. In some other nations respondents gave answers that were culture-bound (for example, "In my country, we do this," or "My culture requires"), without implying that others should do likewise.

In sum, our experience with the professional surveys leads us to conclude that international survey research is possible, though the researcher must be flexible with regard to methods, samples, and instruments in different countries and must be prepared for unannounced innovations on the part of foreign colleagues. Sticklers for absolute comparability of samples or concepts will be frustrated. Nevertheless, such research is worthwhile. Its goal is to provide a basis for further discussion of the issues by giving a general illustration of what most people think. Our research has already led to discussions in national and international professional societies, the World Health Organization, and some legislatures. We encourage others to conduct such research, keeping in mind the possibility of creating social change.

NOTE

1. The Ethical, Legal, and Social Implications Branch of the National Center for Human Genome Research (National Institutes of Health) provided funds for the 1993–1994 international survey. The Medical Trust, one of the Pew Memorial Trusts, and the Muriel and Maurice Miller Foundation provided support for the 1985–1986 survey. My colleague, Professor John C. Fletcher, Director of the Center for Biomedical Ethics at the University of Virginia, Charlottesville, originated the idea for both surveys and acted as a collaborator throughout. Robin Gregg and Wanda Hunt coded a mountain of qualitative data and offered suggestions.

REFERENCES

Beauchamp, Tom L., and James F. Childress. 1994. *Principles of biomedical ethics*, 4th ed. New York: Oxford University Press.

de Tocqueville, Alexis. 1951. [1835]. *Democracy in America*. Vol. 1. Edited by P. Bradley. New York: Knopf.

Gilligan, Carol. 1982. *In a different voice: Psychological theory and women's development*. Cambridge, Mass.: Harvard University Press.

Jonsen, Albert R. 1991. Of balloons and bicycles or the relationship between ethical theory and practical judgment. *Hastings Center Report* 21 (September-October): 14–6.

Locke, John. 1977. *Two treatises*. In *The Locke Reader*, edited by J. W. Yolton. New York: Cambridge University Press, 289.

Macer, Darryl R. J. 1994. *Bioethics for the people by the people*. Tsukuba, Japan: Eubios Ethics Institute.

Marteau, Theresa, Harriet Drake, Margaret Reid, Maria Feijoo, Marta Soares, Irma Nippert, Peter Nippert, and Martin Bobrow. 1994. Counselling following prenatal diagnosis of abnormality: A comparison between German, Portuguese, and UK geneticists. *European Journal of Human Genetics* 2(2): 96–102.

National Society of Genetic Counselors. 1992. Code of ethics. *Journal of Genetic Counseling* 1(1): 41–4.

Reed, Sheldon. 1974. A short history of genetic counseling. *Social Biology* 21: 332–9.

Schama, Simon. 1987. *The embarrassment of riches: An interpretation of Dutch culture in the golden age*. Berkeley: University of California Press.

Sorenson, James R., Judith P. Swazey, and Norman A. Scotch. 1981. *Reproductive pasts, reproductive futures: Genetic counselling and its effectiveness*. New York: Liss.

Walters, Leroy, and Dorothy C. Wertz. 1989. Ethics and genetics in the United States of America. In *Ethics and human genetics: A cross-cultural perspective*, edited by Dorothy C. Wertz and John C. Fletcher. Berlin: Springer-Verlag, 419–56.

Wertz, Dorothy C. 1997. Is there a "women's ethic" in genetics? A 37–nation survey of providers. *Journal of the American Medical Women's Association* 52(1): 33–8.

Wertz, Dorothy C., and John C. Fletcher, eds. 1989a. *Ethics and human genetics: A cross-cultural perspective*. Heidelberg: Springer-Verlag.

Wertz, Dorothy C., and John C. Fletcher. 1989b. Moral reasoning among medical geneticists in 18 nations. *Theoretical Medicine* 10: 123–38.

Wertz Dorothy C., and John C. Fletcher. 1991. Privacy and disclosure in medical genetics examined in an ethics of care. *Bioethics* 5 (3): 212–32.

Wertz, Dorothy C., John C. Fletcher, and John J. Mulvihill. 1990. Medical geneticists confront ethical dilemmas: Cross-cultural comparisons among 18 nations. *American Journal of Human Genetics* 46(6): 1200–13.

CHAPTER NINE

To Enrich Bioethics, Add One Part Social to One Part Clinical

**Eugene B. Gallagher, Pamela Schlomann,
Rebecca S. Sloan, Jessica Mesman,
Julie B. Brown, and Anna Cholewinska**

Bioethics has, since the late 1960s, become an established presence in American medical care, the American academy, and in American life. Having won acceptance, bioethics now needs to be broadened. How do emergent realities in health care policy impinge on bioethical discourse? What must bioethics do to keep its relevance as a critique of modern medicine? Can bioethics move toward greater social relevance without losing its analytic force?

To help answer these questions, we first look at how bioethics developed, starting in the early 1960s. We then present instances of ethnographic observation that offer rich material for bioethical reflection but that, given the present stance of bioethics, are defined as out of range. We hope to show that a bioethical imagination charged with insights drawn from sociology and nursing is not a gratuitous or self-serving extension of the field but a valuable resource for fulfilling the promise of bioethics.

THE ROOTS OF BIOETHICS

Accounts of the beginnings of bioethics usually trace it to the 1960s. James Sorenson and Judith Swazey in their overview of ethical issues in medical care write:

> Although most of the issues being examined in bioethics are old ones philosophically, its emergence in the United States as an area of applied ethics dates from the 1960's . . . bioethics has developed around and focused attention on a particular cluster of values and beliefs, which are very American in character . . . The major value orientation of bioethics has involved individualism, focusing on concerns about autonomy and individual rights. (1989, 494)

Other influential bioethicists, such as David Rothman (1991), place it earlier, with attention to crucial events during and immediately following
World War II. Patricia Flynn concurs:

> The discipline of bioethics is dated by most historians to begin with events of
> the 1960s. However, I maintain that it was under the penumbra of events of the
> 1940s that it emerged, especially the Nuremberg medical trials . . . The trials
> provided a wedge which allowed wider negotiations about the medical moral
> order to occur and were integral conditions for the construction of bioethics.
> (1991, 147–8)

Like other students of bioethics, Flynn agrees that individualism and
autonomy are now dominant themes in bioethics, but her historical probe
takes her back to an earlier, prebioethical era when these themes were
scarcely recognized. In that time clinical medicine had very limited powers
to alter the medical fate of individuals. The great medical advances of the
nineteenth century and the early decades of the twentieth century were in
the domain of public health—improvements in sanitation, nutrition, and
prevention of disease through immunization. Conflicts between the individual and the public interest remained latent but with a strong tilt toward
public—that is, state—power when they erupted into open view. The analytic concepts concerning individual sentience and responsibility that had
been so actively shaped by Enlightenment philosophers such as Locke and
Hume, found no special application to medical situations in the pre-
bioethics period. Under the subsequent mandate of bioethics, however, all
the vigor and acuteness that had earlier been invested in notions of "economic man" and "political man" were now matched by an intense refinement of concepts, centered on the notion of a universalized "biological
individual" as the bearer of disease and a recipient of medical treatment.[1]

Even if Flynn and Rothman are right in tracing the early roots of
bioethics to the Nuremberg medical experiments rather than new technology, technology and research played an important role in the emerging
institutional apparatus of bioethics, including national study commissions,
hospital ethics committees, administrative definitions of brain death, and
informed consent procedures in medical research.

For example, transplantation technology for solid organs generates a
host of ethically charged questions. Since there is a shortage of such organs,
the limited supply must be distributed among a host of potential recipients.
What criteria will govern the selection of recipients? How will the donor
organs be obtained? For cadaver donors, what definition of death will prevail? For live donors, is it ethical for physicians to remove organs that might
impair the biological integrity of the donor?

These are familiar questions, which have been dealt with by bioethicists. We raise them here not to grapple substantively with them but to show
that they entail a style of analysis and response that is congenial to bioethics

as a branch of ethics and philosophy. We believe that in its embrace of existence-of-technology issues, bioethics has been slow to deal with other issues, such as those stemming from maldistribution of medical resources and the interprofessional power dynamics of medical personnel.

These latter issues are rich and evocative and require a focus on social context. The need to pay attention to context might explain why these issues have been ignored by bioethicists. Bioethicists are ill suited to consider issues arising from unequal access, professional and administrative power, or economic and social (dis)advantage.

CLINICAL BIOETHICS AND SOCIAL BIOETHICS

Ethics has traditionally been concerned with questions of right conduct. How ought the individual live his or her life? How can one's conduct be brought under the mandate of ethical scrutiny and analysis? What ethical principles should guide decisions? What authority should these principles be derived from?

Transporting these concerns into the realm of medical affairs, bioethics has tried to bring medical behavior into the pale of ethical observation. From the events and bustle of care in clinics, nurseries, operating theaters, and consulting rooms, it has put forth the injunction: "Wait a moment! Can you as health professionals describe and justify what you are doing—your decisions, and their consequences—in terms of the values of autonomy, mutuality, fairness, and honesty?" Bioethics attempts to explore rationales for behavior and for decisions that transcend purely technical, means-end considerations. It creates a decisional posture or scenario of choice in which an intelligent, moral actor can, given the factual parameters of a situation, make justifiable decisions.

This framework of thinking has dominated the evolution of bioethics. As a branch of philosophy, ethics reflects on episodes of human conduct that would otherwise be enacted according to routine practice, tradition, or habitually accepted authority. Directed to medical events, the ethical framework becomes bioethical. Bioethics probes, as it were, the tissue of a clinical situation to locate a "bioethical lesion," which it then attempts to formulate and resolve according to its mode of analysis.

Clinical bioethics takes the scenario as a given. In contrast, social bioethics asks how the clinical scenario came to be: What were the social forces motivating and informing the actors in the situation? What are the attributes of the actors as characterized according to age, gender, marital status, race, socioeconomic status, and educational attainment? For the patient bearing the illness, what medical and social events led up to the present situation? Does the illness have important social determinants? For the health professionals, what are the salient aspects of their training, orientation to practice, professional values, and professional prerogatives? Medical sociologists will immediately recognize these questions as moving in directions that structure their discipline.

Such questions, and the general matrix of inquiry that motivates them, have policy relevance for the total society and subsectors of it. For example, if an inebriated homeless person diagnosed with congestive heart failure is brought to a frantic metropolitan hospital emergency room, triage questions may occur within the clinical bioethical framework: What resources should be directed toward this patient right now? In contrast, the social bioethicist will be concerned with two other aspects of the case that lie outside the purview of clinical bioethics.

First, the social bioethicist will trace out the impact of social factors that lead to this scenario: Such factors would include the public housing facilities of the metropolis, the employment situation, the patient's neighborhood and social contacts, the patient's family background and kin connections, and medical care history.

Second, in what might be taken by the clinical bioethicist as a gratuitous incursion into the clinical situation, the social bioethicist will examine the patterns of communication and role dynamics that prevail among the personnel who deal with the patient. Whereas the clinical bioethicist is concerned with the content of clinical decisions and their supporting philosophical rationales, the social bioethicist is concerned with the sociomedical factors in society that bear upon clinical situations, the social structure of decision making, and the concrete implementation of decisions.

Social bioethics links clinical or philosophical bioethics with ethnographically oriented social science. Moreover, social bioethics connects microsocial perspectives with macrosocial knowledge. From its linkage of situational with societal factors, social bioethics gains a "political" leverage that clinical bioethics lacks.

THE NURSE AS SOCIAL BIOETHICIST

Among the ranks of health care professionals, it is physicians who have legal authority and responsibility for major decisions and who have the broadest, though not always the most immediate or sustained, access to clinical and social information concerning the patient. Thus, it is not surprising that, from their base of professional dominance, physicians have exerted enormous influence in the development of bioethics.

Although their voice has yet to be heard at the forefront of bioethical thinking, since the mid-1980s nurses have carried out provocative research that addresses ethical issues. From their intimate contact with patients and families in a wide variety of clinical situations, nurses are often in a better position than physicians to observe and interpret the diffuse human aspects of disease and treatment. As Renée Fox notes, "The nurse's professional role brings her . . . closely and continuously in contact with other members of the medical team, and with what it is like to be sick and a patient" (1985, 9).

In contrast, the physician's role as formal authority and specialized technical expert in medical care often puts blinders on what he or she can see and report. From their less constricted vantage point, nurses have infused vital data and insights into bioethical thought. Frequently, their research has, befitting their professional stance, the flavor of ethnographic fieldwork carried out by sociologists or anthropologists who have access to clinical situations. The data we present are derived from nursing research. These data show that ethical concern is never far from the center of nursing research, even when the primary focus is not avowedly ethical. The ethical slant of nursing research lies in the direction of social rather than clinical bioethics, being drawn from and addressed to the social surround of the hospitalized patient and to the role relationships of the medical care providers.

Over the next several pages, we present three pieces of nursing research and briefly consider their ethical implications. The first, by Rebecca Sloan, examines the situation of chronic hemodialysis patients and their disposition toward the possibility of receiving a renal transplant. The second, by Pamela Schlomann in the United States and Jessica Mesman in the Netherlands and in the United States, studies critical decision making in neonatal intensive care units (NICUs). The third study, by Julie Brown, focuses on the kinds of rewards and compensations that are offered to research subjects in the clinical research unit of a major teaching hospital. After describing these studies, we focus on the ethical quandaries they present and call for bioethics to adopt a broader view of its task.

THE HEMODIALYSIS FLOOR: PATIENTS WHO DECLINE RENAL TRANSPLANTATION

Sloan's research (1995) was conducted in a large hemodialysis clinic where over 180 chronic renal failure (otherwise called end-stage renal disease, or ESRD) patients received treatment. The clinic is managed by a national corporation that maintains many other similar facilities. Almost all the patients received treatment three times weekly, for three to five hours at each session. The clinic, located in the southeastern part of the United States, is affiliated with a medical school. In addition to treating patients, it is a teaching base for medical students and residents, and it carried out research in nephrology (for example, testing new drugs for their potential in alleviating complications of long-term dialysis). Sloan's position as research nurse in the clinic gave her a strategic vantage point from which to formulate the issues and questions that she studied.

Sloan interviewed thirty patients and their families in a broad-ranging investigation that explored the impact of renal failure and its treatment. Some of the patients had already received a transplant; most, however, were receiving long-term dialysis. Sloan was especially concerned to delve into a peculiar and striking phenomenon that she discovered through her ongoing work in the clinic: Many patients were notably disinclined toward receiving a transplant. A secondary, related phenomenon of concern was that, in reaction to patients' rejection of a "golden opportunity," some staff had come to hold negative feelings toward those patients.

Patients' disinclination toward transplant was a phenomenon that had escaped attention in earlier sociological studies of renal patients despite its sociological interest, its practical bearing on the supply and distribution of treatment resources in ESRD, and its bioethical implications. As will be seen, Sloan was able to demonstrate that this was a genuine, widespread happening and not the stuff of mere speculation or rumor. However, her interest lay less in assessing its precise extent than in interpreting it and linking it to other aspects of patient and staff experience in the clinic.

A few facts concerning ESRD treatment and expense will provide a context for Sloan's work. First, the federal government through Medicare pays approximately 80 percent of the cost of treatment of ESRD. Currently, the government's share of the cost of hemodialysis comes to about $30,000 per patient annually. Also, dialysis patients commonly have acute crises necessitating hospitalization, which adds to the expense as well as the risks associated with that modality.

Transplantation is cheaper than dialysis. The initial high cost of the transplant surgery is followed by the much lower cost (about $6000 annually for the government's 80 percent share) of the immunosuppressive drugs that are necessary to ward off rejection of the kidney.

From the standpoint of the patient's quality of life, transplant again has a clear advantage. Though the patient must take the drugs necessary to maintain the transplant, this burden is light compared with being tethered thrice weekly to a dialysis machine.

Transplantation is also the superior treatment as judged by patient survival. The *1994 Annual Data Report* of the U.S. Renal Data System (National Institutes of Health [NIH] 1994) shows, like its predecessors, that transplant recipients live longer than do hemodialysis patients, once age, race, and diagnosis are controlled. The 1994 national figures (NIH 1994, 81) show that, of all patients receiving a cadaver transplant, 92 percent lived for one year, and 87 percent lived for two years. The corresponding figures for hemodialysis patients are 76 percent and 60 percent.[2]

Given the powerful advantages of transplantation, why do many dialysis patients refuse to consider it? Sloan found that three major factors accounted for patients' reluctance. First, fear of surgery and further hospitalization. Second, uncertainty and anxiety that the transplant will be rejected. Third, concern that, through rejection, the kidney would be "wasted." Each of these factors is credible in light of the clinical and social biography of most ESRD patients. Let us consider them in greater detail.

Whether or not any given patient is fearful of more surgery, *no* patient enters hemodialysis without an extensive treatment history, including surgery; every patient has the potential for aversion toward more treatment. The treatment history typically begins with treatment for incipient renal decline—the medical effort through drugs and diet to stave off end-stage for as long as possible. When end-stage is reached, dialysis cannot start until, by means of a surgical procedure, an access point is established for the patient's blood to flow out into the dialyzer and then back into the patient's body. The blood access aperture and tubing sometimes become clotted or infected, necessitating heavy antibiotic treatment and surgical clearance—or, in the worst case, the surgical creation of another access point.

The survival statistics suggest that every medically eligible patient should be positively disposed to transplantation. Although patients are, as a rule, given these statistics to consider as they make their decisions, the figures alone are often not compelling enough to motivate them actively to seek transplant. Even if a patient could be certain of longer survival on transplant than dialysis, he or she might nevertheless, on rational grounds, recoil from the prospect of more surgery. Additionally, most dialysis patients know or have heard of transplant recipients whose kidney rejected. Sometimes the recipient expires in the rejection process; otherwise, if survival prevails, it is necessary to return to dialysis. It is also true that dialysis patients are exposed to the hardships and deaths of some dialysis patients in their midst, but dialysis as a repetitive, socially shared, and "known" process seems less dramatically dangerous than the "unknown"—socially and spatially remote—transplant surgery. Further, some of the dialysis-providing staff may themselves hold a very negative attitude which they freely express to patients toward transplant as a treatment modality; Alfred Drees and Eugene Gallagher (1981), for instance, discovered such influences at work in a large German dialysis clinic.

Our picture of dialysis emphasizes the tedium and drudgery of the process—transporting oneself to and from the dialysis site thrice weekly and sitting confined to a chair and a machine for three or four hours on each occasion. However, the "dialysis lifestyle" also has significant, positive aspects for many patients. From an ethnographic study of several clinics, Eugene Gallagher concluded: ". . . many of the patients lead lives that contain little social contact. Coming to the clinic is a social event that punctuates the routine of their daily existence. Elderly patients and those living under economically straitened circumstances probably gain an extra 'social activation benefit' from their clinic time" (1994, 86). Even if the transplant outcome were a "sure thing," many patients might still prefer the familiar routine of dialysis.

A third deterrent to transplant that Sloan found in her study was the scruple that many patients had about "wasting" a kidney. They had the sense that a transplant would not last very long for them; rather than lose a valuable cadaver kidney, they would prefer that another patient have a chance at it.[3] This source of transplant reluctance is related to the uncertainty of outcome—the second factor—but it reveals additional aspects of the life situation of patients.

Many of the patients in Sloan's clinic were poor inner-city residents of the surrounding metropolitan area. Many lived with hardships related to racial disadvantage, economic status, lack of education, unemployment, inadequate housing, family disruption, emotional stress, drug abuse, and conflicts with law enforcement. Life was a daily grind and struggle. They had little experience of success or accomplishment in life as the dominant middle-class orientation of American society views it; instead they saw themselves as a hapless group whose life and medical experiences consisted of "if anything can go wrong, it will!" Sloan's clinic perhaps had an unusual concentration of lower-class patients: however, a national survey reveals that "40% [of dialysis patients] are poor enough to qualify for Medicaid" (Eichenwald 1995, A12).

Although the hemodialysis treatment did enable them to live, the treatment experience of many patients did not lift their spirits or improve their picture of their life. Few were "ideal" dialysis patients in the eyes of staff. Dialysis as a treatment exposes patients to demanding expectations. Perhaps the most difficult for most patients is the drastic restriction on fluid intake between treatment sessions. For many patients the limit is one liter of liquid daily. When patients reported for treatment "overloaded" with water, it meant that more water had to be "pulled" from them by the dialyzer during the session, with greater physiological stress on their body.

Many patients were diabetic; in addition to the demands of dialysis treatment, they were expected to adhere to the dietary discipline imposed by diabetes. Many other patients suffered from hypertension, with its own treatment demands.

From the foregoing, it is obvious that there were many junctures at which patients could fall short of being "ideal" patients, and correspondingly many occasions at which staff could label them as noncompliant or unappreciative.

Of course, not every element in this general scenario of life and treatment applies to every dialysis patient. Nevertheless, it forms a context within which, for many patients, the wish not to try for a transplant kidney becomes understandable. The ongoing struggles with hemodialysis are enough. The hemodialysis-providing staff, fully preoccupied with their own tasks, do not typically foster in patients any great desire to "improve their lot" by transplant. Further, although hemodialysis patients do not have any regular contact with transplant physicians and nurses, they are aware of the latter's attitude that "if you mess up on dialysis, then transplant is not for you."

Observing the transplant situation at the Virginia Commonwealth University, James Levenson and Mary Ellen Olbrisch observe: "The intense fears generated by the perceived scarcity of organs and the long waits may lead to misconceptions in patients and families . . . One common misconception is that the patient who has the best 'connections' will get priority for the next available organ" (1987, 401). There are widespread rumors that celebrities and persons of high social status are favored over lower-status patients. Whether or not these are utter misconceptions, they prevail among patients who have sought transplant and been placed on an active waiting list.[4]

We believe that many lower-class dialysis patients are daunted at the prospect of seeking a transplant. Their expectations about failing with the transplant as they have with other life endeavors are, ironically, matched by mirror-image concerns on the part of families of cadaver transplant donors. Many cadaver organs issue from young people in good physical health who succumb in motor accidents, violent deaths, suicides, homicides, or other misadventures. Their family's grief is exacerbated by the apprehension that their deceased relative "wasted" his or her life and the hope that the unknown (to them) recipient of the donated organ will, in receiving it, "redeem" the young life lost.

Sloan's research and other corroborating studies point to problems in treatment that should occasion bioethical disquietude among professionals providing ESRD treatment. Whatever the precursor conditions that lead to ESRD, the research examined here suggests that, once hemodialysis treatment is begun, many patients accommodate to it in ways that limit their medical prospects and life chances. Their disinclination toward transplant is one such limitation. However, as we have pointed out, this disinclination does not spring from a vacuum but is a piece of other attitudes and values in their lives that flow against the dominant American motif of active achievement. Some staff, especially those involved in transplant, are imbued with enthusiasm for the life horizons opened up by transplantation. They implicitly condemn patients who easily settle for less. They slip into negative stances with patients who care little about rehabilitation and who do not share the staff's optimism.

Let us reflect on this research as it bears on the clinical bioethics/social bioethics dichotomy. The ESRD case offered here calls into question the relevance of autonomy as a dominant ethical principle. Clearly, every hemodialysis patient, hooked indefinitely and dependently to a machine, should prefer the far more autonomous position of the transplant patient. The fact that so many patients do not have this preference clearly shows that in practice rational arguments are often less powerful than such emotions as fear and anxiety. From this we infer that the conceptual apparatus of clinical bioethics is not always adequate to assess the reality of the phenomena they discuss. In contrast, social bioethics comes closer to accepting patients in their varied environments, human individuality, and illness.

THE NICU: CLINICAL AND ETHICAL DISCOURSE WITHIN A HIERARCHY OF PROFESSIONAL POWER

Our analysis of ethical issues in neonatal care derives from the work of Schlomann (1994) and Mesman (1994). Schlomann's study is based on six months of intensive ethnographic observation in a fifty-bed NICU that served both as a regional center, taking referrals from less comprehensively equipped NICUs, and also as a teaching unit for medical and nursing schools. Prior to her research, Schlomann had worked for ten years as a neonatal nurse, thereby acquiring a thorough familiarity with current neonatal care.

Schlomann's study builds on a sizable social science literature on NICUs conducted by nurses and social scientists since the mid-1980s. Schlomann interprets many NICU phenomena by drawing on basic concepts in medical sociology, such as the sick role, professional hierarchies in hospitals, and the physician-patient relationship.

Schlomann's research focuses on the fateful decisions whether to initiate and to continue life-sustaining treatment for severely compromised infants.[5] During the six-month period of Schlomann's study, there were 423 admissions. Of this total, 404 infants survived and 19 died (this includes infants who died either during hospitalization or within twenty-eight days of discharge). It was not within the compass of her study for Schlomann to grade all survivors according to the severity of their problems. Every infant admitted had at least one medical problem of neonatality (including, especially, prematurity), but many had "routine" complications. Those that had "exceptional" complications included the 19 who succumbed and another, perhaps larger, group who though surviving experienced severe crises and permanent functional limitations.

Schlomann's study offers a series of case studies in which infants were either intensively treated on a long-term basis or, with life support withdrawn, allowed to die. She makes close comparisons of seemingly similar cases in which divergent decisions were made. She presents "paradigms of argumentation" that were advanced to support decisions. The medical staff, junior medical staff, nurses, and parents were all parties to the dialogue, though not with equal weight. Schlomann's analysis is as much concerned with the inner logic of the argumentation as with who propounded it. The latter question—who says what—is, however, also important; for example, religious justification ("God's will") that the infant survive or die was offered by parents frequently, sometimes by the nurses, and never by the physicians.

Schlomann looks sharply at the circumstances under which *ethical discourse* arises in the care of the infants. Ethical discourse embraces considerations of the neonate as a human being (or "person") rather than a physical body; the infant's prospects in the near and more distant future; how others view and value the infant's existence; the infant's reaction to painful stimuli (such as needle sticks for blood drawing); the infant's physical appearance; and the demographic and sociopsychological characteristics of the parents. Ethical discourse deals with questions of life and death: How much is the infant suffering? If the infant surmounts the present crisis and intensive intervention, does he or she face still more crises? Will the present effort move the infant to a plane of greater enduring viability? Alternatively, does the infant "need to die"?

Ethical discourse can be contrasted with clinical (or technical) discourse. The latter consists of diagnostic certainties, probabilities, and conjectures; treatment protocols; the monitoring of physiological parameters; and other factual concerns (even though they may involve guesswork). Clinical discourse is incremental and partial; if an infant has been given physiologically disruptive antibiotics for a week, the clinical view can easily disregard that history and think only of the next step. In contrast with immersion in the present, when caregivers think about the infant's long-run survival and prospects as a human being, their discourse becomes ethical. We do not mean that ethical discourse necessarily implies a decision to withdraw treatment—only that the patient is being considered as a whole human being with a potential future, not merely as a biological response system that responds in measurable ways to specific interventions.

The prevailing mode of discourse in the NICU is clinical. Ethical discourse is a perspective or way of talking that attaches to or builds onto the ongoing clinical perspective about an infant. When ethical discourse does appear, it may persist or subside, reemerging later or not at all.

Schlomann found that ethical discourse took form most readily in regard to infants who were seen as "monsters"—whose physical frame, the face especially, was deformed, disfigured, or incomplete. Even then the discussion was not framed baldly as "Shall we intervene vigorously to save this infant, or let it die?" but couched in terms of its viability.[6] No matter how grotesquely deformed an infant, its life would be supported if its physiology—respiration, cardiac function, digestive system—were sound. But if massive prolonged intervention was necessary to save a deformed infant, the discussion would turn ostensibly to its viability. Concern about the "monster" qualities would be overtly voiced at times, but more often it appeared to lie latent in the consciousness of the participants. Viability, based on medical prognosis, was easier to talk about. Discussions of viability are a mode of clinical discourse that draws on technical knowledge about lab values, drugs, biochemistry, physiology, anatomy, neurology, and many other parts of medical science. Schlomann notes that discussion of viability lies mainly within the province of the NICU physicians; it is a paradigm of argumentation that is controlled and displayed most forthrightly by the physicians, to a lesser extent by the nurses, and scarcely at all by the infant's parents, who lack the requisite knowledge and vocabulary.

Schlomann discovered that ethical discourse was less likely to emerge concerning premature infants than about those who were deformed. NICUs in general have many more "preemies" than deformed infants. Though they may be tiny and wizened, most preemies meet normal expectations concerning the physiognomy and anatomical proportions of the human infant. Nevertheless, their early birth may be associated with invisible neurological and cognitive damage, sometimes congenital and sometimes iatrogenic in the course of the strenuous interventions necessary to keep them going. Although some infants born long before term go on to live normal lives, others are permanently disabled and go on to live dependent lives. From the standpoint of long-run social impact and heavy parental burden, preemies probably pose a greater problem than deformed infants. By discovering the greater ethical concern with deformed than premature infants, Schlomann's work shows that discourse in the NICU is governed by priorities and logic that do not comport with the long-run social consequences of decisions made there.

Like Schlomann, the Dutch nurse and anthropologist-of-ethics, Mesman, focused on the distinction between clinical and ethical discourse and came to similar conclusions from her own observations in both Dutch and American NICUs (Mesman 1994). Mesman notes that public discussions of neonatal ethics, such as occur in the media, invoke explicit precepts: "the right to live," "do no harm," and "let the parents decide." On the ward, however, ethical vocabulary is muted. The staff on the ward have their own mode of discourse and their own preoccupations. The problem of "who is a human being?" is not a major overt preoccupation. Discourse remains at the clinical or technical level most of the time.

Mesman argues, however, that despite outward appearances in the NICU, ethics is a continuous latent presence there and throughout all of medicine. Within concrete medical situations, however, ethical concern is felt in a more contextualized and subtle gradient than in highly crystallized, explicit debates of bioethicists in journals or in the mass media. Some notions are expressed both in public/philosophical debate and in the medical arena, but they have different connotations in each arena. Mesman and Gerald DeVries (1991) offer two such notions.

Pain.   To the bioethicist, pain is often used as a criterion in judging quality of life. In ethical discourse, the patient suffering from interminable, irreducible pain is in a strong position to appeal for ending his or her life, as in assisted euthanasia. The medical infliction of pain through treatment can also be a criterion for withholding or withdrawing treatment: Painful surgery can be justified if there is good prospect of benefit, but if the patient is terminally ill and moribund, the principle "do no harm" may come into play.

In the ordinary clinical discourse of medicine, however, pain is viewed as a technical problem to be dealt with by use of the appropriate analgesic agent. However, painkillers sometimes do not work, or they cannot be given safely to fragile patients. If, in the NICU a great deal of pain is imposed on the neonate for treatment or diagnosis but the baby's viability is much in doubt, then the discussion may move from the technical to the ethical level. Staff may first disagree about how much pain the infant is experiencing, but if agreement can be reached that there is great suffering, then the ethical question comes into view: Do the future prospects of the infant justify the continued infliction of pain?

"Let the parents decide."   Bioethicists agree along with everyone else that an infant's parents are the appropriate persons to speak and decide for the infant. However, as laypersons without technical knowledge, the parents are often marginal to medical thinking and strategies. How to involve patients and other laypersons is a problem throughout much of medical care; however, the complexities and uncertainties of NICU care add a layer of difficulty to the problem.[7]

Parents of compromised infants are sometimes torn by indecision over whether aggressive treatment should be continued or stopped. NICU staff generally regard this as an understandable, reasonable posture rather than an evasion of parental responsibility. Behind the staff's perspective lies the supposition that the parents would become ridden with guilt if they were to take a decisive stance to stop treatment. In this tragic situation the physicians will decide among themselves to interpret the infant's condition to the parents and to set out their own view that continuation of treatment would be futile, emphasizing the unanimity of their opinion. By keeping initiative and responsibility on their side, the physicians thus try to relieve the parents of a moral burden (see Mesman and DeVries 1991; Anspach 1994).

THE CLINICAL RESEARCH CENTER: HOW ARE RESEARCH SUBJECTS COMPENSATED?

Whether or not they were the most crucial event in the founding of bioethics, it is clear that the Nazi war-crime trials led to the Nuremberg Code, which "created ethical guidelines for the conduct of medical research throughout the world" (Altman 1987, 17).

This code for the first time prescribed in writing a set of ethical practices, many of which medical investigators had followed earlier on their own. A key element is the principle of informed consent, whereby the investigator apprises the research subject of the risks connected with participation and of any benefits or compensation that the subject will receive. The subject's participation is to be free, voluntary, and uncoerced (qualities that are, of course, inherent in the notion of consent). Since 1966 U.S. medical centers that receive federal research funds have been required to establish ethics boards (often called institutional review boards), which monitor and protect the ethics of research conducted at each center. Attention has focused on the language used in describing the research protocol to the subject and the risks that will be faced. Little attention has been paid, however, to the actual consent process—the informative, communicative interaction by which the written document is exhibited to the patient and the patient's consent is obtained.

Here we address another neglected issue: How are research subjects motivated to participate, and how are they rewarded? Some research is conducted without any tangible reward; subjects in such research are motivated by their own intrinsic interest to take part in the research problem, or they have an altruistic desire to benefit science, medical care, and future patients. Obtaining gratification for these psychic motivations is an intangible reward. More often, however, tangible rewards are offered as an incentive for participation.

It would be ethically defensible to argue that no tangible reward should ever be given; even a small reward might distort the process of obtaining truly voluntary consent. However, much medical research requires effort and time from subjects; without a reward few people would volunteer. Also, some research exposes subjects to an appreciable degree of medical risk; again, it arguably seems "fair" to compensate them for their assumption of risk.

An important principle is that compensation, if offered, should not be coercive. Besides guarding against coerced consent, this principle often has scientific warrant. For example, if a very large amount of money is offered for participation, poor people might be more likely to "volunteer" than better-off people, leading to a skewed sample. Further, anyone attracted by a large monetary reward might be tempted to falsify his or her medical history in order to be accepted and to receive the compensation.

The foregoing discussion concerns healthy subjects. Much medical research, however, is of necessity carried out with sick persons. Monetary rewards would have value for them also. The compensation for them often takes the form of free treatment and hospital care.

These issues have been discussed only rarely in the bioethical literature and in the media (see, however, Morrow 1996). Social bioethics takes these issues seriously. Using material provided in a research nurse's account (Brown 1995), we are able to advance and expand the discussion of experiments and coercion.

Brown served as research nurse for a three-year period at a clinical research center (CRC), which occupied one wing of a 500-bed university teaching hospital. The center was one of a number of centers that were funded by the National Institutes of Health (NIH) for the purpose of enabling medical school faculty to conduct research.[8]

The center had a central committee that evaluated applications for research, including plans for obtaining informed consent from, and compensating, research subjects. Because this was an institutional block grant, applicants could obtain funding without going through the more laborious and competitive process of applying to NIH at the national level. Most of the research studies funded drew upon the inpatient facilities of the center; some, however, were conducted on an outpatient basis.

Here we present brief accounts of seven typical research studies and the subjects' compensation. The first three studies used healthy subjects; the last four used patients.

Three Studies Using Healthy Subjects

The first study assessed the cardiovascular response of young healthy persons to a condition of simulated weightlessness. It was conducted for the benefit of NASA (National Aeronautical and Space Agency). The protocol simulated weightlessness by suspending the subject in a fully inverted position (head down, feet up) for twenty-four to seventy-two hours. Invasive monitoring was carried out through a bloodline into the brachial vein. Noninvasive measurements were carried out on respiratory and urinary output, blood pressure, and oxygen utilization. Cardiovascular medications were also administered to study their effects; although these drugs had some risk when used therapeutically with patients, their application under the "weightless" condition heightened the risk to the healthy subjects.

The ten subjects were all medical students, who were excused from their classes in order to participate. The compensation was $1200. An important intangible reward was the social recognition that they received from peers and medical faculty, who visited them during the study. Later they were congratulated as "survivors" for their courage and steadfastness.

This was an extremely demanding research protocol. All subjects had difficulty in eating, urinating, and, in some cases, breathing. They also had pain from the inserted venous probe and from an external pressure chamber mounted on their chest to monitor breathing. Although all the subjects were initially highly committed, two dropped out early, receiving a payment prorated to the elapsed time of their participation. One subject sustained significant injury to his skin and brachial vein.

The second study used normal subjects as a control group for the evaluation of a zinc supplementation diet intended for patients with eating disorders. The subjects remained in the center for three days, eating only prepared foods, documenting their intake and excretions, and participating in psychological and metabolic studies. The latter consisted of repeat blood studies and a core body–temperature measurement, which involved swallowing a plastic-covered temperature probe that transmitted readings to an external receiver.

There was virtually no medical risk in this study. Subjects experienced minor discomfort from consuming a lower calorie diet (1500–1800 calories) than they were accustomed to and also from excreting the temperature probe at the conclusion of the study. For their participation subjects received $400. Lacking the cachet of the weightlessness study, this study did not lead to any notable social approval for the participants.

The third study compared the metabolism of a widely used cardiovascular drug in healthy young men and healthy older men. The research protocol involved the insertion of two intravenous lines—one for the administration of the drug, the other for taking blood samples.

The drug's ordinary therapeutic effect is achieved by slowing the heart rate while strengthening the heart contractions, to benefit patients with congestive heart failure. Although the basic mechanism of the drug was already well known, other aspects of its functioning were not. The purpose of this study was to compare the clearance rate of the drug over time (the rate at which the blood returns to its preexperimental composition) in the two age groups. The study took one full day to complete, during which the subject remained in bed and ate nothing. There was a moderate medical risk. One subject's heart rate dropped into the thirties, at which point the supervising physician removed him from the study. Another subject was dismissed because he fainted when his intravenous lines were being inserted.

The compensation was $150. Several subjects who were members of the pharmacy faculty at the university, however, declined the compensation. Other subjects, not affiliated with the university, accepted the $150 reward.

For the faculty members, this study was a mode of "self-experimentation" in which a physician or other scientist uses himself or herself as a subject. In this instance an important nonmonetary reward existed for the subjects, namely, peer approval and the academic opportunity to generate subsequent publications from the research.

Four Studies Using Patients

None of the patient-based studies provided a monetary reward. The motivation of the patient-subjects was mixed between self-oriented (albeit nonmonetary) components and altruistic components. The self-oriented component lies in the patient's hope of personal therapeutic benefit (which may exist even when the subject is explicitly advised that the study would be of no personal therapeutic benefit) and in receiving exemplary medical care while serving as a subject. The altruistic component lies in the patient's desire to contribute to medical knowledge and the benefit of future patients.

The first study looked at the generalized brain dysfunction, or encephalopathy, that commonly occurs among patients suffering from alcoholic hepatitis. It evaluated the effectiveness of a dietary supplement in improving the subjects' cognitive functioning. The subjects agreed to accept thirty days of hospitalization, regular medications and prepared meals, daily blood draws, psychometric tests, and health care as needed. No invasive somatic tests were carried out. Postdischarge outpatient follow-up was also offered for as long as the patient adhered to the study protocol. During the hospitalization, the patients were strongly counseled to stay away from alcohol—a difficult avoidance for chronic alcoholics.

The study involved no medical risks. All patients were seriously ill and required medical care aside from participation in the study; whether or not the dietary supplement had a specific therapeutic effect, their health benefited from the care they received. The time commitment of thirty days was a major demand. However, many of the subjects were unemployed and had no family responsibilities.

The weekly psychometric tests required considerable mental effort. Although the test items, simple and repetitive, are easy for persons without encephalopathy, they were difficult and discouraging to the patients. Brown notes, "While working with these patients, I was saddened to watch their . . . struggles with what they knew they should have been able to do" (1995, 11). By posing these tasks for the patients, the study perhaps lowered their self-esteem; many probably had a fairly low level of self-esteem (which was not assessed) prior to the study.

A major benefit that emerged for all the subjects in the course of the study was a positive emotional attachment to the center staff. Brown writes, "In most cases, we became the family that the subject had never had" (1995, 11).

In the second study a supplemental diet was evaluated for patients with late-stage amyotrophic lateral sclerosis (ALS, also known as Lou Gehrig's disease). The study required hospital care for five days every three months, during which patients participated in nutritional, metabolic, and neurological studies to evaluate their physical condition. The subjects ranged in age from twenty-four to the late sixties; not all of them lived to complete the study.

There were no medical risks to the subjects. Subjects were all told that the supplemental diet was not curative but might be palliative, to slow down the relentless nerve degeneration that characterizes the disease. A major, wholly unintended benefit of the study was the periodic respite that it gave to the patient's family from the demanding responsibility for care. Families at first seemed hesitant about "abandoning" their member to the care of strangers when there was no prospect of cure or other major medical benefit. "However," Brown writes, "once the families understood that the CRC staff would provide high-quality compassionate nursing care to their family member, they appreciated the time off" (1995, 12).

The third study was the experimental group counterpart to the second study for healthy individuals. The subjects suffered from anorexia nervosa or bulimia. Their study participation consisted of a thirty-day hospitalization. Besides the zinc supplementation diets, they received the customary eating-disorder treatments: psychological counseling, behavior modification, and medical management of malnutrition and electrolyte imbalances. Periodic urine and blood specimens were taken from the patients.

The medical risks in the study were limited to the slight risk that goes with the drawing of blood. The subjects, however, perceived great risk in the blood draws and urine collection. Their exaggerated perception was due to their distorted body image—a characteristic feature of eating-disorder syndromes; their perception illustrates the divergence that can occur between "objective" risk as judged by researchers and "subjective" risk as felt by subjects.

The fourth study, conducted on an outpatient basis, used hypertensive subjects age sixty-five and older to evaluate the effectiveness of a drug designed to lower diastolic hypertension. The subjects were randomly assigned either to the experimental group or the counterpart placebo group. There were minimal medical risks in the study. Patients who developed critically high blood pressure were removed from the study and given routine medical treatment.

The subjects were not given money or any other benefit such as free hospitalization. It is possible that those in the experimental group benefited from the drug, just as those in the control group may have benefited from a placebo effect. Probably the greatest reward was intangible—the long-term relationships that the subjects established with the center staff.

Having laid out the seven studies (see Table 1), we wish to look into these questions: Were the compensations appropriate, and were they fair in comparison with each other? As noted, ideally, research subjects would volunteer on a merely altruistic basis; compensation would be unnecessary. Some research is indeed accomplished on this basis, but a more realistic posture allows for moderate compensation. One logical position is that the compensation should not be greater than whatever is necessary to motivate the subject to participate; beyond that, it becomes "coercive." The net reward could be calculated as the actual reward minus the cost, the latter being a composite of the risk faced, the effort required, and the time spent.

The appropriateness of rewards is difficult to assess. It is, however, easier to discuss in relation to monetary compensation (the studies with healthy persons) than compensation in the form of health care (the studies with patients). The $1200 reward in the weightlessness study (study 1) is relatively high but must be balanced against the fact that it put the subject in a position of considerable risk and discomfort over an extended period. In comparison, the $400 that the control group subjects (study 2) received in

TABLE 1   **Compensation of Research Subjects in the Seven Studies**

With Healthy Subjects	*Compensation*
Weightlessness	$1200
Control group for eating-disorder study	$ 400
Effect of age on metabolism of a cardiovascular drug	$ 150
With Patients	
Effect of dietary supplement on patients with alcoholic hepatitis	Hospitalization and experimental diet (with potential benefit)
Effects of dietary supplement with ALS	Hospitalization and experimental diet (with potential benefit)
Effect of dietary supplement with eating-disorder patients (experimental group for study #2)	Hospitalization and experimental diet (with potential benefit)
Experimental and control group of (outpatient) hypertensive patients	For the experimental group, potential benefit from the drug; for the control group, potential placebo effect

the zinc diet study was acquired with much less personal imposition. They were exposed to no risks and only minor discomfort.

The cardiovascular drug study (study 3) had a $150 reward. It was a one-day study; the risks and discomfort were of smaller magnitude than in the weightlessness study, but they were substantially greater than in the zinc diet study (which lasted three days). The $150 reward seems considerably low by comparison with the zinc diet reward of $400. Of course, many of the subjects—indeed, every one of the pharmacy-faculty subjects—declined to accept the reward. One interpretation of that would be that they acted from an altruistic motive, but another possible interpretation is that $150 was too small for them to "bother with." A larger reward, say $300, might in contrast have been too valuable for them to turn down.

Intangible, nonmonetary rewards in the form of peer approval were noted in the weightlessness study and the cardiovascular study. We will not attempt to assign a measure to these rewards. Since the pharmacists declined their $150 reward, we might argue that the intangible reward was all it took to motivate them. By comparison, it seems that the medical students who were the weightlessness subjects would not have participated without a substantial monetary reward, though the approval of peers and superiors was clearly also important to them.

The foregoing analysis shows inconsistencies in the scale of compensation. One might ask, "Well, now, does it really matter as long as research gets accomplished and subjects are not abused, misled, or coerced?" Perhaps it doesn't matter, but we believe that the issue deserves more study for the following reason. Medical research is coming under the influence of many new forces. One such influence is the increasing volume of research that is sponsored jointly by public nonprofit entities and by profit-oriented corporations. Another is the vast scope—multi-institutional, multistate, and multinational—of testing of new drugs and procedures. Whether the local-ized institutional review boards can continue to deal with the new pressures is a question raised with increasing frequency (Edgar and Rothman 1995).

Does the trend toward larger-scale, more statistically oriented investi-gation harbor a greater possibility for the depersonalization of subjects? If so we must remember that the dark places in the history of biomedical research show that the distance from depersonalization to abuse is not very great.[9]

DISCUSSION

Recognizing the established position that the bioethical enterprise has achieved in modern society, we wish to energize the bioethical imagination in the "postacceptance" phase of its existence. Our strategy for doing this lies in sharpening the focus on social aspects of medical phenomena: look-ing especially at social factors that affect access to medical care, differences between patients and health professionals (and differences among profes-sionals) in their power and their control of information, and the connec-tions between ethical issues and health policy. We have laid out events and processes ripe for bioethical analysis in three domains of medical activity: the hemodialysis clinic, the NICU, and the CRC (clinical research center). None of these is a stranger to bioethics. Our effort here has not been to open up new frontiers but rather to colonize, with new questions and con-cepts, domains that have been to varying extent previously mapped.

Of the three domains, two—the NICU and the CRC—have been much visited by bioethics in recent years. The NICU has been a virtual forcing bed for concepts pertaining to the definition of life and personhood, the social and legal control (for example, through the Baby Doe regulations) of tech-nology, and the proper locus of life-or-death decision-making authority.

The CRC has been the impetus for the institutional implementation of procedures for informed consent. Beyond formal procedures, it has also stimulated new thinking about the meaning of autonomy for the research subject. The CRC environment has also contributed to thinking about the distinction between the medical research subject, who as somatic and psy-chic "object" contributes to generalized biomedical knowledge, and the medical patient, whose individual welfare is of primary importance both to the patient and to the responsible health professionals. The fact that a cer-tain diagnostic or therapeutic intervention with a given patient would yield valuable knowledge for biomedicine is not, absent probable benefit to the patient, sufficient warrant for carrying it out.

In contrast, the hemodialysis clinic has been of much less concern to bioethics in recent years. Before federal legislation mandated the underwriting of treatment expenses for virtually all ESRD patients, bioethicists used questions about dialysis to establish their importance. The questions of that era were twofold. First, who has the authority to make life-and-death decisions related to access to care? Second, what criteria concerning patients are to be used in selecting those to receive treatment?

With the burgeoning expense of treating ESRD patients, however, questions of the "can society afford it?" type are once again beginning to surface. Even if such concerns congeal into a concerted political force that challenges the prevailing policy of inclusive access to treatment, the resulting debates will probably not lead to the dramatically etched "who shall live?" questions that dominated the previous era.

In our own address of ESRD issues, the perspective was on the opposite side. Instead of being concerned about the potential scarcity of treatment resources, we wondered why it is that many hemodialysis patients do not want transplant treatment. Aside from the way in which more widespread use of transplantation would reduce the economic burden of the expensive dialysis modality, we were concerned by the fact that many patients were rejecting a mode of treatment that most health professionals regard as the superior mode.

Why did many patients have this attitude? The answer to this question lies somewhere between the patient's altruistic impulse to let other patients have a chance for transplant and the patient's dispirited reluctance to try anything new and less burdensome for oneself. Whatever the answer, it becomes necessary for bioethicists to consider and categorize the influences that shape patients' attitudes and to use their analysis of those influences to weigh questions of cost, access, and treatment decisions.

The bioethical focus on NICU phenomena has, as noted previously, swirled around concepts of human status and personhood; although these concepts have other applications and origins outside the NICU context, within it they owe their emergence entirely to the capability of technology to save neonates who in earlier eras would have died. Bioethical rationales for "pulling the plug" (or not inserting it—that is, not initiating treatment—in the first place) are as a rule devised in view of the neonate's prospects and the degree of cognitive/bodily impairment and suffering that may be experienced in later days. Such rationales are arguments concerning quality of life—the expected poor quality of life that is thought to await many NICU graduates forms the basis for questioning the strenuous treatment methods.

In contrast, little apprehension has been expressed in bioethics about the high expenses of NICU care. Greater apprehension is expressed in regard to ESRD expense; this probably depends on the fact that, unlike NICU payers, ESRD has a unitary, centralized payer—the national government—from which complete remuneration is routinely gathered. Even in the ESRD case, however, it is conceptually difficult for the bioethicist to convert "high expense" into an ethical posture for withholding treatment from individuals who have a clinically determined need for it. Suffering and low quality of life appear to be more acceptable rationales for limiting or stopping treatment, especially when patients themselves (or their representatives) are able to judge and decide on the worth of their own lives. In other words, the bioethical principle of individual autonomy reigns. While acknowledging this we nevertheless believe that work needs to be done to create an ethically legitimate space for the recognition of social and public priorities in medical care.

Our attention to clinical research fastened on the compensation of research subjects, a topic neglected by bioethics but fraught with ethical implications. The neglect is particularly notable in comparison with the intense focus on informed consent for research subjects. We noted that compensation for research participation can lead to distorted sampling and thus has scientific and ethical implications. Past excesses and unethical episodes in biomedical research have regularly revealed that the subjects were socially captive or disadvantaged people. Bioethics must develop a fully social model of compensation, recognizing among other factors the meaning of participation to subjects. In several of the CRC studies that we covered, nursing observations pointed to socioemotional rewards of considerable value that had accrued to participants. Yet these rewards—a nonmonetary compensation—were not part of the formal record of scientific results in the research.

We suggest that in all three medical domains bioethics should attend more to the "voice of the patient." To valorize the patient's voice, it will be necessary to find bioethical categories that transform the patient from object to subject, thereby allowing the patient not only a clinical diagnosis but also a social endowment and opening the mind and the senses of medical authority to what it is that patients feel and say.

CONCLUSION

Within the intellectual development of ethics itself, there is good precedent for the challenge that we pose here to bioethics. At its most fundamental, ethics seeks to evaluate human conduct in the light of moral criteria. *Human conduct* has been taken to refer to the purposeful behavior of the individual, asking whether or not his or her behavior conforms to various alternative ethical standards such as those that might emanate from religious authority ("God's will"), political authority ("the good of the state"), or abstract principles such as utilitarianism's "greatest good of the greatest number." In the early part of the twentieth century, a social ethics movement arose in the United States and England. It was connected with a contemporary political liberalism and sought to direct public and academic attention toward what it saw as the evils of capitalist excess, such as poor housing, low wages, abuse of workers' rights, preventable communicable disease, and widespread poverty. These evils, in the view of the social ethics movement, came about as the result of businesspeople and property owners who as individuals might be "ethical" in the narrow sense of financial honesty and adhering to contracts, but whose economic and social power would lead to bad social outcomes unless checked by an enlarged social ethics and related social legislation.

Like the general field of ethics, bioethics started out as a critique of individual conduct within the field of medicine. New trends in scope of medical research and in the application of technology to treatment stretched and frayed the relevance of traditional guides to medical conduct. Bioethics proposed new criteria, individualistic in their perspective and striving for contradiction-free and ambiguity-free philosophical rigor. This was the realm of what we call here *clinical bioethics*. In our view clinical bioethics is good as far as it goes—but it does not go far enough. Even at the price of some ambiguity, bioethics must incorporate into its criteria closer attention to the social processes involved in the delivery of medical care.

Further, bioethics must recognize as both a strength and a limitation of its own approach that successful clinical endeavors occur in the absence of explicit ethical formulations and guidelines. A telling example comes from our own examination of the ongoing work of the NICU. Effective "everyday" communications and decisions were made in the NICU without sustained "ethical" awareness. Only in critical junctures did discourse become ethical; and even then overt technical discourse seemed to carry the burden of ethical concern that was felt more than it was expressed (for example, bioethics in the clinical sense might have some difficulty countenancing and sharply defining the notion of "monster," even though it did figure in the thinking and decision making of NICU participants).

It is at this point—assessing the connections between what is felt and what is expressed, evaluating the social power of the various clinical actors, and understanding the background and context of clinical decisions—that social bioethics steps in. It is a rich perspective and a way of looking at medical phenomena that will strengthen, not supplant, clinical bioethics.

NOTES

1. For a philosophical work that is systematic and rigorous in the abstracted, decontextualized formulations of bioethics, see Beauchamp and Childress (1994).

2. These figures make dialysis appear to be somewhat more risky than it actually is, for the following reason: Not all dialysis patients are eligible, by medical criteria, for a transplant. Some are transplant-ineligible because their immune system would not tolerate the inserted kidney and because their age and associated fragility contraindicate major surgery. Transplant-

ineligible patients as a group will not survive as long on dialysis as transplant-eligible patients. The hemodialysis survival figures given include the transplant-eligible and the transplant-ineligible, which makes the overall hemodialysis patient survival figures "too low" for the comparison we seek here.

3. We note here that Sloan's study was based on a broad hypothetical request to the patient, which in effect said, "Tell me about your decision to seek (or not to seek) a kidney transplant." It was not as if the declining patients had been on an actual waiting list and declined at the point of being offered a kidney. Their response in the research situation, though hypothetical, nevertheless registers meaningful features of their life experience and self-concept from which flow important consequences for their career as patient.

4. A small minority of renal patients receive transplants from live donors. The waiting-list phenomenon and ordeal does not apply to them. Very occasionally, a patient in incipient renal failure receives a live donation without being previously dialyzed.

5. With so much attention focused, understandably, on the fate of the infant, it is easy to overlook the fact that any NICU is, like other parts of contemporary hospitals, a place where skilled professionals do their jobs in a predominantly workaday atmosphere. Social scientists could, though it rarely happens, examine other features of NICU functioning besides treatment decision making. One exception is a study that dealt with the question of whether new and inexperienced pediatric house staff in an NICU ordered more lab tests than more experienced staff (Griffith et al. 1994).

6. Concern and speculation about the viability of the infant, or any other seriously ill patient, is a virtual constant in the practice of medicine. It has been much explored in medical sociology (Anspach 1994; Bosk 1992; Fox 1957; Guillemin and Holmstrom 1986; Hafferty 1991).

7. Studies of NICUs give varying pictures on the part that parents play beyond agreeing that parents are often not well informed about the baby's status and treatment options, nor invited into decision making. In general, staff expect that parents, the mother especially, will play an affectionate and nurturing role with her infant; they tend to condemn mothers who for no apparent reason fail to appear with some regularity. However, parents are sometimes seen as being "in the way" if they begin to play a more active role. Of course, staff rules formally control entry onto NICU premises; further, through informal interactional cues, visitors can be made to feel welcome or unwelcome. A study by Heimer and Staffen gives a differentiated picture of staff attitudes; they write: ". . . because of the fundamental interdependence between medical care providers and parents, parents must be reformed rather than excluded" (1995, 635). They found that NICU staff, in judging the moral worth of parents and their potential for good parenting, made allowances for their circumstances and situation in life. They felt more negative toward a mother who "has advantages" yet failed to perform well than toward another mother who lacked advantages.

8. These centers can be regarded as small-scale extramural copies of the prototype 600-bed Clinical Research Center located on the intramural campus of the National Institutes of Health in Bethesda, Maryland. One important difference is that the Bethesda center is devoted fully to research; it is a *research hospital* in which every patient is recruited and admitted as a research subject. The extramural center we examine here is, however, like the Bethesda campus in that it is maintained mainly by federal funds—that is, NIH appropriations. Formerly, this center accepted no payment by any outside sources, such as patients, third-party insurance payers, or patients themselves. The ban has recently been relaxed so that now payments are accepted from pharmaceutical companies. The earlier stricter ban was based on the fear that outside funding might compromise the integrity of research. The recent policy change benefits the center in that the outside payments help it use its resources (personnel, beds, research equipment) more steadily.

9. We note a peculiarity in the usage of the word *consent*; we regard it as pointing to a stultifying routinization in the meaning of *informed consent*. In the CRC, it frequently happens that a research director asks his or her assistant, "Have you consented the subjects?" The semantic clue lies in *consent* as a transitive verb, not a noun. Ordinarily, one "obtains consent" or "gives consent." In the research situation, however, A "consents" B. One wonders whether B was really giving his or her knowledgeable, informed, voluntary consent or whether B's act was one of perfunctory, routinized compliance. The institutional review board as a rule closely scru-

tinizes the wording of the consent form but pays no attention to the process of obtaining the subject's consent (i.e., "consenting" the subject).

REFERENCES

Anspach, R. 1994. *Deciding who lives: Fateful choices in the intensive-care nursery.* Berkeley: University of California Press.

Atman, Lawrence K. 1987. *The story of self-experimentation in medicine—Who goes first?* New York: Random House.

Beauchamp, Tom L., and James F. Childress. 1994. *Principles of biomedical ethics.* 4th ed. New York: Oxford University Press.

Bosk, C. 1992. *All God's mistakes: Genetic counseling in a pediatric hospital.* Chicago: University of Chicago Press.

Brown, Julie B. 1995. Medical research subjects: Case studies of rewards. Unpublished paper. Lexington: Department of Behavioral Science, University of Kentucky.

Edgar, Harold, and David J. Rothman. 1995. The institutional review board and beyond: Future challenges to the ethics of human experimentation. *Milbank Quarterly* 73(4): 489–506.

Eichenwald, Kurt. 1995. Death and deficiency in kidney treatment. *New York Times,* 4 December, A1.

Flynn, Patricia. 1991. The disciplinary emergence of bioethics and bioethics committees: Moral ordering and its legitimation. *Sociological Focus* 24(2): 145–56.

Fox, Renée C. 1957. Training for uncertainty. In *The student-physician,* edited by Robert K. Merton, George C. Reader, and Patricia Kendall. Cambridge, Mass.: Harvard University Press, 207–41.

———. 1985. Reflections and opportunities in the sociology of medicine. *Journal of Health and Social Behavior* 26(1): 6–14.

Gallagher, Eugene B. 1994. Quality of life issues and the dialectic of medical progress illustrated by end-stage renal disease patients. In *Advances in medical sociology,* Vol. 5, edited by Gary Albrecht and Ray Fitzpatrick. Greenwich, Conn.: JAI Press, 67–90.

Griffith, C. H., N. S. Desai, E. A. Griffith, J. F. Wilson, K. J. Powell, and E. C. Rich. 1994. Housestaff experience and resource use in the NICU. *Clinical Research* 42:275A.

Guillemin, J., and L. Holmstrom. 1986. *Mixed blessings: Intensive care for newborns.* New York: Oxford University Press.

Hafferty, F. 1991. *Into the valley: Death and the socialization of medical students.* New Haven, Conn.: Yale University Press.

Heimer, Carol A., and Lisa R. Staffen. 1995. Interdependence and reintegrative social control: Labeling and reforming "inappropriate" parents in neonatal intensive care units. *American Sociological Review* 60 (October): 635–54.

Levenson, James L., and Mary Ellen Olbrisch. 1987. Shortage of donor organs and long waits. *Psychosomatics* 28(3): 399–403.

Mesman, Jessica. 1994. Morality in the making—A sociology of medical ethics in a neonatal intensive care unit. Unpublished paper presented at First World Congress: Medicine and Philosophy: Sciences, Technologies, Paris.

Mesman, Jessica, and Gerard DeVries. 1991. Management of doubt in neonatal practice. Unpublished paper, Department of Philosophy, University of Limburg, Maastricht, the Netherlands.

Morrow, David J. 1996. Human guinea pigs line up to get sick. *International Herald Tribune,* 30 September, A1, A7.

National Institutes of Health. 1994. *1994 annual data report—United States renal data system.* Ann Arbor: Kidney and Cost Center of the University of Michigan.

Rothman, David J. 1991. *Strangers at the bedside.* New York: HarperCollins.

Schlomann, Pamela. 1994. Initiating and sustaining ethical discourse in a neonatal intensive care unit: An ethnographic study. Ph.D. diss., Department of Sociology, University of Kentucky, Lexington.

Sloan, Rebecca S. 1995. A hermeneutical study of the medical treatment decision for end-stage renal disease patients and their families. Ph.D. diss., Department of Sociology, University of Kentucky, Lexington.

Sorenson, James R., and Judith P. Swazey. 1989. Sociological perspectives on ethical issues in medical and health care. In *Handbook of medical sociology*, 4th ed. edited by Howard E. Freeman and Sol Levine. Englewood Cliffs, N.J.: Prentice Hall, 492–507.

CHAPTER TEN

As Time Goes By: An Intellectual Ethnography of Bioethics

Bette-Jane Crigger

As bioethics approaches its fourth (on some accounts, fifth)[1] decade, voices in many quarters press questions about the field's disciplinary, professional, and institutional identity. What is bioethics? What are its practitioners' commitments and competencies as professionals? Whom does bioethics serve? What, in fact, does bioethics do?

To answer these questions fully would be a massive task, one I have no intention of taking on. The present more modest inquiry seeks, rather, simply to begin the project, to consider how one might go about answering such questions and examine what kinds of evidence are available to the task. Specifically, my aim is to explore how bioethics has constituted itself as a discipline in and through its professional literature. The premise should be clear: I take as my point of departure the understanding that at its core bioethics creates itself in its writing and discourse.

This perhaps calls for some defense, however, for clearly bioethics is a thriving oral culture these days, as well as a literate one. First, to say that bioethics creates itself in writing is not to deny that bioethics as a discipline has also penetrated clinical settings and plays an active role in contemporary health care practice. Whether in the form of ethics committees or ethics consultation services, bioethics today clearly is a significant bedside presence—indeed, the Joint Commission on Accreditation of Healthcare Organizations now requires facilities to have in place formal mechanisms for resolving ethical dilemmas. Seeing bioethics as a kind of clinical practice or as having an important role to play in clinical contexts is in no way incompatible with characterizing it as a discipline of discourse, for its task at the bedside on all accounts is analytic and interpretive in just the same ways.[2] The conversations it sets itself to foster may at some times more directly and immediately inform concrete health care decisions in particular circumstances than at others, but bioethics' fundamental goal remains one of identifying what's "at issue" in the intersection of medicine, the life sciences, and the human life cycle and clarifying how to think well about it.

Just as importantly, *clinical ethics* in its contemporary form is historically an outgrowth of bioethics as a discipline of discourse. In its early years bioethics talked about and wrote about issues; it did not address them at the bedside, as natural as that development may have been. It moved into the clinical setting in response to rather particular historical developments, such as the recommendations of the New Jersey Supreme Court in *Quinlan*[3] that conflicts regarding withdrawal of life-sustaining treatment might better be addressed in institutional ethics committees than brought before the courts. And even clinical (bio)ethics continues to shape itself through the written word—witness the emergence in recent years of journals like *H[ospital] E[thics] C[ommittee] Forum* or the *Journal of Clinical Ethics*.

For such reasons I take seriously the project of understanding the discourse of bioethics as a way of understanding the field itself. What follows is a brief "intellectual ethnography," that is, an examination what sorts of concerns ("issues" in the natives' language) have animated bioethics and helped the discipline define itself as a distinct intellectual endeavor.

MADNESS IN THE METHOD

A few caveats are in order, however, about the ways in which this undertaking has been carried out and the sources on which this exploration is grounded. There is, of course, an extensive literature available for the task—rather too extensive a literature to be in fact manageable. I have restricted myself to considering journal publications. I think this is sound, though it admittedly yields a thinner history than might otherwise be developed, for I take the relationship between journal articles and monographs or books to be essentially evolutionary: ideas tend first and most regularly to reach the field through journal publication and to be subsequently elaborated, refined, and formalized in book form. Granted, this rule will not hold universally; but it holds often enough.

Moreover, I rely on publications I take to be editorially devoted to bioethics. By that I mean publications whose content addresses ethical concerns arising from the development and deployment of biomedical science, whether these concerns have greatest force at the level of individual health care decisions or at the level of public policy and societal values.[4] Further, I take bioethics journals self-consciously to embrace a variety of disciplinary perspectives, paradigms, and methods as appropriate to their interests and topics—of clinicians and other caregivers, philosophers, theologians, humanists, lawyers and legal scholars, policymakers, social scientists, and all the interested others who might wish to join the conversation. This is not, of course, to suggest that individual journals may not themselves have a core disciplinary profile. I doubt anyone, for example, would take serious issues with characterizing *Bioethics* or the *Kennedy Institute of Ethics Journal* as primarily "philosophical" or with speaking of the *Journal of Clinical Ethics* as having a dominantly clinical cast. So too I understand a properly "bioethics" journal to be directed toward a multidisciplinary audience, though again, different publications may seek a somewhat different disciplinary mix among their readers.

The primary source, then, has been the *Hastings Center Report* (hereafter referred to as the *Report*), a publication that I have been privileged to be associated with for over a decade in one capacity or another. This is neither a strategy of favoritism, nor even a matter of simple convenience. Rather, the *Report* is the oldest publication devoted exclusively to bioethics (launched in 1971) and has the broadest circulation of any of the discipline's journals. It was launched specifically to provide a forum for the conversations the Hastings Center wished to see develop around issues raised by emerging biomedical and biological technologies and social practices. And I take seriously its twofold mission: to identify emerging issues (or, to problematize issues for the first time) and to reflect the state of play in the field.

In part this inquiry grew out of work in developing a comprehensive cumulative index to the *Report* and thus to some extent reflects the particular needs and limitations of that effort. Thus, the issues identified here take their origin in the classificatory categories developed to meet the needs of the index. In the first instance, the topics are built up from categories in annual indexes, whose scope became increasingly problematic over the life of the journal. The introduction of a new category heading thus may just as well represent having attained a "critical mass" of articles on a topic already of longstanding interest as the emergence of a new focus for the discipline. This analysis tries to take account of such possibilities in offering general reflections on the topical history. It is also based on issues addressed in full-length articles and regular features, such as case studies and columns of legal or policy commentary, but excludes shorter notes and letters, whether in the *Report* or other publications.

Other sources on which this intellectual "ethnography" draws are the journals *Law, Medicine & Ethics*[5] and the *Journal of Philosophy and Medicine* (launched in 1975) for the early years of the field, *Bioethics* (1987), the *Journal of Clinical Ethics* (1990), the *Kennedy Institute of Ethics Journal* (1991), and the *Cambridge Quarterly of Healthcare Ethics* (1992) for its more recent history. Though it might be considered to be devoted more centrally to the history and philosophy of medicine per se, *Theoretical Medicine* (1980) has also figured as an important professional forum in bioethics, especially in the last decade.[6]

The analysis itself focuses on the subject matter covered in these publications. I do not pretend to have read each and every article with the kind of attention required to catch nuances and subtle shifts in modes of argumentation over time. Intriguing as it is, that is a project for another day. Focusing at the level of subject matter rather than on details of analysis, of course, obscures much; the degree of difference across articles on "the same" topic can be considerable. In the case of the *Report*, for example, articles focusing on in vitro fertilization (IVF) in the late 1970s tended to address potential harms to children born of this intervention, whereas later articles (under the growing influence of the women's movement and feminist analysis, surely) have addressed concerns about the "expressive force" of reproductive interventions. Direct physical (more rarely, psychological harms) have given way to the commodification of reproductive capacity, exploitation of women, and distortions of kinship relationships as the dominant issues under the deceptively uniform heading "IVF."

This makes it more difficult to assess how refinement of the discipline's analytic toolkit alters how bioethics addresses issues or indeed identifies particular questions as "issues" in the first place. For all these reasons, then, consider this no more than a prolegomenon to an intellectual ethnography of bioethics.

AS TIME GOES BY

On the strength of the *Report* first, what can one say about the intellectual evolution of bioethics? Reasonably clear patterns emerge when one looks at what, and when, particular issues have been addressed. To offer a crude taxonomy, there are five sorts of life cycles that issues may live out in the field. In the first cycle, particular concerns may endure over time (however much the analysis brought to bear on them may change)—they are "classics." In the second typical cycle, issues may emerge only to be supplanted by related but not identical concerns; call them "changelings." In yet a third pattern, issues may capture scholars' attention only to disappear within a relatively short period—the "shooting stars" in the disciplinary skies. In the fourth cycle, issues may go through patterns of efflorescence and decline, dominating attention for a span, subsiding, then reemerging. To pursue the astronomical metaphor, think of these as "pulsars." And in a fifth pattern, to shift the metaphor, "families" of issues may differentiate into "genuses" and further into "species" as scholars parse questions with ever greater analytic delicacy and elaborate their understandings of given domains. I want to argue, ultimately, that this last both picks out the kind of issue that is most central in defining the discipline and best describes the dynamic at bioethics' intellectual core.

Classics

It should hardly be surprising that some topics remain perennial concerns for bioethics as a field. The discipline has importantly set itself the task of exploring the moral character particularly of those moments of intersection between medicine and biomedical science and the human life cycle that are among the most highly charged philosophically, theologically, emotionally, and politically. Bioethics is, moreover, professionally committed to recognizing moral ambiguity—indeed, its very existence as a liberal, secular enterprise hinges upon just that activity. A bioethics that took itself to have resolved contested issues, once and for all and for all parties, seems scarcely plausible.

One perennial topic in the bioethics literature has been abortion. From the mid-1970s articles on the ethics of terminating pregnancy have appeared in a steady stream, first in the *Report* and *Journal of Medical Ethics* but as well in the other core journals of the field as they have come on the scene. Yet that stream has been a rather modest one, certainly in comparison to the political saliency of the issue: rarely more than three articles in any given year and often only one, among all the journals reviewed here (Figure 1). The pattern suggests that the field has been more dutiful in attending to the question than passionately engaged by it.

The *Report*'s publishing history suggests that bioethics' interest in and professional engagement with the ethics of abortion often waxes and wanes rather closely with the legal fortunes of the right to choose. The flush of articles in the early years of the *Report* and *Journal of Medical Ethics* can plausibly be linked to the legal debates—and, of course, the political ones with which abortion is inextricably entangled—that culminated in the U.S. Supreme Court decisions in *Roe* (1973)[7] and *Danforth* (1976):[8] the *Report* brought out nine articles between 1973 and 1977, and the *Journal of Medical Ethics* published three articles in its first two volumes (1975 and 1976). Legal challenges to the freedom to terminate a pregnancy as established in *Roe* (especially challenges that reach the Supreme Court) seem to prompt ethicists to return to the topic and invite them to reiterate the moral foundations of the debate and to assess the implications of the immediate legal arguments. Thus again, the *Report*'s interest in the topic was renewed in tandem with *Webster*[9] with five articles in 1989, while *Law, Medicine & Ethics* (*Law, Medicine & Health Care* as it then was) ran four articles on the decision in its winter 1989 issue.

This is not to suggest that the bioethics literature always and only follows the law, of course. Triggers can come from within the health care setting as well, as evidenced, for example, by the fall 1992 issue of *Law,*

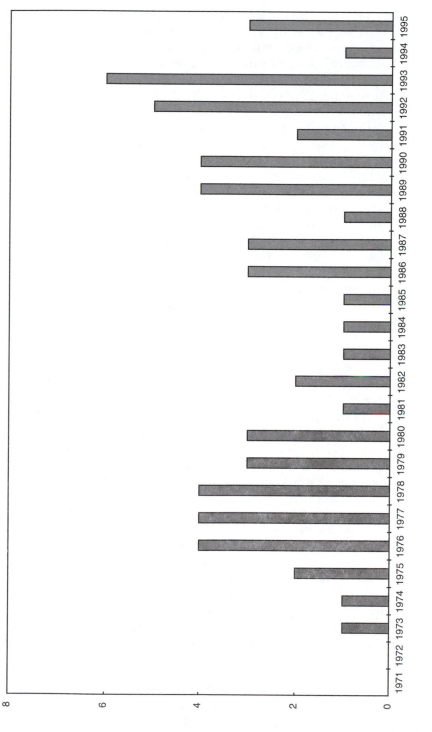

FIGURE 1 Articles on Abortion

Medicine & Health Care devoted to the "abortion pill" RU-486 (with some sixteen articles) or the set of articles on perinatal ethics committees and abortion discussions brought out by the *Journal of Clinical Ethics* in 1992. I want only to observe that, in this as in other areas, bioethics is scarcely uninfluenced by the dynamics of the broader political and legal context. There may indeed be domains in which the field sets the agenda for societal debate, but this seems not to be one of them.

And that needn't be surprising. Though they did not have constitutional imprimatur before *Roe,* the terms of the abortion debate were in a sense already well in place by the time bioethics began generating its own regular literature: The debate would be conducted, with more or less heat and passion, between privacy and the sanctity of life, between a woman's right to choose and the moral character of the human embryo/fetus. Unless bioethics can bring a substantially different lens through which to view the matter, offer new ways in which to parse the arguments or a significantly new and "better" definition of what's at stake, as an issue for the field, abortion is likely to remain closely linked with legal developments.

This pattern of steady but largely undemonstrative affection for a topic is not the only one characterizing domains of perdurable interest, however; there are considerably more volatile patterns to be found as well. Issues surrounding organ transplantation have likewise been enduring themes in the bioethics literature, but to judge by the number of articles devoted to the topic, interest has been both more intensive and has fluctuated more strongly over time (Figure 2). And while developments in the policy arena have clearly significantly affected the level and character of attention, in contrast to abortion, the focus in transplantation is driven at least as much by changing science and technology. Articles in the early 1980s on the artificial heart gave way in the mid-1980s to discussions of fetal tissue transplantation—a conversation effectively cut short in the United States by the Reagan administration moratorium on federal funding for such research and not much resumed when the moratorium was lifted. In recent years the question of xenotransplantation has emerged as salient, once again following the curve of technological developments. In this instance, the focus is on transplantations of baboon livers into human patients and efforts to develop genetically modified pigs to provide organs for human transplantation.

There is a core set of issues in transplantation, however, that has captured the field's attention throughout. Ethical concerns about how organs are procured—including such questions as directed donation and presumed consent—and distributed have been addressed repeatedly over the years. For example, of the more than fifty articles that have appeared in the *Report* over twenty-five years, some twenty-one were devoted expressly to procurement issues: two between 1977 and 1980, seven in the period 1981 to 1984, eleven between 1985 and 1988, and one each in 1989 and 1990. And

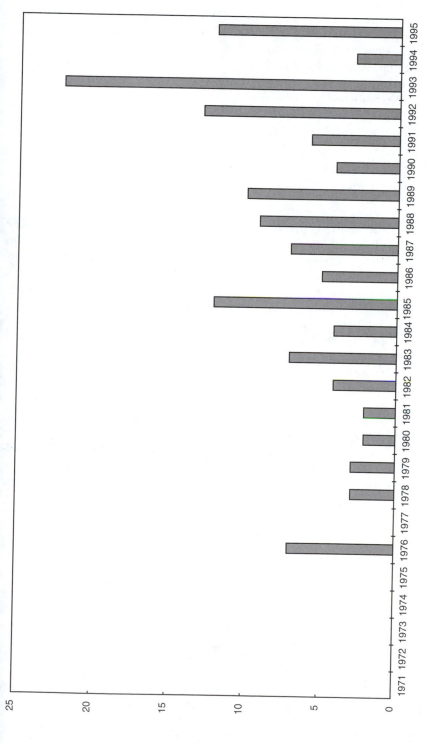

FIGURE 2 Articles on Organ Transplantation

indeed, procurement issues have defined entire journal issues, such as the *Kennedy Institute of Ethics Journal,* which in June 1993 devoted a full issue (vol. 3, no. 2) to the "Pittsburgh protocol" for obtaining organs from "non-heart-beating cadavers," the most recent procurement question to attain prominence during the period surveyed here. Given that organ transplantation seems well established as the sort of good society wishes to pursue and that there will always be a shortage of donor organs relative to need, the issue of procurement will surely remain a significant focus of attention for bioethics.

Changelings

Granting that how we classify issues or themes is in part a function of just how broadly or narrowly we define our categories and that this materially shapes the analysis, the *Report*'s history picks out a further "issue life cycle," that of the "changeling." What I have in mind here is the pattern in which once-privileged issues give way to different but fundamentally related concerns. The leading example from the *Report* is the treatment of reproductive ethics over the years, in which initial engagement with questions of population policy and preventing births has given way—in a nice paradox—to debate over the ethics of helping the infertile give birth.

Between 1971 and 1976 (that is, vol. 1–6), the *Report* carried fifteen articles on population issues and only one on assisted reproduction. Over the following four years (vol. 7–10), the balance began to shift, as significantly more articles (thirteen) were devoted to assisted reproduction and significantly fewer (eight) to population control. That the initial interest in population reflects and was in good measure prompted by broad societal concern in the late 1960s and early 1970s about the threatened "population explosion" seems certain. Analysis was couched fundamentally in the familiar terms of tensions between autonomy and beneficence, between the moral weight of private reproductive decisions and public policy concerns with societal and individual welfare and the legitimate boundaries of state coercion of individual behavior. The attention given to population issues in the *Report* reflected, in no small measure, the interest in the topic of the Hastings Center more broadly, one of whose earliest working groups addressed precisely such questions.

This is not to argue that early interest in reproductive issues was entirely confined to questions of contraception and population control. The inaugural issue of the *Journal of Medical Ethics* in 1975 focused on issues at the opposite end of the reproductive spectrum, so to speak, with a collection of five short articles on artificial insemination by donor.

In the late 1970s, however, the attention of the bioethics community was firmly captured by assisted reproduction with the development of IVF and the birth of the first "test tube baby" in 1978, which produced much debate and a flurry of articles[10] (Figure 3). The shift in focus meant further

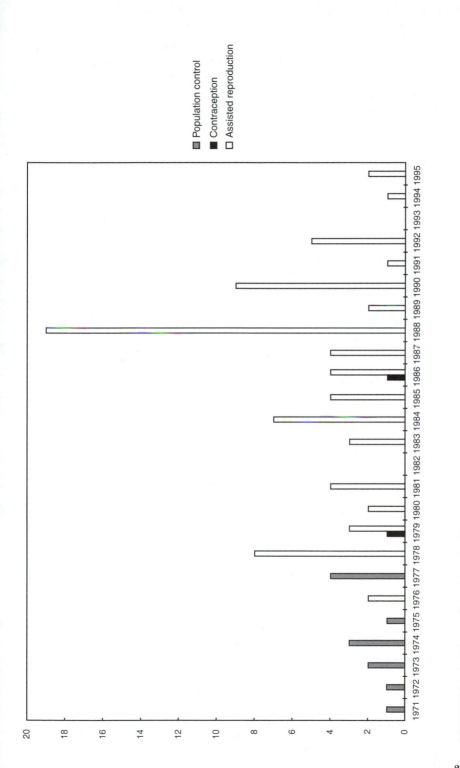

FIGURE 3   Articles on Reproductive Issues

that concerns at least partly rooted in a sense of global crisis gave way to a narrower domain of potential harms to identifiable individuals, whether the test tube babies themselves or their parents.

The saliency of assisted reproduction as a domain of inquiry for bioethics since has been sustained less by the development of new technologies, however, than by the evolution of new social arrangements in which to deploy those technologies and enable infertile individuals or couples to have children to whom they are biologically related. Thus, for example, four of the eight articles on assisted reproduction published in the *Report* between 1981 and 1984 addressed "surrogate motherhood" (now more commonly "contract pregnancy" or "contract gestation"). So too did six of eight articles between 1985 and 1988, largely under the impetus of New Jersey's "Baby M" case,[11] while *Law, Medicine & Health Care* devoted a double issue to the topic in 1988 (vol. 16, no. 1 and 2).

The pendulum may again be shifting, however, as explicitly public policy issues again come to prominence. The *Journal of Clinical Ethics,* for example, in its second issue (summer 1990) presented a special section of articles, "Perinatal Chemical Dependence," examining legal and policy responses to the problems of drug abuse by pregnant women, including issues of court-ordered contraception. And in the *Report,* the exclusive focus on assisted reproduction generally continued though another eight articles in the period 1989–1992 but returned to issues of contraception with the publication of a special supplement on new long-acting contraceptives in 1995. Policy issues predominated, including not only court-ordered use of contraceptives in the criminal justice system but also the ethics of offering various financial and other incentives to teenagers and disadvantaged women to use contraceptives, especially newly approved long-acting methods like Depo-Provera and Norplant. Once more, the ethics literature seems to be tracking both emerging case law and evolving technology.

Shooting Stars

While there is perdurable professional interest in subjects like abortion, organ transplantation, and a variety of reproductive issues, other concerns seem to emerge, dominate attention for a greater or lesser span, and then disappear from the bioethics horizon completely. The best metaphor to describe this pattern may be astronomical: These are the "shooting stars" among issues, brilliantly visible in their meteoric rise to prominence but short-lived.

Perhaps the clearest such example in the *Report*'s history is behavior control, one of the animating issues in the early days of the Hastings Center and one of its original project areas (Figure 4.) Over the first six volumes of the *Report* (1971–1976), fully nineteen articles and/or supplements were

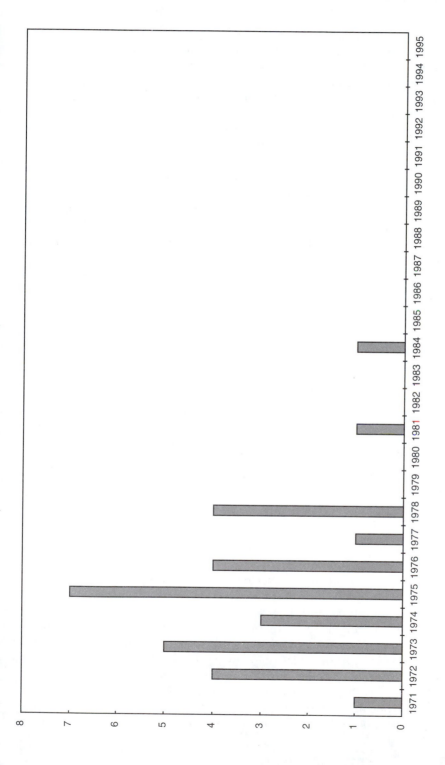

FIGURE 4   Articles on Behavior Control

devoted to the topic, notably to the ethics of psychosurgery. Yet over the next six volumes, the journal offered fewer than half that many discussions, bringing out only seven articles altogether. Since the mid-1980s, the topic appears not to have been salient for the field, though the ethics of psychiatry remains a significant focus for some publications, particularly the *Journal of Medicine and Philosophy*.[12]

Once again, this diminishing attention parallels changing medical practice. What role, if any, specifically ethical arguments played in the demise of psychosurgery as a therapeutic intervention (and the decline of electroconvulsive therapy) is a question far too complex to be addressed here, but as the use of explicitly medical means to control individual behavior waned so, not surprisingly, did interest on the part of ethicists.[13]

There have been topics with far shorter lifespans in the field, of course, a notable one being the ethics of life-sustaining treatment for brain-dead pregnant women. A 1993 case in Germany,[14] soon to be followed by cases elsewhere, first raised the question of whether a pregnant brain-dead body ought to be maintained on life support in order to attempt to bring the fetus to term. Widely noted in many forums, the cases also prompted two article-length treatments in *Bioethics* in 1993 and 1994 and one in the *Journal of Clinical Ethics* in 1993.

Whether, in the end, such issues have truly reached a stable consensus or whether they somehow lacked the depth that would sustain ongoing analysis—or bioethics has lacked the analytic toolkit properly to plumb them—is not clear. With respect certainly to "postmortem pregnancy" as it was labeled, the boundary to bioethics' interest may lie with the inability of technology actually to carry out its intended project—until and unless sustaining a developing fetus in a brain-dead body becomes truly technically feasible the field may simply have more compelling questions to ask elsewhere.

Pulsars

To pursue the astronomical metaphor a bit further, other constellations of issues in bioethics may be better likened to variable stars than meteors. By this I mean to describe those life cycles in which bioethics begins to probe a new domain of analysis, aggressively engages issues it discerns there for a time, and then disengages only to return to the issue periodically with renewed intensity. In a sense this might be taken to be the pattern evinced by organ transplantation, of course, and might yet prove the best description of behavior control. Yet surely the more compelling example is that of genetics, which has been a focus of professional attention from the earliest years of the field (Figure 5).

What began as an early interest in the new recombinant-DNA technology in and of itself quickly grew into a vigorous discussion of its impli-

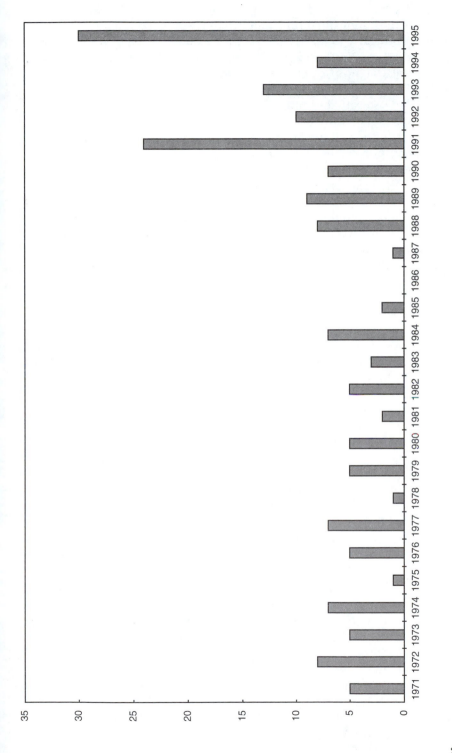

FIGURE 5 Articles on Genetics

cations for both individual reproductive decision making and social policy. Articles in the early to mid-1970s—in, for example, *Law, Medicine & Ethics* (then *Medicolegal News*) and the *Report*—addressed "Medicolegal Issues in the Prenatal Diagnosis of Hereditary Disorders" (*MN*, vol. 1, no. 1, 1975) and "IQ, Race, and Public Debate" (*HCR*, vol. 2, no. 2, 1972). Notably, virtually all the issues that would be addressed in regard to genetics were laid out early in the bioethics literature—prenatal genetic diagnosis, screening, eugenics, patenting of life-forms, "behavioral"genetics (XYY syndrome, or "hypermasculinity"), the creation of transgenic species (chimeras), implications for the concepts of health and disease—only the Human Genome Project (HGP) itself couldn't be grappled with early on, for the obvious reason that it hinged on technological developments yet to come.

As genetic technologies have evolved, for example, with the development of gene-splicing techniques (polymerase chain reaction, or PCR) and the genome-mapping project it made possible, bioethics has reshaped and refined its analysis in coming to terms with new prospects. And as the social climate has changed, some perspectives on the core issues of genetics have become more salient—for example, policy concerns about the confidentiality of genetic information and possible discrimination by employers and insurers. The larger point, however, is that the overall dimensions of genetic issues were essentially in place from the outset of the conversation in the bioethics literature. So too the way scholars look at individual decision making in the context of prenatal screening is increasingly sensitive to the concerns of disability rights advocates about the kinds of discriminatory messages the very existence of screening tests can send to those who have genetically based disabling conditions.[15]

The more realistic a prospect gene therapy has become,[16] the more the issues raised by both somatic and germ-line therapy have penetrated the set of concerns captured under the general heading of "genetics"—witness articles beginning to appear in the *Journal of Clinical Ethics* in 1991, the *Kennedy Institute of Ethics Journal* (1992), and *Law, Medicine & Ethics* (1992), for example. The HGP itself has added yet another topic, one particularly attended to in its own right in the early years of the program—for example, in articles in the *Report* (1989 and 1990), the *Kennedy Institute of Ethics Journal* (1991), and the *Journal of Clinical Ethics* (1991). And as genetic screens proliferate with the successes of the HGP and are increasingly likely to become widely available in primary care settings, the scope of analysis is changing: The focus is widening to include issues of professional competence as well as distributive justice and health care policy. The common thread throughout is the way in which the evolving technology significantly drives the focus of ethical analysis.

Another telling example is the life cycle of AIDS and HIV disease evidenced in the *Report* and other publications (Figure 6). AIDS began to garner attention in the bioethics literature in the mid-1980s, following

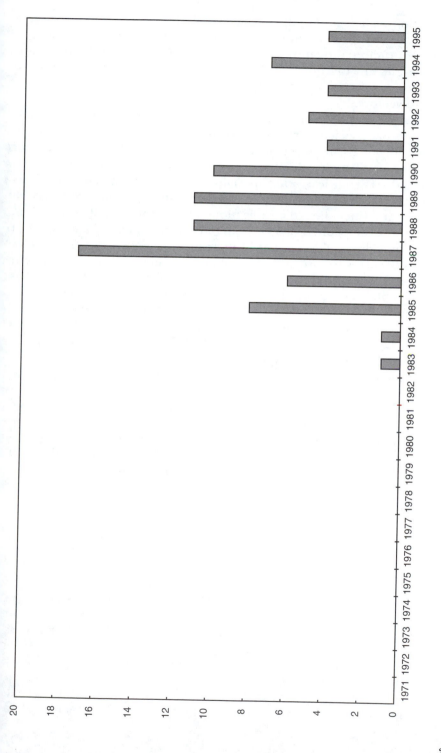

FIGURE 6 Articles on AIDS

recognition of it as a new, distinct syndrome by the Centers for Disease Control. Professional discussion of the ethical challenges of the epidemic—confidentiality, duties to warn or to ascertain one's HIV status (or the right not to know), and the like—grew up in tandem with the public policy responses to emerging scientific evidence on transmission rates and vectors.

Over the late 1980s and into the early 1990s, focus shifted gradually from the broad, societal tension between protecting the civil liberties of infected individuals and safeguarding the public health to rather narrower concerns—for example, about the roles of health care professionals in response to HIV, not least what special obligations may fall on caregivers who are themselves seropositive. At the same time, questions of justice in access to care (including the obligations of employers and insurers) in large measure supplanted debate centered on the behavior and rights of infected individuals. These issues in their turn have given way to broader questions of access to care and health care reform, dimming the spotlight on AIDS in the journal literature of bioethics. So too as the epidemic has become familiar and the initial policy questions have been resolved, discussion has shifted out of general bioethics publications into more specialized fora, particularly journals with clinical and research focus.[17]

New research findings, both basic and therapeutic, briefly capture attention as they emerge, but whatever their potential clinical significance, on the evidence of the literature such developments are not taken to raise fundamentally new issues to engage ethical debate. (Most recently, the issue of testing has returned to prominence with proposals for—or enacted legislation requiring—mandatory testing of pregnant women and/or newborns.) If the ethics conversation is to identify new issues and be reinvigorated, it seems likeliest to be linked to emerging reunderstandings of HIV/AIDS as a chronic, rather than an acute, uniformly lethal disease.

Family, Genus, Species

Although these patterns—the life cycles of classics, changlings, shooting stars, and pulsars—do seem to characterize distinctive ways in which bioethics has engaged issues it identifies as properly within its purview, they may be the least interesting and least significant for the field. Surely the more compelling pattern in the bioethics journal literature is an evolutionary one, of the continual elaboration of new issues within a broad domain through ever more finely differentiated analyses reaching ever greater levels of delicacy. This might be called a pattern of speciation: Over time, clusters of issues that form a "family" differentiate into identifiably discrete lines of inquiry ("genuses"), which in their turn give rise to even finer distinctions and the emergence of "species" as increasingly specialized discussions focus on issues raised in ever more narrowly circumscribed domains. This pattern, I suggest, seems best to capture the dynamics at the intellectual core of bioethics as a discipline, to pick out its most defining issues.

Arguably one such evolutionary family is that of health care policy and delivery. Analysis early on tended to focus on general considerations of health policy and of health care as a right. Over time, these broad issues became much more differentiated internally. Questions of health care as a right, for example, became further refined and elaborated in the analysis of access to care as a distinctive species of issue (with its emphasis on questions of justice), on through to the species "allocation/rationing" that is a prominent focus of the current literature.

Yet to appreciate the way in which this general domain has become increasingly refined and analysis increasingly technical and "local," one must look beyond the core bioethics literature to the proliferation of bioethically informed policy articles in other publications. There is in fact an extensive specialty literature spanning the boundary of "bioethics," "public policy for health care," and "economics." *Milbank Quarterly* (1923) is the oldest journal of this type. In the 1980s *Health Affairs* (1982) and *Health Care Financing Review* (1986) began publication, and even more recently, publications such as *American Journal of Managed Care* (1995) and others targeted to a very particular industry audience have appeared.

What has driven this evolutionary trend? Surely a major external impetus has been the growing perception of cost crisis in health care, along with increasing disparities in access to care. (Recall, in an American context, the emphasis on the growing number of uninsured during debates around the Clinton health care reform and plan and calls for universal access.) But a second strand would seem to have been the long-standing concern in the discipline itself with the character of medicine as a profession and its appropriate goals. "Goals talk" as such has only recently entered the conversation perhaps, but the underlying concerns seem to have animated the analysis of health care systems from the outset. To a certain extent then, we might say that in this domain the fit between issues central to bioethics (the philosophical nature of medicine as a profession) and the social and political context in which the field has developed has prompted a "natural" evolution within the discipline.

Even this may not best illustrate the central intellectual life of bioethics, however. For if this pattern does indeed capture those central dynamics, virtually nowhere is it more clearly and fully evident than in regard to end-of-life issues.

The family "death and dying"—to use the original category established for the *Report*'s first index—has been one of the most dynamic of any within the field, as even the most cursory perusal of the literature makes abundantly clear. To press the metaphor, the main genuses within the family are, roughly put, care of the dying and decision making. These have both proven vital, dynamic lineages, differentiating into several new species, each with its own subspecies: hospice, termination of treatment, assisted suicide and euthanasia, proxy decision making, and advance directives.[18]

What began in the early years of the *Report,* the *Journal of Medicine and Philosophy,* and other publications as a general concern with attitudes toward death and broad questions about the kind of care dying patients receive has gradually developed more sophisticated inquiries in more narrowly defined domains—the ethics of withholding and withdrawing life-sustaining treatment, of "futility," of decision making for patients who are not competent, and the various standards and mechanisms through which care plans may be developed for these patients—of assisted suicide and euthanasia. Each of these has become the domain of independent, vigorous analysis, seen to be characterized not only by broadly shared ethical concerns—how best to respect patients as persons, for example—but just as importantly by specialized issues created by particular local features—for example, to what extent preferences expressed by a once-competent individual in an advance directive continue to define that individual's most significant interests and ought to govern the care of the now-incompetent patient.[19] New issues are themselves the product not simply, nor even necessarily most importantly, of new technologies or strategies of care but of the very ethical analyses that preceded them. Earlier analysis of the right to refuse life-sustaining treatment gave rise to questions about how to honor those rights for patients unable to express preferences at the time decisions must be made. The resulting recognition of advance directives led to further questions about the interpretation and implementation of living wills, to whether surrogate decision makers best fulfill their responsibilities to the patient by working within the framework of best interests or substituted judgment, and to questions about who should serve as proxy when the patient has no "bonded surrogate" or never appointed a health care proxy (see Figure 7).

Respect for persons has now been pressed through the analysis of whether an individual could choose to forgo life-sustaining treatment or request that such treatment be withdrawn, to the issues of physician-assisted suicide and euthanasia. And just as the earlier discussion of the "right to die" in reference to termination of treatment gave rise—and indeed continues to do so—to several distinctive issues, such as what if any moral weight attends a distinction between withholding and withdrawing life-sustaining treatment, or whether artificial nutrition and hydration fall within the interventions about which patients or their surrogates may properly choose, or the questions of do-not-resuscitate (DNR) orders and "futility," so the species-assisted suicide and euthanasia has differentiated its own special areas of inquiry, including the distinction between active and passive euthanasia (or killing and letting die, the form in which the dichotomy links this species to its relative), whether the professional commitments of

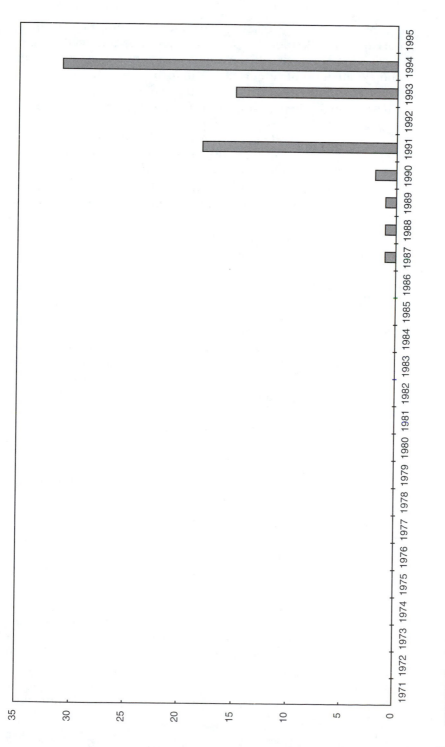

FIGURE 7   Articles on Advance Directives

211

caregivers require them to actively aid patients in dying or specifically refrain from doing so, whether the practices should be tolerated or legalized, and what sorts of safeguards must be in place to protect against the coercion and exploitation of vulnerable patients in either situation.

Note that I attribute this rather dramatic evolution not to the development of new biomedical technologies, or to aspects of the broader political climate in which these issues are discussed, but to philosophical reflection on the injunction of respect for persons. I do so quite deliberately. Context surely has influenced the shape of the conversation and made it perhaps easier for some issues to distinguish themselves than others, and without respirators, and vasopressors, and all the rest of intensive care technology many of these questions would take very different forms. The point I want to suggest, however, is that bioethics' intellectual resources are precisely the sort that enable just this kind of elaboration of issues—the parsing of situations as forms of moral arguments and the pursuit of their implications. And just this sort of refinement is the task it has set for itself, though perhaps not always explicitly.

Stephen Toulmin (1982) noted that, in responding to the "demand for intelligent discussion of the ethical problems of medical practice and research," in the 1960s philosophers perforce had to shift from the theoretical, metaethical analysis that had dominated academic ethics in mid-century to debate couched "in practical, concrete, even political terms . . ."[20] The result was not only a shift away from theory but also, more particularly, a focus that required philosophers to

> substitut[e] a new preoccupation with situations, needs, and interests; it required writers on applied ethics to go beyond the discussion of general principles and rules to a more scrupulous analysis of the particular kinds of "cases" in which they find their application; it redirected that analysis to the professional enterprises within which so many human tasks and duties typically arise; and, finally, it pointed philosophers back to the ideas of "equity," "reasonableness," and "human relationships," . . . . (Toulmin 1982, 737)

Bioethics seems to have found that kind of deep engagement especially in the realm of medical care at the end of life. The more deeply engaged bioethics becomes, the more it finds to become engaged with; the better it parses situations, the more complex they become. And the more deeply engaged bioethics becomes, the more it refines its own analytic resources, allowing it to open up new domains of inquiry. Indeed, the field's reflections on and development of its own theoretical and analytic repertoire are another example of this evolutionary pattern. Broadly speaking, to the rootstock of principlism have been grafted increasingly vigorous strains of communitariansim, feminism, and narrative ethics; and in recent years, casuistry and virtue ethics have staged something of a comeback.

There is, I think, an important difference lurking here between the way in which "death and dying" has enabled (bio)ethics to create and recreate itself as a discipline and the way in which the domain of health care policy has not. For the moment I can only suggest how we might understand the difference: The attention to cases and particulars that the family "death and dying" sustains has rather less purchase in regard to health policy. This is not precisely, or not solely anyway, the problem of a lack of identifiable individuals around whom policy issues could focus, the absence of a patient in the bed for whom decisions must imminently be made. Poster children for policy questions could certainly be found. Rather, the problem lies in finding sufficiently analytically sophisticated ways to engage the individual as token of a type of situation, need, or interest, of moving from the identifiable individual to the community or society or the public domain.

That calls for a more finely grained kind of theory than bioethics yet seems to have available to it—or perhaps better, in this realm, ethics has not yet made the theoretical moves of which Toulmin spoke. It hasn't figured out well enough how to make theory work at the level of public policy. Perhaps this is in part a function of the fact that a marriage of theoretical traditions is called for, an effective synthesis of the analytic paradigms of ethics and of political philosophy that could at least bridge, ideally integrate, the two domains. Without those tools in hand to enable new concerns to emerge from its own analysis, the issues bioethics engages in the policy domain and the ways in which it does so will likely continue to hinge on external factors. The work is going forward, as increasing interest in communitarian philosophy makes clear; with those tools in hand, "health care policy," I suspect, will prove to have as evolutionarily rich a life as death and dying now enjoys.

EPILOGUE

If these preliminary analyses of the lives of issues in bioethics are at all persuasive, they suggest an obvious next step: a more fine-grained exploration of just how bioethics has brought its theories to bear in each of these cycles. Just what has the discourse of bioethics sounded like in engaging different topics? And how has that engagement helped refine the theory available to the discipline?

Large questions those, best left to another occasion.

NOTES

1. See, e.g., Jonsen (1993).
2. A similar point is developed in Crigger (1995).

3. *In re Quinlan,* 70 N.J. 10, 355 A.2d 647 (1976).

4. We should acknowledge a practical concern at this point, however. There may well be a disjunction between the emergence of disciplinary and/or public interest in a topic and its appearance in the published literature of bioethics, a disjunction that can be as much an artifact of publishers' production constraints as of any other factor. Not only do schedules not always accommodate "breaking stories," but so simple a thing as length will dictate what is covered in any given number of a journal—like other resources, pages must be allocated among competing topics.

5. Launched in 1973 as *Medicolegal News,* this publication has gone through several changes over its history. It began carrying "bioethics" articles prominently in 1982, when it became *Law, Medicine & Health Care.* In 1993 it changed names again, to the current *Law, Medicine & Ethics.*

6. This does not exhaust the range of possible sources. There are further highly specialized publications devoted to particular dimensions of bioethics, such as *IRB: A Review of Human Subjects Research* (1979), or *HEC Forum* (1989), along with a host of newsletters produced by various bioethics centers throughout the world. And journals "outside" the field now more or less regularly offer articles germane to bioethics, among them publications directed primarily to clinical audiences, such as *JAMA,* the *New England Journal of Medicine, Archives of Internal Medicine, Annals of Internal Medicine, Generations,* and the *Journal of the American Geriatric Society.* So too publications directed toward a policy audience are a significant locus of publication for bioethics issues, for example, *Health Affairs* or *Milbank Quarterly.* Another obvious source not mined here is presentations at meetings of the various professional societies that "bioethicists" are associated with: the Society for Health and Human Values, the International Association of Bioethics, the American Association of Bioethics, or the Society for Bioethics Consultation. Finally, there are electronic sources such as the Medical College of Wisconsin's bioethics bulletin board, which increasingly serve as forums for conversation and "publication" of issues." And indeed, at least one book-length piece has been released on the Internet: Benjamin Freedman's *Duty and Healing,* which can be found at this web address: http://www.mcgill.ca/CTRG/bfreed/.)

7. *Roe* v. *Wade,* 410 U.S. 113 (1973).

8. *Planned Parenthood of Central Missouri* v. *Danforth,* 428 U.S. 52 (1976).

9. *Webster* v. *Reproductive Health Services,* 492 U.S. 490 (1989).

10. The lead note in the column "Report from America" in the December 1978 issue of the *Journal of Medical Ethics* was entitled "Louise Brown—A Storm in a Petri Dish."

11. *Matter of Baby M,* 537 A.2d 1227 (N.J. 1988).

12. Recall, as well, the launch of *Philosophy, Psychiatry & Psychology* in 1994. Despite the lack of attention in the recent bioethics literature, it may be too soon to declare the topic dead as a matter of significant concern. Issues of behavior control may soon reemerge in a new guise with the growing interest in "behavioral genetics."

13. Beyond, that is, isolated moments, such as an article in the fall 1994 issue of the *Journal of Clinical Ethics.*

14. See, e.g., Anstötz (1993).

15. Indeed, there is now a "quasi-bioethics" journal devoted to disability-related issues, *Issues in Law and Medicine,* launched in the summer of 1995.

16. That gene therapy is a reality is only underscored by the launch of a specialty journal devoted expressly to the new molecular medicine, *Human Gene Therapy* (vol. 1, no. 1, spring 1990).

17. E.g., *AIDS Clinical Care* (1989) and a host of others, ranging from patient information newsletters to policy and scientific periodicals.

18. Again, I use the index categories set up for the *Report* to identify these lineages.

19. See, e.g., the running debate between Ronald Dworkin and Rebecca Dresser (Dresser 1995).

20. Toulmin (1982).

REFERENCES

Anstötz, Christoph. 1993. Should a brain-dead pregnant woman carry her child to full term? The case of the "Erlanger Baby." *Bioethics* 7(4): 340–50.

Crigger, Bette-Jane. 1995. Negotiating the moral order: Paradoxes of clinical ethics consultation. *Kennedy Institute of Ethics Journal* 5(2): 89–112.

Dresser, Rebecca. 1995. Dworkin on dementia: Elegant theory, questionable policy. *Hastings Center Report* 25(6): 32–8.

Jonsen, Albert R. 1993. The birth of bioethics. Special supplement. *Hastings Center Report* 23(5, suppl.): S1–4.

Toulmin, Stephen. 1982. How medicine saved the life of ethics. *Perspectives in Biology and Medicine* 25(4): 736–50.

CHAPTER ELEVEN

Changing Society, Changing Medicine, Changing Bioethics

Karen G. Gervais[1]

NEW CHALLENGES FOR BIOETHICS

Bioethics in the United States has been a professional field since the late 1960s. It has become such a complex field that, as in medicine, professionals both share a broad base of expertise and have their distinctive specializations. The agenda was set in the early 1970s with the specification of a framework of ethical principles centered in patient and research-subject autonomy, or self-determination. Thus began the emphasis on patients' rights, as opposed to physician paternalism, and of human subjects' rights to make informed decisions about their participation in research. The other principles, beneficence and justice, completed the framework.

The essential thrust of this ethical framework in the medical arena was to enable patients to make decisions about medical choices in accordance with their personal values and beliefs, particularly decisions to withhold or withdraw life-sustaining treatment at the end of life. As medical technology advanced, increasingly complex situations arose—situations posing value dilemmas on which there was no social consensus. Thus, it was thought that decisions should be made by those who would be directly affected.

Conflicts have often arisen concerning whether to honor the principle of autonomy, beneficence, or justice in a given situation, but deference has usually gone to autonomy (see Wolpe, this volume). Indeed, some claim that if we don't know what a patient would have wanted, we are not free to do what the vast majority would choose in such a situation or would agree to be in the patient's best interest! The ethical agenda has been to develop the implications of what has been considered to be the weightiest principle of the three, patient autonomy. In a sociopolitical system centered on the

216

premise that the individual comes first, this comes as no surprise. But the downside of this emphasis on autonomy and its implications has been that we never developed this three-principle framework adequately. In its imbalanced state, it has set the ethical agenda and been the standard currency of ethical debate for many years.

Principlism, as adherence to this framework is called, has had its opponents. Bioethics is now rich with alternative theoretical approaches to ethically informed decision making, but the early principles cannot be entirely set aside or ignored. They do keep before our minds the central moral requirements associated with health care situations: Patient and family values are honored, a high standard of professional faithfulness or fidelity to patients (to actively seek their good and to avoid harming them) is the professional's guide in addressing the inherent vulnerability of the patient, and fairness in access to the essential good of health care is ensured. So rather than set aside this framework, I will concentrate on two substantial social changes that call upon us to "strike the set" and recast and refine our ethical framework. As it has been developed thus far, this framework is poor equipment for addressing ethical issues associated with (1) our culturally diverse society and (2) the changing relationships and dynamics of our health care system. I will focus on these areas of ethical challenge in order to show the deficiencies of our framework in its established incarnation and to suggest directions for recasting and refining it.

Some social changes are so radical that they require an entire reconceiving of the ethical framework—a task we now face in relation to changes in the financing and delivery of health care. In the late 1990s we need a population-based, patient-centered ethic that enables sound health care relationships between patients and professionals while providing—from a population perspective—cost-effective, medically appropriate health care. How can the moral requisite of professional fidelity to patients be ensured in a system that increasingly seems to place physicians in the position of a double agent, serving patient and population simultaneously? In short, our ethical framework must become a more balanced one: Justice and autonomy must be defined and understood relative to each other, and the duties of beneficence must be clarified in ways that will bring the benefits of health care to all.

Other social changes require an enlargement of what we value and a reinterpretation of key ethical principles. Increasingly, our society has a new face. Significant immigrant communities bring alternative perspectives on self, community, and health and illness to health care settings and encounters. Often, these communities do not share the explanatory paradigms and ethical goals that are the common currency of Western medicine and the bioethics movement. When the health care encounter becomes an intercultural encounter, what can and must be done to enable patients and families to make ethically informed health care decisions?

Since an ethically informed health care decision is one that is based on an understanding of the physical, psychological, familial, social, spiritual, and economic consequences of the decision made, and is consistent with the values, beliefs, and desires of the patient (and/or their family), it is clear that health care professionals need to learn the skills associated with "cultural competency." In short, our ethical framework must be recast and refined to remove the presumption that all health care encounters are unicultural.

Let us look at these two social changes and the challenges they pose to the traditional ethical framework of bioethics. First, we will ask how we can ensure that our framework succeeds as an ethic for intercultural relationships. Then we will turn to the question of how to interpret and protect the professional duty of beneficence and fidelity to the patient as our system increasingly applies population-based reasoning to resource-allocation decisions.

THE CHALLENGE FOR BIOETHICS: DEVELOPING AN INTERCULTURAL HEALTH CARE ETHIC

The field of bioethics has been rooted in post-Enlightenment philosophical traditions and consequently reflects the values and assumptions of the dominant culture. The model for ethically informed health care decision making it has generated is a decidedly Western model, centered in the ethical principle of patient autonomy and supported by an individualistic concept of self and a rationalist model of decision making.

Arguably, this model does not always serve mainstream patients that well. Even clearer, though, is the inadequacy of this model and its associated practices (for example, decision making and informed consent requirements) for members of other cultures.

Yet an underlying assumption of the field of bioethics has been that patients and families must be enabled to make health care decisions consistent with their deepest understandings of the meaning and value of life, for otherwise they will be "at odds with themselves" in potentially harmful ways. For this reason some families of patients in permanent vegetative state are allowed to determine that their loved one receive ongoing life-sustaining care, while other families are allowed to have such life-sustaining treatment discontinued.

We need to develop and apply a decision-making model that respects the values, beliefs, and practices of our society's special cultural groups so that their decisions about health care will be authentically grounded in their ultimate sources of meaning and value. Such a model is essential to promote conditions of understanding and active respect, essential elements of effective healing relationships.

An Application of an Intercultural Health Care Ethic: Promoting Culturally Competent Health Care for the Hmong

Our practical problem is to learn how to implement an intercultural health care ethic in relation to people whose views of the self, family, community, time, causality, and spirituality depart from the temporally bounded, individualistic, and mechanistic perspectives that prevail in Western culture. The Hmong people are an especially powerful example of this cultural disconnect—a disconnect that is ethically significant because it threatens to disrupt the Hmong from their central sources of meaning and communal support at times when they are, like any of us, most vulnerable, needy, and fearful.

Some ethicists have begun to address (1) the specific issue of promoting culturally competent health care for the Hmong and (2) the broader bioethics concern of building a model ethical framework that might be applied to intercultural health care relationships generally. This intercultural ethic for health care relationships will clarify the elements of information, interaction, and communication essential to promote ethically informed decision making. As the theory behind the practice of culturally competent health care, it will continue to be influenced by the practical experience gained through working with the Hmong community to educate health care professionals in the perspectives of the Hmong people so that these professionals will know, concretely, how to implement their commitment to culturally competent care for the Hmong.

Cultural homogeneity and intercultural respect.   Significant debate surrounds the extent to which a multicultural society should go to promote the conditions of cultural survival for its nonmainstream communities. Some hold the view that a liberal society should guarantee uniform treatment in accordance with procedural principles to all its citizens, but go no further. Beyond this, a liberal society must leave everyone free to pursue their conception of the good life. Procedural justice, they claim, is guaranteed through the imposition of neutral principles. These principles are considered to be neutral because everyone is treated uniformly under those principles.

Others contend that the notion of procedural justice just described is culturally biased in favor of the dominant group. They also think that the obligations of a liberal society to its diverse cultural communities extend further—to the active promotion of the conditions of cultural survival for nonmainstream groups. They might, for example, argue that bilingual education should be provided for members of a specific culture.

Those who think a liberal society has this stronger obligation to support the survival of its cultural minorities also take exception to the claim that procedural justice is neutral or impartial. They point out that procedural justice may impose a cultural homogeneity that displaces the perspectives, beliefs, and decision-making customs of some cultures. Procedural principles, allegedly culture-neutral, are really not so, as they see it.

To give an example, that there would be a procedural principle that everyone who dies an unexpected death would be autopsied appears to affect equally everyone who dies unexpectedly. But because of Hmong views on the self and the afterlife, this "neutral" principle works a kind of spiritual violence on the deceased Hmong person and family that is unparalleled for "mainstream" members of our society. For the Hmong, autopsy causes the dead further suffering. Alterations in the body affect the self in the next life, since the individual lives on in the next life with the bodily characteristics it died with in this life. From this perspective, procedural equity with respect to autopsy appears to be harmful to the Hmong. Autopsies should not be performed on the Hmong unless absolutely necessary, and a careful and sensitive process of obtaining familial consent should be followed.

Charles Taylor, a leading sociopolitical scholar, writes eloquently on the reason why a liberal society should hold an expansive view of its responsibilities to promote conditions of cultural survival for its minority cultures:

> Our identity is partly shaped by recognition or its absence, often by the *mis*-recognition of others, and so a person or group can suffer real damage, real distortion, if the people or the society around them mirror back to them a confining or demeaning or contemptible picture of themselves. Non-recognition or misrecognition can inflict harm, can be a form of oppression, imprisoning someone in a false, distorted, and reduced mode of being. (Taylor et al. 1994, 25)

The problem we must solve in a liberal society, Taylor claims, is to identify those instances in which the authenticity of persons or groups is undermined by imposing a false homogeneity on them—that is, when norms are imposed on them that make their conformity to those norms a condition of their recognition. Depending on what conformity requires of them, they may lose what they consider to be their souls and therefore their identities in the process. The imposition of homogeneity is a refusal to recognize them and becomes a way of "imprisoning [them] . . . in a false . . . mode of being."

This broader debate about intercultural respect has direct relevance for health care ethics, for nowhere is it clearer than in the health care setting how important it is that people's decisions and actions be consistent with their beliefs, values, and decision-making customs. A failure to address cultural particularity will separate patients and families from their ultimate sources of meaning, human connection, and comfort. It will leave people "at odds with themselves" in harmful ways. The deference given mainstream families should surely be extended to all patients and families, regardless of their cultural identification. Cultural perspectives on the meaning and value of life must be recognized and enabled in the same way any of us would want our defining perspectives to be identified, understood, and honored in health care situations.

Working with the Hmong: A model for the future of bioethics. In 1995 the Minnesota Center for Health Care Ethics (MCHCE) held its first annual Diversity Summit Conference, "Hmong Perspectives on Critical Care." The purpose of this conference was to begin to promote intercultural understanding that would ground appropriate attention to Hmong patients' and families' faith and cultural perspectives by health care professionals. The conference was quite different from the typical conference sponsored by ethics centers. Rather than a heavy focus on refining abstract arguments or teaching caregivers the principles of ethical reasoning, this meeting was intended to give caregivers a chance to listen to their clients.

At the Diversity Summit mainstream members of the health care and allied professions heard and interacted with seventeen representatives of the Hmong community. The Hmong taught conference attendees about their cultural beliefs and decision-making practices for the critically ill and about the barriers the Hmong perceive to culturally competent care. These barriers include:

- The failure to understand the worldview, explanatory paradigms, and decision-making customs of the Hmong.
- The imposition of Western linguistic and conceptual structures on communication with patients and families.
- The discounting of customary Hmong social and spiritual supports.
- The disregard of traditional Hmong healing practices.
- The threat of legal interventions based on Western perceptions of, for example, parental neglect.
- The disregard of Hmong attitudes and etiquette concerning interpersonal relationships.

Three panels of Hmong presenters, including Hmong professionals from the fields of nursing, social work, spiritual care, mental health, children and family services, and senior services broadened understanding about Hmong perspectives on critical illness and the communication needs of Hmong patients and families. Through a shaman and an herbal healer, participants learned about traditional Hmong health practices; and a young Hmong woman needing a kidney transplant talked poignantly of the effects of the clash between Western medicine and Hmong practices on the relationships between herself and her family and community as she sought a transplant. On the second day of the conference, case discussions were led by two Western health care professionals who serve the Hmong.

Three special experiences were also part of the conference. A video (*Western medicine*, 1996) conveyed, through the voices of Hmong patients and families, the difficulties some had experienced in our health care system: the failure to receive adequate explanations or to be allowed to consent to treatment, the concern that they were experimented on, their fear of legal interventions that would disrupt their relationships with their children, and the mistrust and exclusion of their traditional practices in times of medical crisis and major life transitions. A play presented a dialogue between two physicians who were trying to resolve their frustrations and dilemmas in treating a critically ill child from another culture (Cope 1996). The conference closed with performances of Hmong traditional dance, music, and a play retelling the history of the Hmong.

This summit grew out of a rich long-term collaboration between members of the Hmong community and the staff of a health care ethics center. The sort of education needed to promote culturally competent care can only come about through such direct relationship and the strategy of bringing members of the special population into direct contact with health care professionals.

A resounding message came from the speakers at Diversity Summit I. It was, *build trust*. Trust is not an ethical principle that one follows. Rather, it is the outcome of our attentiveness to the quality of our relationships with each other. How can health care ethics help us clarify the kind of attentiveness to the Hmong that will nurture trust? First, a relational model of clinical encounters between care givers and patients must be categorically affirmed. To affirm a relational model of the clinical encounter is to affirm personal connection over abstract principle, to affirm covenant over contract (see May 1983). As one of our speakers so poignantly put it: "By investing yourself in creating the trust of one Hmong person, you will build the trust of many. The loss of the trust of one will lose the trust of many."

Conference speakers made concrete suggestions concerning relationship building with Hmong patients and families. The Hmong appreciate introductions and have an interest in knowing some personal information about their caregiver. Going to a physician is often a last resort for them, due not only to their initial inclination to rely on their own healing practices (shaman rituals, herbal medicine, and massage) but also to their fear of invasive procedures. Their experiences in Laos and as refugees have made many Hmong understandably distrustful of authority. They are particularly concerned that they may be subjects of medical experiments.

For these reasons, relationship building is critical, and every test or treatment option must be explained in detail and given clear reasons. It is important to speak with respect, to smile, to have some words of Hmong in one's vocabulary, to ask open-ended questions like "What brought you here today?" and to avoid language that, when spoken by an authority figure like a physician, might be viewed by the Hmong as having the power of a curse that will result in a particular outcome. For example, rather than saying,

"Your son is dying," it was suggested that indirect references be used, such as "Your family will have a difficult time in the next week or so."

Because the Hmong understand the person to be a unity of body and soul, they fear procedures that alter the body. Such procedures may compromise the well-being of the soul. A person is considered to be ill when he or she can no longer perform his or her communal role; illness is a sign that the soul has left the body. Illness may be due to the impacts of spirits, natural imbalances, organic causes, supernatural occurrences, and magic. Traditional Hmong healing practices will vary depending on beliefs about the source of the illness.

The Hmong people are not saying "We do not believe in Western medicine." They do not, however, hold an explanatory model in which the assumptions and methods of Western medicine always have an easy or acceptable rationale. They are asking for explanations of health care options in terms they can understand. They are asking for clarity about what a treatment is for, why this is necessary, and why they will not improve without treatment. This information enables them to make ethically informed health care decisions. Approaches to explanation that do not require the challenging of Hmong concepts and explanatory structures must be sought. The goal is not to get the Hmong to think as Westerners. Rather, the medical mind-set must learn to explain itself in terms accessible to the Hmong.

For example, for some of the Hmong, many aspects of body structure and function remain a mystery. Also, they have a spiritual understanding of the source of illness, which is considered a departure or wandering of the soul that requires a shaman to "recall" the soul to its place within the body. This recalling of a soul may require bargaining with a spirit to allow its return; thus, a shaman ritual may involve a practice such as animal sacrifice. When traditional Hmong approaches fail, a Western physician's assistance may be sought. The challenge to the physician will be to find ways of explaining what the disease is, what treatment may correct the problem and why, and what the likelihood of success is. Too many tests, without attention to providing rationales for each, will generate suspicion and discomfort. For this reason it is better to parse out the tests that must be performed, taking diagnosis a step at a time.

The Hmong consider illnesses with discernible manifestations (like chicken pox) to have organic origins. These outward symptoms indicate that the body's natural balance is disturbed. The Hmong understand healing measures to restore the body to balance; their herbal medicines are thought of in this way. Particular communication difficulties surround diseases that lack discernible signs. When lab tests confirm conditions that are unseen by the patient, a patient and family may be helped to understand the need for treatment by being shown a comparison between a healthy patient's lab results and their own. A child's heart murmur and need for treatment may require that parents be able to listen to a healthy heartbeat and compare it to their child's heartbeat. Another patient or family that has faced the same issue may be of help in promoting the patient's understanding. Physicians are called upon to find creative ways of demystifying the body and its inner processes for the Hmong.

Surgery and anesthesia are particularly troubling. The Hmong are concerned that (1) both may alter them in ways that will affect them in this life and the next and (2) this may have bad impacts not only on themselves but also their family members. Families of patients for whom surgery or another intervention has failed will feel vulnerable to the spirit of the deceased, who may cause trouble for them.

It is therefore very important to find ways of conveying, concretely, what the surgery involves, what it will do, how this will change health for the better, and the likelihood of success. Increasingly, Hmong who receive thorough explanations will choose surgery to alter disfigurement, improve function, or lengthen life. Because the Hmong fear that the soul will wander when anesthesia induces an unnatural deep sleep, it is also important to provide alternatives to general anesthesia when possible. Patients facing difficult procedures are helped by the presence of family members as well as cultural peers.

As these examples show, a good professional-patient relationship requires time, attention to the explanatory framework and spiritual understandings the Hmong bring to health care situations, and a commitment to developing creative approaches to patient education. The ensurement that traditional Hmong healing practices may continue in tandem with Western medicine is not only a sign of respect but also a great reassurance to patients and families.

A further complexity in this picture is the need for the physician to identify the decision maker(s) in order to include them in the process of explanation. The Western decision-making model centers on the autonomous patient, deciding about health care interventions on the basis of personally held values and beliefs. While there is increasing attention to the patient and family as the unit of care and concern, decision making still revolves around the question of what the patient wants or would have wanted. But this is not a decision-making model that enables the Hmong to make ethically informed health care choices.

The Hmong person is a communal person—a person constituted and sustained by communal ties: family ties, clan ties, lineage ties, ancestral ties. A strong ethic of reciprocity grounds the unity and solidarity of the Hmong community. Would that we all could feel the supportive presence of others in our lives as the Hmong do. And yet, in times of medical crisis, the Hmong confront the individualistic and isolating decisional structures Western bioethics has generated as the antidote to physician paternalism and human-research abuse.

Western patient autonomy is Hmong isolation. We need to address the decisional needs of Hmong patients as communal selves. This requires a sensitivity to the traditional decision-making structures in the Hmong community and means that informed consent should be adjusted to the patient's values. If the patient values decision making by the extended family, then the consultation and explanations must include them. The Hmong then need time for reflection and discussion in order to reach a decision. At the same time that professionals must adapt to a communal approach to decision making, they must remain sensitive to Hmong persons who may be taking on a more Western perspective on health and disease, as well as on decision making.

Toward an Intercultural Ethic of Health Care

Relationships between the Hmong and health care professionals must be guided by the ethical ideal of empowerment. Just as medical ethics originated in the view that patients need empowerment, we must nurture the conditions essential for Hmong empowerment in the health care setting. These conditions must permit Hmong beliefs, customs, and understandings of community and self to be factors in health care communication and decision making. This principle of empowerment is a relative of the autonomy principle but clearly richer in terms of the attentiveness patients and families are due in health care settings.

The field of bioethics has the opportunity to create an intercultural health care ethic that addresses the question, In what ways must cultural difference be addressed in order to create the possibility of effective health care relationships and authentic health care decisions by persons of diverse cultures? We must acknowledge that our norms, ethical principles, and relational and decisional models affect cultured selves, and that this may be harmful to cultured selves when they most need to feel grounded in traditional relationships and structures of meaning.

An intercultural health care ethic will elaborate the conditions essential to cultural respect, conditions that enable ethically informed decision making. Bioethics centers must be prepared to move beyond their academic environments and their comfortable relationships with physicians—they must act as liaisons, helping bring together health care providers and diverse groups in the community. Work with communities of color must provide concrete direction to health care professionals in implementing an intercultural health care ethic—the process we at MCHCE are currently engaged in with the Hmong community. In this way, bioethics will contribute to the evolving of practices that will enable the American "melting pot" to be a mosaic of intercultural exchange and empowerment, rather than a source of cultural confusion and meltdown for the special cultures that increasingly enrich and challenge Western ways.

THE CHALLENGE FOR BIOETHICS: PROTECTING THE PHYSICIAN-PATIENT RELATIONSHIP IN OUR CHANGING HEALTH CARE SYSTEM

As we have seen, health care professionals face the challenge of responding to the different culture-based needs of their patients. They do so in a health care system that increasingly presses them to see more patients and to see themselves as not only patient caregivers but also stewards of health care resources. The emerging arrangements combining the financing and delivery of health care (which will be generically referred to as "managed care arrangements") impinge on physicians in ways that call into question the ability of the physician to be the patient's advocate and even to claim to have clinical autonomy. While cost-containment strategies are essential, are there ways of protecting the physician from the charge and the fact of double agency in our changing system?

Maybe it is the unexpurgated propaganda wreaked on my juvenile brain by the McCarthy hearings years back, or maybe it's the ethicist in me, but a certain dizziness sets in when I contemplate the life of a double agent. On occasion, each of us has to make hard choices between conflicting responsibilities, but we don't think of ourselves as continuously poised on a fault line between inherently contradictory allegiances. Yet if there has been one central ethics complaint against managed care, it is that the physician is cast in the role of double agent, with the dual and conflicting call to promote the best interests of one's patient and to be the steward of the population's health care resources simultaneously. What possibility is there that the physician will remain the patient's advocate and retain the patient's trust?

Although a principled approach to some situations of double agency must be possible, most of us do not want our physicians distracted from our care by such calculations. It is through a personal relationship that the health care system exists for and affects every patient. Each of us goes to his doctor believing that his doctor's focus is on him, not on a population of possibilities, as she listens, examines, tests, evaluates, explains, and recommends.

The caregiver's response to a patient originates in an ethic of virtue, a concept of professional and personal performance directly responsive to a patient's vulnerability, situation, and needs. Centered on the best interest of the individual patient, this ethic is guided by the belief that one can do too little and too much relative to certain ends and that the virtuous performance of one's art depends on understanding the difference and acting accordingly. This patient-centered ethic may dictate health care interventions wildly at odds with interventions that would be chosen from a population-based perspective.

And yet, the need to allocate finite health care resources requires us to decide whether decisions about coverage for health care interventions should be paid for from an individual patient perspective or a population perspective. For all but the very wealthy, access to adequate, lifelong, affordable health care can only be secured through a pooling of a portion of their economic resources and their equitable drawing from those pooled resources to cover the costs of medically necessary health care services. Because the resource pool is finite, drawing equitably from it will require that several constraints be observed: (1) A maximum amount any individual may draw from the pool must be imposed, (2) some health care interventions must be excluded from coverage, and (3) patients with equal health care needs must be treated equally.

Because health care is a basic good and because individuals have entrusted a portion of their resources to the managers of the resource pool, the managers of the pool are stewards of both the resource pool and the pooled population's health. Therefore, the steward has ethical obligations to members of the pool as individuals and to its members as a collective.

What perspective should this steward adopt in making coverage decisions, that of the individual or the population? Only the population perspective is ethically justifiable. If the individual perspective were adopted to determine the extent of coverage for medically necessary care each patient could access, the resource pool would soon be exhausted. The individual perspective is inherently at odds with the rationale that led individuals to pool their resources for health care security in the first place. Adopting the individual perspective would bankrupt the pool, thus depriving those who have made few claims on resources of access to health care, the basic good they thought they had secured through joining the pool. In short, it would be unfair to some members of the pool were the steward to manage the pool from an individual perspective.

More importantly, managing the pool from the individual perspective would also be a deceit to every person who joins the pool: Adopting the individual perspective presents the same threat to the interests of every person who joins the pool, since any one of them becomes vulnerable to the loss of health security were management of the pool from the individual perspective to drain the pool.

However, if the steward were to adopt the population perspective on resource management and therefore make coverage decisions from a population perspective, these two ethical faults, unfairness and deceit, would be avoided. Honesty and fairness in the overall arrangement and its conduct would be preserved.

What has all this to do with the role of the physician and the problem of the physician as double agent? Is the physician the steward just referred to? How can a physician effectively serve both patient and population? Is this the correct way to be framing our understanding of the obligations of the physician in our changing health care system?

As shown previously, because health care resources are finite, they must be allocated on the basis of population-based decisions that will promote the greatest health care good for the greatest number of the population. While this evolution to population-based health care is essential, it is important that the meaning of the word *good*—in the phrase, "the greatest good for the greatest number"—be defined from a patient-centered perspective. Study after study demonstrates that patients value the quality of their relationships with their caregivers most highly. Second on their list is the knowledge and technical skill of their physician. Health care is fundamental to our well-being, and the primary relationship through which we receive it is intensely important to us. Above all, this relationship requires time and continuity. In his poignant book *Intoxicated by My Illness*, Anatole Broyard describes what he wants in his physician:

> Now that I know I have cancer of the prostate, the lymph nodes, and part of my skeleton, what *do* I want in a doctor? I would say that I want one who is a close reader of illness and a good critic of medicine . . . who is not only a talented physician, but a bit of a metaphysician, too. Someone who can treat body and soul . . . [one who is] able to go beyond the science into the person [and] imagine the aloneness of the critically ill . . . I want him to be my Virgil, leading me through my purgatory or inferno, pointing out the sights as we go.
>
> Just as he orders blood tests and bone scans of my body, I'd like my doctor to scan *me*, to grope for my spirit as well as my prostate. Without some such recognition, I am nothing but my illness. (1992, 40–49 *passim*)

It is clear that the physician-patient relationship is an intensely personal and central one from the patient's perspective. The physician's role has been historically understood to be based on an ethic of fidelity to patients. While someone has to assume responsibility for the ethical balancing of population and individual health care interests, surely it ought not be the physician. How, as we make the essential transition to managed care, can the integrity of the physician-patient relationship be protected? Should the fiduciary ethic grounding the physician-patient relationship give way to an ethic of the physician as double agent? Such an ethic, presumably, would provide the physician with rules for bedside rationing. These rules would be necessary to justify a physician's withholding of an obviously beneficial intervention from a particular patient because of the impact providing the intervention would have on the population. Should we take steps to develop such an ethic, or should we take steps to distinguish patient care decision-making standards from resource-allocation standards and clearly place responsibility for those distinct decisions in separate hands?

I believe we must avoid making the physician a double agent of the patient and population simultaneously. Managed care arrangements can be designed ethically in a way that effectively insulates the physician from the threats to the physician-patient relationship.

Since many seem to think that the phrase "managed care ethics" is an oxymoron, I feel I must explain my position. Part of the problem with managed care, I am convinced, is that people do not understand it. Another part is that even those who understand it do not necessarily subscribe to the change in social ethos it requires. I have addressed a need to change our social ethos in the argument that we must adopt a population-based approach to decision making to distribute finite health care resources fairly and honestly. But we need managed care organizations (MCOs) to take a fundamental and decisive step in favor of the individual patient if any of these changes are to be palatable. Managed care must display its ethical mettle by attending to the need to insulate the physician-patient relationship sufficiently to remove the onus of double agency from the physician.

The ethical untenability of the physician as double agent leads me to ask, Whose double-agency problem is it, anyway? Who really needs the ethic for double agency? In fact, I think it is the health plan that has assumed the onerous task of providing population-based, patient-centered care. It is on the health plan that the ethical burden falls most heavily to be the stewards of the resources of their enrolled population and to ensure effective quality care for each enrollee. It is the health plan that requires a new ethic for solving the complex equation represented by the phrase "population-based, patient-centered care." Patients are still vulnerable, and vulnerable in new ways, in managed care arrangements. That vulnerability must be thoroughly characterized and addressed.

When the provision of population-based, patient-centered care becomes the physician's problem, managed care arrangements compromise the ethical centerpiece of health care: the fiduciary relationship between physician and patient. Were double agency to become the fate of the practicing physician, the best analogy to the transformed physician-patient relationship arguably becomes the mechanic—new car (or maybe used car) under warranty. The physician ceases to be a personal caregiver and becomes a diagnostician who identifies the patient's ailment (the car's source of malfunction), the range of responses (scrap heap, part replacement, tune-up), whether the health plan covers it (warrantied or not), what the patient will have to pay in addition to what the plan will pay (the limits on the warranty), and the like.

The physician's problem of double agency in our emerging health plans is brought on by the health plans themselves: The health plans themselves have not behaved as though they have assumed a fiduciary role in relation to a population and its members. Many of them have not addressed the need for a thorough examination of the problems of informed consent created by managed care. They have been unwilling to disclose their incentive arrangements or ensure their enrollees that these arrangements reward quality care rather than undertreatment. Or they have silenced physicians with "gag rules" or the threat of deselection (exclusion from the provider network, that is, loss of job).

It is not the physician's job to resolve problems of double agency. It is the health plan's job to prevent such problems from arising at the level of the physician-patient interaction in ways that compromise the physician's duties of truthfulness and fidelity. The physician should be constrained by medical necessity criteria and coverage agreements, but not silenced by them.

While health care reform at the national level has stagnated, there has been no corresponding slowdown in the restructuring and evolution of our health care financing and delivery system. MCOs are increasingly directing choices that were traditionally made in the context of the physician-patient relationship. As a result, many people are concerned that business goals are dictating health care goals, undermining health care professionals' role as patient advocates, and compromising patient care.

But it can be otherwise. Imagine the MCO that communicated well with its enrollees, giving them important information that would genuinely clarify the basis of their entitlements under a managed care framework, reassuring them about their physician's ability to be attentive to their individual needs. Imagine an MCO informing and preparing its enrollees with the following announcement:

> Given the high costs of health care and the escalating demand for it, some balancing between the interests of individual enrollees and the population of enrollees must occur. This balancing is the responsibility of your health plan, not of your physician. Your health plan covers the costs of medically necessary diagnosis and treatment. The coverage you are entitled to is a function of the benefits package you or your employer purchased. The coverage you are entitled to is for diagnosis and treatment that will permit you to function within normal range. This is basic, essential care, not excessive care directed at personal enhancement. Medically necessary care does not include all medically available and appropriate care, and your benefit contract may contain specific exclusions of medically necessary care (for example, experimental interventions). There may be many medical interventions that might, in a given situation, be of value and benefit to you as an individual but will not be covered by your health plan. Your physician will inform you of the existence of such treatments, as well as an explanation of why they are not covered. To provide a more expansive benefits package would increase the costs of coverage for the group of enrollees of which you are a member, costs that you or your payer has determined are beyond the scope of its responsibility to you. You may wish to purchase a more expansive medical coverage package. For information, please contact our office.

I have already said that I believe care can be ethically managed from a population perspective. I have also recommended that strategies for insulating the physician-patient relationship should be a key ethical goal for MCOs. I do not mean by this that it will be business as usual for physicians. Physicians will not be able to pursue the good for each patient in an unbridled way. But the strategies I have in mind will enable the physician to talk fully and truthfully to the patient and will require the MCO to have ethics processes in place for the analysis of recurrent ethical dilemmas in coverage decisions. To ensure the patient-centered element of the MCO's responsibility, the physician-patient relationship must be protected by an elaborate informed consent framework that addresses everything from enrollment to full disclosure of treatment options and coverage limitations by physicians to their patients.

The new era of managed care is producing a generalized "dis-ease" among health care professionals and the patients they serve. In the traditional fee-for-service arrangement, the understanding has been that the physician is to serve the patient's best interests and be respectful of patient autonomy. All who have felt the shelter and comfort of this special relationship know they do not want to lose it. No wonder managed care creates a sense of dis-ease.

Just as the field of health care ethics addressed the dis-ease that emerged around the life- and death-altering technologies that became prevalent in the 1960s, developing the ethical framework for patient-surrogate decision making concerning life-sustaining treatment in particular, the field of health care ethics has an essential role to play in addressing the dis-ease surrounding managed care.

I have suggested that the first step in this process is for us to acknowledge that managed care itself is the double agent and that managed care needs a new ethic for the complex yet critical social task it has assumed: to provide affordable and high-quality population-based, patient-centered care. Recognizing the centrality of the physician-patient relationship to successful diagnosis, healing, and comfort, MCOs must fulfill their commitment to patient-centered care by sheltering the physician-patient relationship. Through mechanisms ensuring informed consent, full disclosure, and physician security, the potential for humane doctoring of the kind Broyard identified can be protected, even as our health care system reorganizes the financing and delivery of health care.

CONCLUSION

An examination of profound changes in the composition of our society on the one hand, and in the arrangements for the financing and delivery of health care on the other, shows that the autonomy-centered ethical framework generated by the field of bioethics must be substantially retooled. This retooling requires a fuller elaboration of the justice and beneficence principles. In addition, it must be acknowledged that health care is such a central life good that the justice principle must become our central ethical guide: beneficence and autonomy must be circumscribed accordingly. In an individualistic society such as ours, believing that attitudinal change of this magnitude will occur is difficult. Yet the key may lie in the special understanding of the principle of autonomy that multiculturalism requires: Autonomy understood as empowerment may provide security not only for patients with diverse perspectives but also for patients facing a health care system characterized by new relationships and incentives.

NOTE

1. Portions of this article appeared in Karen Gervais, "Double Agent Doctors? Tensions Arise at the Intersection of Patient and Population Care," *Minnesota Physician* (April 1996): 18–19; and "Providing Culturally Competent Health Care to Hmong Patients," *Minnesota Medicine* (May 1996): 49–51.

REFERENCES

Broyard, Anatole. 1992. *Intoxicated by my illness.* New York: Potter.

Cope, Timothy. 1996. *Second opinion.* St. Paul: Science Museum of Minnesota.

May, William. 1983. *The physician's covenant.* Philadelphia: Westminster Press.

Taylor, Charles, et al. 1994. *Multiculturalism.* Princeton, N.J.: Princeton University Press.

Western medicine through Hmong voices. 1996. Produced and copyrighted by the Minnesota Center for Health Care Ethics, Minneapolis. Videocassette.

CHAPTER TWELVE

Why Bioethics Needs Sociology

Raymond DeVries and Peter Conrad

To have a professional interest in bioethics is to be inundated with newsletters, invitations to seminars, announcements of conferences, new books, and inaugural editions of journals. Although we are sociologists and not practicing bioethicists, our desks are covered with a startling array of offers, opportunities, and information. Among the many things that arrived in the first months of 1997: An invitation to a symposium sponsored by the American Medical Association on the occasion of the 150th anniversary of the AMA and its 1847 code of ethics; quarterly newsletters from several "Centers for Bioethics," describing new programs and research agendas; numerous brochures for "training courses" in medical ethics offered in various places including Washington, D.C., Nijmegen, the Netherlands, and a castle nestled in the hills of Tuscany; a subscription form for *Medical Ethics Advisor*, a monthly newsletter that is a "practical guide to ethics decision making"; flyers for books on Jewish approaches to bioethics, Christian approaches to bioethics, and Muslim approaches to bioethics; solicitations for contributions to support the work of various ethics centers, each of which seems to be celebrating some significant anniversary.

All this activity suggests that bioethics is a healthy and expanding field. It also suggests that we may be a bit presumptuous to suggest that bioethics *needs* sociology. What do we sociologists have to offer bioethicists?

Simply put, sociologists can show bioethicists how social structures, cultural settings, and social interaction influence their work. A bioethicist who adopts a sociological imagination (see Mills 1959) can reflect on the practice of bioethics, to understand how the task of bioethics is constrained by disciplinary habits, professional relationships, cultural "ways of seeing," institutional needs, economic demands, and arrangements of power and prestige.

Our aim in this paper is to awaken a sociological imagination in bioethics. We begin this task with a consideration of the goals of the enterprise.

THE WORK OF BIOETHICS

Our claim that bioethics needs sociology presupposes that we know what the work of bioethics is. There is of course disagreement about the proper task of bioethics.[1] These different opinions about the proper role of bioethics stem from different understandings of the origins of the field[2] and from the fact that bioethicists are drawn from disparate professional groups including law, medicine, philosophy, theology, literature, and social work.

Is it possible to find a common thread in these disparate histories and different professional perspectives? Is there a goal for bioethics that is general enough to be ecumenical? We think so. Despite different views of the history of bioethics and different professional interests, nearly all bioethicists would agree that the purpose of bioethics is *to provide an **independent** and **reasoned** voice in medical decision making.*

Here is where sociology can help. Careful *reasoning* requires a full understanding of bioethical transactions, wherever they occur: in the clinic, in the classroom, in the offices of policymakers or legislative halls. Sociology, with its ethnographic approach to social interaction, offers the possibility of a richer understanding of these transactions. Furthermore, the "debunking," relativistic stance of sociology (see Berger 1961) can help preserve the *independent* voice of bioethics by showing bioethicists how their profession is being shaped by existing arrangements of power. Sociology puts ethical decisions in a larger, sociohistorical context. This more detached view of the bioethical transaction calls attention to questions about the distribution of resources, the socialization of medical professionals, and the "professionalization" of bioethics. Seeing the "ethical moment" with sociological eyes allows bioethicists to examine their role and influence in the medical marketplace.

THE BLIND SPOTS OF BIOETHICS

What leads us to believe that bioethicists lack a "sociological imagination"? When a sociologist reads bioethics, watches a bioethicist at work, or looks at the place of bioethics in the health care system, two questions keep presenting themselves, questions that, despite their importance, seem of little

interest to bioethicists: (1) How does an issue get defined as "bioethical"?
(2) Who speaks for bioethics?

Defining Bioethical Problems

It is not immediately clear how an ordinary problem becomes a bioethical problem. Our days are filled with activities that have bioethical import:
Each day we decide, among other things, what to eat, how to travel to work
(do we use fossil fuels? do we wear our seatbelts?), how to exercise our sex-
uality. All these mundane decisions are bioethically significant; they affect
our lives and the lives of other beings on Earth, and yet they are rarely
deemed worthy of bioethical attention. Bioethicists also ignore less mundane moral questions, such as how to allocate responsibility for smoking-
related illnesses.

Where is the bioethical spotlight trained? Not surprisingly, we find a
strong bioethical presence when we enter the hospital. The ethical stakes
are higher there; it is a place where decisions with immediate and profound
ethical consequences are made routinely. But even here, in the hospital, not
all spheres of activity attract bioethical attention.

In her article "What Nurses Stand For," Suzanne Gordon (1997) writes
eloquently of the important role nurses play in American health care. It is
nurses who spend the most hours interacting with patients and their families, wiping brows, emptying bedpans, offering comfort. In the midst of this
routine care, nurses make profound ethical decisions. Gordon recounts the
story of a nurse who resisted the order of physicians to remove the catheter
of a woman dying of cancer. The physicians were concerned about the likelihood of a dangerous urinary tract infection; removing the catheter would
make the infection easier to treat, prolonging the woman's life. From the
nurse's point of view, removal of the catheter was pointless and cruel. It
would cause intolerable pain and might have or might not have added days
to the patient's life. The nurse confronted the physicians: "She's dying anyway . . . her disease . . . is killing her, not a urinary tract infection" (p. 84).
The physicians followed the advice of the nurse, and the woman was
"allowed" to die with her catheter in place.

Just as patients often fail to recognize the important medical work of
nurses, bioethicists do not see the important role played by nurses in ethical decision making. Somehow the ethically resonant work done by nurses
is not labeled "bioethical." Nursing ethics is a minor planet in the galaxy of
bioethics, offering its practitioners little respect and prestige. Daniel
Chambliss reviewed the principal texts in bioethics and found little if any
mention of nursing. He concludes, "[M]edical ethics is geared primarily to
physicians . . . [N]ursing, which will actually carry out many of the decisions
[of physicians], has no place in the discussion" (1996, 4–5).

Only certain medical actors attract the attention of bioethicists. Bioethicists also ignore certain (sociologically) obvious questions about the structure of health care. Consider an important report released by the Hastings Center, "The Goals of Medicine: Setting New Priorities" (Hastings Center 1996). The four-year project involved representatives of fourteen countries. Its objective was to "examine the goals of medicine in light of its contemporary possibilities and problems. Where has medicine been, where ought it to be going, and what should its future priorities be?" (Callahan 1996). Included in the report's recommendations was this statement: "We take it as a given that every civilized society should guarantee all of its citizens a decent basic level of care, regardless of their ability to pay for it." This is a somewhat unexpected recommendation coming from a bioethical task force that included representatives from the United States. Not only is this guarantee lacking in the United States, American bioethics has by and large ignored questions of justice in favor of preserving autonomy. But before we congratulate the Hastings Center on overcoming one of the blind spots of American bioethics, we must consider a page of "dissents" included in the report.

Denmark was among the fourteen countries that took part in the effort. Although they signed the final report, they felt uncomfortable with the assertion just quoted. The nature of their dissent is instructive: "Denmark is committed to a completely egalitarian health care system based on social solidarity and equal access to the public health care system. Accordingly it does not accept the idea of a *decent minimum*, which it believes would be a step backward" (Hastings Center 1996, S25; emphasis added).

The Danish dissent reminds us that different societies have different ways of seeing medicine and the ethical problems it generates. What we Americans see as a step forward is regarded by the Danes as a step in the opposite direction.

Lack of sensitivity to the structure of medical care systems prevents American bioethicists from seeing the way they protect the status quo. As Paul Wolpe (see Chapter 3) points out, the individualistic stance of American bioethics leaves unchallenged the existing system of medicine. Chambliss goes further. He suggests that ethicists and ethics committees serve the interests of medical organizations by deflecting attention away from structural deficiencies in health care, redefining them as limited ethical problems:

> Talk of "ethical dilemmas" diverts attention from the structural conditions that have produced the problem in the first place . . . This is why so many hospitals can readily accept an "ethics committee" and its debates about ethical issues . . . [Threats to powerful hospital staff are] contained by framing issues as difficult dilemmas rather than seeing them as symptoms of structural flaws in the health care system. (1996, 92–3)

Efforts by bioethicists to create "an ethic for managed care" offer another illustration of this structural blind spot. The work of ethicists centers on discovering ways to determine what sorts of treatments the "risk pool" can bear: When 300,000 people pool their resources for medical care, can they afford to pay for certain very expensive but experimental treatments?[3]

Curiously absent in bioethical deliberations about risk pools and managed care organizations (MCOs) is a critique of the administrative costs of these organizations. Bioethicists are busy determining formulas, recommending better informed consent for clients of MCOs, or finding ways to protect the physician-client relationship, but they are *not* asking if an MCO can ethically justify executive salaries over $1 million (before stock options) while denying a member proper instruction on breastfeeding after childbirth.

There is a place for bioethical consultation in the difficult decisions faced by physicians and patients in clinical settings, but a *reasoned* and *independent* voice in medical decision making must consider *all* actors in health care—it must pay attention to the political and economic conditions that influence access to care and generate different levels of health. It is remarkable that American bioethicists have not noticed the ethical problems inherent in the work of those who are not physicians. It is striking that American bioethicists ask so few questions about the conditions that have produced a medical system that consumes one-seventh of the country's gross domestic product while one-seventh of its citizens lack health insurance.

Defining Bioethicists

Just as it is not clear how an "ordinary" question becomes a "bioethical" question, it is difficult to explain how an "ordinary" person becomes a "bioethicist." Our media are full of pronouncements by bioethicists, but seldom do we stop to ponder, "What sort of training or expertise gives one the right speak as a 'bioethicist'?" We live in a world of specialized occupations; we expect that behind every "expert opinion" lies scholarly consensus on the course of study needed to develop expertise, peer review of credentials, and perhaps even government-sponsored professional regulation. None of this exists in bioethics.

If you peruse the electronic mailing lists and bulletin boards of bioethicists, you find sporadic debates about professional education and licensing, but, as of early 1997, there have been no sustained, disciplined, public discussions of who is and who is not qualified to be a bioethicist. Graduate-level programs in bioethics are in their infancy, and, not surprisingly, established bioethicists disagree about what should and should not be included in the curriculum. Some bioethicists insist that the whole idea of professional training in bioethics is misguided; they believe such training is tuu narrow and prefer would-be bioethicists take obtain a degree in medicine, law, or philosophy.

Given the disagreement over professional education and credentialing, and given the formative stage of the field, how does one become an "established bioethicist"? Is it as simple as getting a position with "bioethicist" in the title? It is true that anyone can claim to be a bioethicist, but legitimacy in the role is gained only through public recognition. There are two (related) ways to get this necessary public recognition: (1) acknowledgment by peers and (2) broader public acceptance of one's authority in "bioethical" matters. Bioethicists have prepared the ground for occupational legitimacy by forming professional associations (for example, the American Association of Bioethics, the Society of Bioethics Consultants) and by establishing both private and university-based bioethics centers. Media reliance on members of these organizations to explain "bioethical issues" and government creation of bioethical task forces and commissions[4] enhance the legitimacy of the bioethical profession. As a result of this gradual process of self-identification and recognition, bioethical organizations and their members have become repositories of "bioethical expertise." But is this all a house of cards? Consider the following example.

In November 1996 the board of the United Network for Organ Sharing—an organization that controls the distribution of organs for transplantation in the United States—voted to change the rules determining which dying patients get livers. The new rule gives priority to those with the best prospects for survival, a significant change from the old system where the sickest patients had priority, regardless of the likelihood of their surviving the procedure. The board's decision drew a great deal of media attention.

Journalists looking for someone to interpret the meaning and import of this change turned to bioethicists. Gina Kolata of the *New York Times* called on Arthur Caplan, director of the Center for Bioethics at the University of Pennsylvania, and on Stuart Youngner, director of the Clinical Ethics Program at the University Hospitals of Cleveland. Their comments were a combination of historical observation and personal opinion (Kolata 1996):

> *Caplan:* The new rule "is the first introduction of a policy of giving organs to those who are most likely to benefit . . . They [transplant experts] have got a toe in the water. I think that is good."
>
> *Youngner:* "It seems to me that you ought to extend it all the way. If somebody who isn't at death's door would do better with a transplant than somebody who is, why wouldn't you give it to them?"

Notice that both men were careful to identify their pronouncements *as* personal opinion ("I think . . ." and "It seems to me . . ."). But, because they were recognized as bioethical experts, their opinions gained authority.

Neither man put the decision in the larger frame of bioethical analysis. Neither offered an explanation of the conditions of justice or of the nature of beneficence or autonomy. Neither bioethicist called attention to the way that transplant decisions are made, the way evaluations of "greatest chance of survival" are (or will be) carried out. Of course, the *New York Times* is not a professional journal; it is not the place to make complicated deontological or utilitarian arguments. But questions about the empirical reality of transplantation are critical to understanding this new policy; such questions deserve more than personal opinion and in fact can be better answered by health care providers, medical social workers, or medical sociologists. Given what Caplan and Youngner had to say, it is not immediately clear why the opinions of bioethicists are solicited.

The cloning of a lamb in Scotland offers a more recent example of the same phenomenon. When Dolly, the first cloned mammal, was presented to the world, it was bioethicists who were consulted by the media and the government. The phones of bioethicists were ringing off the hook; newspapers and the airwaves were full of bioethical opinion. The possibility of human cloning led President Clinton to convene the National Bioethics Advisory Commission (NBAC)[5] for the purpose of deciding the proper approach to studying and developing cloning techniques. Bioethicists were deemed the appropriate professionals to sort out the human implications of the cloning breakthrough.

The growing importance of bioethics, represented in these two examples, arouses sociological curiosity. Here is a field whose subject matter is ill defined and whose practitioners come from widely different backgrounds, a field with no universal standards for practice, and yet, somehow, it has insinuated its way into medicine and become an important presence in health care. How has this happened? How is the field changing as it becomes more established? Answers to these questions will allow bioethicists to reflect on the nature of their voice in medicine. If no one examines the process of professionalization in bioethics, the field will be shaped by the existing medical care system. Bioethicists will not represent an independent voice in the discussion of the uses of medical power.

SEEING BIOETHICS: CONTRIBUTIONS FROM THE SOCIOLOGY OF PROFESSIONS[6]

If bioethicists are to understand the situation of their profession, they must understand the social forces responsible for its birth.[7] Most people believe bioethics is the natural response to the explosion of new technology in medicine. The syllogism runs: new technology = new questions = bioethics.[8] Although there is a simple elegance to this explanation, it is empirically false. Ezekiel Emanuel reminds us that questions generated by new technology are not new, they "are as old as man and medicine" (1991, 13). He underscores this point using the words of Kenneth Ryan, chairman of the National Commission for the Protection of Human Subjects of Biomedical and Behavioral Research:

> Although advances in technology have heightened ethical concerns in recent years, the problems of euthanasia, withholding or withdrawing treatment, truth telling, informed consent, and equitable access to health care have long been with us. *They were just never on an open public agenda.* (Ryan 1986; emphasis added)

Furthermore, new technologies are not new to medicine. Medicine has introduced new machines and new techniques regularly over the past century, many of which reframed the moral questions of medicine.

Another problem with the "technology explanation" is that it gives no help in understanding why a new profession of "bioethics" emerged. The mere presence of technology did not demand creation of a bioethical specialty to serve as the arbiter of ethical questions. Several existing occupations could have risen to the call: lawyers, clergypeople, and social workers routinely give counsel in matters of life and death and were available to give counsel on the use of new technology in the 1960s and 1970s.

The technology explanation does not go deep enough. To understand the flourishing of bioethics, we must explain the new, profound public suspicion of medicine and the use of a specialized ethical profession to respond to that suspicion. What characteristics of society allowed and encouraged the growth of bioethics? In the case of the United States, three features stand out: *secularization, pluralism,* and *individualism.* Each of these characteristics created an "opportunity" for the growth of ethics. Because secularized society lacks a foundation for ethical decision making, moral dilemmas, once readily solved with reference to a faith tradition, now require the articulation of nonreligious solutions. Pluralism demands arbitration between cultures—a niche neatly filled by a bioethicist. And the rise of individualism—well documented by Alexis de Tocqueville (1969 [1835]), David Riesman (1962), and Robert Bellah and his colleagues (1985, 1991)—diminishes the role of community in ethical decision making, creating a need for ethical guidance.

These three features of American society came together in the historical moment of the 1960s—where agitation over civil rights, the Vietnam war, and the liberation of women led to widespread questioning of institutional authority and the desire to correct structural injustice (see Farrell 1997). The conduct of medicine did not escape scrutiny; the bioethics movement is the organized offspring of that scrutiny.[9]

Support for the nascent bioethical specialty was found in the state of the occupational world. We Americans are accustomed to specialization; we expect the growth of knowledge to spawn new specialty areas. More specifically, medicine, an occupation fragmented into many specialties, was (and is) organizationally prepared to accept an ethical specialist. Although ethicists are not always welcome at the bedside, the idea of a trained and certified specialist is an ordinary part of medicine and can be transferred to bioethics. Bioethicists use this logic to defend their place in medicine. Thomas May, an ethicist at the Memorial Medical Center in Springfield, Illinois, explains:

> If you're a cardiologist, and a foot problem arises, you may call in a consultant in that particular specialty to help identify the problem. [Similarly, moral quandaries beyond the grasp of doctors] will seem obvious to a philosopher, because, you see, we deal with these concepts every day. (Quoted in Shalit 1997, 24)

Creating Bioethics

These conditions prepared the ground for bioethics in the United States, but to fully understand the field we must examine the ways (would-be) bioethicists responded to the social and cultural climate. The work of creating bioethics can be divided into two categories: (1) It was necessary to do the *intellectual* work of finding a way to speak to American society, and (2) bioethicists had to do a good deal of *organizational* work in order to gain legitimacy and strength.

Looking at bioethics as an *intellectual enterprise*, we find in the work of bioethics an effort to help secularized, culturally diverse, individualistic Americans make difficult choices about medical care. The best known work in bioethics, *The Principles of Bioethics* (Beauchamp and Childress 1994), articulates essential principles that can be used to guide ethical decision making in a society with little common ground. The principlist approach of Tom Beauchamp and James Childress has suffered much criticism but remains the dominant model in the field. Critics of principlism argue that it does not sufficiently respect the diversity of society. The alternative theories they offer—for example, communitarian, feminist, casuistic, narrative— are attempts to find a way of doing ethics that does not impose moral ideas—or principles—on those involved in a moral dilemma.[10] Although principlism and its rivals differ in their ethical strategies, they are sociologically alike in their effort to find a way to speak of what is "right" without violating varied ideas of "rightness" in a diverse society.

In American society, intellectual work alone is not enough to prove expertise or gain recognition. The rise of bioethics from obscurity to prominence is best understood by looking at the field as an *organizational enterprise*. If bioethics was to be a legitimate specialty, it needed the proper institutional accoutrements, including training programs, professional associations, graduate programs, and journals.

The struggle of bioethicists to find a proper, mutually agreeable way of organizing themselves has been more challenging than their efforts to find a proper intellectual framework. Bioethicists have been engaged in a decades-long effort to develop standards for the profession, to create a unified professional association that can speak for bioethics, and to develop a body of knowledge unique to bioethics. According to sociologist Everett Hughes, the organizational work underway in bioethics is typical of all "professions in transition": "[Occupational groups that are] self-consciously attempting to achieve recognition as professionals [must find a way to] separate the sheep from the goats, to set up categories of truly professional and of less-than-professional" (1958, 133–5).

In the case of this "profession in transition," the task of separating sheep from goats is complicated by the fact that the best-known bioethicists have not had professional training in bioethics. The founders of bioethics come from a variety of backgrounds, with degrees in philosophy, medicine, theology, and law. When interviewed in 1992, many of these "original bioethicists" insisted that the proper way to become a bioethicist was to first get an advanced degree in one of these fields and then to come into bioethics. They justified this position by explaining that bioethics was a rich, interdisciplinary field that drew some of its best insights from the conversation between disciplines. Narrowing the focus of training to bioethics would diminish the field.

By 1997 these attitudes were changing. The demand for a professional identity has led many bioethicists to rethink their stance on professional education and to establish university-based masters and Ph.D. programs in bioethics.[11] The creators of these programs go to some lengths to explain how specialized training can coexist with the dogma of an interdisciplinary field. The rhetoric surrounding the creation of a new program leading to a M.Bioethics (Masters in Bioethics) at the University of Pennsylvania Center for Bioethics is particularly revealing. Caplan (1997), director of the center, comments:

> Among all of my colleagues I have been the most vociferous critic of starting an advanced degree program in bioethics. . . . I have long been suspicious of bioethics degree programs because I fear they may lure people to enroll in the false belief that holding an MA degree in bioethics will produce a job as a bioethicist. But my fears . . . have been allayed by the agreement . . . that the students Penn will seek to attract will either have an advanced degree in hand, will be pursuing one simultaneously . . . or will fully understand the need to continue their professional studies beyond the M.Bioethics. (Caplan 1997)

Caplan's confession is sociologically naive. Although he and his colleagues at the University of Pennsylvania are giving full disclosure, the M.Bioethics program will change the face of bieothics. The degree begins the separation of the sheep from the goats; it will become the necessary credential to perform bioethical functions.

This process—a move from a diverse, interdisciplinary movement to a routinized professional specialty—is also visible in the creation of the professional associations of bioethics. In early 1997 there were four major professional associations, each with a slightly different vision of bioethics: the *American Society of Law, Medicine, and Ethics* (ASLME), representing those with a special interest in law and medicine; the *Society for Health and Human Values* (SHHV), a truly interdisciplinary group made up of social workers, pastors, philosophers, clinicians, artists, lawyers, and a collection of other humanists; the *Society for Bioethics Consultation* (SBC), representing clinical bioethicists; and the *American Association of Bioethics* (AAB), representing academic bioethics. For the past few years, these organizations have been holding joint annual meetings, allowing interaction among members of the groups. At the joint meeting planned in November 1997, members of the SBC, SHHV, and AAB will vote on a proposal to merge their three organizations. If the merger is approved, a new 1300-member-strong organization will be formed.[12]

The path to this proposed merger has not been smooth; the debates along the way reveal the tension between those who champion the interdisciplinary character of the field and those wanting to establish a specialized profession. When the AAB was officially launched in 1993—an organization "devoted solely to the advancement of the field of bioethics" (AAB n.d.)— sister organizations were invited to take a seat on the newly formed board. SHHV declined this offer. Then-president Joel Frader (1993) explained this decision to SHHV members:

> I have found some of the interactions around the birth of the AAB confusing and disappointing. In contrast to the inclusive spirit of the SHHV, which attracted me in the mid-to-late 1970s, an entirely different atmosphere seemed to surround many AAB dealings. I sometimes perceived, perhaps wrongly, contempt and disdain for those, like myself, without "proper" credentials.

The problem of professionalization is present in another organizational form important to bioethics: the hospital ethics committee (HEC). HECs were established by administrators to help resolve dilemmas that arise in the life of the institution. Nearly every hospital in the United States has such a committee composed of a collection of care providers, local clergy, community members, and administrators. What qualifies one to participate in ethical decision making? Until recently this question was seldom asked; but as bioethics professionalizes, discussions about credentialing are becoming more frequent.

One debate about the credentials of ethics committee members on the "biomed-l" list serve (biomed-l@listserv.nodak.edu) reflects mixed feelings toward professionalization among practicing bioethicists. The debate began with a simple question:

> [D]o . . . any member[s] of the [hospital ethics] committee need to be licensed/certified?

The responses varied. At one end were those suspicious of licensing:

> [L]icenses . . . restrict more than they liberate . . . Most licenses don't recognize alternative means of securing competency and that a number of professionals and indeed non-professionals can contribute to the ethics committee . . .

Others found licensure to be a useful tool:

> I would recommend some form of credentialling for the committee chairmen. Otherwise there will be risks of the committee decisions being railroaded by someone with the gift of persuasion but with less than complete understanding of ethical principles . . .

> Licensing would add to the credibility of individuals and be an indication of the commitment to the issue.

Still others reflected on the problem of credentialing in bioethics:

> One of the main arguments against [licensing and credentialling] is that the educational background, occupation and experience of all those who participate in bioethical facilitation [are] so varied that there might be no unified basis for judging the . . . competency of any candidate . . . [E]thical decision making is a function that anyone could perform and the opinion of a lay person might be just as significant as that of a philosopher.

The language used by bioethicists reflects the state of their occupation as a profession in transition. Like all occupational groups, bioethics has its own insider language, a language that embodies their technical expertise *and* their way of thinking about their work and themselves. Perhaps the most persistent metaphor in the speech of bioethicists is the use of the word *crowd* to refer to members of their field. The word is sometimes used to refer to all bioethicists, as in an editor's response to a book review one of us wrote for a bioethics journal:

> [W]e appreciate how you have described the significance of this book for the bioethics crowd . . .

Daniel Callahan used the metaphor in the same way in his reflection on the state of bioethics in 1996, entitled "Bioethics, Our Crowd, and Ideology." At other times the "crowd" metaphor is used to distinguish groups or points of view *within* the field: Bioethicists speak of the "Georgetown crowd," or the "narrative ethics crowd," or the "SHHV crowd." The metaphor is particularly apt: Both bioethics and crowds have ill-defined boundaries and are characterized by shifting alliances. In bioethics we find "crowds" coalescing around debates over training, organization, and credentialing.

As bioethics professionalizes, its boundaries will become clearer. Developments in the organizational form of bioethics will lead to increased separation of the "sheep from the goats," the "truly professional from the less-than-professional." These changes will further establish the place of bioethics in American health care.

Responding to Bioethics

Reflection on the intellectual and organizational form of bioethics does not tell us much about the reception and influence of bioethics. The professionalizing project of bioethics is still under way. Has it made a difference in the way medicine is practiced?

Bioethics has been successful in establishing a presence in the medical care system, but it has been less successful in altering the behavior of physicians, medical researchers, administrators, and policymakers. Bioethicists worry publicly about whether they are "watchdogs" or "lapdogs." In an issue of the *Hastings Center Report* marking his retirement as president of the Hastings Center, Callahan expresses his fear about the role of ethics in medicine:

> In the early days of bioethics there was an interesting debate between the views of Joseph Fletcher—who never said no—and those of Paul Ramsey—who usually said no and who argued that the capacity to do so was a test of moral seriousness. It appears that Fletcher won the day. While bioethics creates problems now and then for the mainstream, right-thinking trends, it mainly serves to legitimate them, adding the imprimatur of ethical expertise to what somebody or other wants to do. (Callahan 1996, 3)

He ends with a plea for bioethicists to "cause trouble now and then" (p. 4). But can bioethics be a more forceful, troublesome presence in medicine? There are at least two organizational obstacles to a more powerful bioethics. First, greater bioethical authority brings with it a moral "deskilling" of physicians and others involved in decisions about care. Keeping up with the literature of bioethics is a full-time job; skilled caregivers simply do not have the time to keep current in their own field and bioethics. In this way a well-developed bioethics specialty threatens physicians, undermining their moral authority, relegating physician competence to the technical aspects of medical care. Responsibility for moral decisions is transferred to bioethicists. It is one thing for a cardiologist to admit a lack of knowledge in problems of the foot, but it is quite another for that specialist to abdicate moral authority, to admit to the need for an ethics consult.

Fearing this moral de-skilling, the Mayo Clinic refuses to bring medical ethicists on staff. They regard every interaction between a client and a caregiver as an ethical exchange; hence, they insist all caregivers must be ethically skilled. Instead of a staff of medical ethicists, they have created a medical humanities department that is responsible to organize dramatic readings, plays, and film presentations intended to make the Mayo staff more ethically sensitive.

A second barrier to a more powerful profession of bioethics is found in the occupational inclinations of medicine and bioethics. Decisiveness and action characterize medicine; bioethics is inclined to reflection. Notice how Albert Jonsen, a bioethicist, defends his profession against Callahan's charge of permission giving:

> I am . . . satisfied that most of "our crowd" dwell in the world of intellectual ambiguity and are convinced that solutions must find their way among the least worst options. (Jonsen 1996, 5)

Here is the problem: Ethicists reflect and physicians act. When the world of contemplation and ambiguity meets the world of action, the outcome is fixed. Ethicists lose. They are relegated to the sidelines.

A different way of measuring the effect of bioethics on medicine is to ask, Who are the clients of bioethicists? Whose interests do bioethicists represent? An idealized view of the field, proffered by bioethicists, claims that bioethicists represent the patient, protecting his or her autonomy against the power of medicine. A cynical view of bioethics—represented in Ruth Shalit's journalistic account of the new profession—comes to quite a different conclusion. In answer to her question, "Just whom . . . [are] the ethicists really serving?" Shalit (1997, 25) asserts, "A swelling corps of HMO utilitarians are cashing in on their ethical expertise, marketing their services to managed care executives eager to dress up cost-cutting decisions in Latinate labels and lofty principles."

An empirical answer to that question looks to the organizational location of bioethics. The presence of bioethicists in medical institutions leads to an affinity between bioethicists and other professionals there. The role of a bioethicist is in fact much like that of a public defender in the American legal system. The formal role of each is to represent the interests of a client in a large and confusing bureaucracy, but, like public defenders, bioethicists must maintain good relationships with other members of that bureaucracy, many of whom are working against the interest of their clients. Given this organizational situation, bioethicists will be inclined to represent the interests of medical professionals and medical institutions over those who are merely passing through—patients and families.

Bioethical ways of framing a moral dilemma often put the bioethicist on the side of medicine. This tendency is illustrated by Judith Andre's (1998) story of a laboring woman who locked herself in a hospital bathroom in an effort to realize her desire for a nonmedicated birth. After arranging for a drug-free birth with her obstetrician, she was shocked to be confronted with a nurse insisting on starting an intravenous line. Andre points out that the typical bioethical response to this dilemma is to define the problem as a "maternal-fetal conflict." The actions of the mother are seen as a threat to her child (and its "autonomy"), not as an act of resistance to the medical system.

Bioethics as Social Work

If bioethicists are not quite the watchdogs of medicine they had hoped to be, what are they doing? It seems to us that the work of clinical bioethicists is best categorized as a form of social work. Charles Bosk (1992) observed this in a study of genetic counselors. He described genetic counseling as a "mop-up service"—a way for higher-status physicians to pass off the messy task of dealing with distraught parents. Bosk also noticed that even when physicians would not call on genetic counselors, they would use the bioethical notion of "autonomy" to avoid difficult counseling situations.

In her article "The Week of November 7," clinical ethicist Andre (1998) describes her work. Her week began with a typical case. A physician, faced with a difficult situation regarding a feeding tube for an elderly woman, requested an "ethics" consult:

> Everything about the situation was familiar; the issue (refusal of treatment); the procedure (we listened, we talked, we asked about how [the patient] had lived her life and what she said she had wanted); and the resolution (a patient or her surrogate has a right to refuse treatment, even when refusal risks shortening her life) . . . We listened with attention and respect . . . [we] reminded [the patient's daughter] that she was free to change doctors.

Reflecting on the results of the consultation, Andre concludes:

> Consultations are a slow and expensive process. [The patient's] life was probably shortened slightly . . . [The] daughter felt far better: perhaps that was the major positive result. The physician probably felt more comfortable too.

Andre wonders why she was called in to consult. Was it for legal protection? Was it because the physician was genuinely uncertain about the right thing to do?

Hearing bioethicists talk of similar consults—of being brought in to calm a nursing staff upset over the removal of a feeding tube from a long-time PVS patient, or of helping family members come to terms with the death of a loved one in circumstances that involved transplantation, or the removal of life support—it seems clear that bioethicists are doing social work: listening to patients (or staff), suggesting options, finding ways to reconcile individual and institutional agendas. Perhaps the organizational success of bioethics is related to the fact that bioethicists are willing to do the "dirty work" of medicine.

Seeing Ethical Dilemmas: The Value of Ethnography

A bioethicist who understands the sociological forces at work in the profession of bioethics is prepared to see clinical ethics in the new light of ethnography. Ethnographic research has always been an important part of medical sociology. Using participant observation and in-depth interviewing, sociologists have produced a rich literature on the social organization of, and interaction in, the medical world. These studies have focused on how medical care as a socially organized activity is delivered and how different actors in the scene experience it. Although they collect qualitative data and focus on the subjective world—on the social construction and meaning of social interaction—ethnographers have avoided "ethical" questions per se. There are ethnographic studies of medical "mistakes" (Millman 1976; Bosk 1979; Paget 1985), but this work has not captured the imagination of bioethicists.

The sensitivity to nuance and meaning that is characteristic of ethnography makes an ideal vehicle for examining normative language or decision making. A sociological approach to bioethics involves systematic observation and data collection of what might be called *medical ethics as they are practiced.*

Bruce Jennings was one of the first ethicists to point explicitly to the possibilities of forging new connections between ethnography and bioethics. Jennings (1990) reviewed several ethnographic studies on neonatal intensive care and, using these as an example, outlined the potential contribution of ethnography to the study of traditional bioethical issues. Neonatal intensive care (level III) provided a good case because so much of the ethical discussion has focused on two key issues:

a. the proper process for making decisions about life-sustaining treatment with critically ill and severely impaired newborns; and
b. the use of the "best interest" standard and the nature of the quality of life judgments that are made by providers and parents involved in the decisions (Jennings 1990, 263).

Setting Bioethics in a Real Context

Jennings suggests that observational studies of NICUs should provide important (and not previously available) information on how decisions are made and why. He notes that comparing the ethical and ethnographic literature "leads one to wonder whether the ethnographers and ethicists are talking about the same institutional world" (1990, 266). Jennings sees characterizing the differences as real versus ideal or normative versus descriptive as superficial and narrow. He points to three reasons why ethnographers and ethicists see social action and practice differently, posing these as challenges to the field of bioethics.

First, there is the relative degree of emphasis given to the agent and to the context of agency. As noted, for bioethicists the primary unit of analysis is the individuals who make reasoned and informed decisions. Ethnographers, on the other hand, focus on the context and look more at the process and "agent-shaping power" of the world. The context can be symbolic-cultural or institutional-structural (or both), but it is a primary factor in shaping decisions.

Second, ethnography can unearth a *moral phenomenology*, the process by which moral concepts and categories "are embedded in ongoing forms of social practice and experience . . . " (p. 269). Put simply, how is morality socially constructed by actors in the situation where ethics is being accomplished? How do people create the moral vocabularies they use to make their decisions? For example, how does the moral status of the premature newborn get created in situ, by whom and with what consequences?

Third, ethnography can show ethicists better ways to bring about social change. Most bioethicists assume that rational persuasion, education, or argument will lead to more ethical decision making. Ethnographers, by showing the shadings and complexities of the social process, can identify points where change strategies may need to be different. This may be, for example, the case with the parents' role in decision making:

> Almost all ethical opinion holds that the parents' rights and responsibilities are compelling; it is both wrong and harmful to disenfranchise them. At the same time, the clear message from the studies of the NICU is that parents do not now play a very meaningful role. And without changes in the way NICUs are organized, professionals are trained, and parents are counseled, it is unlikely they ever will. (Jennings 1990, 271)

As Jennings points out, ethicists have not yet understood this since most prescriptive discussions focus on the parent and physician with no reference to the organization and operation of the NICU.

Barry Hoffmaster, a Canadian bioethicist, states the challenge more directly in a 1992 article: "Can Ethnography Save the Life of Medical Ethics?" He sees the field of bioethics in intellectual and practical trouble. He claims that the field has been left theoretically barren because of its reliance on an "applied ethics" approach, and the clinicians' former enthusiasm for bioethics is waning due in part to the persistence of stubborn problems, as well as ethicists' removal and distance from the realities of clinical practice. Here, too, he sees the dominant conception of medical ethics as "applied moral philosophy," with its emphasis on "constructing rational defenses of general principles and organizing these principles into a consistent theoretical system" as the reason for the perilous state of most of bioethics (p. 1421).

A major part of Hoffmaster's critique is the notion "that moral theory and moral practice are discrete" (p. 1422) and that the theory is too far removed from the front lines of the delivery of health care. Though he recognizes that there has been a shift away from this theory-driven, applied ethics approach, a more situational and contextual approach has not yet replaced it (especially in terms of the way bioethics is researched and taught). Hoffmaster suggests that drift away from theory-driven applied ethics opens the way for ethnographic approaches in health care and for a moral theory that is more grounded in the empirical realities of the problems it studies.

Both Jennings and Hoffmaster see the potential of ethnography to supplement and even partly transform the field of bioethics by emphasizing and examining the contextual and situated nature of morality and moral choice. We could then better answer such questions as "why only certain issues come to be recognized as moral problems; how moral problems get categorized or labeled; and how moral change occurs?" (Hoffmaster 1992, 1424). In short, we could focus more on process and outcome and see how what we call bioethics is accomplished by human beings interacting in a social context.

It is true that sociologists have been slow in responding to issues of interest to bioethicists. But medical care is changing, and medical ethicists have become one of the "strangers at the bedside," to borrow David Rothman's (1991) term. Sociologist Erving Goffman often exhorted ethnographers to study where the action is, and that is precisely where the issues of bioethics reside: where the world of technology and the world of values rub up against each other.

Limiting Treatment in ICUs

Robert Zussman (1992) studied two different hospital intensive care units (ICUs) for his book *Intensive Care: Medical Ethics and the Medical Profession.* He spent many months doing firsthand observation and interviewing. He is candid in his view of the potential of sociology for bioethics: "If sociology cannot tell us how matters of medical ethics should be resolved, it can tell us, in fact, how [and why] they are resolved" (p. 3). Specifically, Zussman focuses on how decisions are made to continue or terminate treatment for terminally ill patients. He finds, for example, that occupational position affects decision making. Nurses, who are in the unit all the time and have much more patient contact, are less likely to object to a limitation of treatment of terminally ill patients (see also Chambliss 1996).

The core of Zussman's study, however, focuses on decision making around treatment for the terminally ill. He found that in intensive care physicians treat informed consent as little more than a formality—in the language of medical ethics, emphasizing benevolence over autonomy (p. 85). It is not that physicians always want to treat aggressively; indeed, Zussman suggests that physicians sometimes see their treatments as "torture" for patients. But "much of the drama of intensive care comes from the efforts of physicians to maintain their discretion" over life-and-death decisions—most often to limit treatment—especially since families rarely say they want nothing else done (p. 101). But prognostic uncertainty limits the discretion of physicians. This is particularly manifested in the process by which a patient becomes defined as "terminal."

At both hospitals he studied, "physicians insist [that] they limit treatment only for terminal patients" (p. 132). But it is the process of judging an individual "terminal" that is critical. Zussman found that the Countryside Hospital physicians' definition of terminal was looser than that found in Outerboro Hospital. This results in Countryside physicians limiting at least some type of life-prolonging treatment for one in four patients discharged from the ICU, whereas Outerboro's comparable figure was one in seven. These included both withholding and withdrawing treatment, a distinction that the physicians make regularly and resolutely, even if most ethicists find the distinction wanting. The difference between the two hospitals is not the differing medical or ethical orientations of physicians who work there, for Zussman did not find any:

> Rather, the distinction between withholding and withdrawing treatment, whatever its resonance to some physicians, is imposed on physicians primarily from outside their own culture. In particular, it is imposed by the law or, more accurately (especially in the case of Outerboro), by the hospital administrations' interpretation of the law. Thus, at Outerboro, unit policy forbids removing respirator-dependent patients from respirators not because it is wrong but because the hospital lawyer has declared that terminal weans are, if not illegal, at least legally questionable. (136)

As Zussman notes, the "distinction between withholding and withdrawing treatment expresses limits of the physician's discretion" (p. 137). Physicians at hospitals like Outerboro become "trapped" after they have begun certain treatments; so having prohibitions imposed on them, physicians attempt to develop strategies to "recapture their freedom of action." Physicians may make the designation "terminal" on the basis of which of the "aggressive" treatments, once begun, can be withdrawn. It is not clear, no matter how they are justified, that these designations are always in the patient's best interest.

How Decisions Are Made in NICUs

Renée Anspach, in her book *Deciding Who Lives: Fateful Choices in the Intensive Care Nursery* (1993), presents a study based on sixteen months of participant observation and interviewing at two neonatal intensive care units (NICUs) (twelve months at one, a major teaching hospital; four months at another, a general community hospital). She takes something of a sociology-of-knowledge approach to medical decision making. She calls her approach "a study of commonplace ethics" emphasizing the modes of moral reasoning of ordinary people in everyday life. She argues that decisions are collective (not individual) acts and that people's decisions arise out of their location in the social structure.

A major part of her argument is that

> [Members of the] nursing staff, because of their different work experiences, develop varying views of the "facts" and conflicting expectations of the right thing to do. For example, an infant who is likely to be severely disabled has a different social meaning for a nurse who sits at the bedside than for a physician whose contact with the baby is confined to technical interventions. (1993, 21)

She illustrates the types of "prognostic conflict" that emerge about the different kinds of knowledge physicians and nurses have. The more "subjective," personalistic knowledge of nurses may lead to different conclusions than the more technical knowledge of physicians.

One of the most interesting insights provided by Anspach is her analysis of the process of achieving informed consent. In a brilliant chapter, aptly titled "Producing Assent," Anspach identifies the social organizational barriers to achieving informed consent, focusing specifically on the process by which parents are informed and the context in which their consent is obtained (p. 86). She examines how the organization of an NICU shapes the decision-making process. She outlines two models of decision making: the assent and the (informed) consent model. In terms of assent, the physicians and staff make their decision and then work to achieve family/parental assent to that decision. The consent model, in contrast, presents that information to parents and treats them as the principal participants in the decision making.

In her study Anspach found that, although professionals in both NICUs acknowledged the importance of parental involvement in decision making, the assent model was more frequently used. In case conferences she observed, physicians and others employed a number of practices, unwittingly or intentionally, which "framed or shaped parents' decisions." Parents were included in the decision making only *after* the staff had reached a consensual decision to terminate life support or withhold treatment. Sometimes physicians would use language that frames the "medical facts" in a manner that seems to lead parents to only one conclusion; for example, "suggest[ing] that continuing to support the baby would require an active decision, whereas terminating life support would only be allowing nature to take its course" (p. 98).

> The degree of latitude parents exercised in decision making varied according to a number of social contingencies, including: how the staff viewed the psychological consequences of incorporating parents into life-and-death decisions; how certain the staff were about the correctness of a particular decision; and how the professional perceived the parents' competency to participate in life-and-death decisions. (Anspach 1993)

Staff confidence, potential consequences of decisions, and physicians' judgments about parents' competency are a critical part of decision making and affect the degree to which parents are actually part of the "informed" consent process. As Chambliss suggests in his review, in major medical centers informed consent "represents at best a polite fiction" (Chambliss 1993, 650).

As this ethnography shows, ethical decisions are shaped by the social context in which they are made. Focus on consent as a product of a contract between individuals gives an unrealistic and overly simplistic view on ethical decision making. Decisions and consent are both affected by external factors beyond the physician-patient encounter and shaped by the social context in which they are accomplished. Ethnography helps shift the bioethical gaze from the discrete encounter of individuals to an interactive process that takes place in a social context.

CONCLUSION

All occupations are socially embedded, but the task of bioethics—the delineation of moral behavior in medical settings—gives a certain urgency to the task of discerning the influence of social context. Those who do ethics and those who have ethics "done to them" should understand how moral pronouncements are influenced by social situations.

What would a sociologically informed bioethics look like? Imagine an ethics consult on transplantation. The bioethicist with a sociological imagination would bring to the discussion sensitivity toward the power imbalance between the physicians and the sick, a consideration of the institutional pressures associated with a transplant program, regard for the economic background of the decision, and knowledge of the cultural meaning of transplantation for patient and caregivers. He or she would also consider how this clinical decision affects culture, how, for example, it contributes to the "commodification of organs"—the movement from the donation to the sale of organs (see Fox 1996).

Bioethicists who think sociologically will ask difficult questions about their profession. For example: Does the recent bioethical attention to questions of justice reveal a new concern for the fate of the medically underserved? Is it a response to persistent criticism of the radically individualistic stance of bioethics? Or might this development in bioethics be related to new challenges faced by *physicians* working in MCOs? Has bioethics responded to needy patients or needy physicians?[13]

We sociologists are naturally wary of bioethics as a discipline and a method of medical reform, in part because of its unsociological assumptions and continual decontextualization. As sociologists and ethnographers, we are also skeptical of disciplines that are based largely on deductive and often absolutist principles. It seems to us that the world and people's interaction within it simply are not organized that way. If bioethics is to have an effective, reasoned, independent voice, it needs sociology. Bioethicists must see themselves and their clients as agents in a social context, a context that tugs and pushes and shapes ethical action.

NOTES

1. It would be a sociologically enlightening task to ask a collection of practicing bioethicists and those with a stake in the deliberations of bioethicists (patients and their families, physicians, health care administrators) to define the work of bioethics. The ensuing arguments would be a good illustration of the way social location influences bioethical sensibilities.

2. See Jonsen (1993) for several accounts of the history of bioethics. Conventional histories claim that bioethics emerged in response to technological advances in medicine. Indeed, this is the view promulgated in the founding statements of the first centers for bioethics. According to its literature, the Hastings Center, established in 1969, was created to "fill the need for sustained, professional investigation of the ethical impact of the biological revolution," including "advances made in organ transplantation, human experimentation, prenatal diagnosis . . . the prolongation of human life . . . " (Hastings Center 1973; see also Callahan 1981). If you accept this view of history, the work of bioethicists is to find a way to live with new technology, to find answers to questions that were unimaginable a few decades ago: When is someone "dead enough" to allow the harvesting of organs? What conditions justify creating a human clone? Should there be an upper age limit for in vitro fertilization?

In his history, Rothman claims American bioethics "began with a whistleblower and a scandal" (1991, 15). The whistleblower in question is Dr. Henry Beecher. He created a scandal in the field of medical research in 1966 when the *New England Journal of Medicine* published his article "Ethics and Clinical Research," an exposé of the abuse of human subjects. If Rothman is right about bioethics as a response to questionable practices in human experimentation, the task of bioethics is to protect research subjects and, by extension, patients.

Still others see bioethics emerging from the "rights movements" of the early 1960s. Challenges to established patterns of discrimination in various institutions spilled over into medicine, leading to systematic scrutiny of the actions of physicians and hospitals. This scrutiny evolved into the "bioethics movement." This version of history suggests that the goal of the bioethical project is to extend and defend the rights of the clients of the health care system.

3. Bioethicists are currently struggling with the use of "autologous bone marrow transplantation" in the treatment of breast cancer: Should managed care organizations (MCOs) pay

for this very expensive and as yet unproven therapy? In certain cases, policies of MCOs have caused sufficient public outcry to cause the government to step in and demand coverage. Federal legislation mandating coverage for a twenty-four hour stay after normal childbirth is perhaps the best known example.

4. Perhaps the most important of these is the National Bioethics Advisory Commission (NBAC), created in late 1995 by order of President Clinton. The commission consists of eighteen members, appointed by the president for the purpose of "provid[ing] advice and mak[ing] recommendations . . . on bioethical issues arising from research on human biology and behavior, and the applications, including clinical applications, of that research." For further information on the NBAC, visit their Internet web-site address:

http://www.nih.gov/nbac/nbac.html

5. See note 4.

6. Our reflections here are based on preliminary fieldwork on the bioethical profession. Included in our data sources are (a) field notes and interviews collected at bioethical events, ranging from bioethical colloquia to gatherings of bioethicists; (b) review of the documents of bioethics, including newsletters, web sites, and other brochures and advertisements; and (c) interviews with practicing bioethicists.

7. We are not attempting to provide a complete history of bioethics here. Rather, our goal is to give a brief sociological rendering of its emergence and professionalization.

8. See note 2.

9. One might also argue that demographic shifts in America have produced questions at the "edges of life" (Ramsey 1978; see also Callahan 1987, 1990). Both the "graying" of America and delayed childbearing by baby boomers create large interest groups that must face ethical choices about life support and medical intervention that were uncommon a generation ago.

10. See Pellegrino (1993) for a thirty-year retrospective on the theories of medical ethics.

11. Visit the following web site for a listing of programs offering advanced degrees in bioethics:

http://www.med.upenn.edu/~bioethic/

12. More information about the merger can be found at

http://www.iphh.cal.edu/shhv/CONSENS.htm

or on the web site for the American Association of Bioethics

http://www.med.umn.edu/aab/

13. Consider the following verses, taken from a poem published in the *Journal of the American Medical Association*. These lines reflect physician contempt for the new constraints of HMOs (Parker 1996; © Copyright 1996, American Medical Association):

With HMOs—Well, Who Really Knows?

What we hope now prevails is a lifting of the veils
　　to reveal the HMOs' greed,
To see through the sell and pull out of hell
　　subscribers who are truly in need . . .

But God save your soul if you've a bad mole
　　or are losing your body hair . . .
If you've a strange rash, then you'd better have cash
　　for a skin doc you'll never see;
You'll first be deterred from being referred
　　for medical necessity.
It takes a magician to get past that physician
　　your primary care designee . . .

On them you depend, but they must defend
　　the profit; on them is the onus

To keep the costs low (as to treatment you go)
  so executives share in a bonus.
Now physicians who care feel great despair
  that they must so closely ration,
But if they want work, they should act like clerks
  and try to stifle all passions.
If they want to be good, then like Robin Hood
  they steal from the lords of risk pools.
It's not treating disease or suffering to ease,
  it's the almighty dollar that rules.

If the clients of bioethicists are physicians, then the growing bioethical concern with the injustice of HMOs is best interpreted as a response to the needs of doctors, not patients.

REFERENCES

AAB (American Association of Bioethics). n.d. *AAB: American Association of Bioethics.* Pamphlet. Salt Lake City: AAB.

Andre, Judith. 1998. The week of November 7: Bioethics as practice. In *Philosophy and medicine series, Vol. 50,* edited by Ronald Carson and Chester Burns. Dordrecht: Kluwer (forthcoming).

Anspach, Renée. 1993. *Deciding who lives: Fateful choices in the intensive care nursery.* Berkeley: University of California Press.

Beauchamp, Tom L., and James F. Childress. 1994. *The principles of biomedical ethics.* 4th ed. New York: Oxford University Press.

Bellah, Robert, R. Madsen, W. Sullivan, A. Swidler, and S. Tipton. 1985. *Habits of the heart.* Berkeley: University of California Press.

———. 1991. *The good society.* New York: Knopf.

Berger, Peter. 1961. *Invitation to sociology.* New York: Doubleday.

Bosk, Charles. 1979. *Forgive and remember: Managing medical failure.* Chicago: University of Chicago Press.

———. 1992. *All God's mistakes: Genetic counseling in a pediatric hospital.* Chicago: University of Chicago Press.

Callahan, Daniel. 1981. The Hastings Center: Origin and History. Unpublished paper.

———. 1987. *Setting limits: Medical goals in an aging society.* New York: Simon & Schuster.

———. 1990. *What kind of life? The limits of medical progress.* New York: Simon & Schuster.

———. 1996. Bioethics, our crowd, and ideology. *Hastings Center Report* 26(6): 3–4.

Caplan, Arthur. 1997. From the director: The M. Bioethics. University of Pennsylvania, *Center for Bioethics Newsletter* 2(2): 1, 7.

Chambliss, Daniel F. 1993. Is bioethics irrelevant? *Contemporary Sociology* 22(5): 649–52.

———. 1996. *Beyond caring: Hospitals, nurses, and the social organization of ethics.* Chicago: University of Chicago Press.

de Tocqueville, Alexis. 1969. [1835]. *Democracy in America.* Translated by George Lawrence and edited by J. P. Mayer. Garden City, N.Y.: Doubleday.

Emanuel, Ezekiel. 1991. *The ends of human life: Medical ethics in a liberal polity.* Cambridge, Mass.: Harvard University Press.

Farrell, James J. 1997. *The spirit of the sixties: Making postwar radicalism.* New York: Routledge.

Fox, Renée C. 1996. Afterthoughts: Continuing reflections on organ transplantation. In *Organ transplantation: Meanings and realities,* edited by Stuart Youngner, Renée Fox, and Laurence O'Connell. Madison: University of Wisconsin Press, 252–74.

Frader, Joel. 1993. President's letter. *Bulletin of the Society of Health and Human Values* 23(3): 1–2.

Gordon, Suzanne. 1997. What nurses stand for. *Atlantic Monthly* 279(2): 81–8.

Hastings Center. 1973. Masthead. *Hastings Center Studies* 1(1): inside cover.

———. 1996. The goals of medicine: Setting new priorities. *Hastings Center Report* 26(6, suppl.): S1–27.

Hoffmaster, Barry. 1992. Can ethnography save the life of medical ethics? *Social Science and Medicine* 35: 1421–31.

Hughes, Everett C. 1958. *Men and their work*. New York: Free Press.

Jennings, Bruce. 1990. Ethics and ethnography in neo-natal intensive care. In *Social science perspectives on medical ethics*, edited by George Weisz. Philadelphia: University of Pennsylvania Press, 260–77.

Jonsen, Albert R., ed. 1993. The birth of bioethics. *Hastings Center Report* 23(6): S1–15.

———. 1996. Bioethics, whose crowd and what ideology? *Hastings Center Report* 26(6): 4–5.

Kolata, Gina. 1996. In shift, prospects for survival will decide liver transplants. *New York Times*, 15 November.

Millman, Marcia. 1976. *The unkindest cut*. New York: Morrow.

Mills, C. Wright. 1959. *The sociological imagination*. New York: Oxford University Press.

Paget, Marianne. 1985. *The unity of mistakes*. Philadelphia: Temple University Press.

Parker, Deborah S. 1996. With HMOs—Well who really knows? *Journal of the American Medical Association* 276(13): 1006.

Pellegrino, Edmund D. 1993. The metamorphosis of medical ethics. *Journal of the American Medical Association* 269(9): 1158–62.

Ramsey, Paul. 1978. *Ethics at the edges of life*. New Haven, Conn.: Yale University Press.

Riesman, David. 1962. *The lonely crowd*. New Haven, Conn.: Yale University Press.

Rothman, David. 1991. *Strangers at the bedside: A history of how law and bioethics transformed medical decision making*. New York: Basic Books.

Ryan, Kenneth. 1986. Tradition and change in the teaching of bioethics: Observations from the field. *Harvard Medical Alumni Bulletin* 60 (summer): 25–7.

Shalit, Ruth. 1997. When we were philosopher kings. *New Republic* 216(17): 24–8.

Zussman, Robert. 1992. *Intensive care: Medical ethics and the medical profession*. Chicago: University of Chicago Press.

CHAPTER THIRTEEN

Autonomy and Difference: The Travails of Liberalism in Bioethics

Bruce Jennings

To comprehend the sociology *of* bioethics, one must appreciate the sociology *in* bioethics. By that I mean the understanding of self and society bioethics conveys. Bioethics has attained considerable social influence during the last three decades owing principally to the broadly ideological functions its discourse has performed in Western society, particularly in the United States. In this essay I explore one facet of the ideological work of bioethics, a facet that has to do with the normative reconciliation of corporate and technological power with individual, personal freedom. This reconciliation is essential for the legitimation of political and professional institutions in late capitalism (Habermas 1973). American bioethics offers a conceptual framework for this reconciliation by conceptualizing individual autonomy, and an autonomy-centered ethic, in such a way that social and cultural realities should be seen (from a moral point of view) as resources of the self, as the means of realizing individual will and purpose. This notion of autonomy in bioethics carries with it a corresponding understanding of culture and society as an external environment of use values, epiphenomena as it were, ontologically and morally secondary to the rational individual.

Recent critiques of the use of autonomy by bioethicists lead us to a reconsideration of the sociology in bioethics and beyond that to the ways in which bioethics is a microcosm of philosophical and ideological cross-currents within contemporary American liberalism itself. One such critique is being developed by a group of researchers whom we might call "bioethnographers," to suggest a term suitably parallel and in tension with "bioethicists." A second critique grows out of the newly emerging political theories of liberalism that stress difference, pluralism, and multiculturalism rather than the universalism of autonomy, rationality, and rights. This is the tension between what I refer to as *autonomy liberalism* and *difference liberalism*. I will explore these two lines of critique, show how they converge, and consider how they bear on mainstream bioethics and the autonomy-oriented liberalism that is its native soil.

THE LIBERAL HERITAGE OF BIOETHICS

The year 1997 marked the fiftieth anniversary of the Nazi doctors' trial at Nuremberg, and 1947 is as good a date as any to set as the beginning of the modern revival of biomedical ethics. The spirit and principles that grew out of the postwar examination of Nazi atrocities have been (1) periodically renewed in bioethics during the ensuing decades and (2) extended to cover not only medical research with human beings but also clinical medicine, the use of biomedical technologies and their social implications, and public policy reform in the financing and delivery of medical care.

Bioethics was born at the zenith of twentieth-century autonomy liberalism, and it has shared the fate of that public philosophy, at least in the United States, ever since. This is what makes bioethics a sociologically and historically important object of study. Bioethics was forged in the ideological (and not just military) victory of the Allied powers and in the formation of the cold war era Western alliance. Bioethics has grown out of and is unimaginable without the moral triumph and vindication of an open society: that is, a society respectful of individual rights and interests; dedicated to a moral style of reasonable moderation, compromise, and mutual accommodation; and optimistic about the possibility of creating and sustaining a system of individual privacy, freedom of choice, equality of opportunity, and ordered liberty under law. The open society tolerates pluralism and difference, to be sure, but only to bide the time. Ultimately, it believes in moral progress, ecumenicalism, and enlightened cultural convergence.

This moral sensibility was particularly well suited to the progressive liberalism and consumerism of the late 1960s and 1970s, when medical paternalism came under attack from many quarters—such as the women's health and home-birth movements—and when advances in medical technology seemed to offer compelling ethical dilemmas and value conflicts that neither prevailing social norms nor legal precedents were adequately prepared to resolve. Bioethics has become a new discipline and a new profession rapidly and successfully because it has performed an essential ideological service to the public philosophy of postwar American liberalism. It has fashioned a moral identity, a style of acting in the life world of high-technology medicine, and an intellectually rigorous discourse of conceptual analysis, each centered around the notion of individual autonomy. It has rescued autonomy from the libertarian radicals of both the right and the left and turned it into the linchpin of a mainstream ideological accommodation. This accommodation of mainstream liberalism, and hence of what has become mainstream bioethics, involves a modus vivendi between the structures of power in capitalist medicine and biotechnology (which progressive liberalism wishes to control but not to challenge fundamentally), on the one hand, and the social ideal of the competent, self-sovereign, and unencumbered individual, on the other. Joining with other parallel cultural forces since the early 1970s, bioethics has participated in the social construction of the autonomous person—a thin self who leads a rich life (Emanuel 1991). And the quotidian work of bioethics is to devise an ethical system that will respect and protect this self.

BIOETHNOGRAPHY VERSUS BIOETHICS

One of the most telling critiques that can be mounted against mainstream bioethics is to question the philosophical coherence, the moral adequacy, or the practical feasibility of this modus vivendi between corporate technological power and individual freedom. This is what bioethics promises to reconcile, and the legitimacy of its discourse will be eroded if it fails to deliver the ideological goods. Presidential commissions, hospital ethics committees, and practicing clinicians need arguments and reasons; they need a working vocabulary of value concepts that will allow institutional practices to continue and not grind to a halt.

An impressive edifice is this bioethics and one that has an impressive track record in the courts, in the professions, and in the public policy arena (Bulger et al. 1995). Yet, especially in the last few years, some cracks have begun to appear. For instance, there is a divisiveness and an unsettledness in bioethics around issues such as human gene therapy, embryo research, and the legalization of physician-assisted suicide and euthanasia. This divisiveness was not so evident in the 1980s when equitable access to health care or the right to refuse life-sustaining medical treatment were being discussed.

The ideological and institutional subtext of the debates within bioethics in each of these areas deserves its own careful exploration, but that is beyond the scope of this essay. Here I propose to examine yet another fissure in the ideological structure of mainstream bioethics, one that is, I believe, more generically revealing for a sociology of bioethical knowledge. The crack I refer to is most apparent within the context of clinical decision making in urban medical centers serving ethnically and culturally diverse patient populations. And the critique of bioethics it represents has been largely brought to the fore by social scientists using grounded approaches and qualitative sociological and ethnographic methods. These scholars and researchers are the new bioethnographers.

It is not surprising that bioethnography should be critical of bioethics (and vice versa). Bioethnographers are working in many of the same settings as bioethicists and are asked to respond to many of the same dilemmas.

It is natural that a certain tension and rivalry should spring up, for bioethnographers have their own legitimation tasks to worry about. ("How much are you getting paid, and what have you done for me lately?" ask medical school deans.) As social scientists, although they may also be moderate liberals, bioethnographers are characteristically disposed to frame the dilemmas in other terms than those most natural to the analytic philosophers and lawyers who fill the ranks of mainstream autonomy bioethics.

In substantive terms the bioethnographic critique has a moral point of view of its own (often left implicit) and has to do with the relationship between autonomy and pluralism. It is predicated on the insight (and I think it *is* that) that the ideal of autonomy cannot easily be reconciled with other moral ideals associated with social and moral pluralism, such as respect for difference, recognizing and validating the identity of others, and tolerance. This critique holds that bioethics reflects a culturally biased conception of moral value and rationality in its clinical recommendations and policy prescriptions (Fox 1987). According to its critics, an autonomy-centered bioethics emphasizes notions of individual choice and future-oriented planning that are foreign to the lived reality of the poor, the marginalized, and people of color in a multicultural society like the United States.

The bioethnographic critique goes on to make a second important point. By normalizing and universalizing a particular set of cultural assumptions and privileged behaviors and a class-specific conception of rational moral choice, bioethics makes both a practical and an ethical mistake. Practically, bioethics is unable to give adequate clinical and public policy guidance to professionals who confront culturally diverse patients and citizens. These people are rendered invisible and voiceless by bioethics, and their special needs are not met. Ethically, bioethics fails to respect persons because it erases their particularity and their culturally constituted identities.

Finally, the bioethnographic critique concludes that mainstream bioethics must become more sensitive to the culture-bound assumptions that lie at the heart of its own conceptual and philosophic framework; it must purge that framework of notions that erase difference or that fail to provide equal respect for the inassimilable "other." With this conclusion, one might note in passing, bioethnography also creates an intellectual niche and justification for its own discourse. For it is precisely the "difference-sensitive" vision of bioethnography that can provide a difference-blind bioethics with the intellectual distance and perspective it needs.

A LIBERALISM OF DIFFERENCE

In this debate between bioethics and bioethnography, it is not difficult to recognize echoes of a broader debate now taking place within liberal political theory itself. William Galston has aptly characterized this as the tension between the enlightenment project in liberalism and the reformation project (Galston 1995). The enlightenment project is to discover the universal principles of justice and reason, and with them to liberate the universal human potentiality in each of us. The reformation project is at once more modest and more political. It is to devise a means for common and cooperative life among individuals and groups who have radically divergent, even incommensurable, value systems and ways of looking at the world. In the recent flowering of creative work in political theory, the universalistic, rationalistic ethics of the enlightenment heritage, autonomy liberalism, has been called into question from many angles—feminist, gay and lesbian, ethnic, multicultural, and religious. For those who remain committed to liberalism but who take this critique seriously, another type of liberalism is emerging, difference liberalism.

The central concept of autonomy liberalism is a common, colorless humanity that we all possess qua human beings. The core of that humanity is, at least according to this powerful strand of the liberal tradition, the condition of being self-sovereign and exercising rational and responsible freedom of choice. The central concept of difference liberalism, by contrast, is respect for and the validation of identity that adheres precisely in difference rather than universality. The core is on the surface, and the surface is the core of the self. Difference liberalism will not accept assimilation as a moral goal, even if it is assimilation into a regime of universal enlightenment or reason.

Three different versions of difference liberalism are developing: (1) difference as incommensurability, (2) difference as justice, and (3) difference as self-identity.

Difference as incommensurability.   This position leans heavily on epistemological skepticism or relativism, and this view is widely congenial to many in the ethnographic social science disciplines today (Rorty 1989). It holds that the universal understanding of humanity essential to autonomy liberalism is an illusion. Philosophy and reason will never discover the truth about our humanity (either because they lack the capacity to do so or because there is no final truth to be found), and universalizing and totalizing discourses such as this are historically exposed as impositions of power used by one privileged group to dominate more vulnerable groups. The discourse of enlightenment, in other words, turns out to be a betrayal of liberalism because it leads to domination rather than liberation.

Difference as justice.   A second version of difference liberalism takes its bearings from a moral rather than an epistemological perspective (Young 1990). It holds that genuine liberal justice requires respect for difference and treating persons as equals, with equal dignity and respect, *not despite their differences but precisely because of them.* It is no moral achievement to live with and to respect those whom I regard as fundamentally the same as myself. But to respect the rights and freedoms of those whom I find to be strangers, challenging, unsettling, perhaps threatening—that is an admirable and just mode of relationship (in both political and professional life) and more in keeping with liberalism's historical tradition of dissent and idiosyncratic diversity.

Difference as self-identity. Finally, there is a sophisticated version of the critique of universalistic liberalism that does not pit the reformation strand against the enlightenment strand but rather collapses them and reads them into one another. It argues that the proper understanding of autonomous individualism requires pluralism rather than universalism (Kymlicka 1989; Taylor 1991; Taylor et al. 1994; Moon 1993). This argument is based on the notion that human self-realization comes in and through life lived in culturally meaningful practices, not by abstraction or escape from those practices. It follows then that it is ethically and philosophically incoherent to require individuals to shed their culturally, ethnically, or religiously specific skin and to adopt a universal mode of reasoning and decision making and a universal code of behavioral norms as the price of entry into the liberal society. For one thing, it is not just shedding superficial wrapping to do so but eviscerating the very things that give us identity and make us human in the first place. Giving up our humanity cannot be the price of preserving and protecting it.

Moreover, the formalism implicit in the tradition of autonomy liberalism works to its own disadvantage when we appreciate the emptiness of freedom of choice or even the exercise of human rights sheerly for their own sake. What makes choice or the protection of rights meaningful to the self who has them—and to the moral theory that defends them—is the culturally specific and thick traditions, practices, institutions, and forms of life that constitute the object of choice or the context of protected interests and freedoms. If the self that is given freedom of choice must first be a thin or culturally unencumbered self, then freedom of choice has little moral value because such a self has little or nothing of independent worth or value to choose. Worth comes from the particularity and culturally situated nature of the self's relationships and commitments, and not from the abstract universality of having and exercising freedom or choice as such.

THE PLAY OF DIFFERENCE IN BIOETHICS: THE CASE OF CLINICAL DECISION MAKING

While it has been somewhat influential in policy debates and in broader social discourse about medical and scientific questions, the most significant impact of bioethics has thus far been in clinical settings. It is therefore understandable and fitting that clinical settings and quandaries have been the venue in which bioethics has had to confront the broader cross-currents of liberalism that I have just reviewed. To gain a better purchase on the ideological work of bioethics in medicine, it is useful to look at these clinical quandaries more closely.

An economical way to do so is to consider an editorial by Lawrence Gostin (1995), a prominent and distinguished bioethicist, that appeared in the *Journal of the American Medical Association (JAMA)* accompanying the publication of two empirical and ethnographic studies of cultural difference in outlooks of medical treatment and decision making. These articles reflect the developing critique of mainstream autonomy bioethics. One of the studies (Blackhall et al. 1995) compared attitudes toward informed consent and decision making among white, African American, Mexican American, and Korean American patients and families; and the other (Carrese and Rhodes 1995) studied traditional Navajo beliefs about health, sickness, and medical care. Both studies questioned the appropriateness of mainstream ethical and legal standards in obtaining informed consent and in the ways clinicians should relate to patients and families in the face of serious illness and significant medical decisions. In essence, these researchers raised questions about the universal validity of the principle of respect for autonomy and the individual human right to control medical decisions that affect one's health, body, and interests in significant ways.

These two articles and the accompanying editorial are noteworthy for several reasons. First, the fact that these articles and this exchange took place in the pages of *JAMA* is itself significant. When aspects of disagreement ordinarily found in the professional bioethics literature spills over into the mainstream professional medical literature, that is one indication that the issues in question have attained a sociopolitical status greater than a mere family quarrel or intradisciplinary dispute. Bioethics has always struggled to gain the ear of the medical profession, and when it has that ear, it must be careful what it says. In this case, physicians (and other readers of *JAMA*) were being made aware of an argument to the effect that the bioethics framework (against which physicians have often bridled but were now coming to accept, sometimes with the overzealous enthusiasm and rigidity of new converts) was asking something of patients and families that was very difficult for them to fulfill, at best, and was perhaps disrespectful and overweening, at worst.

The editorial was framed to represent the response of mainstream bioethics to this potential disruptive and delegitimating criticism. In reading Gostin's serious, even ingenious, response to this legitimation challenge, we learn much about both the flexibility and the blindness of autonomy bioethics.

The editorial is structured in four parts. Initially, it sketches the autonomy paradigm and its historical background, subtly linking informed consent to the major international human rights codes of the postwar period. One does not question informed consent lightly, for it has the moral weight of the international community behind it. It is a hard-won step forward in the moral progress of enlightenment.

Second, Gostin reviews the findings of the papers in conventional fashion for such editorials, accurately if selectively stating the reservations about the model and the practice of informed consent the paper authors present. In this discussion, Gostin makes a move that is not simply an explication of the arguments of the articles but represents a substantive intervention in the debate itself. He implicitly distinguishes between the form of informed consent and its substance or content and then suggests that the problems lie with an overly legalistic and rigid application of the form of informed consent doctrine and patient autonomy, not with the moral or philosophical substance of the doctrine itself. This is a distinction that is foreign to the bioethnographic critique of mainstream bioethics. Part of the bioethnographers' point is that one cannot easily separate the form and the content of autonomy because the very way in which the concomitants of autonomy, like informed consent, are structured in practice—signing forms, direct communication between the sick patient and the physician—inherently conveys cultural significance that may not be normatively acceptable to members of different traditions and groups. Nonetheless, this distinction allows Gostin to locate the problem in a much less disturbing place than the bioethnographic critique would have it. If there is a problem, and Gostin readily acknowledges that there is, then it lies not at the conceptual core of bioethics, with the very concept of autonomy itself, but in the procedural means employed to implement this universal value. And fixing that becomes a technical problem, a problem of clinician sensitivity and education. Sensitivity, consciousness raising, and clinician education, of course, are the *forte* of bioethics, which can carry on with yet more work to do, its mission secure.

Third, having acknowledged the problem and given it a nonradical gloss, Gostin then reaffirms the foundations of autonomy bioethics by pointing to the dangers of an individualized and sensitive approach to cultural difference. Does sensitivity, he asks, imply that there are no "core standards of humanity that must be honored universally?" That question he answers with a resounding no: "Ethical norms or human rights are universal not because they are recognized by certain countries or cultures, but because the human dignity in which they are grounded is universal" (1995, 844). This is an exceedingly strong statement of the enlightenment project and autonomy liberalism. The battle lines are drawn.

In the final section of the editorial, however, he holds out the olive branch by interpreting the challenge of difference in a very subtle and important way. In an intellectual sleight of hand, cultural difference becomes an aspect of individual preference. Thus, while Gostin rejects the notion of difference as incommensurability and rejects the notion of difference as justice, he carves out a position that is compatible with the insights of what I have called difference as self-identity. We are not fundamentally alien beings to one another; nor does justice demand that we abandon the individualistic, patient-centered ethic that has characterized mainstream bioethics. But ethnic background, cultural membership, and religious affiliation and belief are subjectively important to people, and a respecter of autonomy and dignity ought not ride roughshod over them— least of all when the form of informed consent rather than its moral substance is at stake.

At the close of the editorial, Gostin speaks for the perspective of mainstream bioethics at its most characteristic when he proposes essentially a procedural solution to the conundrum: When clinicians are faced with an ethnic family or patient who presents a challenge of difference to the standard American moral rules, an ethical review process should be sought, allowing persons knowledgeable about the ethnic group in question to be consulted. Note that the purpose of this, however, is not to make physicians more connected to the value of a different tradition or form of life as such but only to enable physicians to do with their Mexican, Navajo, or Korean patients exactly what they are supposed to do with their white patients: to have a sympathetic understanding of their beliefs, values, and preferences as individuals and to respect those preferences unless doing so seriously conflicts with the physician's duty to safeguard the medical welfare and best interests of the patient. In this way, autonomy bioethics is not challenged in any fundamental philosophical or conceptual way; it is simply made more cosmopolitan.

WHERE DOES BIOETHICS GO FROM HERE?

One conclusion to be drawn from this discussion is that the tension between bioethics and bioethnography—or, differently stated, between autonomy bioethics and difference bioethics—is a complex and multidimensional one. It is partly sociological and structural: What disciplines and what methods will control the value-laden discourse about biomedicine and biotechnology in the coming decades? But it is mainly ideological and philosophical: Can the individualistic and universalistic moral framework of liberalism remain viable in the face of increasing cultural diversity in the United States? This ideological aspect itself is open to several conflicting interpretations.

Gostin's treatment of the problem is intelligent and cogent as far as it goes. I think it represents the most plausible response that autonomy bioethics can make to the challenge of difference liberalism. By constructing cultural difference as a circumstance of the individual's distinctive per-

sonal interests and needs, the challenge is largely neutralized on the theoretical or philosophical plane and transformed into a procedural and institutional glitch in need of repair. The autonomy framework of mainstream
bioethics can accommodate itself to cultural difference in this sense quite
readily. Cultural difference is employed to attack a narrow form of American
middle-class ethnocentrism that bioethics naturally eschews.

But we may still wonder whether this response goes far enough and
how long it can keep the specter of ideological delegitimation at bay. At the
very least, I think autonomy bioethics cannot continue to be quite as con-
ciliatory as Gostin is, nor quite as indirect in acknowledging the moral conflict that exists between autonomy bioethics and difference bioethics.
Defenders of the enlightenment project today, no less than in the eighteenth century, will have to be prepared to stand up and say that certain
beliefs and cultural practices are simply wrong. Perhaps, after all, that is not
so outrageous a stance as it is often portrayed as being, but it is difficult to
defend something that gets labeled as a "hegemonic, totalizing discourse."
Perhaps, after all, the assertion of moral disagreement is not the denial of
otherness but the first step toward acknowledging and respecting it.

Still, theoretical problems remain. If bioethics takes them seriously,
each of the three versions of difference liberalism will pose challenging
problems for mainstream bioethics. In distinctive ways each position questions the very tendency of mainstream bioethics (and more generally autonomy liberalism itself) to abstract from particularity or singularity in order to
reach commonality or a universal humanity.

How can we think about this tension more productively, take the challenge seriously, and not abandon views that, as Gostin rightly points out,
represent moral progress? I close with a story that may help point us in the
right direction.

As an undergraduate in 1970, I was privileged to participate in a semi-
nar with Bayard Rustin, the prominent civil rights leader of the 1960s. At
that time Rustin was at odds with more radical black power advocates. He
was severely criticized for his less than complete rejection of Richard
Nixon's "Black Capitalism" program. In many ways the debates then taking
place among African American leaders were reminiscent of the debate two
generations earlier between Booker T. Washington and W. E. B. DuBois. In
any case Rustin favored attacking the problem of racial inequality and injustice in America as an economic problem first and foremost rather than as a
racial and cultural one. At one point he said that the best hope for African
American progress and equality lay in the fact that the white man "loves
green more than he hates black." This comment bears on both the sociology of bioethics and the ideological work bioethics performs.

Rustin's cynical and pragmatic comment suggests a flaw in both autonomy liberalism and difference liberalism. People, particularly the dominant
majority, will never "love black"; they will never accept and respect differ-

ence for its own sake. But by the same token, they will never love in a color-blind way either; they will never recognize the common humanity behind the superficial otherness. They will only love instrumentally, self-interestedly; they will only love the use that others can be to them.

This is neither the liberalism of the Enlightenment nor the liberalism of the Reformation; it is the liberalism of the marketplace. It is the version of liberalism (mistakenly called conservatism) that is becoming dominant in American health care today. I believe the most important ideological work for bioethics in the next generation is to develop a framework and a vocabulary that put countervailing pressure on this domination by marketplace liberalism. Bioethics will also have to reconsider the ideological work it has been doing, for no viable answering response to marketplace liberalism will come from a moral philosophy that fails to understand the reality of culture and the power of institutions.

Autonomy bioethics cannot do this by holding fast to the assumptions that were serviceable during the 1970s and 1980s but no longer exist. A critical yet constructive engagement with the moral claims of difference and pluralism in bioethics is essential, particularly those views that construe difference as self-identity and justice. This engagement can strengthen the capacity of the entire field to respond to marketplace morality.

How might this be done? In looking for commonality in an underlying human essence, as autonomy liberals do, and in looking for justice or respectful recognition in currently existing forms of behavior, belief, lifestyle, and self-presentation, as difference liberals do, perhaps we have been looking for commonality and respect in the wrong places. Perhaps, if we are to find them at all, we will find both differences to respect and commonalities to nurture bubbling up from action rather than pouring down from theory. We will find the secret to pluralistic community in the shared activity of dialogue and problem-solving praxis in civic institutions and communities of human scale. Bioethicists should strive to imagine and design these communities; bioethnographers should strive to understand how they work and can be sustained.

Are any of us likely to find two more vital tasks?

REFERENCES

Blackhall, L. J., S. T. Murphy, G. Frank, V. Michel, and S. Azen. 1995. Ethnicity and attitudes toward patient autonomy. *Journal of the American Medical Association* 274(10): 820–5.

Bulger, R. E., E. M. Boddy, and H. V. Fineberg, eds. 1995. *Society's choices: Social and ethical decision making in biomedicine.* Washington, D.C.: National Academy Press.

Carrese, J. A., and L. A. Rhodes. 1995. Western bioethics on the Navajo Reservation. *Journal of the American Medical Association* 274(10): 826–9.

Emanuel, E. 1991. *The ends of human life: Medical ethics in a liberal polity.* Cambridge, Mass.: Harvard University Press.

Fox, R. C. 1987. *Essays in medical sociology.* 2nd enlarged ed. New Brunswick, N.J.: Transaction Books.

Galston, W. A. 1995. Two concepts of liberalism. *Ethics* 105(3): 516–34.

Gostin, L. O. 1995. Informed consent, cultural sensitivity, and respect for persons. *Journal of the American Medical Association* 274(10): 844–5.

Habermas, J. 1973. *Legitimation crisis.* Boston: Beacon Press.

Kymlicka, W. 1989. *Liberalism, community, and culture.* New York: Oxford University Press.

Moon, D. J. 1993. *Constructing community: Moral pluralism and tragic conflicts.* Princeton, N.J.: Princeton University Press.

Rorty, R. 1989. *Contingency, irony, and solidarity.* Cambridge: Cambridge University Press.

Taylor, C. 1991. *The ethics of authenticity.* Cambridge, Mass.: Harvard University Press.

Taylor, C., et al. 1994. *Multiculturalism: Examining the politics of recognition.* Princeton, N.J.: Princeton University Press.

Young, I. M. 1990. *Justice and the politics of difference.* Princeton, N.J.: Princeton University Press.

CHAPTER FOURTEEN

Afterword:
The Sociology of Bioethics

Renée C. Fox and Raymond DeVries

During the two years it took to assemble this book, Professor Fox, a pioneer in the sociology of bioethics, and co-editor DeVries carried on a conversation about the articles that were submitted. This extended conversation reviewed the state of the sociology of bioethics and the biases and perspectives of those working in this new field. This afterword is a product of those conversations. It summarizes the themes developed in the book and reflects on the work that remains for the sociology of bioethics.[1]

The essays collected in this book open a new chapter in the relationship between bioethics and social science; they mark the beginning of the systematic study of bioethics and its role in modern society. Although bioethics has existed as an organized movement since the late 1960s, it has attracted very little sociological attention. For the most part, when sociologists entered the world of bioethics, they entered in the role of consultant, lending sociological skills to the bioethical task. In this volume we find social scientists (and philosophers with a social scientific bent) using bioethics not as an opportunity to offer their skills but as the subject of sociological analysis. It is appropriate, then, that we close this book with a review of the patterns and themes found in these groundbreaking articles, calling attention to their strengths *and* their weaknesses.

All the essays place bioethics in the framework of society, culture, and historical circumstance. This commonality is somewhat surprising, given the diversity of the topics covered (the genesis and evolution of bioethics; the cognitive concepts, problematics, modes of reasoning, and facts used by bioethicists; the value orientation and ethos of the field; the founders of and influential participants in bioethics; the institutionalization of the profession and its impact on medicine) and the varied backgrounds of the authors (sociology, anthropology, philosophy, political science, and various hybrids of these fields).

Nearly all the authors invoke *social constructionism* and *interactionism*. In a manner common to the sociology of knowledge, they underscore the fact that the moral issues and type of philosophical deliberation used by bioethics are socially constructed. The rich historical detail offered by Rob Houtepen (Chapter 7) in his essay on euthanasia in the Netherlands exemplifies this emphasis, although, interestingly, he takes the "Dutch-ness" of some of those details for granted. His oversight is instructive. Because we Americans are unfamiliar with Dutch culture, we can see the part of the story he does not explain. Those who study bioethics in the United States would do well to adopt this "outsider's perspective," looking for the "American-ness" of American bioethics. We return to this point later.

The authors pay particular attention to the way the changing social characteristics of medicine in the United States structured the contours, context, and substance of bioethics. Special importance is attributed to increasing bureaucratization, corporatization, and commercialization of the delivery of medical care; the accelerating dominance of managed care; and (to a somewhat lesser extent) the deployment of an increasing amount of heroic, high technology and "halfway" technology. The concomitants of these developments, they imply, include a more distant and depersonalized physician-patient relationship, a notable loss of a sense of calling or vocation on the part of physicians, a diminution of trust between patients and physicians, considerable degradation in the quality of patient care, and a reduction both in the professional autonomy of physicians (including their role as arbiters of ethical matters in medicine) and the rights of patients. Jeanne Guillemin (Chapter 4) and Jonathan Imber (Chapter 2) devote the greatest amount of attention to these phenomena. Imber presents the sociohistorical background to the current role of bioethics as "public relations" spokespersons for medicine, as "clarifiers" and "consolers" of the medical world. Guillemin is highly critical of the inherent conservatism of U.S. bioethics—impugning it for what Max Weber would have called its "blinders." She contends these blinders have deflected the attention of bioethics from the two most crucial developments in modern health care—the "rampant depersonalization" of patient care and the "free-market takeover of health care."

As a result of their fresh, sociological look at the field, virtually all the contributors fault bioethicists for a failure to recognize the social, cultural, and historical influences on their ethical thinking. Bioethicists are also criticized for not considering the consequences of their outlook for policymaking and for the larger society. A more sociological perspective, the authors imply, would rectify bioethical shortsightedness and provide better, more workable solutions to the moral questions and problems being pondered. However, the authors are more critical than they are constructive: They provide no models or solutions for consideration by bioethicists.

The authors are unanimous in their vehement critique of what Paul Wolpe (Chapter 3) terms "the triumph of autonomy" in American bioethics. The meaning ascribed to this "triumph of autonomy" varies from author to author. In these articles we find four separate but interdependent definitions being used:

1. Most common is the reference to the overweening weight given to an autonomous, self-determined conception of individualism and individual rights by the predominant conceptual framework of American bioethics—the "principlism" of Anglo-American analytic philosophy. In their classic monograph (now in its fourth edition), *Principles of Biomedical Ethics,* Tom Beauchamp and James Childress developed the principlist approach with great richness and subtlety; but in practice, the four principles—autonomy, nonmaleficence, beneficence, and justice—are used in a less sophisticated way. People without training in philosophy often wield the autonomy-centered ethical paradigm like a stripped-down catechism or mantra. When this version of autonomy enters the bureaucratic world of medicine, it allows caregivers to abdicate responsibility for processes they set in motion on the grounds that patients ought to be "free" to exercise their "autonomy."

2. Other contributors focus on how the ideology of American bioethics is persistently intertwined with the notion of autonomy. Bioethicists in the United States attribute high intellectual status to what one of the founders of the field, philosopher Daniel Callahan calls a "coolly rational mode of analysis."[2] As such, they exclude serious consideration of the play of "nonrational" social and cultural factors in moral life. As Donald Light and Glenn McGee (Chapter 1) point out, this highly rational notion of autonomous individuals leads bioethicists to ignore what sociologist Harold Garfinkel might have termed "good sociological reasons for bad bioethical outcomes."

3. For Bruce Jennings (Chapter 13), the idea of autonomy underlies the propensity of American bioethics to regard culture and society as "external . . . epiphenomena" that are "ontologically and morally secondary to the rational individual."

4. Other contributors find autonomy to blame for the difficulty American bioethicists have with our pluralistic society. Those who seek to forge and hold on to a universal, rational, and autonomous mode of analysis have a good deal of trouble recognizing and respecting social, cultural, and moral pluralism. Jennings sees this problem residing in the tension between what he calls "autonomy bioethics" and "difference bioethics." Like Guillemin, he regards the leaning of bioethics in the direction of autonomy to be ideologically and politically conservative.

The strong sociological critique of autonomy highlights an inevitable conflict between bioethicists and social scientists. Social scientists preach the value of "contextualization" while bioethicists anguish over "sinking into cultural relativism." Callahan's reflection on the state of bioethics offers an apt illustration.[3] If bioethicists cease to "float above culture and class," he says, the result will be "subservience to the interests of class and tribe, to our crowd and the passions of the moment."

The article by philosopher-bioethicist Karen Gervais (Chapter 11) suggests that there *is* a way to get involved with culture without giving in to "interests" or "passions." Working with representatives of a Hmong community, Gervais and her colleagues at the Minnesota Center for Health Care Ethics created an "intercultural health care ethic." Her description of that process demonstrates how such an ethic can be developed and why it is both practically and morally important to do so.

Many contributors highlight the value of ethnography for bioethics. Among sociologists working in the field of bioethics, it is taken for granted that the method par excellence of conducting socially and culturally cognizant and sensitive bioethical research is ethnography. Eugene Gallagher and his colleagues (Chapter 9) even go so far as to make "ethnographically oriented social science" coterminous with "social bioethics," which they claim "links clinical and philosophical bioethics" and "connects microsocial perspectives with macrosocial knowledge." Dorothy Wertz (Chapter 3) is the only contributor who writes about the potential of survey research for enlightening bioethical issues. She suggests, on the basis of her own experience with a thirty-seven-nation study of ethics and genetics, that international, cross-cultural surveys are not only feasible but also empirically fruitful and a useful way of promoting desirable social change.

Two authors use the concept of ethnography in new ways. In his discussion of ethnographic methods and ethnographers, Jennings starts with a broad definition of the method: For him, all qualitative social science research about bioethical matters that uses a "grounded approach" qualifies as ethnography. He goes on to coin the neologisms "bioethnographers" and "bioethnographic critique," equating ethnography with a critique of the overly individualistic, rational, acultural, universal, and olympianly abstract and dispassionate methods of bioethics. This conflation of ideas is interesting on one level but worrisome on another. To say that a method of gathering information necessarily generates a critique of a given field can prompt useful reflection on the way theory implicates method. But we have noticed that it has become fashionable in the bioethics literature to envision ethnography, in the words of philosopher Barry Hoffmaster, as a way of "sav[ing] the life of medical ethics."[4] Bioethicists are enthusiastic about going into the field to do firsthand ethnographic studies, although they have little understanding of what this type of research involves and promises. They have an insufficient sense of the kind of training it takes to do a proper ethnographic study; few have knowledge of the anthropological and sociological studies and the vast methodological and monographic literature generated by ethnographic analysis. With her training in anthropology, we can be sure that Bette-Jane Crigger (Chapter 10) clearly understands ethnography but, like Jennings, she chooses to expand the idea. She uses the idiosyncratic term *intellectual ethnography* to characterize the content analysis she has done. In so doing she has taken liberties with the traditional meaning of ethnography, liberties that can expand the value of the method but can also further misunderstanding about it among the uninitiated.

A considerable number of the chapters in the volume are historically grounded. These include Imber's, Wolpe's, Guillemin's, Jonathan Moreno and Hurt's (Chapter 5), Charles Bosk and Joel Frader's (Chapter 6), Houtepen's, and Crigger's contributions. Historical scholarship provides a longitudinal and comparative perspective that is of considerable help in understanding the past *and* present situation of bioethics. Nevertheless, certain limitations and problems characterize the historical accounts in this volume. Crigger presents an intriguing taxonomy of five patterns or "life cycles" that have marked the dynamic unfolding of different bioethical issues over time, but this taxonomy is not accompanied by more than a passing analytic interpretation of what accounts for these different cycles. Despite the fact that it is a "thicker," more detailed historical account than Crigger's, the same is true of Houtepen's account of the debate on euthanasia in the Netherlands. His careful history of the back-and-forth movement of this debate between the realms of medicine, religion, government, law, and the public sheds much light on present-day Dutch medical ethics, but Houtepen never explains why euthanasia played this role in Dutch society and culture. These are only two examples among numerous others in the book that are stronger in historical outline than they are in analysis.

The collection also suffers from the minimal amount of macrohistorical analysis. Only one article—by Raymond DeVries and Peter Conrad (Chapter 12)—attempts to place the escalating interest in medical ethics since the late 1960s in the larger framework of parallel patterns in other professional fields. There is little reflection on what theologian James Gustafson terms "ethics as a growth industry." The contributors give insufficient attention to what the growth of bioethics means for society as a whole and its cultural tradition. A particularly striking example of an omission of this sort is the lack of serious consideration of the work of Alexis de Tocqueville. Early in the nineteenth century, de Tocqueville observed and wrote brilliantly about the emphasis that American society placed on individualism and individual rights, identifying the problems this posed for the development of social solidarity and a societal community in the new American nation. This cultural history is integral to the present-day "triumph of autonomy" in American bioethics. To fail to consider this is to fail to see the "American-ness" of American bioethics.

In some ways, most intriguing of all are the inconsistencies in the authors' historical accounts of certain aspects of the development of bioethics. They are interesting because they reflect a considerable amount of historical revisionism that has crept into the "story" of how bioethics has unfolded. Two major points of discrepancy in the authors' presentations concern the history of the concept of *informed consent,* so pivotal to bioethics, on the one hand, and the relationship of bioethics to religion and secularism, on the other.

Typical of a general tendency in the bioethics literature, Wolpe alleges that the term *informed consent* was first introduced in 1957 in the legal case of *Salgo* v. *Leland Stanford Jr. University.* Moreno and Hurt, clearly the more accurate historians, demonstrate that the Atomic Energy Commission first used the term ten years earlier, in 1947, before the Nuremberg Code was promulgated. Furthermore, after a thorough review of the approximately 400,000 government documents to which the President's Advisory Committee on Human Radiation Experiments gained access, Moreno and Hurt were able to establish that, contrary to the "conventional wisdom about the history of federal requirements" (to which most bioethicists, including numerous of the contributing authors subscribe), "high officials in the Atomic Energy Commission . . . articulated and communicated requirements for consent and therapeutic intent that surpassed even today's standards." It is important to note that these requirements were never fully implemented, but the research of Moreno and Hurt complicates the easy view that early experimenters with radiation cared little for their subjects.

The "conventional bioethical wisdom" about the history of American bioethics vis-à-vis religion is that bioethics was nurtured in the long-standing religious traditions in medical ethics. This view asserts that theologians dominated the young field of bioethics and that as the field matured it became increasingly secular. This is the understanding that Wolpe presents in his paper. Guillemin, however, challenges this conventional history, contending that "secularism ruled" in the founding years of bioethics. Both the Kennedy Institute and the Hastings Center recruited an ecumenical group of theologians and philosophers, and in those pioneering settings, particularly at the Hastings Center, secularism was dominant. Based on the historical record and on Renée Fox's early involvement in the bioethics movement, we believe that Guillemin's account is the more correct one. Imber's concept of "cultural repression" offers a useful way of explaining the systematic forgetting and distortion involved in the historical revisionism to which some of the contributors to this volume succumb.

Finally, we are both struck by the authors' lack of sociological reflection on their own work. With the exception of one comment by Guillemin about the secularism of sociologists and the ways in which the field of sociology shares what Weber called the rationalized "disenchantment of the world," these essays do not apply the same kind of analysis to the characteristics of their own profession and professional outlook that they do to bioethics and bioethicists. As we already noted, the contributors offer a "fresh, sociological look at bioethics," but when it comes to their own work, they wear the same blinders as bioethicists: They fail to recognize the social, cultural, and historical influences on their sociological thinking. There is a dearth of "sociology of sociology" in what they have produced. We learn nothing about what has drawn them to study bioethics or about the place of this work in the field of sociology. The need for this is apparent both in accounting for the commonalties of perspective that are present in these essays and in the differences in viewpoints, analyses, and interpretations that they display.

This book is an exciting first step in the sociology of bioethics. These essays advance our understanding of the practice of bioethics and—on a somewhat grander scale—they deepen our understanding of the social sources of morality. We have no doubt that this volume will lead to further work by these authors and others. This work will—among other things— clarify the value of ethnography for bioethics, dissect the system of ethical consulting, define the relationship between bioethics and medicine, explore the economic influences on bioethics, and analyze the structure of the new profession. This growing literature in the sociology of bioethics will shed new light on ethical decision making and should give bioethicists pause.

NOTES

1. The dual role of DeVries as editor and commentator requires some explanation. Because the sociology of bioethics is a field in process, DeVries and Subedi refrained from using their editorial power to persuade the contributors to adopt a particular perspective on the field. Detailed editorial comments were made about the content of the pieces, the logical flow of arguments, the need for additional examples or references, but the editors made no attempt to shape the authors' perspectives or to "correct" their views of bioethics. More "meddlesome" editors would have eliminated inconsistencies and corrected oversights, but DeVries and Subedi were interested in presenting an accurate picture of the field as it exists today. In this afterword, DeVries removes his editor's cap, and, along with Fox, comments on the content and perspectives of the authors.

2. See Daniel Callahan, 1997, "Bioethics and the Culture Wars," *The Nation* 264(14): 23–4.

3. See note 2.

4. Barry Hoffmaster, 1992, "Can Ethnography Save the Life of Medical Ethics?" *Social Science and Medicine* 35:1421–31.